Deeper Learning with Psychedelics

Deeper Learning with Psychedelics
Philosophical Pathways through Altered States

DAVID J. BLACKER

Cover Credit: AI (Artificial Intelligence) concept. 3D rendering. Shutterstock

Published by State University of New York Press, Albany

© 2024 State University of New York

All rights reserved

Printed in the United States of America

No part of this book may be used or reproduced in any manner whatsoever without written permission. No part of this book may be stored in a retrieval system or transmitted in any form or by any means including electronic, electrostatic, magnetic tape, mechanical, photocopying, recording, or otherwise without the prior permission in writing of the publisher.

For information, contact State University of New York Press, Albany, NY
www.sunypress.edu

Library of Congress Cataloging-in-Publication Data

Name: Blacker, David J., author.
Title: Deeper learning with psychedelics : philosophical pathways through altered states / David J. Blacker.
Description: Albany, NY : State University of New York Press, [2024] | Includes bibliographical references and index.
Identifiers: LCCN 2023048140 | ISBN 9781438498126 (hardcover : alk. paper) | ISBN 9781438498140 (ebook) | ISBN 9781438498133 (pbk. : alk. paper)
Subjects: LCSH: Education—Philosophy. | Hallucinogenic drugs—Therapeutic use. | Cognition—Effect of drugs on. | Learning, Psychology of.
Classification: LCC LB14.7 .B562 2024 | DDC 370.1—dc23/eng/20231218
LC record available at https://lccn.loc.gov/2023048140

10 9 8 7 6 5 4 3 2 1

*For those who have been imprisoned
for the crime of exploring their own minds*

Yesterday's weirdness is tomorrow's reason why.

—Hunter S. Thompson, *The Curse of Lono*

Contents

Preface	ix
Acknowledgments	xv
Introduction: Psychedelia's Third Wave	1
Chapter 1: Overview	21
Chapter 2: Epistemic Loosening	57
Chapter 3: Hypertrophic Identification	103
Chapter 4: Psychedelic Envelopment	149
Chapter 5: Doxastic Enhancement	205
Conclusion: Some Parting Thoughts	239
Notes	247
References	297
Index	331

Preface

Psychedelics are often claimed to yield profound insights. In fact, the very neologism "psychedelic" means, literally, "mind manifesting," a phrase that itself portends deep revelations about self and world. But there is a problem. It is notoriously difficult to articulate psychedelic insights with much specificity beyond a platitude or two, such as "everything is connected" or "it is all about love." While there is no harm in such ineffability per se, it is certainly curious from an educational point of view, because the very existence of the alleged insight would imply that some form of learning has taken place. Under ordinary circumstances where, say, I have figured out right triangles with the Pythagorean theorem ($a^2 + b^2 = c^2$) or ascertained the precipitating causes of the US Civil War, I can explain what I have learned in detail with lots of relevant examples of triangles and references to historical events. Yet psychedelic insight does not seem to work this way. Granted, there are copious "trip reports" that typically include plenty of detail about what people remember about their psychedelic journeys and what went on during them. Such psychonautical reportage can be inherently interesting—to the point that it represents an emergent online literary genre unto itself. As rich and suggestive as these first-person narratives may be, however, the morals of all these stories, the accounts of the "lessons learned" from them, seem disappointing by comparison, at best a kind of "you had to be there" situation. If it indeed represents genuine learning, why is psychedelic insight so comparatively ineffable?

One answer is that psychedelic insights are peculiar; they are different in kind. More, it is sometimes said they belong mostly to the religious and therapeutic realms and are therefore more like conversions on the Road to Damascus or psychological gestalt shifts that occur at some meta-level; they enable new ways of thinking in a more holistic manner. This may be. Still, the question remains: What is the *educational* nature of these insights, where those claiming them indicate that they have learned something significant yet cannot communicate it very well? Experiencers can tell you at length about the wild happenings in the trippy "otherworld," but, again, disproportionately little about what exactly was gained and the ultimate significance of the adventures. For patients with trauma and believers with spiritual concerns, none of this might matter much, mental health and faith being their own rewards. If it works it works; articulating its specifics is a secondary matter at best. But what about those outside the concerns of therapy and religion? Say we stipulate what recent clinical studies worldwide seem to be showing, namely, that psychedelics are promising for alleviating a host of psychological debilities such as depression, PTSD, addiction, and even death anxiety among terminal cancer patients. And say we stipulate further that the "plant teachers" and "flesh of the gods" are integral to the religions and cultures of communities around the globe—and have been for millennia. But what about the vast majority of users of psychedelics in the modernist west not looking for a specific cure or to enact religious rites pertaining to a specific cultural lineage? What might they get out of it?

My question, then, is this: If one lacks a definable trauma or psychological condition and does not style oneself a spiritual seeker along religious lines, can one still learn from psychedelics? And, if so, if they can catalyze educational processes and effects not reducible to medicine and theology, can these be more fully described—beyond game but vague one-liners like those cited above? My goal in this book is to make headway toward answering these questions. As a predictable spoiler alert, let me be clear that it would be ludicrous for me to suggest I've found "the answers" to these hard questions. But I think more can be said than has been.

It is a humbling task, though, because psychedelia is dauntingly multidisciplinary such that no single researcher can pretend to anything close to comprehensive expertise. There are superstars in neuroscience, pharmacology, psychology, chemistry, botany, classics, anthropology, art, music, literature, religious studies, philosophy, and many other disciplines all making regular contributions. But nobody is truly a jack of *all* those trades. My own approach is philosophical in its basic orientation, meaning that it references many philosophers, uses philosophical terminology, and lingers over questions characteristic of that discipline. Despite the need for interdisciplinarity, as a researcher, one must still be rooted in some intellectual tradition or other. And philosophy is not a bad one for investigating psychedelics: it opens possibilities for inquiry that are unique to it, and adjacent investigations seem to lead inevitably to deep and abiding philosophical topics such as the nature of the self, how we know what we know (if we know anything), what is real, and what is the good life for a human being. Though scientists get the grant money, philosophers certainly get more than our share of the best questions. Yet, like any other discipline, philosophy has its limitations as well. The days are long past when grand "systematizers" in the history of philosophy could posture as being above the disciplinary fray and pronounce to everyone else from on high. Rightly, nobody buys that anymore, especially the philosophers themselves. A healthy academic humility now comes with the territory.

So, on a multifarious topic like psychedelics, one does one's level best to recognize disciplinary limitations yet also incorporate relevant findings wherever they arise. Accordingly, despite philosophy being its leading element, this book is heavily informed by—and deeply indebted to—a host of other researchers in other disciplines and approaches. Early in my doctoral studies in philosophy, I was told it was advantageous to become "narrow but deep," that is, to strive to become the world's leading expert in some small niche: the philosophy of adverbs, Kantian aesthetics, or Plato's middle period (these three still being broader than optimal). Then one could truly be "original," a trailblazer, albeit of a tiny and pretty lonely technical footpath. On the nineteenth-century German university model of specialization and contemporary academia's realities of "publish or perish," this professional advice still makes good sense. With psychedelics, though, narrowness of this sort simply will not do. It would consign one's efforts to irrelevance and, even worse, an inexcusable dullness.

While flouting my early mentors' advice about narrowness, I aim to bring philosophical considerations to bear in two main ways: 1) making philosophical questions about the educative nature of psychedelic insight central to the present inquiry and 2) enlisting selected canonical philosophers from the western tradition to help illuminate the topics discussed. The first will be obvious throughout. As for the second, although other major thinkers like Plato are discussed in each of the book's sections, I specifically insert four "philosophical pathway" excurses into chapters 1–4 that feature, in turn, Martin Heidegger, René Descartes, Hans-Georg

Gadamer, and David Hume. Though psychedelics are not directly discussed by any of them, certain central theses of theirs turn out to be highly relevant. This is one of the main burdens of my argument and hopefully the reader will feel I have satisfied it by showing that these canonical philosophers can contribute a great deal to the discussion. In addition to the eastern and indigenous traditions that have tended to dominate discourse about psychedelics—providing unparalleled perspectives—it is also the case that the multi-layered western tradition also has copious resources for exploring the many philosophical questions that are raised. This should not be too big a surprise, as the usage of psychedelics is a cultural universal and a global inheritance; and as such, it generously invites many different approaches. One may certainly seek enlightenment from traditions far distant from one's own upbringing. From an educational point of view, it is salutary and enriching to engage in this kind of voluntary self-alienation.[1] But traditions closer to hand should not be neglected either. We should examine all of them and psychedelia should be claimed by *everyone* as a precious cultural inheritance that ties us to one another as well as to *each* of our distant pasts.

Technical Note

One technical note. This is hardly a work of neuroscience or pharmacology, but for clarity's sake, unless otherwise specified, by "psychedelics" I am indicating what are sometimes termed "classic psychedelics." This isn't really a scientific category but a convenient shorthand that cobbles together elements from neuroscience and chemistry with the histories and cultures of psychedelic usage; it is not a precise classification. Generally speaking, in terms of their neuropharmacology, the classic psychedelics are those that are serotonin (5-HT) receptor agonists (mostly, it is thought, at the 2A receptor, but sometimes others).[2] The family of classic psychedelics, my default meaning when using the term "psychedelics," are:

1. **psilocybin**, a.k.a. "magic mushrooms" (psilocin, 4-hydroxy-N,N-dimethyltryptamine, is the active agent, orally consumed);

2. **LSD**, a.k.a. "acid" (lysergic acid diethylamide, orally consumed);

3. **N,N-DMT** (N,N-dimethyltryptamine, usually inhaled but sometimes injected);

4. **ayahuasca** (DMT combined with a monoamine oxidase inhibitor, usually into a digestible brew);

5. **5-MeO-DMT** (5-methoxy-N,N-dimethyltryptamine, an agonist for the serotonin 1A receptor, usually inhaled);

6. **ibogaine** (12-methoxyibogamine, receptors and action mechanisms are various and not fully understood, orally consumed); and

7. **mescaline** (3,4,5-trimethoxyphenethylamine, active at multiple serotonin receptors, orally consumed).[3]

The first six of these belong to the tryptamine class or group of compounds, a reference to their basic chemical structure, while mescaline is a phenethylamine. Each of these drugs has both a natural source (counting LSD as a derivative of ergot, a naturally occurring mold [*Claviceps purpurea*] afflicting cereal crops, especially rye) and also exists as lab-synthesized analogs.

There are other psychoactive compounds discussed, some of them serotonergic and some of them not, that operate via both similar and different pathways, such as MDMA (3,4-methylenedioxymethamphetamine, a.k.a. "ecstasy" or "molly," and not really hallucinogenic but mood- and emotion-affecting), ketamine ((RS)-2-(2-chlorophenyl)-2-(methylamino) cyclohexanone, hallucinogenic and operating primarily on non-serotonin receptors), and salvinorin A (highly hallucinogenic with an absurdly long chemical name, an oddball agonist for the kappa opioid receptor).[4] But the seven listed above are the classic psychedelics, somewhat due to their internal properties and mechanisms of action but also somewhat because of their popularity and societal influence. Many others are perfectly legitimately called "psychedelics," such as the serotonergic compounds 2C-B (4-bromo-2,5-dimethoxyphenethylamine, like MDMA a phenethylamine) and DPT (N,N-dipropyltryptamine, a tryptamine), and many, many others—hundreds, at least, and, in principle, indeterminately many potential "designer" variations. But none of these is as common or has enjoyed the contemporary cultural impact of the listed seven.

In sum, while it is related to their chemical structures, the phrase "classic psychedelic" is an imprecise fusion of science and non-science; it is really just a lexical designator that has become popular through repeated usage. But for reasons of efficiency and economy of prose, it is hard not to use it (hence this note.) It is important to realize, though, that classic psychedelics are just the tip of an indefinitely large chemical iceberg, with novel psychoactive compounds being synthesized and discovered constantly (so many, in fact, that even chemists must have trouble keeping up with them all). Also, the neuroscience of all of this is very young, very fluid, and so subject to alteration as more is discovered. It would be the soundest of wagers to bet on new breakthroughs regarding basic aspects of psychedelics in the years to come. Not even those with the highest levels of scientific expertise can yet speak with much confidence about the totality of what, at any level, is really going on here.

Acknowledgments

These acknowledgments are briefer than usual. When I started on this topic, I was under the impression that it was still somewhat taboo in my academic circles, especially in education, where talk about the possible educational benefits of "drugs" might be thought somehow to imply an endorsement of their use by children. (Early on, I received some accusatory questions implying as much.) Any such implication is of course completely false. This book, and I personally, take no normative stance whatever on individuals' use of these substances; their usage in any form is neither encouraged nor discouraged. One should, as they say, consult with one's physician and, probably, one's lawyer. This situation, combined with the concurrent Covid crisis, which suspended normal academic life for a few years, created a situation in which I kept this project largely off the radar while incubating it. It is incredible how things have changed in just a few short years, however. As discussed in the following pages, the amount of research now bursting forth from prestigious institutions has opened the gates of legitimacy for everyone; the previous caution is no longer necessary, even in sensitive areas like education. (It might even be weird now in certain sub-disciplines *not* to have any interest in psychedelics.) For obvious reasons, though, my above-mentioned stance of neutrality regarding usage remains fully in force and nothing in this book should be taken to imply the endorsement of anything drug related. My main educational guidance for children is decidedly conventional: "stay off drugs and stay in school, kids."

That said, several individuals, groups, and institutions helped make this book possible, and I will thank them in no particular order. Please note that acknowledgment does not, of course, imply agreement with anything advanced herein. These people might not like what I say at all.

I thank my home institution, the University of Delaware, for employing me, in part to do research, and continuing to deposit paychecks into my bank account. Without that, I doubt I'd have much time for this sort of thing. I am also grateful to McGill and Concordia Universities in Montreal for supporting some of the early work on the project. Over the years, I have been provided with valuable feedback on various bits and pieces: audiences at the aforementioned universities of Delaware, McGill, and Concordia, the Philosophy of Education Society (US) and the Philosophy of Education Society of Great Britain, along with Kevin McDonough, David Waddington, Laura Desimone, Kristyn Hatfield, Chris Higgins, Abby Hughes, Josh Blacker, Bridget Goodfellow, Mikel Elam, Mike Watson, Doug Lain, Alpesh Maisuria, Alex Safos, Walker Stewart, Corey Greenberg, Catherine Arnold, Bryan van Gronigen, Bob Hampel, Stephanie Del Tufo, Chris Phillips, certain other individuals, the proprietors of a few farms and ranches outside of Austin, Texas, what used to be known as the Laguna Gloria Art Museum (also in Austin), three sets of inquisitive seniors in my legal studies seminars, two specific unnamed groups back in the 1980s, a more recent unnamed entity, an unnamed presence (who I think is still there), a JVC stereo (red), various backyard honeybees (now deceased; they don't live very long), Ottorino Respighi (1879–1936), a few more people I'm not going to name, and my late Dad, a neurosurgeon and neuroscientist who explored neglected realms of the mind way ahead of his time.

Finally, above all the other gratitudes is what I owe my wife, Carolyn Blacker, whose visionary art also discloses the hidden and who was an incredibly good sport about the continual flow of manuscript drafts I kept inflicting on her.

I am also very thankful to Richard Carlin, editor par excellence at SUNY Press and author of great books about music. Richard was remarkably encouraging and helpful from the beginning of this project. Also at SUNY Press, I thank several anonymous peer reviewers for their very helpful comments and Aimee Harrison, Ryan Morris, and James Harbeck, the latter for superb copyediting. Lastly, as noted in the body of the text, though in substantially altered form, portions of the Descartes and Hume subsections used as raw material a few passages previously published in my *Democratic Education Stretched Thin: How Complexity Challenges a Liberal Ideal* (Albany: State University of New York Press, 2007). Also, as is customary with academic work, dribs and drabs of the material originated as invited talks and conference papers over the years. Lastly, the faults and errors in this book are mine alone.

Introduction

Psychedelia's Third Wave

> The discovery of psychedelics by the Western world was first met with wonder, followed by an excited anticipation of their potential as tools for exploring the mind and treating psychological disease, and then by misinformation, suspicion and suppression. Ignorance, misunderstanding and fear form a dark thread through the history of psychedelics in the late 20th century. Fortunately, this thread is finally beginning to fray.
>
> —Andrew Gallimore, *Reality Switch Technologies*, 3–4

First Wave (1940s–1950s)

Psychedelics are back. They never exactly went away, certainly not for many indigenous peoples with intact cultural lineages worldwide. But for the more economically developed countries (MEDCs) a major hiatus in their above-ground use ensued with the Johnson-era *Drug Abuse Control Amendments of 1965* (Public Law 89-74) and the more comprehensive Nixon-era *Controlled Substances Act of 1970* (Section 201 (c), (21 U.S.C. § 811 (c))), which banned psychedelics in most research venues and categorized them as "Schedule 1," designating them as unsafe, with a "high potential for abuse" and lacking any legitimate medical use. Around this time, spurred by the United Nations *Convention on Psychotropic Substances* (1971), most other countries adopted similar bans. Previously, especially since the 1950s, there had been a great deal of institution-based research on psychedelics in both the West and former Soviet bloc, mostly concerning psychiatric applications of LSD and to a lesser extent mescaline.

This included large-scale covert military research, most notoriously the CIA's sinister Project MK-ULTRA (1953–1973), among whose victims were novelist and counter-cultural icon Ken Kesey, mathematician and terrorist Ted Kaczynski, Boston mobster Whitey Bulger, and, as is now known, cult leader and murderer Charles Manson. Also among the program's 149 clandestine subprojects were widespread abuses of prison inmates, including mind-bogglingly inhuman nonconsensual experiments, with LSD and other substances, on black prisoners in the Louisiana State Penitentiary from 1955 to 1956, conducted through Tulane University.[5] MK-ULTRA's abuses were revealed by Congress in the Church Committee hearings of the 1970s, bringing public attention to the need for ethics protocols to protect human subjects in government research.

As historian Mike Jay has documented, immediately prior to the first wave, there had been a noteworthy history of psychoactive compounds being explored by highbrow "psychonauts," mostly via self-experimentation, such as Sigmund Freud (cocaine), William James (nitrous oxide), and W. B. Yeats (hashish).[6] But what became the most popular and emblematic "classic" psychedelic of the first and second waves, LSD, was not discovered until during World War II by Swiss chemist Albert Hofmann (1906–2008) as one of several synthetic ergot derivatives being investigated at Sandoz Laboratories, a chemical company based in Basel. Ergot is a toxic fungus afflicting rye and other grain crops exposed to excessive moisture, such as during early frosts. It had long plagued European harvests, particularly in cooler regions. When ingested, usually by peasants who could not afford to discard the fungally tainted "bread of the poor," it caused the hallucinatory and sometimes lethal affliction medievals and early moderns knew as "St. Peter's snow" or "St. Anthony's fire," among other names.[7] It was a probable cause of periodic outbreaks of ecstatic fervor, including violent witch manias, as late as the Salem witch trials in 1692, according to the analysis of historian Mary Matossian.[8] LSD's curious psychotropic properties became known by Hofmann himself when he took a leap of faith one April afternoon in 1943 and, out of scientific curiosity, dosed himself with it and then took a very strange bicycle ride home that has become iconic in psychedelic lore.[9] ("Bicycle Day" is now celebrated by psychedelics enthusiasts every April 19.) Sandoz eventually began offering free samples of LSD to researchers worldwide in hopes finding commercial uses—a kind of early crowdsourcing—an offer especially taken up in the former Soviet bloc, which gave rise to large-scale research there among psychiatrists, particularly focusing on alcoholism and depression. This included the influential maverick Czech (and later American) psychiatrist Stanislav Grof (b. 1931) (stangrof.com), who supervised thousands of LSD-assisted therapy sessions in the 1950s and 1960s and later became a founder of transpersonal psychology. From these sessions, Grof distilled a framework for understanding the psychological patterns he observed within LSD and other non-ordinary experiences, in particular what he terms "perinatal matrices" having to do with the reliving of birth trauma. After the outlawing of LSD for research, Grof developed "holotropic breathwork" as a non-chemical mechanism for altering consciousness.[10]

Prior even to LSD, another powerful psychedelic, mescaline, was originally derived from the columnar cactus of Peru and the peyote and San Pedro cacti of the Mexican and American desert Southwest. It had long been present among the indigenous people of the New World at the time of the Spanish Conquest and was actively suppressed by missionaries and viceroys. Peruvian, North American, and European researchers eventually learned of the mescaline-yielding plants and the compound was fully lab synthesized by Austrian chemist Ernst Späth (1886–1946) in 1919. (It had been extracted from peyote by German chemists in the early 1900s.) Soon thereafter, mescaline was manufactured and distributed by the German pharmaceutical giant Merck and it then served as an entrée into psychedelics for a continental milieu of intellectuals and avant-gardists.[11] This included German philosophers Ernst Bloch (1885–1977) and Walter Benjamin (1892–1940), French Surrealist poet Antonin Artaud (1896–1948), and French philosopher Jean-Paul Sartre (1905–1980).[12] Sartre's psychedelic foray was short-lived. After a massive overdose of mescaline in 1935, the future Nobel Prize awardee spent a bizarre and terrified year convinced he was being followed around Paris by giant lobsters.[13] It is hard not to see the hand of his earlier psychedelic experiences just a few short years later, in the novel that launched existentialism, *Nausea* (1938). In the famous mirror scene, Sartre's protagonist confronts his own visage in a suspiciously mescaline-like manner, losing his grip on reality:

> What I see is well below the monkey, on the fringe of the vegetable world, at the level of jellyfish. It is alive, I can't say it isn't. . . . I see a slight tremor, I see the insipid flesh blossoming and palpitating with abandon. The eyes especially are horrible when seen so close. They are glassy, soft, blind,

red-rimmed, they look like fish scales. . . . The eyes, nose and mouth disappear: nothing human is left. Brown wrinkles show on each side of the feverish swelled lips, crevices, mole holes. A silky white down covers the great slopes of the cheeks, two hairs protrude from the nostrils: it is a geological embossed map. And, in spite of everything, this lunar world is familiar to me. I cannot say I *recognize* the details. But the whole thing gives me an impression of something seen before which stupefies me.[14]

This may be the most famous depiction of a "bad trip" in the history of philosophy. Mescaline was also the experiential basis for English author Aldous Huxley's (1894–1963) classic psychedelic-themed trilogy *Doors of Perception* (1954), *Heaven and Hell* (1956), and *Island* (1962). Huxley was so devoted to psychedelics that he requested LSD from his wife and took it during his last hours on his deathbed.[15]

Along with mescaline and LSD, the other main psychedelic of the first wave was so-called "magic mushrooms," whose main psychoactive ingredient via oral ingestion is the alkaloid psilocybin (which breaks down via digestion into its psychoactive counterpart psilocin). Though psychedelic mushrooms are ubiquitous worldwide, their unusual properties had long been mostly forgotten in the MEDCs, despite ample evidence of their use in ancient Europe and elsewhere. The most familiar of these is the iconic red-capped and white-spotted toadstool *Amanita muscaria* (or fly agaric), which is moderately poisonous but also contains a non-psilocybin hallucinogen (muscimol, which operates along different neural pathways from psilocin). It is curiously prominent in older religious imagery and fairy tales such as that of Santa Claus (Siberian shamans filter it through reindeer urine).[16] Psychoactive mushrooms of the psilocybin variety were brought to modern mainstream attention by way of Gordon Wasson (1898–1986), an eccentric polymath who was, at different periods, a Columbia University English professor, a J.P. Morgan executive, and, later in life, an amateur ethnobotanist and anthropologist. Wasson and his wife, Russian pediatrician Valentina Pavlovna Wasson (1901–1958), popularized mushrooms in North America via a 1957 *This Week* magazine article documenting their participation in a traditional mushroom ceremony in Oaxaca, Mexico, conducted by the now-famous Mazatec *curandera* María Sabina (1894–1985).[17] Psilocybin was later synthesized for research purposes by Hofmann at Sandoz (modern research on psilocybin is usually conducted by injection with the synthesized form, as this allows for precise dosing).

Worth noting in any discussion of the recent history of psychedelics is that, in an unfortunate echo of colonialism, the Wassons' Oaxacan adventure ended up being damaging to Sabina and her family, as Wasson seems to have inadequately safeguarded Sabina's confidentiality. This resulted in hostility from local authorities and unwanted and destructive tourism when the magazine piece placed Sabina's remote mountain village (Huautla de Jiménez) in the public eye.[18] This extractivist pattern of cultural and environmental damage, however inadvertent in this case, should be kept firmly in mind. Indigenous peoples' ancestral knowledge continues to be appropriated in ways that are often reckless and harmful. Along these lines, two current environmental concerns in desert areas of the southwestern US and northern Mexico are the endangered status of the mescaline-yielding peyote cactus and the Sonoran Desert toad, whose venom is one of the primary sources of 5-MeO-DMT. Nicknamed the "God molecule," 5-MeO-DMT is arguably the most powerful known psychedelic. It is finally now being widely acknowledged how the *curanderos* of Amazonia and Mexico (and shamanistic figures around the globe) have served to preserve the knowledge of these essential substances, not unlike the role played by monastery monks (and other scholars) in preserving literacy and classical learning during the European Dark Ages. Without this appropriated knowledge, the current psychedelic renaissance would not have been possible or even, really, imaginable. While organizations such as the International Center for Ethnobotanical Education, Research, and Service (iceers.org) and the Chacruna Institute for Psychedelic Plant Medicines (chacruna.net) have arisen to assist in safeguarding these interests, the indigenous and environmental impacts of psychedelics' globalization remain concerning.

Second Wave (1960s–1970s)

In the decades that followed the first-wave psychedelic discoveries of the German mescaline chemists, Hofmann, and Wasson et al., a second wave ensued that was characterized by a bursting forth of psychedelia onto the vast canvas of popular culture. Before the mid-1960s, psychedelics tended to be limited to the above-mentioned avant-garde figures such as Huxley and miscellaneous creative types such as writer and artist

William S. Burroughs (1914–1997), who experimented with mescaline, LSD, and even a version of ayahuasca in the Amazon.[19] There were in addition high-profile Hollywood notables like film director Stanley Kubrick (1928–1999) and actor Cary Grant (1904–1986), the latter undergoing around one hundred LSD therapy sessions at the Beverly Hills Psychiatric Institute. Grant claimed that LSD "saved my life."[20] Also part of this emergent southern California scene, many early LSD sessions were also conducted at UCLA by psychiatrist Sidney Cohen (1910–1987), whose patients included Bill Wilson, the founder of Alcoholics Anonymous. Wilson became convinced that LSD was the best way to treat alcoholism by providing the non-religious with a vivid sense of the "higher power" necessary in twelve-step programs (his contemporaries in AA were hostile to the strategy of using one drug to overcome another).[21] Cohen, along with English/Canadian psychiatrist Humphrey Osmond (1917–2004), who coined the term "psychedelic" in correspondence with Huxley, were part of Huxley's circle.[22]

Things then radically changed as psychedelics exploded into popular consciousness in the 1960s via cultural entrepreneurs such as Ken Kesey, with his proto-hippie Bay Area entourage known as the Merry Pranksters and their warehouse "acid test" parties—with music provided by an upstart local band eventually called the Grateful Dead.[23] Other noteworthy popularizers included Harvard psychologists Timothy Leary (1920–1996), Richard Alpert (later Ram Dass, 1931–2019), and Ralph Metzner (1936–2019), and—not to be forgotten—some enterprising underground distributors and chemists. These latter included a motley assemblage of colorful individuals, such as the shadowy inventor, bootlegger and intelligence operative "Captain" Al Hubbard, dubbed the "Johnny Appleseed of LSD," who widely distributed Sandoz-created LSD worldwide, and the clandestine chemist and Grateful Dead sound engineer "Acid King" Stanley Owsley, the first known freelancer to produce LSD, by his own admission creating 5 million doses between 1965 and 1967.[24] A few years later there was also the prolific renegade chemist, initially at Dow Chemical and the DEA, Alexander Shulgin (1925–2014), who introduced the empathogen MDMA to therapists and discovered many compounds such as the psychedelic phenethylamine 2C-B.[25] In large part due to bridging figures such as these, psychedelia soon bolted from the corporate chemistry labs and elite intellectual circles to become near ubiquitous in the MEDCs. To say the least, psychedelics and their associated aesthetics profoundly shaped the 1960s in art, music, literature, politics and, really, the entire vast hippie and hippie-adjacent cultural scene, including a vibrant and roughly concurrent Black Psychedelia, associated with Sly and the Family Stone, George Clinton, and many others. Perhaps the cultural apotheosis was reached with the release of the Beatles' chart-topping concept album *Sgt. Pepper's Lonely Hearts Club Band* (1967), one of the best-selling albums of all-time, which did not even pretend to disguise its essence as an intricate ode to LSD.[26]

Yet as Leary's ludic slogan "turn on, tune in, drop out" permeated the counterculture, and that counterculture then dovetailed with anti–Vietnam War sentiment and political protest, the subsequent Nixonian normie backlash was all but guaranteed. The whole emergent ragtag ensemble—from Haight-Ashbury to Woodstock—appeared alien and menacing to traditional straitlaced America. The hallucinogenic drugs that seemed to have corrupted the minds of large segments of American youth—particularly among the affluent and college-educated—had to be contained to halt a generation feared by older mainstream authorities to be literally out of control. Authorities coalesced against this cultural threat and ultimately the naïve and laid-back "Age of Aquarius" hippie vibe was no match for their multi-pronged onslaught. The psychedelic utopianism of the 1960s thus gave way—with powerful assists from heavily negative press coverage (sometimes warranted) and from events themselves, like the murders perpetrated by Manson's California LSD cult—to the disillusionment and cultural and spiritual fragmentation of the 1970s and beyond. Psychedelia then became on the whole less collective and publicly visible and more privatized and introspective, inflected with more of a self-help New Age spiritualist ethos than with the "we can change the world" mood of the 1960s.[27] Gonzo journalist and drug enthusiast Hunter S. Thompson summarized this rather abrupt cultural turn in his inimitable style: "That was the fatal flaw in Tim Leary's trip. He crashed around America selling 'consciousness expansion' without ever giving a thought to the grim meat-hook realities that were lying in wait for all the people who took him seriously. . . . All those pathetically eager acid freaks who thought they could buy Peace and Understanding for three bucks a hit."[28]

The Nixonian backlash period also resulted in the termination of almost all ongoing above-ground research on psychedelics, much of it focused on as alcoholism, drug addiction, and mental illness. The Maryland Psychiatric Research Center (an extension of previous work done at the Spring Grove State Hospital near Baltimore) was the last outpost of LSD research until it too was scuppered in 1975. What came to be known as the "war on drugs" thus pushed psychedelics—and the knowledge base that had been accumulating since the first wave—almost completely underground. While psychedelics were never eradicated and continued to exert strong influences on pockets of the culture, particularly among the artistic, musical, and zine subcultures of this period, political demonization and increasingly aggressive drug enforcement succeeded in stigmatizing them such that psychedelics were placed mostly out of bounds for polite society and "respectable" scholars.[29] As a result, for a generation, from the early 1970s to the 1990s, academics whose research took these substances seriously, even in remote contexts such as ancient history, like Boston University classicist Carl A. P. Ruck (b. 1935), found themselves ostracized and professionally blackballed. Conventional wisdom and the police power of the state together erected a powerful wall of taboo and fear that stood firmly in place for decades.

Third Wave (1990s–present)

This deflationary period lasted for a generation until a third wave began to form.[30] Integral to this process were two harbingers of a new sensibility toward psychedelics who are hard to categorize but were (and are) massively influential: speculative thinker and essayist Terence McKenna (1946–2000) and the non-affiliated mycologist Paul Stamets (b. 1955).

McKenna, brother of the noted ethnopharmacologist Dennis McKenna (b. 1950),[31] was a prolific writer but perhaps was—and still is—mostly encountered via his talks and lectures, where he employs a singular voice and speaking style that combines personal psychonautical tales with wry humor and a brainy playfulness. McKenna vividly conveys that psychedelics are not just aesthetic and spiritual tools but they also invite an intellectual adventure that can help us grapple with deep questions about human existence.[32] Still much discussed is his highly speculative (and hyperbolically named) "stoned ape theory" that suggests psychedelic mushrooms were key catalysts for human brain development and consciousness, particularly alongside the human expansion out of Africa. This journey, so the theory goes, involved hunter-gatherers' wider search for food sources. If one tracks animals for a living, one becomes intimately acquainted with animal scat, which, under certain conditions, serves as a fecund substrate for psychoactive *Psilocybe cubensis* mushrooms.

It is difficult to imagine that archaic humans did not stumble across these dung-growing psychedelics and eventually, with the development of agriculture and the domestication of cattle, the requisite dung became all the more ubiquitous. Cow and horse dung are still a major substrate for *Psilocybe cubensis*. I personally recall undergraduate students in 1980s Austin, Texas, collecting garbage bags full of *Psilocybe cubensis* from local pastures in springtime—while keeping lookout against farmers intent on chasing off "the hippies." Unbeknownst to them, according to McKenna, these students may have been engaging in one of the most ancient of psychedelic traditions. This theory remains highly speculative and it has not gained much traction among mainstream academics. It is, however, a typical kind of thought exercise for McKenna, who was self-aware enough not to claim he was "proving" a thesis like this and was merely, as he did across a wide range of topics, inviting engagement and curiosity—which he certainly has. It is an interesting intellectual role to play in the culture, one that the incentive structure of contemporary academia mostly discourages.

More soberly scientific than speculative and literary, Stamets represents a rare type in the modern era, a "gentleman scholar" throwback to earlier periods in the history of science: the high-level self-taught amateur who, as an academic outsider, nonetheless makes important contributions to the field. Regularly cited in the scholarly literature, he was recognized in 2014 as an "Innovation Ambassador" by the American Academy for the Advancement of Science for his work on subterranean fungal networks and his many mushroom-related patents.[33] Stamets's research, writings, and online lectures have served as key resources for mycologists and for the psychedelic community.[34] In his bestselling 2020 book, *Entangled Life: How Fungi Make Our Worlds, Change Our Minds and Shape Our Futures*, Cambridge biologist Merlin Sheldrake recognizes that Stamets's "definitive" works "continue to provide a crucial reference for countless mycologists, grassroots or otherwise," and that Stamets "has done more than anyone else to popularize fungal topics outside university biology departments."[35]

Inspired by these and other forerunners, the third wave proper began in the 1990s with the visionary efforts of above-ground medical researchers, especially psychiatrist Rick Strassman (b. 1952) at the University of New Mexico and, a few years later, neuroscientist Roland Griffiths (1946–2023) at Johns Hopkins University.[36] Ironically funding his initial research from federal "war on drugs" programs, Strassman worked with the powerful psychedelic tryptamine DMT. DMT is a naturally occurring compound endogenous to humans and other mammals and was discovered by scientists at various stages at midcentury (its hallucinogenic properties were discovered in the modernist West by Hungarian chemist Stephen Szára in 1956).[37] This discovery again occurred with an assist from several indigenous Amazonian peoples who have long utilized it, most famously in the form of ayahuasca, a tea ingeniously combining the DMT-laden leaves from particular rainforest plant species with the bark of a certain liana vine that inhibits DMT's normal breakdown in digestion. (DMT can be chemically synthesized as well.) This compound, along with others such as psilocybin/psilocin and LSD, was reliably provided during these decades to researchers such as Strassman and Griffiths through the rigorous efforts of the unassuming yet quietly radical chemist David Nichols at Purdue University's College of Pharmacy. (Nichols is a relatively unsung hero of psychedelia's third wave, characterized as it has been by a cautious securing of academic legitimacy—as unlike Timothy Leary as it could be.)[38] Along with UCLA psychiatrist Charles Grob (b. 1950) during the early 2000s, Griffiths conducted his experiments at Johns Hopkins mostly with mushroom-derived psilocybin. Strassman and Griffiths administered these serotonergic tryptamine compounds via injection to patients in therapeutic settings and achieved highly noteworthy results almost immediately. In their psilocybin trials, for example, Griffiths and Grob and colleagues were able significantly and durably to reduce death anxiety in terminal cancer patients and to help alleviate generalized anxiety, depression, PTSD, and various addictions at rates far higher than other known treatments.[39] Ongoing studies like these have created an atmosphere of legitimacy and optimism, and, as their results have filtered through the popular press, have greatly increased public curiosity concerning psychedelics research.

Although they are still illegal in most jurisdictions, psychedelics' general reputation and legal status have continued to evolve at a rapid pace since the initial findings by Strassman and Griffiths. Every month seems to bring news of new studies and potential applications. Major psychedelics research operations now include, not only Johns Hopkins Center for Psychedelic and Consciousness Research (hopkinspsychedelic.org), but Imperial College of London's Centre for Psychedelic Research (www.imperial.ac.uk/psychedelic-research-centre/), New York University's Center for Psychedelic Medicine (med.nyu.edu/departments-institutes/psychiatry/research/center-psychedelic-medicine), and many other prominent research centers, including Harvard, Yale, UCLA, Wisconsin, Mount Sinai School of Medicine (New York), Baylor College of Medicine (Houston), and Massachusetts General Hospital (Boston).[40] (At this point it seems difficult to find a prestigious university that is not at least planning to open a new psychedelics research unit, as are, for example, the University of Texas at Austin and the Berkeley, San Francisco, and San Diego campuses of the University of California.) Finding early funding through independent research foundations such as the Multidisciplinary Association for Psychedelic Studies (maps. org) and the Beckley Foundation (UK) (beckleyfoundation.org), these efforts involve a range of drugs, especially MDMA and psilocybin, both of which seem poised to win Federal Drug Administration approval for PTSD and other treatments.[41]

Along with this burgeoning research activity, there is currently a strong trend toward decriminalization and legalization of psychedelics, spearheaded by a few countries like Canada and Australia (MDMA and psilocybin), and some US cities and states (largely modeled on cannabis legalization), most notably at present in Colorado and Oregon, where, post-legalization (via statewide referendum), regulatory frameworks for the therapeutic use of psilocybin are underway, as well as large amounts of private investment capital currently flowing into psychedelics research (there are now many publicly traded psychedelics startup companies).[42] In 2022 the Biden Administration, via the Assistant Secretary for Mental Health and Substance Use (US Department of Health and Human Services), announced it was considering a "Federal Task Force" on the "complex issues" around "emerging substances such as MDMA and psilocybin."[43] Also at the federal level, a bipartisan Congressional Caucus to explore psychedelics research was launched in 2022.[44] It should also be noted that there is a wide and ever-expanding variety of additional psychedelics currently being prescribed and researched. Among the best known of these are ketamine, a synthetic hallucinogen currently used above-ground to treat anxiety and depression at clinics nationwide, and, at an earlier stage of research, ibogaine, a very powerful botanical psychedelic from the environs of Gabon in West Central Africa, which is currently being investigated for the treatment of opioid addiction.[45] Though ibogaine has long been known in Central Africa, it has been little researched thus far; its safety and therapeutic efficacy remain uncertain.

Considering these shifting pharmaceutical sands, one may summarize that, whereas the first psychedelic wave was characterized mostly by mescaline and LSD and the second wave by LSD and mushrooms, the third wave is characterized by mushrooms, DMT/ayahuasca, and a heightened curiosity and innovation regarding additional compounds. (Though it has its advantages in terms of ease of use and is still prevalent, LSD is less popular in research and recreation because of its lengthy time of action: around twelve to fourteen hours, compared to around four to six hours for mushrooms and ayahuasca and a mere fifteen to thirty minutes for inhaled DMT.) Psychedelia is rapidly becoming more variegated and complex, as private investor and researcher activities continue to expand in this space, including the ongoing synthesis and discovery of new psychedelic compounds. Appropriately, skeptical voices still urge caution, but overall popular sentiment—particularly among the young and the non-religious—seems also to have shifted more favorably toward psychedelics, as evidenced by increased usage among adults, including the rise in certain fashionable circles of "wellness" approaches involving so-called "micro-dosing" (usually psilocybin or LSD).[46] Psychedelics' improved reputation has also been enhanced by an outpouring of sympathetic journalism, spearheaded by the high-profile articles, books, and Netflix series by bestselling science journalist Michael Pollan (b. 1955) (michaelpollan.com). New media is also awash in psychedelics conversation, headlined by comedian and DMT booster Joe Rogan (b. 1967), purveyor of the world's most downloaded podcast, where prominent psychedelics researchers and experiencers have been regularly featured in long-form interviews. And social media platforms are replete with psychedelic resources. Notable among these are emerging digital artists who have skillfully replicated the visual and auditory sensations associated with DMT and other psychedelic experiences: see for example the astonishingly accurate trip simulations on the YouTube channel Symmetric Vision (www.youtube.com/@SymmetricVision). Mainstreaming is further fostered by major sports figures such as world champion boxer Mike Tyson (DMT and 5-MeO-DMT) and football quarterback Aaron Rodgers (ayahuasca), who have publicly lauded their psychedelic experiences, Rodgers going so far as to credit ayahuasca for his back-to-back NFL MVP awards in 2020 and 2021.[47]

As a result of these developments, it no longer comes across as eccentric to study psychedelics, and the flood gates are opening in both academia and the culture at large. An exciting aspect of this phenomenon in academia is the interdisciplinarity permeating this area of study. Just about every academic discipline is implicated in some way or other, beginning with the STEM fields, particularly chemistry, biology, and medicine (especially psychiatry, psychology, and neuroscience). Psychedelics are also being approached anew across the arts and humanities, social sciences, and applied fields: from botany to classics, psychology to philosophy, education to archaeology, nursing to theology, anthropology to legal studies, journalism to ethnic and area studies—to name just a few. There is a bull rush of journal articles and books across all of these fields and others. This includes urgent and manifold ethical and equity concerns, such as the aforementioned situation of indigenous peoples, environmental and species endangerment, and the alarming potential for patient/client abuse in therapeutic settings. As articulated by Columbia University psychiatrist and drug addiction researcher Carl Hart, there are also critiques of class snobbery in the "psychedelic chauvinism" alleged in the bourgeois elevation of psychedelics as agents of spiritual enlightenment in heightened contrast to the scary "bad people" street drugs of abuse like opioids and methamphetamine—with matching drug enforcement and sentencing biases.[48] Relatedly, there are also edgier legal and political debates around "cognitive liberty" or "neurocognitive self-determination," that is, the freedom to alter one's own consciousness, with sufficient resonance to preoccupy both libertarians and intersectionalists alike.[49] The list goes on. We are already seeing papers on the "queering of psychedelics" and cis normativity, as in "how psychedelics can help with gender identity and transition."[50] As an area study, psychedelia is truly becoming a full-service microcosm of academic trends.

And as noted regarding Stamets, research innovation has not been limited to the university. As have other fields, for example archaeology and botany, psychedelics is amassing a tradition of valuable amateur contributions. A striking recent case is the physical substantiation of long-held suspicions of ancient Greek ceremonial use associated with the Eleusinian Mysteries by a determined attorney and amateur classicist, Brian Muraresku (brianmuraresku.com). (Muraresku discovered "psychedelic beer" chemical residue in ceremonial chalices at a Greek outpost in Catalonia, Spain.)[51] At the experiential level, because of their long periods of illegality, the knowledge base of the effects of psychedelics continues to be highly indebted to amateur psychonauts and others. In terms of the first-person cataloging of events, individual users have copiously chronicled their experiences via crowd-sourced online databases like the trip reports meticulously cataloged at Erowid (erowid.org), an invaluable resource for curious members of the public and academics alike. These "experience reports" remain valuable data reservoirs because the legal and scientific machinery of institutional research grinds far too slowly to keep full pace with the wild proliferation of new compounds and novel usage practices. (There are *many* more, lesser-known psychedelic compounds currently being used informally than the more famous classic psychedelics discussed in this book.) Along these same lines, there are publicly accessible ongoing analyses of a wide range of psychedelic compounds, such as that provided by Mindstate Design Labs (UK) psychedelics researcher (and YouTuber) Josie Kins, who has developed a helpful Subjective Effects Index (EffectIndex.com), "which features a granular taxonomy of the subjective psychedelic experience" aimed at "developing a universal terminology set for discussing and describing that which was previously ineffable."[52] Kins's ongoing experiential database and associated frameworks are the most comprehensive currently available (I utilize her work in chapter 2).[53] There are also exemplars of extremely effective public communication about psychedelic science, such as neuroscientist Manesh Girn's valuable YouTube channel and podcast "The Psychedelic Scientist" (www.youtube.com/@ThePsychedelicScientist), which provides highly accessible content on a range of relevant topics.

As important for third-wave psychedelia as academic research is the religious and spiritual front, where psychedelics are tied to sacramental "entheogenic" usage by indigenous groups and both traditional and emergent religious communities.[54] In the US, the pan-tribal Native American Church (NAC), among whose founders was the important historical figure—and peyote devotee—Comanche Chief Quanah Parker (c. 1845–1911), has long used peyote as part of its sacred rituals and has undergone a winding path toward securing the legal status to use it as part of their free exercise of religion.[55] Specifically exempted from drug enforcement actions by the DEA since 1981, the NAC's right to use peyote is now safeguarded by federal statute as part of the Religious Freedom Restoration Act of 1993 (P.L. 103-141). A highly noteworthy additional legal accommodation of entheogenic psychedelic use is the unanimous 2006 Supreme Court ruling in favor of the União do Vegetal (UDV) Church's right to use DMT-containing ayahuasca and, a few years later, the extension by a federal appeals court of an analogous right, also with ayahuasca tea, to members of the Brazilian Santo Daime religion.[56] A major First Amendment Free Exercise Clause carve-out has thus emerged for native religions to use psychedelics ceremonially within their churches, at least from traditional and low-abuse-potential sources like peyote and ayahuasca. As discussed in later chapters, the next legal frontier has to do with non-indigenous congregations and individuals—including the question of what exactly defines a constitutionally qualifying "religion"—and how future religious exemptions might be extended.[57] It is a complex legal situation involving a number of factors and at present it is unclear how this area of law will evolve. What is clear, however, is that the psychedelics exemption for indigenous religions is a significant development that was unthinkable until recently. Depending on the slipperiness of its slope, it is bound to have an influence on the culture at large. At present there is no documented harm from their traditional usage of "plant medicines" to long-time NAC, UDV, or Santo Daime congregants that would justify restrictions on safety grounds. These communities' ongoing psychedelic practices may therefore be able to provide tradition-based models of responsible use based on collective responsibility and culturally resonant post-experience psychological integration.

On a much larger potential scale, there are already religionists more mainstream to American traditions incorporating psychedelics as entheogens, for example the Shefa Jewish congregation in the Bay Area (shefaflow.org) and the Ligare Christian Society based in Savannah, Georgia (ligare.org). In a sense, these contemporary groups build on older insights from the famous Good Friday Experiment, conducted in 1962 by Harvard psychiatrist Walter Pahnke (1931–1971) as part of his religious studies doctoral thesis, in which theology students were given psilocybin at Boston University's White Marsh Chapel. As against a placebo group, almost all of the student-participants reported Christianity-inflected "mystical" experiences, thus reinforcing psychedelics' entheogenic capabilities within the context of an individual's particular religious background experience and predilections.[58] In this connection, it is worth noting that these entheogenic aspects have been an important focus of widely read thinkers in the field of religion, such as MIT and University of California philosopher of religion Huston Smith (1919–2016), himself a participant in Pahnke's experiment, and the influential Buddhist writer and teacher Alan Watts (1915–1973).[59] It should be noted that there are also strong suggestions of traditions of psychedelic usage in Islam, especially among Sufi mystics.[60]

To summarize, the most visible currents in the ongoing third wave of psychedelia involve 1) a burgeoning global medical-therapeutic research nexus increasingly characterized by commercial interests, 2) academic attention across a wide range of additional fields, 3) increasing visibility across popular culture, and 4) in the US, at least, a growing legal religious accommodationism centered around indigenous communities, but possibly poised for extension by a US Supreme Court friendly to the free exercise of religion.

Beneath the Wave

> To deny philosophers of mind psychedelic substances is tantamount to denying instruments to musicians.
>
> —Peter Sjöstedt-Hughes, *Noumenautics*, i

But this is only the visible surface of the third wave. There also persists what has always been quantitatively by far the largest current of psychedelic use, that variously designated as "informal," "recreational," or illicit use. Spurred perhaps by the legitimating aura emanating from the medical and religious areas described above, psychedelic use is currently on the rise among adults, according to 2022 polling. Over a quarter of Americans surveyed report they have tried at least one "real" psychedelic drug such as mushrooms, LSD, or DMT (i.e., not just cannabis), including significantly higher percentages among millennials (35–44) and the college-educated.[61] A National Institutes of Health survey finds that "hallucinogen use among young adults [19–30] reached [an] all-time high in 2021," with usage almost tripling in the last decade.[62] These are mostly private individuals and small groups of friends ingesting psychedelics for entertainment and/or personal growth. As they are neither members of indigenous communities nor, for the most, part ingesting psychedelics to address a specific trauma, addiction, or mental illness, they are essentially making well visits to the psychedelic realm. These visits are sometimes undertaken for considered intellectual, spiritual, or wellness reasons but sometimes not for any "serious" reason at all. Though with these powerful substances, intent and outcome are assuredly not identical, as it is very possible to enter into it in one frame of mind and come out of it with a decidedly different one; while there are patterns to these experiences, they are never wholly predictable. As religion scholar Erik Davis (techgnosis.com) comments, "some psychedelic trips—they begin as a lark, a perceptual dérive, and end up with gods and devils and the screaming abyss."[63] Whatever users' intents and outcomes, the overwhelming majority of psychedelic usage is conducted in non-ceremonial and non-medical informal venues.

What about the experiences of this majority of extra-legal experiencers? Surely it would not be justified to sideline inquiry into them for reasons of respectability—or even safety: if there is something dangerous going on in society it should be studied from multiple perspectives. Just as urgently, a large number of individuals—some of them very young—are seeking psychedelic experiences to learn something about their lives and life in general, and many of them claim to have done just that, even if they usually have trouble articulating it. What precisely might they be learning?

This is where education and philosophy can serve important roles, not just for the benefit of knowledge accumulation for its own sake and/or authorities' regulatory designs, but also, it is to be hoped, for enhancing the self-understanding of the experiencers themselves. Putting "party drug" uses aside—while remaining mindful that play can have its serious sides—it is striking how typical it is for psychedelic users to report they have undergone significant and even profound *learning* experiences, either during the trip itself and/or in the course of psychologically integrating the experience afterwards. These are situations not necessarily specific to recovery from X, Y, or Z condition or trauma or understood through the ceremonial scripts of X, Y, or Z religious tradition. But nonetheless they culminate in an "afterglow" feeling—of indeterminate duration—of having gained worthwhile insights of great personal significance, often a hard-to-articulate existential gestalt shift in self-understanding and an altered perception of one's place within a larger scheme of things. At the more meaningful end of the spectrum, psychedelic experiences thus commonly possess a decidedly *educational* if not inchoate *philosophical* character, one not reducible to their cognitive, aesthetic or emotional character. Philosophers have begun to explore this territory, with compelling pioneering work by Australian philosopher Chris Letheby (University of Western Australia) in the philosophy of mind, British philosopher Peter Sjöstedt-Hughes (University of Exeter) in the history of philosophy and how philosophy can be utilized in the psychedelic therapy context, and, a bit earlier, Canadian philosopher of education Kenneth Tupper (University of British Columbia [plantteachers.com]), who was an early advocate for considering psychedelics as "cognitive tools" for catalyzing educational experiences of "wonder and awe."[64]

But such inquiries are only beginning. And this is as it should be, for, properly understood, this is not a niche topic for a narrow range of specialists. The desire deliberately to alter consciousness is a cultural universal manifest across a wide range of human experience; it cannot be exhausted within any one disciplinary perspective or set of interests. Across that wider set of concerns, psychedelics are neither medical nor religious phenomena exclusively; although these two are indispensable entrees, they are hardly comprehensive. Psychedelic experiences can also be understood as often having a distinctly *educational* character with patterns that are not reducible to situations of therapeutic recovery or religious mysticism. These patterns are in turn further distinguishable and greatly illuminated by describing them in traditional philosophical terms. The philosophical lens is not a *superior* way of looking at psychedelics, but it is well suited to doing so and it has been severely underappreciated. In the following pages, along with certain others, I argue that psychedelics are, in Grof's phrase, "non-specific amplifiers"—that is, they are essentially protean and elusive of any determinate *telos* or fixity of purpose, though their intimate directive power can fool one into thinking otherwise.[65] In contrast to what seems to be a prevailing hippie folk wisdom, psychedelics are not inherently environmentalist or Gaia-oriented, loving and politically progressive, oppositional or counter-cultural, spiritually healing or emotionally beneficent. They may certainly be those things on specific occasions for certain individuals (and I have personally experienced those manifestations). But they also may not be.

While psychedelic experience indeed has some identifiable deep structural features, my argumentative burden will be that these features do not point it in any particular direction; psychedelics do not by themselves give us *answers* to anything. Their philosophical and educational value lies elsewhere and this book's aim is to explain that contention. One of the virtues of a philosophical approach is that it can help us better to look beyond our subjective predilections and personal projections. Success along these lines is only ever partial, of course, as we are necessarily situated within interpretive horizons that are always embodied, enculturated, and bounded by geography and history and much else. The eastern and western philosophical traditions are very obviously themselves cases in point of this situatedness.

Still, it is just as much a part of us that we constantly struggle to see beyond those very horizons as well, the admittedly impossible attempt to do so being one way of looking at the philosophical enterprise as a whole.

Though our finitude guarantees perpetual failure, the equally perpetual struggle to "fail better" shows we are also always capable of *learning* and in so doing pushing outwards against our circumscriptions—not against all of them at once, but in places here and there.[66] Used wisely and with a constant eye toward safety, psychedelics can be potent allies in this endeavor, a philosophical and educational adjuvant that can augment both questioning and dissociation yet also re-affiliation and re-connection, fostering—among other things—a dynamic that neuroscientists term "neuroplasticity." To be sure, this is a Goldilocks situation where, akin to a Vygotskian "zone of proximal development," one wants neither too much nor too little neuroplasticity; one does not want one's mentality either stuck in ruts or amorphously malleable.[67] And neither does one want plasticity for plasticity's sake (traumatic brain injury and methamphetamines augment brain plasticity as well); obviously, what is needed is an adaptively *beneficial* plasticity rather than one that is debilitating.[68] This is where a philosophically informed educational framework can be useful. It can help provide a normative scaffolding from which to make a more distanced assessment of the worthwhileness and coherence of these experiences. As always, it would be ridiculous to aim at a definitive or final understanding of these phenomena, but a greater understanding is always an appropriately modest aim. Humility aside, though, these are extremely powerful "reality switch technologies," in chemist and neuroscientist Andrew Gallimore's words, that demonstrably act on our neuronal networks as "world-building machines," what Watts calls the very "chemistry of consciousness."[69] The stakes here for our sense of ourselves and how we perceive our ultimate purposes are high.

All learning involves a temporal dimension anticipating mortality—however obliquely—in that it separates oneself from one's (previous) self to at least some small extent, constituting a new and altered self that now includes that which has been learned; out with the old you and in with the new one. This is why the passage of time provides the possibility of looking back on one's former self with a degree of detachment, as if that younger self were, to a degree, a separate being, the distance between being filled with what has been experienced and learned in the interim. There is an intimate poignancy in such reflections, especially over a long span, as it is inevitably a kind of lived *memento mori*, a reminder of approaching death. In German philosopher Arthur Schopenhauer's (1788–1860) words, "Every separation gives us a foretaste of death—and every reunion a foretaste of a resurrection."[70] Perhaps there is an intimation of both of these in the "ego death" reported in some of the most intensely dissociative states, such as that commonly described with 5-MeO-DMT, as an unsettling total "whiteout" of consciousness, the return from which is, strangely enough, often reported to result in deep and durable feelings of serenity and gratitude. Even if one has no desire for psychonautical adventure, chemically aided non-ordinary states of mind are interesting and beg for further inquiry. Maybe they're mere illusions, maybe they're truly profound, maybe they're deeply worthwhile, and maybe some are better off never having had them. And maybe, somehow, they are all of these things. There are no guarantees in this realm. My purpose here is not to proselytize or recommend anything to anyone. Please consult your doctor, shaman, priest, or rabbi—or your lawyer—but certainly not your philosopher. Psychedelics are not for everybody. Nothing is for everybody. But there is nothing from which somebody cannot learn.

Chapter 1

Overview

Ultimately, the quest is to find out who we are.

—David E. Nichols, in Morris,
"Conversation with Dr. David Nichols"

Learning from Psychedelics?

There is an apparent universal human need for deliberate consciousness alteration. We seem to be creatures for whom unadulterated reality has never been quite fully sufficient. As journalist Michael Pollan writes, human beings are perpetually inclined "to stimulate or calm, to fiddle with or completely alter, the qualities of our mental experience."[1] Among the most potent of these mental alterations are the ancient psychoactive substances that have been documented as having accompanied our ancestors for millennia and into the mists of prehistory.[2] In addition to a "worldwide association of psychedelics with spiritual traditions,"[3] anthropologists have speculated that hallucinogens such as psilocybin and other mushrooms even predate anatomically modern humans, "perhaps from the dawn of the human presence on the planet," and seem to have been adaptive for millions of years along the course of our evolutionary history, as the "incidental inclusion of psychedelics in the diet of hominins, and their eventual addition to rituals and institutions of early humans could have conferred selective advantages."[4]

The thesis that humanity has a deep history with psychoactive substances is lent further credibility by the fact that we share our consciousness-altering propensity with non-human animals. Psychopharmacologist Ronald Siegel affirms that "intoxication with plant drugs and other psychoactive substances has occurred in almost every species throughout history. There is a pattern of drug-seeking and drug-taking behavior that is consistent across time and species."[5] Among the many examples:

> After sampling the numbing nectar of certain orchids, bees drop to the ground in a temporary stupor, then weave back for more. Birds gorge themselves on inebriating berries, then fly with reckless abandon. Cats eagerly sniff aromatic "pleasure" plants, then play with imaginary objects. Cows that browse special range weeds will twitch, shake and stumble back to the plants for more. Elephants purposely get drunk on fermented fruits. Snacks on "magic mushrooms" cause monkeys to sit with their heads on their hands in a posture reminiscent of Rodin's *Thinker*. . . . Monkeys and baboons, which share our tastes and temperaments, learned to use hallucinogens and tobacco to relieve boredom with all the shrewdness and zest of human users.[6]

Even pigs apparently enjoy the psychoactive properties they experience from henbane.[7] This widespread and abiding—and apparently pan-species—implied dissatisfaction with everyday consensus reality indicated by such instances is an abiding mystery that modern inquiry is only beginning to explore. As physician and writer Oliver Sacks remarks, "To live on a day-to-day basis is insufficient for human beings; we need to transcend, transport, escape; we need meaning, understanding, and explanation; we need to see overall patterns in our lives."[8] But why, one wonders, is "normal" reality not enough? From whence comes this shadowing insufficiency?

While such questions may never be answered fully, much exploration is taking place amidst the current "renaissance" of interest in psychedelic compounds.[9] This has been spearheaded by promising medical research on the therapeutic capabilities of psilocybin ("magic mushrooms") and the synthesized "empathogen" MDMA. (MDMA is not a "classic" psychedelic like LSD or psilocybin mushrooms due to its subjective effects being mainly non-visual; as an empathogen it might be thought of as *emotionally* psychedelic in that it is associated mainly with enhanced intersubjective feelings, mostly of a prosocial type, such as sentiments of interconnectedness.) Additionally, both inside and outside medicine and therapy, there is renewed interest, even to the point of having become fashionable, in experimentation with additional powerful psychedelics. Some of these have been preserved in indigenous cultures and are now becoming more widespread, such as orally ingested ayahuasca (usually a digestible Amazonian brew combining a monoamine oxidase inhibitor from the stalk of the *Banisteriopsis caapi* vine with DMT from the leaves of the *Psychotria viridis* shrub), 5-MeO-DMT (originally from parotid gland secretions of the Sonoran Desert toad [*Incilius alvarius*]), ibogaine (from the African shrub *Tabernanthe iboga*), *Salvia divinorum* (a highly psychoactive and unusual plant native to Mazatec regions of southwestern Mexico), various *Datura* species (a very dangerous hallucinogenic plant with an ancient global lineage), mescaline (originally sourced from several cacti of the Americas, including the peyote [*Lophophora williamsii*] and San Pedro [*Echinopsis pachanoi*] varieties), and many others, including lab-created LSD, DMT, ketamine, and the aforementioned MDMA.[10] There is also an indefinite number of synthesized "designer" psychedelic compounds, with new ones surfacing constantly.

For the history-minded, there are also exciting discoveries and informed speculations about ancient history that suggest, among other things, the presence of psychoactive substances in ceremonies foundational to western culture, most notably the ancient Greek Eleusinian Mysteries, estimated to have been practiced for over one thousand years (ca. 1500 BCE to 392 CE) and the early Christian Eucharist, which may have been modeled on Eleusis.[11] These and other developments—such as a reexamination of the prevalence of entheogenic mushroom motifs in early and medieval Christian iconography throughout Europe—have created a renewed general interest by classicists and other experts in the "central role of psychoactive herbalism in the religious and cultural life of pagan antiquity and its assimilation into Christian traditions."[12] In Eastern religion, too, equally if not more anciently, there has long been speculation as to the nature of what is vividly represented as a psychoactive ritual drink called "soma" that is mentioned prominently in the foundational Hindu scriptural hymn the *Rig Veda* (written ca. 1000–2000 BCE).[13] There are many candidates for soma's identity, including the possibility of a psychedelic mushroom or plant.

At a more personal level, although everyone knows about "good trips" and "bad trips" and that psychedelics have long been utilized as party drugs, there is commonly more claimed for them than for other mind-altering but somewhat more somatic substances like cocaine, opioids, alcohol, and marijuana (although each of these can have very potent hallucinogenic effects). Psychedelics are said to be especially capable of providing insights that are wrenching, perspective-shifting, and yielding of life-changing spiritual meaning. Such characterizations seem to imply an *educational* claim that one has *learned* something as a result of the interaction, including the processing of that experience afterwards; while one may learn something from having a "good time" with a party drug, there is clearly something more specific being communicated here—something weightier and more durable is meant. This appears to be the situation uncovered by Roland Griffiths and colleagues at Johns Hopkins University's Center for Psychedelics and Consciousness Research (hopkinspsychedelic.org), who have, in multiple studies, established that psychedelic experiences can be of deep significance to patients with severe trauma. In the clinical setting, subjects reported their encounter with psilocybin to be among the "five most personally meaningful and among the five most spiritually significant experiences of their lives," comparable to the birth of a child, and that, astonishingly, the *psilocybin encounters significantly and durably reduced death anxiety among terminal cancer patients*—all of which obviously implies that something very powerful indeed had been learned.[14] When anything at all—substance or not—so profoundly effects as basic an element of human existence as death anxiety, it is time for everyone to sit up and pay attention. This demonstrable pedagogical power also accords with the customary veneration of psychedelics in indigenous contexts as sacred "plant teachers" and the like.[15]

These therapeutic discoveries are undeniably hopeful, but psychedelics may also be conceived as educational tools *outside* of the medical frame. What then might be hallmarks of a truly *educational* experience with psychedelics, one that might not only help with trauma but provide a learning experience for just about *anyone*? Trip reports often emphasize that psychedelic experiences are to be set apart because something takes place with them that is more profound than simply a good time; those claiming to have found some sort of epiphany or enlightenment via psychedelics are making a claim that something important has thus been *learned*. But what are we to make of a claim like this? It is difficult to know exactly, especially since, as is admitted by all parties, the descriptions are rarely as impressive as the supposed insight. It is a difficult problem. Although much has been published on psychedelics, the precise nature and quality of the specifically educational insights they are said to enable has been underdiscussed. Drugs and therapy addressing injury and trauma should be left to qualified medical practitioners. But psychedelics, conceived as *educational* technologies, have a much wider field of application than this.

Consciousness Alteration as Readiness to Learn

> Clearly there are monsters down there in the underworld. But there are also treasures. By lowering the threshold of consciousness, psychedelics allow people to intervene in habits and patterns that are usually subconscious, automatic, and chronically resistant to conscious efforts to change. They bring insight, help people confront and accept repressed experiences or emotions, and allow them to choose to think, feel and live differently.
>
> —Jules Evans, *The Art of Losing Control*, 105

What is an altered state altered *from*? Nobody really knows. A naïve realism might circularly take "normal" everyday consciousness to be bedrock, like in the comical story about Samuel Johnson's refutation of idealism, the so-called "appeal to the stone," which consisted of his "striking his foot with mighty force against a large stone, till he rebounded from it—'I refute it *thus*.'"[16] In philosophy, there have always been non-realist views, such as the Berkeleyan subjective idealism that Johnson sought to refute to coherentist views of truth of many varieties that disallow any external reality "out there" to which our mental processes might correspond. In psychedelic circles it is fashionable to speak of (merely) "consensus reality" or (merely) "adaptive consciousness" in order to emphasize these ontological uncertainties. ("Dude, I just had this idea: maybe the altered state is 'more real' than the normal one . . . whoa!") These core philosophical problems will not be solved here, except to note that simply rhetorically elevating the altered state and demoting that of the baseline state solves nothing either: it only remits the problem to one remove further because maybe the consensus and/or the adaptations are *truer*. (It would be fair to suggest, however, that a high dose of any classic psychedelic would render Dr. Johnson's rock kicking far more hysterically comical.) Equally worrisome, and more pertinent to the present inquiry, is that anyone wishing to analyze altered states of consciousness *from the inside* is faced at the outset with a parallel problem of distinguishability: how to delineate the *feel* of the "ordinary" from that of the "altered" consciousness. Conceiving of something as having been altered implies a baseline conception of the thing in its unaltered state. The alleged alteration would not register otherwise. Unfortunately, what philosopher David Chalmers (1995) calls the "hard problem" of consciousness, that is, how to explain the qualitative first-person dimension of the phenomenon—the qualitative feel of it from the point of view of the experiencer (i.e., its "qualia")—has thus far also proven elusive.[17] (It is almost as if philosophers never solve the problems they raise, an accusation which would, of course, be correct—at least since Socrates.) It is prudent therefore to rope off this area of intense, even obsessive, philosophical interest and step gingerly around it. A rough and pragmatic phenomenological account that is ontologically agnostic will have to suffice.

For that account, I turn to the still-unsurpassed picture of ordinary experience provided in the early writings of Martin Heidegger (1889–1976), the philosopher *par excellence* of assessing consciousness in terms of its lived experience in what he calls, in his magnum opus *Being and Time* (1927), the "existential analytic of Dasein (being-there)."[18] In Heidegger's sense, "average everydayness" (*Alltäglichkeit*) is the default mode of experience wherein we have, as it were, our heads down going about our business immersed in the countless serial and concurrent projects that populate our waking hours. This mode where we encounter the world as ready-to-hand "equipment" (*das Zeug*) constitutes our normal mentality most of the time: as a goal-directed teleological flow that is bothered only occasionally by an eruption of reflection either concerning the worthwhileness and directionality of particular projects or onto ourselves introspectively (16). What we "see" normally are our own projects and purposes, and the instruments and tools by which we realize those projects are largely invisible. They only become visible and stand out for us when they break down in some way, in which case they stand out for us as entities that are "present" in a way that they can be contemplated independently. When I'm scrolling through my social media feed I don't think about "my phone" as such unless, say, the battery runs out or something else goes wrong. Then all of a sudden "my phone" becomes present to me in a way that it was not before when it was, to my mind, thoroughly sunken into my mental background while it was working smoothly. These eruptions of objects becoming present-at-hand—and the modal switching we constantly perform between ready-to-hand and present-at-hand—are indispensable for analyzing the structure of lived experience, how we cut through the world from the point of view of the one actually doing the cutting through. That "one," the first-person experiencer, in Heideggerian terms, is "Dasein."

Continuing with Heidegger, one of humanity's signal "ontical" properties is that we are "ontological," meaning that, for whatever evolutionary reasons, we possess a capability of self-awareness regarding our own contingency—our limitedness and mortality—an occasional reflexivity that, when it occurs, opens a space for the deepest questioning and doubts. "The ontical distinction of Dasein lies in the fact that it is ontological" (12). Within this liminal space, often pursuant to what we may experience as a reorienting resolve of the will, we find ourselves considering what is the point or worthwhileness of X, Y or Z project and, ultimately, this may lead us to follow through by wondering, "What is the point of *all* our projects in the ensemble?" If sustained long enough, this sequential questioning leads inevitably to a confrontation with the unmovable reality of our own limitedness and finitude. Pursuing those "whys?" until they lead us into the vastness of space and time inevitably raises the question of one's ultimate significance. For Heidegger, one of the key descriptive facts about us as organisms is that we tend to contemplate our own mortality; not only will we die someday, but we are also *aware* of this eventuality. This simultaneously terrible and exhilarating existential capability is a core defining experience for a human being, and a sustained focus on it is perhaps the major unifying theme among other mid-century "existentialist" philosophers like Jean-Paul Sartre.

In these broad existentialist terms, psychedelic consciousness alteration would seem to involve precisely this kind of modal shifting, a kind of toggling of consciousness back and forth between the purposiveness and project-centeredness of everydayness and the quantitatively rarer (but undeniable) temporary cessation of purposiveness, during which a range of non-ordinary experiences is made available. Psychedelic experience is certainly not the *only* way one might achieve purposiveness cessation. Other candidates include aesthetic contemplation, such as Immanuel Kant's (1724–1804) account of the experience of "the beautiful" as involving "purposiveness without a purpose," Buddhist loving-kindness (*metta*), Christian unconditional love (*agape*), "pure" scientific curiosity, Heideggerian "releasement" (*Gelassenheit*, "letting beings be"), Stoic and Epicurean tranquility (*ataraxia*), many meditative and trance-like states, and a long list of other "archaic techniques of ecstasy."[19] This is where definitionally true "out of the box" thinking is made possible via a potential releasing of a Pandora's box of out-of-the-ordinary experiences. When we gain release from the "in-order-to's" of the everyday project orientation and into what Kant called the "free play of the imagination," a new world of possibilities is *literally* opened, including the potential for sublime experiences "transcending every standard of the senses."[20]

In the history of educational thought, this departure from everydayness is central to Plato's famous dialogue-within-a-dialogue about learning, the *Meno*. In their conversation, Socrates's eponymous interlocutor likens the feeling of being jolted out of his everyday attitude by Socrates's questioning to being stung by a "torpedo-fish" (*narkē*), literally a numbing drug-fish (probably a colorful way of describing a type of stingray). This pedagogical intervention causes Meno finally to be rid of his conceit to knowledge, thereby rendering him "perplexed" but ready to learn:

> MENO: Socrates, I certainly used to hear, even before meeting you, that you never did anything else than exist in a state of perplexity [*aporia*] yourself and put others in a state of perplexity. And now you seem to be bewitching me and drugging me and simply subduing me with incantations, so that I come to be full of perplexity. And you seem to me, if it is appropriate to make something of a joke, to be altogether, both in looks and other respects, like the flat torpedo-fish of the sea. For, indeed, it always makes anyone who approaches it grow numb, and you seem to me now to have done that very sort of thing to me, making me numb [*narkan*]. For truly, both in soul and in mouth, I am numb and have nothing with which I can answer you.[21]

This teacher-induced perplexity is the famed state of mind of Socratic ignorance that is generated via teacher-student dialogue. It illustrates how the removal of a student's conceit to knowledge is one of teaching's greatest tasks. It is not, as is often thought, the *removal* of ignorance that is to be most highly prized, but rather the *achieving* of it. From the Socratic point of view, the pupil's state of ignorance is more even than one pedagogical accomplishment among others: it supplies a necessary condition for any learning whatsoever. One is closed to the inherent novelty of the learning experience when one thinks one already knows.

As with Socratic dialogue, the destructive precondition for learning, the fostering of the requisite perplexity, may certainly be arrived at through natural means. But under the right conditions, it seems able to be chemically induced as well, as the numbing drug-fish himself, a devoted and enthusiastic participant in the drugged rituals of the Eleusinian Mysteries, was undoubtedly personally well aware.[22] One may practice meditation, holotropic breathing, or fasting, dance or drum oneself into a trance, lose oneself in an orgasm, drift away in a reverie, be swept up in a work of art or literature, fuse one's identity with a social group, become numbed by a gestalt "aha," achieve a feeling of mystical union with God-or-Nature, become swelled by Freud's "oceanic feeling"[23]—along with countless other states of mind where one is liberated from the default purposive state of mind and into the *aporia* of which Socrates speaks. These experiences—and countless more—may catalyze a moment of respite from the above-mentioned circuitry of in-order-to's that characterize most of waking life.[24] In this broad existential sense, there is probably nothing at all ontologically special about psychoactive drugs.

From time immemorial, however, they have provided an efficient opportunity, paradoxically, to plan to have an experience of the unplanned, deliberately and reliably to induce extra-pragmatic states of mind that are otherwise available (mostly) exclusively to those of unusual mental powers—shamans, *curanderos*, mystics, and prophets—capable of the requisite spiritual discipline. For those of us who are not yet superstars of spirituality, these molecules represent a significant convenience. But as their adoption by traditional cultures indicates, their relative ease of use—including their predictable temporal duration—also renders them potentially far more inclusive and therefore capable of informing *collective* imaginaries and shaping *shared* lifeways—rather than being an elite possession only for the few. In a way, psychedelic drugs might be said to represent a *democratization of spirituality*. They are not distributable in mass society along the same exact communal lines as a traditional Navajo peyote ceremony or, indeed, as recent archaeo-chemical research has suggested, the Eleusinian Mysteries and early Christian Eucharist (and the latter's suspiciously "fortified" ceremonial wine).[25] In these models, members of the community more or less equally participate in the altered state together rather than it being sequestered as the secret possession of a shamanic or priestly caste who, although they typically administer and shape the interpretation of the sacramental substance, are no longer its sole direct experiencers. In fact, as Carl A. P. Ruck and

Mark A. Hoffman discern, in ancient civilizations, customs involving severe priestly restrictions of entheogens seem "to be characteristic of the decadent stages, when the sacrament is deemed too dangerous for the lower class of peoples or social groups, and is reserved only for elites with the proper preparation."[26]

The Sensorium Let Loose

> The rabbit-hole went straight on like a tunnel for some way, and then dipped suddenly down, so suddenly that Alice had not a moment to think about stopping herself before she found herself falling down what seemed to be a very deep well.
>
> —Lewis Carroll, *Alice's Adventures in Wonderland*, 10

The foregoing suggests that provoking Socratic perplexity and *aporia* might be one sense in which psychedelics can help preface learning experiences. Let us explore further features of the psychedelic lesson plan.

What we are after is a substantive *learning* experience rather than one that is merely entertaining. Not to knock entertainment—it has its place and should not be underestimated. Fun can have serious effects: play is crucial to child development, comedians are among our most astute social critics, and "the Trickster" is a universal cultural archetype.[27] But many in the psychedelic community are at pains pointedly to emphasize a depth dimension to what they have experienced and to draw a distinction between the putative profundity of their journey and the mere oohing and aahing over the cool visuals and general trippiness. Admittedly, the perceptual circus can be highly diverting: intense colors, kaleidoscopic geometric patterns, a distortive "waviness" or "breathing" quality to one's perceptual field, lingering tracers when tracking moving objects, a heightened ability to notice a wider-than-normal range of goings-on around one, a busier-than-usual buzzing of sounds, perceptual and emotional blending, etc. Sometimes the sheer fun of these sensorial bedazzlements (or the discomfiture if one is alarmed by them) is quite enough for many individuals and they wish to go no further. Yet many of those psychonautically inclined enough to try higher dosages are unsatisfied with just the perceptual showtime shenanigans; something central to the experience would be missing if that were *it*. Reports make clear that there are stranger and more profound happenings taking place beyond the play of the sensorium.

People commonly report that they have been *educated* by psychedelics in the sense that they have learned impactful lessons with durable consequences for their subsequent lives. Often these can be boiled down to a single key moral insight—for example, "don't take yourself so seriously" or "be there for your loved ones" or, very often, large-scale generalizations like "everything is love," "we are all connected," "we must care for the earth," etc. Subjects are often aware that these sound like trite inspirational wall poster quotes, which can lead to frustration—or amusement—that they can do no better at articulating exactly *what* they have learned; there seems often to be an ineffability about these experiences that eludes full description. There is a frustrating mismatch between the experience's magnitude and its description. Certain artists have perhaps done better on this score—one thinks of the hallucinogen-inspired paintings of Alex Grey (www.alexgrey.com/art/) or the abstract "imagined landscapes" of 2020 Guggenheim Fellow Barbara Takenaga (www.barbaratakenaga.com)—but still, as evocative and visionary as they may be, these artworks seem more suggestive than specifically instructive, at least from a philosophical point of view that craves more definition.[28]

I'll first approach these experiences phenomenologically, noting how they do in fact initially appear and refraining from making extrapolating judgments as much as possible. The data for this analysis are found among the copiously available trip reports, clinical studies, literary descriptions, artistic visions, and personal experience. A phenomenological account would not look too quickly past psychedelics' initial perceptual adumbrations. As an external observer, it would seem easy to take on a spectator's perspective at the parade of perceptual stimuli, as if one were merely watching an especially good light show. But this approach is limited because, with psychedelics, the sensory inputs are also accompanied by obverse and multifarious sub rosa *feelings*, which can register as delightful (or in rare cases as terrifying), and normally provide one with a decided *attitude* about what is going on.[29] (It would be very unusual to have an affect-less psychedelic experience.) One is pointedly *not* just a disinterested observer; one is *being-there* in the Heideggerian sense of being fully engaged in undergoing it. Appreciating this being-there aspect is like appreciating the obvious difference between watching a kiss in a movie and actually kissing. In both cases one "knows" a kiss is going on but in only one case is one actually experiencing the kissing for oneself; one could even become a knowledgeable "expert" on movie kisses without ever having kissed anyone oneself. Likewise, an account of psychedelic experience is limited if it is presented exclusively in the manner of disembodied or disinterested observation. Despite all the surface shimmer, beneath it all one is also undergoing a total experience in a more holistic sense. Along with the sense perceptions and cogitations, it has mood and emotion attached to it: it makes one *feel* a certain way. As ethnobotanist Giorgio Samorini remarks, the "contents and sense of a human psychedelic experience reach far beyond the visual and auditory hallucinations that accompany them."[30] This mirrors Heidegger's more general observation that the feel of an experience is not just an occasional matter but a ubiquitous accompaniment to all human experience: "in every case Dasein always has some mood [*gestimmt ist*]"; "we are never free of moods" (134, 136). Despite this, our rationalist inheritance causes an overemphasis on empirical sense data and the purely cognitive contents of experience; we tend to think we truly understand an experience only if we can categorize and count it. Yet there is still that persistent *feel* lurking beneath it all, stubbornly eluding all the analyses and calculations: that first-person "insider" sense of it, what philosophers call "qualia." In Heidegger's summation, "ontologically mood is a primordial kind of Being for Dasein, in which Dasein is disclosed to itself *prior* to all cognition and volition, and *beyond* the range of disclosure" (136). In psychological terms, integrating something momentous that has been undergone involves achieving knowledge about it (e.g., cognitive behavioral therapy) but it also involves a more holistic affective appropriation. Understanding a psychedelic experience from the inside in terms of its qualia necessarily requires this double-barreled approach too. As a participant in an Imperial College London psilocybin trial for depression expressed it, "I think psychedelics are the difference between knowing something and then really absorbing and feeling it."[31]

This aspect of the phenomenon seems important. It suggests that what is occurring is a lived sense of expansiveness that brings to the fore what the existentialists would describe as the contingency of one's own being-in-the-world. More specifically, the perceptual fluctuations occasion something akin to an inferential psychological process where one starts to see that what one has been taking for granted as perceptual bedrock reality is actually, let us say, more flexible than previously assumed. Again, some find this epistemological funhouse aspect exhilarating, whereas others are alarmed by it. And there is ample room for both attitudes to cycle in rapid sequence within the same trip. But wherever one lies on the pain-pleasure spectrum regarding these disequilibrating feelings, one is viscerally reacting to an *induced apprehension* that things may not actually be as they seem ostensibly. One gains a highly vivid sense that there's somehow something more "out there" than meets the everyday eye. We already know this intellectually beforehand from regular perceptual distortions: the stick that looks bent in the water, I could have sworn I heard footsteps outside the tent last night, etc. As with the movie kiss, though, there is a vast difference between knowing something intellectually, such as the fact that I will die someday, versus knowing it in the sense of accepting it as an intimate and comprehensive reality *for me*. A surgeon who knows all about mortality statistics and has even seen many people die may nonetheless have great difficulty when actually confronted with evidence of her *own* impending demise, say, when instead of giving the terminal diagnosis to a patient, the tables are turned and she receives it *herself*.[32] More, as philosopher and psychiatrist Jonathan Lear explains, Heidegger has "shown us that we typically use phrases such as 'We are all going to die someday' or 'We are all mortal' as cliches to *tranquillize* us out of any real encounter with how what we are saying targets us. Although we say 'we,' a stealthy 'I' slips the noose."[33] In a way, there is existential comfort in keeping our finitude at a distance; a fuller *felt* experience of contingency is worlds away from apprehending it merely cognitively.

I call this ensemble of the *lived* experience of perceptual distortion combined with the self-questioning it can engender "*epistemic loosening*" (explored in depth in the next chapter). It is an existential state wherein sensory perceptions alter such that one starts to feel a vertiginous mistrust of them that one does not normally encounter in normal everyday mode. One is made to wonder: was the epistemic trust misplaced all along? What *else* should I mistrust? And down Alice's rabbit hole we go: "Down, down, down. Would the fall *never* come to an end?"[34] One does not need to fall very far, though, to experience epistemic loosening. Even those slight visual "drifting" perturbations are sufficient for occasioning *at some level* the requisite sense of perceptual contingency and bemused skepticism. In this key manner, the moment of epistemic loosening—usually the initial encounter of a psychedelic trip—seems closely related to the numbing perplexity of the ready-to-learn moment of Socratic ignorance. In both, the conceit to knowledge is to varying degrees troubled.

In standard psychedelic terminology, "setting" has to do with the immediate environment within which the trip occurs. Is it at home? In a park on a beautiful day? At the mall? "Set" has to do with one's mindset going in. Is the incipient tripper worried about something? Depressed? Feeling okay about her life overall? I would suggest that one's favorable or unfavorable *attitude* toward this Socratic-like epistemic loosening, if it can be identified in advance, should be considered an important aspect of the set in this context. Some welcome it and some do not, and the same person may have different propensities at different times. But one disposed to enter that Socratic state of readiness to learn will, I think, tend to have a very different experience from one who is not. This is a ubiquitous theme among psychedelic guides across the spectrum from the traditional shamanic to modern therapeutic contexts. It also seems to be settled common sense among psychedelics users: one needs to have an attitude of openness toward the experience and let it go whither it will rather than trying to control it. "Fighting it" almost guarantees a bad outcome; someone embarking on a high-dosage LSD trip—let alone ayahuasca or DMT—with the mindset of being in command of how it will unfold is laughable, just as it is laughable when one of Socrates's interlocutors tries to control an on-form Socratic dialogue, which typically ends with consternation and/or someone storming off. (The most dramatic example of this is the main interlocutor of Book I of the *Republic*, the brash and aggressive Thrasymachus, who exits from the dialogue out of frustration with Socrates's challenges.)[35] Starting with the perceptual wobbles and/or slight unease one first notices at the onset of a trip, this destabilizing epistemic loosening is a key initial clue to locating the educative element that lies within it. Beneath all the surface bells and whistles and akin to the unsettlements of Socratic ignorance, it readies the mind for novelty and so positions it as *ready to learn*.

Smaller Selves, Larger Identifications

> A second factor is required for truly durable change: the discovery of new forms of self-modelling during the experience, and the consolidation of these during the subsequent period of integration. It's not just the plasticity—it's the way you use it.
>
> —Chris Letheby, *Philosophy of Psychedelics*, 147

Epistemic loosening can become extreme enough that it can be described as "dissociative," perceptions becoming so out of whack that one loses one's bearings more comprehensively. On the extreme end there are phenomena such as the so-called "k-hole" of ketamine that is described as like an out-of-body experience. At perhaps the farthest dissociative edge are the bizarre happenings found with 5-MeO-DMT where, during a relatively short trip of 10–20 minutes, subjects undergo what is described as a more or less complete "white-out" dissociation from their sense of self, their ego—sometimes blissful, sometimes terrifying, sometimes both—after which they sometimes report returning with a new sense of connection with other people, living organisms, and even nature as a whole.[36] To these extreme dissociative experiences, one might add what Terence McKenna called "heroic doses" of psilocybin mushrooms (5 grams dried) and very high doses of LSD (in the range of 500 micrograms), and also robust ayahuasca and DMT trips.[37] Here "epistemic loosening" would be so euphemistic as to be inaccurate. Users describe it (non-pejoratively) as more like an epistemic crisis where the borders of the self are perceived to have dissolved and the ego radically reduces its prominence—some go so far as to use the metaphor of "ego dissolution" or "ego death" to relate the feel of it. Unsurprisingly, this blurring of the boundaries of self and world very commonly gives reciprocal rise to a holistic realization of connectedness to what previously appeared to be "outside" and "other," like humanity as a whole or nature and cosmos writ large. When all goes well, an ancient paradox ensues: a process whereby one finds oneself by losing oneself; as in the saying of medieval Japanese Buddhist sage Dogen Zenji (1200–1253): "To know yourself is to forget yourself."[38] The diminution of the ego associated with extreme epistemic loosening allows it then to reconnect and integrate with something previously perceived as external. This "amazing grace" paradox ("I once was lost but now I'm found") is a core experience of the world's mystical traditions and is hardly a unique feature of psychedelia. Nonetheless, it does appear that epistemic loosening can function as a relatively easy entrée into what such mystical experiences feel like.[39]

The common so-called "unitive" or "unitive-mystical" experience in psychedelics seems to be built up out of these sentiments of connection, as in "we are all one," "everything is connected," "it's all about love," etc.[40] The altered sense of self apparent in such moments, however ephemeral—it doesn't always last for long—is a visceral version of what

I'll analyze in chapter 3 as *hypertrophic identification*, where one identifies with a more encompassing entity like the earth, nature, the cosmos, God, etc. In the history of philosophy, a close analog may be found in certain branches of Stoicism and Epicureanism, like those associated with the Roman poet Lucretius (c. 99–55 BCE). In his famous poem *The Nature of Things*, one achieves a kind of immortality—and comfort from the terror of death—via the contemplative identification with the laws of science and their manifestation in the natural world:

> Thus, in this way each man is running from himself, yet still
> Because he clings to that same self, although against his will,
> And clearly can't escape from it, he loathes it; for he's ill
> But doesn't grasp the cause of his disease. Could he but see
> This clear enough, a man would drop everything else, and study
> First to understand the Nature of Things, for his own sake:
> It's his condition for *all time*—not for one hour—at stake,
> The state in which all mortals should expect themselves to be
> After death, for the remainder of eternity.[41]

In a Platonic or perhaps Pythagorean vein vis-à-vis mathematics, one overcomes the anxieties and imperfections of the sublunary world by participating *in mente* with that which is itself unchanging. Psychologically one achieves a release from anxiety in this manner through what Hellenistic philosophers called *ataraxia* (variously translated as "tranquility" or "equanimity").[42] (If you have identified yourself with what is immortal, the idea goes, the "small stuff"—almost everything in everyday life by comparison—is no longer so worrisome.) Spinoza (1632–1677) has a version of this as well, where he counsels in his magnum opus the *Ethics* to perceive matters "*sub specie aeternitatis*," that is, from the perspective of eternity, where we "sense that our mind, insofar as it involves the essence of the body under a form of eternity, is eternal, and that this aspect of existence cannot be defined by time, that is, cannot be explicated through duration."[43] (This is the philosophically nuanced source of the broad colloquial advice to "look at things philosophically"). For the ancient Stoics and Epicureans, the royal road to *ataraxia* is mainly through science and logic, for the Pythagoreans and Platonists it is mathematics, and for the Spinozans it is a broader based "geometrical" inquiry into first principles leading to an "intellectual love of God" (*amor Dei intellectualis*).⁴⁴ For Christians, this move away from the ego may evolve sharply differently into the *moral* goal of a life dedicated to emulating Jesus, the so-called "imitation of Christ" that Thomas à Kempis (c. 1380–1471), in his influential devotional text of that title, saw as a personal project at the imperative core of the religion.⁴⁵ There are of course many other strategies generative of this kind of hypertrophic identification, including, one should add, ethical acts of altruism, self-sacrifice, and, in extreme cases, martyrdom, representing countless objects with which it is possible to identify.

Most striking for present purposes is that hypertrophic identification does not occur in a vacuum, but rather is dependent on some pre-existing doxological substrate; it grafts itself hermeneutically onto a framework of beliefs—the deep mindset—already held at some level by the experiencer. I have seen no credible reports of a psychedelic experience at one fell swoop inserting into anyone's head an entirely novel worldview. The hypertrophic identification enabled by epistemic loosening seems instead to works *opportunistically* with whatever pre-existing ideational material is lying around. In suggesting this polymorphousness, I mean to cast doubt on the view that the identification is more determined, that it is inherently nature-oriented or peace-loving or some such. This undoubtedly occurs, but it is clearly not inevitable. The hypertrophic identification could be taken in indeterminately many directions, including much darker ones like human sacrifice, witch hunting, or fascist politics, where a predisposed subject might identify herself even more fanatically with any number of larger causes. Hypertrophic identification is definitely playing with fire, as the CIA's MK-ULTRA experiments alone demonstrate. In a way, Nixon was right to fear psychedelics as potentially highly destabilizing.⁴⁶ It all depends on the nature of the pre-existing doxastic material with which identities are fused.

In the established terminology of psychedelia, if what we have been discussing so far has to do with philosophical aspects of set, this attention to a subject's latent belief systems transitions into a focus on deep aspects of setting. Both set and setting therefore must be included when considering the conditions for durable insight. Psychedelics can help make one ready to learn by minimizing the ego in preparation for the risk of hypertrophic identification. But, whether salutary or not, good trip or bad trip, how might this be made a *memorable* event? What might make it stick?

Beyond Set and Setting

> My epiphany came slowly and gradually—in line with my methodical clinical approach. Psychedelics taught me how to best conduct science. But might they, I wonder sometimes, have taken me to the same place as the hippies?
>
> —Ben Sessa, *The Psychedelic Renaissance*, 2

One hallmark of a worthwhile learning experience is *durability*. We forget a great deal and perhaps we forget most of what we have learned in the long span of life. Against what is commonly thought, this does not mean that the learning was pointless, however. We might not remember the capitol of Moldova, but in studying a wide range of subject matter, we indirectly acquire habits of mind, patterns of thought and an "allusionary base" of symbolic tools, as philosopher of education Harry Broudy (1905–1998) termed it.[47] Yet surely there should be at least *some* shelf life to an alleged learning experience to qualify it authentically as such. Pure effervescence would seem disqualifying. This is why it is senseless to say one has learned something from an unrecalled dream. There may be subconscious goings-on, of course, and these assuredly control our behavior to a significant degree. But learning as commonly understood implies some element of *conscious* appropriation, and consciously appropriating something must always have at least *some* temporal dimension that can allow for at least *some* period of rumination. One may certainly learn from an event lasting a split second; and people spend their lives trying to "learn the lesson" from, say, a tragic moment of violence or a fateful split-second decision. But it is the reflection upon and incorporation of the event that constitutes the learning part of it, and that part extends over an indeterminate period of time.

The same is true with psychedelics. The dazzling funhouse and entity encounters of a breakthrough 15-minute DMT trip may be the subject of a lifetime of contemplation for some people. But for others it might not be. And also, it should be noted, these experiences are notoriously easy to forget—like dreams. My point here is that for significant learning to take place from these experiences it seems that some post facto temporally extended process of psychological *integration* is necessary (as has become conventional wisdom in psychedelic therapy). Otherwise, they are likely to remain submerged into one's subconsciousness, at best perhaps a vague and receding memory of a divertissement undergone once upon a time. In terms of what has been previously discussed, in such a case one would have gotten the epistemic loosening and the readiness to learn—but without really learning anything much. I think this happens frequently with psychedelics and many if not most of the trip reports one sees are of this ilk: weird and wild images and emotions that are unintegrated into any larger or more durable meaningful lesson. Sound and fury signifying very little in the end. If we want to locate the learning elements in it rather than merely catalog its passing phantasmagoria, we need to attend very carefully also to the *externalities* of the psychedelic experience as well as to the *internalities* that occur during the relatively short pendency of the trip itself. Although "set and setting" is perhaps the leading catchphrase in the literature on psychedelic guidance, there is no bright line separating the two, any more than one could neatly separate the psychological from the social or the individual from society. But further attention to setting's temporal dimension allows for a needed enlargement of perspective from an educational point of view.

Accordingly, I propose further terminological updates to complement an appropriately more detailed typology of setting, including the general phrase "*psychedelic envelopment*" detailed in more depth in chapter 4. But a short précis of the many dimensions of envelopment here at the outset may be helpful to the reader:

First, with the most ancient lineage, is the *entheogenic* envelopment. I use Ruck's neologism "entheogenic," meaning, roughly, "divine inspiration giving," because it heavily emphasizes the religious or spiritual-visionary aspects of psychedelics and is usually associated with organized ritual usage (and often higher dosages as well).[48] The term "envelopment" is meant to stress the ideational and sociocultural contexts through which these experiences are interpreted by those supervising and/or undergoing them. Along with epistemic loosening, these envelopments not only shape individuals' psychedelic journeys, but they also provide necessary conditions for learning anything from them. If epistemic loosening renders a psychedelicized subject *ready* to learn, then the envelopment within which the "lesson" takes place preconditions and shapes whatever subsequent learning actually might occur.

The most iconic and traditional subcategory of entheogenic envelopment is the shamanic envelopment. Here psychedelic access is mediated through some sort of guide representing an accumulation of cultural wisdom and know-how regarding the use and interpretation of relevant events. The paradigmatic figure would be the indigenous tribal shaman or *curandero* (there are as many terms in world history for this role as there are cultural traditions) who may serve variously in roles onlookers from industrial society might categorize as convener, guide, therapist, priest, doctor, doula, nutritionist, storyteller, master of ceremonies, and more—all rolled into one. Following Romanian anthropologist of religion Mircea Eliade (1921–1986), who was himself borrowing from Nietzsche on this point, this situation was a more or less scripted "eternal recurrence of the same," in the sense that it is typically an age-old passed-down ceremony that recapitulates archetypal themes (much like the old pagan elements of modern holidays that are still "repeated" annually).[49] This is of course a broad and ancient category, largely accessible to researchers in the annals of anthropology and history, and there are as many variations on it as there are cultural lifeways. In this light, it is important to recognize that the shamanic envelopment does not designate *only* indigenous contexts. There are also archaic contexts sometimes accessible via historical accounts (e.g., the plethora of ecstatic cults in the ancient Greece and Rome) along with persisting undercurrents within western traditions (e.g., Arctic Sami reindeer herders, [probably] Viking berserkers, and other surviving neo-pagan traditions such as Wicca and druidism with their extensive esoteric understanding of exotic plant-based "potions" and the like). Taken together as a global inheritance past and present, these shamanic envelopments are by far the most important storehouses of knowledge and meaning regarding entheogens. And much remains to be learned from them.

An additional adjacent subcategory is the theological envelopment. It is probably much rarer in the long span of human history because it tends to arise only at scale within severely hierarchical societies rather than among smaller hunter-gatherer bands. Here, a threshold level of societal division of labor allows a move beyond subsistence to support a priestly caste authorized to distribute and ritualize psychedelic usage, typically under liturgical conditions prescribed by a sanctioned religious orthodoxy. This higher level of doctrinal formality is why it is a *theological* rather than a shamanistic envelopment. It is further distinguishable by its relatively greater institutionalization and establishment vis-à-vis some larger political entity like a kingdom or empire. Not always though: it could be partaken underground *within* a larger political entity that may even be hostile to it, as in the case of a dissident religious sect such as, arguably, the early persecuted Christians in their catacombs and house churches.[50] In the theological envelopment, the purpose is to enliven some preferred religious belief system, to inculcate a more robust sense of religious devotion, and to accommodate the mystical impulse toward a more personal ecstatic experience that runs alongside every major world religion, for example Sufism in Islam or Kabbalism in Judaism. The western archetype of this envelopment is the Eleusinian Mysteries, practiced sedulously for almost two thousand years and, despite the shroud of secrecy around it (what happened to initiates in Eleusis was to stay in Eleusis on pain of death), it was clearly massively important in the classical world and regarded as indispensable by such luminaries as Socrates, Plato, and Cicero.[51] As indicated previously, the ceremonies held at Eleusis itself and at the far-flung Mediterranean outposts of Magna Graecia seem to have included ritual psychedelics.[52]

In a kind of hybrid with their shamanic pasts, there are also, currently, syncretistic indigenous and indigenous-inspired churches such as the North American Native American Church (NAC). The NAC's long battle with the federal government concerning ceremonial peyote use represents a different kind of theological envelopment: an outgrowth of the shamanic envelopment that has evolved into a more standardized and institutionalized form out the need to obtain legal protection for the purpose of sheer cultural survival. Relevant protections were also extended, in *Gonzales v. O Centro Espírita Beneficente União do Vegetal* (2006), the "UDV" case, where the US Supreme Court unanimously sided with an immigrant indigenous Amazonian Church and their right to drink ayahuasca as part of traditional religious observances.[53] Conforming to the constitutional requirements for protection *as recognized religions* (including their syncretism with Christianity), has caused indigenous groups like the NAC and UDV to slide from their original shamanistic provenance toward elaborations more characteristic of the theological envelopment.[54] In their more formally institutionalized settings they are more akin to mainstream church congregations, albeit with a very distinctive experiential twist at Communion.

A second major category is the *medical* or *therapeutic* envelopment. This in a sense replaces the entheogenic envelopment for modernized societies where, for better or worse, science and technical bureaucracies provide epistemic legitimacy, a role once reserved for ecclesiastical authorities. "Legitimate" drug use is now mediated by medical experts in the take-home form of prescriptions (e.g., medical marijuana) or in highly scripted clinical settings like government-approved trials. As psychedelics are active mostly upon the mind, the medical-therapeutic envelopment is heavily weighted toward psychiatry, with a telos of healing trauma (e.g., PTSD, anxiety and depression, OCD, substance abuse) and, at the vaguer end of the spectrum, the many tentacles of the wellness industry and its growing set of claims for the ability of psychedelics to improve individuals' lives (e.g., micro-dosing, enhancement of creativity, partner intimacy, even gender transition).[55] What is definitive of this envelopment overall is that it is conducted with the explicit goal of *healing* individuals: specific diagnosed conditions in the case of the medical establishment and vaguer lifestyle recommendations for the wellness industry. Given the realities of modern medicine as involving both a research apparatus and its distribution as a commercial good (especially in the US), this envelopment is not separable from the powerful profit-based imperatives of the business world (psychedelics have become an active investment arena).[56] The norms of "pure" medical research are thus not wholly dominant in this envelopment and it would be naïve to think of it as entirely composed of disinterested medical researchers and earnest physicians. These individuals exist, but their research products and clinical expertise tend to be quickly capitalized on (literally) by corporate interests who then will dictate the terms of access and distribution for psychedelic "pharmaceuticals" and therapies. At the moment, the more disinterested norms of medical research predominate, but this is an "early days" function of psychedelics' restricted legal status that gives researchers a temporary distributive monopoly. As the legal situation changes and commercial interests move in, they will inevitably shape the space according to their own priorities. Psychedelics also raise internal professional ethics challenges distinctive to this envelopment, as new normative territories emerge regarding therapist-patient interactions. Indeed, as a recent study concludes, "psychedelic psychotherapy is rife with unique ethical challenges that require self-awareness and practical approaches that go beyond the training of a conventional psychologist."[57] More seriously still, there have also been allegations of sexual abuse among underground psychedelic therapeutic operations, underscoring the need for more serious attention to legal and ethical issues in psychedelic guidance and counseling.[58] There will be more on these challenges in chapters 3 and 4.

Distinguishable from both the entheogenic and medical envelopments, there is also an *intellectual* envelopment, which, although quantitatively much smaller, tends to be outsized in influence. Most of this book's introduction is devoted to the exploits of individual thinkers in this category across the three waves of modern psychedelia. The unifying theme within this envelopment is that the psychedelic journey is undergone with a plan to advance some agenda in the realm of ideas: scientific, philosophical, political, aesthetic, etc.

An offbeat example at the margins is political envelopments across the ideological spectrum that seek to commandeer psychedelics to further their own platforms and agendas. There is an "Acid Left," mostly an online phenomenon, which seeks to advance its particular critique of the capitalist status quo, environmental groups that see entheogens as giving impetus to a sense of connectedness to nature pursuant to earth-friendly lifestyles and ecological activism, and even plenty of right-wing groups who have used psychedelics to foster group cohesion and ideological devotion.[59] There are also miscellaneous collectives, including intentional communities who have provided psychedelic envelopments pursuant to their own idiosyncratic ends. Sometimes these can turn nefarious: as Johns Hopkins psychedelics researcher Matthew Johnson notes, "The powerful subjective nature of psychedelic experiences can be leveraged toward explicit harm, as in the extreme case of Charles Manson and his followers."[60] Less troubling and more prevalent are relatively benign but also cultish communities like Ken Kesey's Merry Pranksters, which gave way to those created by Deadheads, the itinerant sub-culture of Grateful Dead followers and successor bands like Phish. Whatever the level of commitment of their fans and followers, musicians and artists have long provided such reservoirs for psychedelic energies; modern psychedelia is in fact unimaginable without them. The designation "intellectual" might seem like a stretch for such groups. But the broad sense in which it is meant would include those intentionally following a guiding cultural ideal of some kind, however fuzzily defined, along the lines of the original meaning of the Greek educational term *paideia* (viz., the self-conscious pedagogical pursuit of a cultural ideal).[61] So, as is obvious to anyone who attended a Grateful Dead concert in their heyday, there is a major difference in this regard between the true Deadheads and the audience members just there for the show. The people who have banded together and organized their entire lives around the Dead's version of psychedelia are up to something different from the (mere) showgoers, somewhat analogous to the difference between residential monastery initiates and holidays-only churchgoers.

For intellectuals of a more academic bent, in addition to the literary coteries centered around luminaries like Huxley, there have also been intellectual envelopments that are scientific and even philosophical in nature. Some of the main litterateurs and scientists are cataloged in my introductory chapter, from Terence McKenna and Michael Pollan to Alexander Shulgin and David Nichols. An ancient philosophical example would be the circle around the philosopher-mathematician Pythagoras, who was also described at times as a shaman, where the religious and the philosophical are not at all separable. Figures like Pythagoras represented, as classicist E. R. Dodds writes, "a very old type of personality, the shaman who combines the still undifferentiated functions of magician and naturalist, poet and philosopher, preacher, healer and public counsellor."[62] By definition, all of them veterans of Eleusis, the Pythagoreans provide an interesting example of an intellectual envelopment emerging out of an entheogenic one, suggestive of how communities of inquiry might develop and evolve new modes over time. Plato's thought was certainly deeply shaped by his involvement with them.

Perhaps the most widespread envelopment of all—or maybe it represents an *absence* of envelopment—lies in the realm of what is commonly labeled "informal" or "recreational" use. I will primarily use the latter term and call it the *recreational* envelopment. "Recreational" is sometimes thought to be a pejorative, but this need not be the case if the term is taken literally, as a scene for the "re-creation" of something. A sub-theme of this book is that it is mistaken to assume this envelopment is frivolous and unworthy of analysis because the experiences going on within it are not "scientific" or "spiritual" enough. Surely, if the study and practice of psychedelics teach anything, it is that profundity can lie in the strangest and most unlikely places; it does not have to be in the Amazon, at Eleusis or at Johns Hopkins to count as "real" or "serious."

This is where individuals or ad hoc micro-groups of friends and acquaintances partake of psychedelics for amusement, out of curiosity or maybe DIY personal development—with or without a "trip sitter" for safety—and their experiences play out indeterminately according to their variegated sets and settings. Derivative as it is from cultural assumptions about leisure time, and also largely relegated to the private sphere due to the currently illegal status of most psychedelics, the recreational envelopment tends to be ideologically framed by a default libertarian and/or consumerist ethos where what a freely choosing subject personally gains from the experience is paramount: it is about an individual's choice to pursue insight and/or enjoyment. Servicing some of these choices is a growing psychedelics tourism industry (e.g., mushrooms in Jamaica, ayahuasca in Peru) that provides a niche example of recreational use.[63] "Authentic" or not, participants in these tourist conclaves often report meaningful experiences.

It must be stressed that there are not bright lines between the envelopment categories. The entheogenic envelopment obviously often has medical-therapeutic elements; within those cultures the relevant plants are commonly revered as "plant medicines," and individuals in indigenous communities will also sometimes seek these rituals to heal personal traumas. Similarly, the wellness approach often blends with a quasi-religious envelopment when it incorporates religious motifs from whatever tradition, from New Age sensibilities to eastern-inspired meditation and breathing techniques. And psilocybin clinical trial participants often report religious experiences right there in the hospital. There are, have been, and will continue to be countless hybrids and blends. In fact, it may be more appropriate to speak of an "envelopment profile" for any given instance: X trip was partly therapeutic and partly artistic (intellectual); Y trip was partly entheogenic and partly romantic (recreational); Z trip was partly psychonautical self-experimentation (intellectual) and partly to get out of a mental rut (therapeutic/medical). Envelopment categories are blunt instruments and do not provide surgical delineations. But I believe they help us begin to map the different ways in which larger contexts of psychedelic usage beyond just "setting" help to fix lasting meanings into experiencers' minds. As indicated, each envelopment will be discussed in much greater detail, primarily in chapter 4.

Worldview Acceleration

> What is important is not creating something out of nothing. What my friends need to do is discover the right thing from what is already there.
>
> —Haruki Murakami, *Killing Commendatore*, 260

A central axiom of the philosophical school known as phenomenology, founded by Edmund Husserl (1859–1938), is that all consciousness is *consciousness of* something in particular.[64] When we hear, see, or touch something we always are hearing seeing and touching some-X; there is never pure unadulterated hearing, seeing, or touching per se. We never just have "a thought" either, one that is just a thought *simpliciter*; when thinking, we are always thinking *about* something or other. For Husserl, consciousness therefore always has "intentionality" in this orientational sense.[65] (Even a more general sensation like pain is *felt* as locatable somewhere in the body—even "inaccurate" phantom limb pain.) It is the same with tripping on psychedelics. One never just "trips": there is always some thing (or some things) *in particular* going on within the temporal flow of the tripping—even if all of one's perceptions, including that very temporal flow, seem distorted beyond anything familiar.[66] The phenomenological point is that since there is perceiving going on, however bizarre, one is always perceiving X, Y, and Z. Even where the psychoactivity has upturned the epistemic apple cart, such as in cases of synesthesia (e.g., hearing colors, seeing sounds, etc.), one is never just perceiving per se. Our conscious brains continuously train a *focus* on this-and-that by perpetually distinguishing figure from ground (without which we would suffer catatonia from an indistinguishable riot of incoming sensation), and those focused-upon thises and thats always—inevitably—marshal forth our interpretive faculties; we can't help but *make sense* of our perceptions as *about* something or other. As is true of experience generally, both set and setting collaborate hermeneutically and fuse themselves with one another. And we can't help it: it isn't possible for us to refrain from *interpreting* what happens to us; even the bare linguistic act of *naming* a perception sends one down this interpretive road.

In terms of psychedelics, there is the initial epistemic loosening—sometimes quite destabilizing—that has the effect of causing us, perhaps for the first time in our lives, to withdraw full trust from our perceptual apparatus. We have the unsettling lived experience of Descartes vis-à-vis his famous "evil genius" who, in the *Meditations*, arrives as a thought experiment to dramatize that we could be deceived about everything and so must embrace a hyperbolic doubt concerning the totality of our senses in order to then figure out what to trust.[67] (Cartesian doubt is the topic of chapter 3's "philosophical pathway.") With psychedelics, even at lower doses, we are not just led to entertain the fleeting intellectual fancy that our senses could in principle be wrong; we are made to suffer the actual experience that they are *in fact* not as reliable or comprehensive as we had thought. This *lived dissonance* can provoke strong emotions. Mild psychedelic trips usually begin and end in this realm, where perception—and accompanying emotions—get a bit fluxy and weird and nothing much else happens. Substance and dosage, however, sometimes push further into a categorically different realm of "true hallucinations" (i.e., a hallucination perceived as external and real) and other extreme oddities; one can hallucinate and be *aware* one is hallucinating, but sometimes a threshold is crossed where this metacognition vanishes. A sufficient dose of DMT will do this and then some. Novelist Tao Lin well captures this compound's DMT's otherworldly intensity: "If death by comet was unexpected, and departing Earth nonphysically like I did on psilocybin was, after decades in the same metaphysical place, beyond unexpected, my experience of smoked DMT was beyond beyond unexpected. It was around two ontological corners. It was closing closed eyes twice, or waking, incredibly, thrice. It was a mental sneeze that kept intensifying, ludicrously, instead of ending in a second."[68] At whatever intensity, though, epistemic loosening, as the opening of an aperture of doubt, can provide an effective basis for becoming ready to learn in the classic Socratic sense.

In terms of any durable learning, and beyond personal idiosyncrasies having to do with an individual's mindset, what happens next depends in my view on the controlling psychedelic envelopment. Lasting meaning is made during the post hoc integration process, but it is the envelopment that determines the specific nature of that integration. This is where even intense psychedelic experiences seem often to fall short of educational expectations; especially within the envelopment of recreational use, they often begin and end at mere entertainment and endure only as future cool stories to tell. Plenty of weirdness and fragmentary visions and fluid plot lines—much like an especially colorful crazy waking dream, but nothing of much lasting significance. But we are trying to locate *durable* learning experiences, the type hinted at in the claim by neuroscientist and psychologist Christopher Timmermann and colleagues that "psychedelics alter metaphysical beliefs," where psychedelic users in an ersatz ceremonial context were "inclined" to change their "metaphysical beliefs" (i.e., their basic assumptions about the nature of reality) and that the "observed changes were enduring, persisting for up to 6 months in most domains."[69]

These kinds of deeper alterations, I think, are enacted as the tripping experience is filtered through the governing envelopment. The initial epistemic destabilization, though highly fecund as a source of insight on its own terms, is really merely a prelude. It creates the flexibility and openness needed for a novel interpretive integration, a fluid putty-like state that is especially primed for what philosopher Hans-Georg Gadamer

(1900–2002) termed a hermeneutic "fusion of horizons" of set and setting that might take any number of forms.[70] There seems little warrant for the view that there is any *inherent* context-independent direction to psychedelic experience—any particular shape or direction the putty *must* take. This goes against what is commonly implied in the folklore of psychedelia and seems to function as conventional wisdom among enthusiasts. (Though it is hard to say, an exception may be some of the spookier claims about DMT, e.g., encounters many claim to have had with McKenna's machine elves, the "purple lady," or any number of other entities, usually encountered in groups and typically benign and/ or indifferent.)[71] One hears of how *psychedelics* (inherently) promote a feeling of oneness and connectedness and a sense of harmony with nature and so on, the mystical-unitive experience, where at varying levels of explicitness a quasi-Gaian worldview is embraced.[72] No doubt these can be heartfelt realizations (I have felt them myself). Without diminishing such realizations' poignancy and their potential applications to individuals' lives, it seems unlikely that it is the drug *per se* that drives the process. Instead, it is the interaction of the drug with a priori latent factors already extant in the individual operating dynamically at the multiple levels of set, setting, envelopment, etc. There are patterns, but just as is often the case with educational experience, there is too much complexity and too many variables to *guarantee* specific outcomes.

For it seems much more likely to be a projection from a set of previously held convictions (perhaps not altogether consciously) on the part of the subject herself. Those of us already prone to what philosopher Jules Evans terms "ecstatic environmentalism" will in a sense project what we want to see when interpreting what we have undergone.[73] In the clinical setting, where the envelopment has been under therapeutic supervision and focused on overcoming past trauma—literally targeted sessions with the therapist before and after the prescribed trip—it is proportionately likely, as intended, that any lesson absorption will center on the trauma that has been the therapist and patient's collaborative focus. (This is why expert guidance is recommended for optimal therapeutic integration in the first place.) By the same token, in the shamanic envelopment, it is unsurprising when the entheogenic visions come packaged in the idiom of the cultural imaginary of its particular milieu. It should therefore not be surprising that in a theologically enveloped scene like Pahnke's famous psilocybin Good Friday Experiment (1962), the divinity student subjects reported theologically tinged mystical experiences, including ecstatic visions of the Messiah.[74] None of these Christian theology students saw Ba'al or Dionysus or UFOs or the Maya God Itzamná; predictably, they saw Jesus. That their ecstasies came pareidolically robed in their pre-existing theology seems hardly coincidental. I emphasize that this relativism of setting does not by itself render trip-gained insights false any more than the fact that one is thirsty and seeking water makes the water "false" when one finds it; the veridicality of any alleged insights is an altogether different question and it is separable from their epistemological provenance.[75] (It would be a genetic fallacy if otherwise.) It's just that one must be mindful of the hermeneutical principle that any insight or understanding whatsoever must presuppose the set of pre-existing mental frameworks and assumptions that are inevitably carried into the psychedelic experience.

We have a very strong tendency to see what we are primed to see; we continuously project ourselves and promiscuously confirm our biases. This can lead to confabulation and illusion, certainly. But it is also a precondition for any kind of understanding; it is just how the mind works and how the learning of *anything* takes place. As in the Gadamerian formulation, "understanding is always the fusion of these horizons," and so learning necessarily involves various scaffolding processes where we absorb novelties by making them cohere with our prior framework of assumptions.[76] This hermeneutical conception implies that there was a kernel of truth to Meno's paradox about the apparent impossibility of learning if it were wrongly conceived as the input of wholly novel information: "it's impossible for a man to search either for what he knows or for what he doesn't know: he wouldn't be searching for what he knows, since he knows it and that makes the search unnecessary, and he can't search for what he doesn't know either, since he doesn't even know what it is he's going to search for."[77] One hundred percent pure novelty by definition would not be understandable *as* anything at all because we would be, literally, unable to *relate* to it. The *purest* novelty would be, ex hypothesi, unable to generate any understanding or insight at all; if no sense can be made of something it cannot be psychologically integrated.

This dependency of learning on the learner's pre-existing horizons suggests what Grof calls the "pluripotency" or "non-specific" nature of psychedelics.[78] On this view, they are fundamentally protean and therefore what one learns from them is less a function of a drug's internal pharmacological properties than it is of the revelatory contours created by one's governing context and how that context is utilized to make the trip into something meaningful for an actual individual's life. The quality of the experience is not just an internal function of drug chemistry per se but also always a combined function with environing factors, not just of set and setting as conventionally understood, but of deeper and more latent factors hidden "inside" the individual simultaneous with indeterminately large "outside" factors; under even light conceptual analysis, the set-setting dualism falls apart pretty quickly upon examination, as the tripping self is ultimately constituted by infinite indeterminacies all the way down and all the way up. Psychedelics are therefore better conceived as *quantitative accelerators* (in Grof's terminology, "catalysts" or "amplifiers") in the service of *whatever* combustible worldview elements are ready-to-hand and able to be surfaced from within and assimilated from without.

This indicates a fourth major factor in locating the learning element within entheogenic experiences: what I'll call *doxastic enhancement* (the subject of chapter 5). I use the term "doxastic" to specify that it is an individual's extant belief structure or worldview, supported by whatever sociocultural and material factors, that seems to be the main determining factor when ascribing durable meanings—real learning—to these experiences. (Otherwise, we are back to the mere cataloging of a string of disconnected perceptions—all those trip reports as just sound and fury but signifying very little.) My suggestion is that psychedelics can provide novelty in that they serve to enhance and enliven an individual's *pre-existing* belief structures, like pouring fuel on a smoldering fire; they function as worldview accelerant. They do not *provide* the beliefs *de novo* so much as they can *animate and enliven* them, paradoxically via an initial loosening of perception. I would speculate that in the best case they do not harden pre-existing beliefs so much as they extend those beliefs roughly in the directions they are already oriented toward by a particular envelopment. In this scenario, the sensation of novelty with the psychedelic experience has much to do with a rejuvenating pulse that it sends through one's existing network of belief—like illuminating a dense mesh of Christmas lights—that simultaneously grows new connections both to itself (recombinant loops) and into new territory, facets of what neuroscience terms "neuroplasticity."[79]

Continuing in neurological terms, psychedelics may help foster a *goal-directed plasticity* of mind, a creative and educational sweet spot where we are rendered highly receptive to absorbing deeper "archetypal patterns" to which, unaided, our cultural and religious traditions provide us only partial access.[80] One might think of this as a kind of Vygotskian "zone of psychedelic proximal development" where, if we are already primed for it, we could be bootstrapped into learning something worthwhile.[81] Neither plasticity nor goal-directedness *alone* supplies a proper goal for learning: an excess of the former would result in an unproductive mental spasticity, while an excess of the latter can deteriorate into an equally unproductive rut of unreflective rule-following. Goal-directed plasticity represents having a *general* trajectory, in this case a *general* worldview (however acquired), that is also able to maintain maneuverability within that trajectory. As in good philosophical inquiry, one might be "seeking answers" to particular questions while simultaneously being open to alterations of those very questions. I am reminded of Nietzsche's aphorism about composer Georg Friedrich Handel's peculiar genius as "freedom under the law"—a good way to word this Goldilocks situation in which creativity does not go off the rails because it is constrained (but not cowed) by a tradition; the true creative innovates *within* a set of accepted rules and becoming enabled by them, rather than seeing them as simple obstacles to be eliminated or "dropped out" from.[82] Kant's influential account similarly characterizes the creative imagination, paradoxically, as "free lawfulness" and "lawfulness without a law."[83] In an allied sense, psychedelics could be described as catalyzing a kind of playful and imaginative neo-animism where, via doxastic enhancement, assistance is rendered in learning to *re-enchant* the traditions of our existing world, a world that has for too many on the contemporary scene grown morally cold and void of meaning. We may have stumbled upon a valuable ally in helping us to enliven a physical world that for centuries has been conceived by serious thought as a set of dead and indifferent mechanisms.

A Framework for Psychedelic Learning

> The mind, bound up within imperfect and half grown organs, *is not even aware of its own existence.*
>
> —Jean Jacques-Rousseau, *Emile*

To summarize: in this book, I try to make sense of widespread reports that psychedelic experiences are not merely entertaining and one can *learn* important things from them. The problem is that it appears to be difficult to communicate just exactly what these allegedly important things are. Approaching the psychedelic experience as an educational process yields what I hope are helpful categories for identifying the learning aspects of these experiences that are durably worthwhile. These can be listed as:

1. an *epistemic loosening*, a Socratic dishevelment of unexamined assumptions that renders one "ready to learn";

2. pursuant to a tendency toward *hypertrophic identification*, where the destabilized subject is impelled toward an identification with some entity perceived as larger and more durable than the melting ego;

3. all of which unfolds under the aspect of a particular *psychedelic envelopment*, reflecting the range of sociocultural and ideational frameworks of belief where the compounds are actually administered and interpreted;

4. leading in the best case to a *doxastic enhancement*, where the participant's previously existing worldview is simultaneously challenged, enlivened, and extended.

Elaborating these four phenomena is the main subject matter of this book. In its course, I defend the Grofian thesis that *psychedelics do not contain any determinate message or specific "teaching,"* despite the widespread conventional wisdom that they *inherently* usher us toward a unitive feeling of connectedness with nature and the like. (To be clear: I do not dispute that such sentiments occur, only that such a telos is directed by anything inherent in the substances.) Rather, as I will explain in greater detail through subsequent chapters, I think that the moment of ego dissolution associated with a threshold intensity of epistemic loosening promotes a plasticity of mind that concomitantly tends toward a nonspecific hypertrophic identification. Immediately with ego dissolution comes a reconstitutive push that seeks to "heal" the self-oblivion via a curative mimetic fusion with some larger and/or more meaningful entity (e.g., Platonic forms, imitation of Christ, Gaian Living Earth).[84] This reconnection constitutes a moment of extreme potential vulnerability, where subjects are, as neuroscientist Robin Carhart-Harris and colleagues have shown, "suggestible" and disposed to want to latch onto whatever set of stable-seeming meanings is closest to hand.[85] As will be elaborated, there are therefore clear dangers associated with this temporary disequilibrium and things can easily go sideways. By themselves, then, such experiences will not "save the world" and should not even be regarded as necessarily beneficent.[86] Abusive persons can too easily construct envelopments designed to twist these transient malleabilities into serving their own interests.[87] What is key is a salutary managing of the fusion of one's psychological profile with one's enveloping horizons—realizing that both of these have vast depths that are usually hidden but some of which are surfaced in psychedelic experience; in the manner of Jungian archetypes, these horizons are iceberg-like in that typically we are consciously aware of only the tiny visible tip. And the enterprise of therapy attests that the project of accessing and becoming more explicitly aware of one's most abiding and deepest motivational patterns is no small thing. In this vein, Tupper suggests the exciting idea that psychedelics may thus allow for deeper kinds of educational experiences than have been typically allowed in recent times, perhaps helping learners grasp what philosopher Kieran Egan called "somatic" and "mythical" forms of understanding that have become much less accessible to the modern mind.[88]

The spear point of the learning process, then, lies in the doxastic enhancement phase where integrative reconnections are formed between self and at least some subset of its heretofore obscured motivating beliefs, initiating a process of reacquaintance with something like archetypal patterns of meaning. This is the point at which some find Spinoza's "God, or Nature" (*Deus, sive Natura*)—among other "big insights" they might embrace.[89] However grand this process sounds, though, it also implies that psychedelics, however powerful as catalysts or accelerants, are not a substitute for "normal" learning experiences, before and after the psychedelic episode, where one expands one's understanding of one's world by conventional means; ex hypothesi, for the maximum pedagogical effect, the more usable mental material one brings to the table, the better. Sorry to be a psychedelic scold, but *one must still do one's homework*. The richer an understanding of one's own motivating worldview, the more durably significant the learning experiences based on that understanding are likely to be. The existence of psychedelics is no excuse for intellectual laziness or lack of inquisitiveness about one's social and natural environment and ancestral inheritances. These powerful mental peripherals may help efficiently jump-start awareness—and this can be spectacular under the right circumstances—but apart from that they are not really a shortcut to anything in particular. Under the right conditions and if all goes well, they may help one exhume, revive, and reconstruct one's latent worldview, but they will not enable one to build a new one ex nihilo. This is consistent with what many indigenous cultures appear to have known for ages: ensconced ceremonially in cherished rituals, entheogens tend to have a culturally integrative and stabilizing effect rather than the "tune in and drop out" disintegrative and destabilizing effects with which they have become associated in modern individualist societies, as when hippies and other 1960s types saw LSD and mushrooms as allied with their antagonism toward the mainstream of their own culture. Against the assumption that they are inherently countercultural, there may be ample room to consider a *psychedelic traditionalism* that is ultimately more attuned to the needs of the human psyche for intersubjective connection and intergenerational frameworks of meaning.

Along the way, though, given the hermeneutical structure of the learning experience as a multilevel fusion of personal and cultural horizons, the maxim "garbage in, garbage out" is likely still to obtain. Superficial people who are uninterested in the world around them will have superficial and uninteresting trips. (And this observation is to be understood with the full humility of recognizing that "depth of understanding" is not at all to be equated with academic knowledge; credentialed snobbery in this arena is a sure sign of foolishness.) A durable psychedelic insight, grounded in the conviction that something deep and meaningful has occurred—even if inarticulable—consists in this reconnection and perhaps even in the mere *attempt* at forging a reconnection. For the attempt *itself* can indicate an advance and a deep learning experience, where there is perhaps no success in the sense of a final result for this grand endeavor. As Gadamer writes, a "reconstructed question can never stand within its original horizon," so new horizonal fusions of set and setting are not to be regretted ultimately as so many failures.[90] Although it can never be complete, there is no reason to view it as futilely Sisyphean because this ongoing dynamic of fusionism is simply how the human mind works and what makes any learning possible. As philosopher John Dewey (1859–1952) stated, "mind is primarily a verb. It denotes all the ways we deal consciously and expressly with the situations in which we find ourselves."[91] The etymology of Humphrey Osmond's neologism "psychedelic," meaning "mind-manifesting," is strikingly consistent with Dewey's sentiment, the idea that learning and insight are things we *do* in an ongoing manner more than they are artifacts of inert and external information that is transmitted to us in a final form.

Profound gestalt-like realizations do not occur in every single psychedelic trip. But every trip gestures toward them. Ultimately, I contend that psychedelics do not so much *give* us insight as they may *allow* insight to occur; they may help us reach for meaning but they themselves do not provide it. Augmenting our reach is no small matter, though, and we sorely need the help.

Chapter 2

Epistemic Loosening

> This feeling—a sense of wonder—is perfectly proper to a philosopher: philosophy has no other foundation, in fact.
>
> —Plato, *Theaetetus*, 155d

Epistemic Loosening as Philosophy

The realization that perception may mislead drives a founding impulse of western philosophy. The pre-Socratics, the earliest recorded exemplars of this impulse, were animated by the quest for a deeper reality beneath appearances. The mysteriously sourced conviction that there simply *must* be such a reality generates an imperative toward philosophical inquiry when it is twinned with a nagging nonacceptance of the accuracy and completeness of sensory ephemera in general; if the senses can deceive, then reality is (at least) sometimes hidden from us. As "substance monists," the earliest philosophers pursued this suspicion by trying to uncover what lies below the perceptual surface and then hypothesizing about what that substrate might be. Usually credited as the very first Greek philosopher, Thales (fl. 580 BCE) put forward water as fundamental, but other thinkers proposed alternatives, such as Empedocles's (fl. 450 BCE) more heterogeneous substrate composed of air, fire, earth, *and* water.[1] Probably the most important of the pre-Socratics, Heraclitus (fl. 500 BCE), took a different approach altogether by prioritizing change and flux *themselves* as the fundamental reality, imperfectly represented to us in the dynamism of fire or more abstractly in his oft-repeated aphorism that "one cannot step twice into the same river" due to its ceaseless change.[2] Whatever its variety, this quest for some underlying ontological bedrock implies a chronic dissatisfaction with a state of affairs whereby what we perceive around us in our everyday attitude via the effervescences of our sensorium is *all* that there is. Whether the considered philosophical conclusion is, à la the pre-Socratics, "all is X" or "all is flux," there now exists a chasm to be bridged between mere appearance and (putative) reality; out of the mists of pre-history, a philosophical *problem* thus arises.

As Heraclitus famously states, "the true nature of things tends to hide itself."[3] This line encapsulates the core originating narrative of western philosophy (and science) as involving a persistent curiosity toward this hiddenness and, the other side of the same coin, an abiding skepticism about the trustworthiness of appearances. What is it that underlies it all? Since our sensory organs not only yield an incomplete account of the world but also often outright mislead, how could we use those same untrustworthy organs even to begin to find out? Whatever first caused it to arise among the pre-Socratics (was it literacy? brain changes? economics? intercultural borrowing?), chronic epistemological perplexity caught on with the classical Greek avant-garde and provided the questioning cultural milieu responsible for Pythagoras, Socrates, Plato, and Aristotle. Yet the disposition to allow wonder need not be perceived as exclusively elite or esoteric; as a state of mind, it is potentially available to just about anybody. Admittedly, it's a bit of a mystery why anyone falls into it. It may happen one fine day or it may not. And it may befall the smart and not-so-smart alike. Common experience shows that philosophical puzzlement does not seem to be a function of a person's cleverness, beyond perhaps a certain minimal cognitive threshold. The simplest among us, such as very small children, regularly express a greater wondering curiosity than most of the wizened adults around them. In principle, epistemological skepticism can beckon universally.

At the creek edge, I dip half of my stick into the water to make it look bent yet *I know* it is actually straight—as verified by extracting and re-examining it. And . . . I may then ask myself: why the illusion? Why does it look different in the changing creek water contexts? Or I confuse dark blue and black and pick the wrong shoes. And . . . I may ask myself, what *are* these colors anyway? How do I know what I see as one color is the exact same felt qualitative experience as when *you* see that same color? Maybe we see it differently and just attach the same words to different perceptual experiences. How would one ever know? Or, I thought I heard something out there in the darkness, but later upon reflection maybe I didn't hear anything after all. And . . . I may ask myself, if my companion also heard it, does that mean it was real? Could we *both* be wrong? Everyday life is rife with large and small perceptual dissonances and conundrums like these, each one of them potential epistemological quagmires. It does not require the verbal machinery of academic philosophy to fall into them. All it takes is a disposition to notice them at their inception, that is to say, to identify, and isolate them from amidst their flowing ubiquity—they are *always* present, lying in wait for us—and then the dogged will to keep on asking questions—and, depending on the width and depth of the questioning, a willingness to press the bounds of convention and sanity. The royal road to philosophy is simply to take these perceptual quirks and puzzlements seriously enough to obsess over them and begin to wonder hyperbolically whether *anything at all* can be trusted—*ever*.

Philosophy is distinguished only by the monomaniacal zeal with which it selectively explores these passing cognitive fissures that are in principle available to everyone at every single conscious moment. A survival-positive penchant for psychic groundedness prevents most of us from falling down into the fissures because we normally have the good sense to get on with life. But for those with the will—or disposition or addiction or illness—to do so, that particular Yellow Brick Road is there to be followed. Just like with the Munchkins in the Land of Oz, it is common knowledge that the road is there to be taken and is not too hard to find *if one chooses to*. Though Dorothy does have to search a little for it, it does not take her long just to find the Yellow Brick Road and merely to get started. But staying on it though the twists, turns, and adventures all the way to the Emerald City is quite another matter.

Relatedly, the desire for consciousness alteration involves an implicit epistemological recognition of an appearance-reality distinction. And since that desire is observably a cultural universal, therefore, the implied awareness, at some level, of an appearance-reality distinction is a cultural universal as well. The pre-Socratics gave early voice to it, but they were in no way the sole keepers of such questions. However rut-stuck in our thinking we may become at times, what I am calling "epistemic looseness" is natural to most everyone and it is probably especially strong in small children who have not yet become busy enough in life to sideline certain thoughts as "distractions." Psychiatrist Stanislav Grof's hypothesis from thousands of LSD therapy sessions in the 1950s and '60s, that psychedelic trips often involve a pattern of "perinatal" regression, basically a re-living of one's own birth trauma, is unsurprising from this perspective.[4] Psychedelic experiences can be full of astonishment and novelty, yet despite all that they can also possess an odd aura of déjà-vu. It is very common, for example, for this phenomenon to be represented in DMT user reports of being greeted by "charming and inviting" entities expressing welcoming kinds of sentiments of the "we're so glad to see you here again" variety.[5] The weirdness so often has such a strangely familiar feel. One can be freaked out, of course, by the unfamiliar and the unexpected. But our mental architecture is such that we are also disposed to feel very much at home precisely when we are nowhere at all near home; as much as we love our comfort and safety, our evolution and history shows that we are fundamentally venturesome primates, too.

Epistemic loosening is the gateway to all of it. Well short of DMT entities, even low-dosage run-of-the-mill psychedelic perceptual distortions do this initial job just fine. In fact, I suspect—and some research seems to suggest—from this perspective that the low-level initiatory distortions can be underrated while the more comprehensive and "mind-blowing" breakthrough experiences can sometimes be overrated.[6] From an educational perspective, the psychedelic gateway of perceptual distortion functions perfectly sufficiently as a crucial initiatory catalyst for occasioning epistemic looseness, "reminding" one, qua a kind of lived experience, of an epistemological problem: that appearance-reality distinction that we always already knew about from direct past acquaintance. The onrush of perceptual distortion—including, it should be said, the (typically) closed-eye geometric patterns and visual bricolage that also nearly always inhere in psychedelic trips of any magnitude—is thus one potent way to help uncover that new-yet-strangely-familiar epistemically winding road and then escort one a few skip-steps down it. This is the essence of epistemic loosening in its function as an announcing mechanism: it signals to us that our accustomed sensory orientations have reached their outer limits and we are about to be ushered into a new realm. Whether that new realm is broken through to or not is another matter—it often has to do with dosage—but either way the perceptual alterations offer a liminal experience that is hard for most people, grounded as they are in practicalities, to reliably generate chemically unassisted.

As for this odd and under-discussed feeling of familiarity: it is not necessarily a specific déjà-vu targeted toward specific aperçus (i.e., remembering *this* thing or *that* thing in particular), but rather a more generalized sense of being ushered back, *once again*, into an opaquely familiar-seeming realm of contingency. It is familiar, in my view, due at least to the aforementioned philosophically generative experiences with perceptual dissonance, that everyone naturally has in the course of living. It is perhaps traceable all the way back to birth trauma as per Grof's theory, though the phenomenon of epistemic looseness does not require this particular origin; the mass of life experience everyone normally accumulates is sufficient as the undifferentiated basis for what is later felt to be "remembered." For epistemic loosening is not about particularized memories. As in: "I recall seeing that swirly colored shape as an eight-year-old in the weave of my neighbor's rug." If the recollection were attached to discrete memories like that, it would actually tend to work *against* epistemic loosening, because it would retrospectively reinforce a conviction of the *accuracy* of one's perceptions, like when one discovers retrospectively that the annoying jingle playing on a loop in one's head was present due to an ad one heard earlier in the evening. There is a modicum of epistemic comfort in knowing the musical earworm's pathology: one is at least aware of its referent and relieved of having to wonder why one conjured such a dumb song. The experience of discovering the provenance of the earworm would be more like an epistemic *tightening* in that it would tend to restore confidence in the acuity and trustworthiness of one's sensory apparatus. Everyone has enjoyed the sense of retrospective forensic relief provided by the discovered sense of an identifiable empirical reality behind what one saw or heard or felt. Though, of course, the disconfirming opposite can bring relief as well, like when that grizzly bear we *thought* we heard at night outside our camping tents turns out to be a squirrel—although this kind of disconfirming relief is really also epistemic tightening, too. It just involves a change of object; the bear-to-squirrel shift is what really provides the relief. Bear-to-unknown would be decidedly less relieving: good that there's no bear but . . . *what* was it?

At any rate, while they can be highly diverting, and also delightful or frightening or whatever else depending on one's mindset, the *specific* distortions or hallucinations are not the main thing. Rather, *it is the trippy sensory fluidity in general that engenders the epistemic looseness*: a sub-cognitive mood perhaps reminiscent of the lost feeling of childhood novelty or, also subject to the opacity of memory, the jumbled bricolage of dreams.[7] A "familiar newness" is paradoxical to a degree, but I mean it literally—and follow the perinatal thesis to this extent—in that it is present from those old echoes of childhood when the world was new (or at least newer) or maybe briefly also glimpsed in novel experiential episodes that generate a momentary occurrence of unstructured vertigo—the "shock of the new," to borrow art critic Robert Hughes's apt phrase—while one "orients" oneself via reconstituted pattern recognition and/or the reestablishment of narrative coherence.[8] These are the rare situations where we briefly recall how things appeared in the "once upon a time" of childhood when the world seemed new; it is a strangely compelling atemporal sensation in this manner, the "wonder years" and the like (including the world of fairy tales) associated with the young mind making order from chaos through the installation of identifiables and archetypes. The odd feeling of familiarity—not exactly déjà-vu and not exactly a specific memory—is attached to the perceptually fluid state of mind *itself* rather than the particular perceptions inhabiting it; though novel, it *feels* like something that one has felt before. An aesthetic analogy may illustrate. One may indeed focus on a single component paisley *boteh* or a single line or square of plaid, but the overall aesthetic *pattern* of the paisley or plaid has its *own* emergent effects, one irreducible to its components; the aesthetic sums are far more than their parts. Hard-wired cognitive mechanisms ineluctably yield up these patterns for us, language and its composite, narrativization, perhaps being the ultimate examples of our drive to impose order on a recalcitrant world so as to make the nonstop bombardment of perceptions more manageable.

Psychedelics create a comparable situation where, yes, there are discrete and memorable happenings, but it is the *overall* panoply of epistemic loosening that seems to leave the most durable impression. Empirical research may suggest something of this kind. In their 2022 paper, "More than Meets the Eye: The Role of Sensory Dimensions in Psychedelic Brain Dynamics, Experience, and Therapeutics," neuroimaging specialists Marco Aqil and Leor Roseman conclude that the often-neglected (by researchers) "low-level" sensory alterations induced by psychedelics have a causal effect on "high-level alterations" associated with "long-term therapeutic (or possibly harmful) changes in the human brain."[9] Such findings support my contention that the psychedelics-induced perceptual alterations associated with epistemic loosening are more existentially momentous than they might ostensibly seem. They should not be written off as merely superficial and/or entertaining diversions. The firsthand and relatively intense experience of perceptual instability—more intense than what most people have previously been through—provided at even low dosages naturally orients the meaning-seeking mind toward higher-level realizations, a means by which one is rendered more ready to learn in the Socratic sense. Robust experiences of perceptual instability like these can vividly disclose none other than the very appearance/reality gap that so concerned the pre-Socratic philosophers, something we grownups all "know about" intellectually but rarely actually experience anymore in our everyday lives. The existential "losing trust" aspect of epistemic looseness (what the researchers are associating with "high-level alterations") illustrates an additional key element: it is not *only* the perceptual distortions that are significant. It is also one's attitude toward them. Walking into a circus funhouse is far less likely to generate epistemic looseness because it is such an isolated visual experience (and also because one knows full well it is the mirrors that are making things look funny). When one emerges from the funhouse and reenters the comparatively normal fairground outside, one might be laughing and a little dizzy, but one's basic *feeling* of epistemic trust in one's senses is not too severely challenged. It is challenged a little, perhaps, but it is not remotely as comprehensive and potentially wrenching as even a moderate trip with a classic psychedelic. Epistemic loosening is thus not perceptual flux alone but it also carries with it an element of existential challenge that is not merely cognitive but is subjectively *felt*; it *troubles* one's conception of reality to an extent rather than merely diverting one's attention.

Psychedelics thus serve as a kind of epistemological crisis machine, a situation the French might call *bouleversé* (lit. "upset"), where basic assumptions about the world surrounding us can become scrambled and thrown haphazardly out of joint from the point of view of the experiencer. Whereas beforehand we know abstractly and propositionally that our perceptual apparatus is imperfect, a psychedelic experience of sufficient dosage makes it inescapable for us to *live* for a time with that fact's vertiginous reality—not unlike the moment while walking along at some great height when one looks down and becomes dizzied by the sudden realization of the vastness that lies below. Individual attitudes toward such existential vertigo may of course vary. As Hunter S. Thompson advises, "Buy the ticket, take the ride . . . and if it occasionally gets a little heavier than what you had in mind, well . . . maybe chalk it up to forced consciousness expansion: Tune in, freak out, get beaten."[10] In this metaphor, epistemic loosening is the start of the ride, when it's too late to go back and you begin to realize what you're in for.

It is worth noting how often such sentiments occur in the beginning phases of a psychedelic trip. They can be very anxiety-inducing for some people. This can be the source of what might be described by effected individuals as a "bad trip," even on a mild dose of a classic psychedelic. While I am sure there are some who freak out in funhouses, it is certainly not merely the perceptual flux that causes the anxiousness. Rather, it is the flux combined with the existential troubling thereby occasioned (i.e., the two elements of epistemic loosening) that causes the difficulty. It is interesting how different individuals have different responses to this: some happy to "take the ride" and some who want to get off it and go home. In this light, the standard mantra of psychedelic guidance that suggests "trust, let go, be open" (TLO) specifically targets the affective dimension of epistemic loosening rather than prompting the wayward tripper on the mechanisms of cognition.[11] It is rather comical to imagine launching into an explanation of serotonin receptors or the chemistry of tryptamines etc. with someone undergoing this kind of bad trip anxiety. What such a person needs in that situation is to be aided in finding the *emotional* acceptance and equanimity that the "TLO" mantra is meant to promote.

All the same, effectively but not uniquely, ingesting psychedelic compounds makes epistemic loosening relatively predictable and repeatable. One does not need to wait passively for a random crisis over the course of one's life—one that may never come—for the experience to occur; it can be intentionally jumpstarted. While there is always an element of unpredictability in any human undertaking—and the best-laid psychedelic plans can notoriously go awry, even for the most experienced psychonaut—one may of course work to augment the probability of a particular outcome. There may be ancient fatalist wisdom involved in waiting for serendipity, to be struck by the proverbial lightning, but modern human beings are disposed to want to use technologies to stack the odds in our favor. It is the difference between waiting to fall down the stairs by accident and choosing to descend them. One gets to the bottom either way. And there are predictable and unpredictable aspects to either scenario. Gravity is present in both, for example, and will predictably be a factor in all possible outcomes. But even in the more controlled volitional scenario the plans could of course go awry: one might slip on a dog toy halfway down and suffer a twisted ankle. As compared with the surprise fall, though, the outcome of the planned descent is far more predictable; assuming a modicum of experience and/or due informational diligence, when one ingests a psychedelic, one can have a pretty good idea of what is likely to happen.

For one thing, epistemic loosening will *in some form* probably occur this time and the next, even while one maintains the understanding that there always remains a possibility of diverging from expectations, perhaps even radically so. But this element of contingency is a feature of every intentional act, not just psychedelic situations. In fact, working to minimize contingency by stacking probabilities in our favor is a defining characteristic of hominins, as attested by our evolving use of tools whose raison d'être is the manipulation of the environment in order to secure chosen outcomes. Considering their ubiquity throughout human history and prehistory and their equally ubiquitous use to achieve desired ends (e.g., healings, mystical insight, communal bonding), psychedelics must be viewed in precisely this light: *as technologies.*

There is some resistance to this notion because, I think, it resonates poorly with much of the surrounding culture that has grown up around psychedelia. It seems cold and impersonal and not very spiritual or otherworldly. A tool-based approach presents as antagonistic to the mood of New Age spiritualism and naturism that has grown up alongside psychedelics since the 1960s, much of which contains an implicit Luddism that views technology as alienating. All this is understandable. But it is misdirected because it underappreciates how basic technology is for any imaginable human experience—not just in STEM-like arenas but across all areas of human activity, including religion, art, poetry, music, etc. Hominins have co-evolved along with our technologies across the broadest possible spectrum, including our very linguistically based mentalities (about which more below). It is literally impossible to conceive of putting it aside. As argued below, a philosophical perspective on technology shows that it is a much deeper phenomenon than that suggested by its ostensible associations with thing-like tools, the image most have of it when first considering the subject. Technologies are incorrectly conceived as a bunch of inert things lying around apart from us. Considered properly, they represent something much more integral with which we are much more intertwined. This is particularly true of mind-altering tools like psychedelics that affect our very intake of sensory inputs.

Andrew Gallimore's phrase "reality switch technologies" helps to reframe the discussion and orient it toward psychedelics' unruly (though also to an extent predictable) *disclosive* power, rather than seeing them merely as simple tools that can uncomplicatedly help us achieve X, Y, or Z predetermined outcomes. To take a pressing example, while they certainly seem to hold clinical promise as therapeutic tools across a range of ailments, this is just the tip of the psychedelic iceberg. Ex hypothesi, psychedelics can do far more than just shepherd individuals back to a conventional a priori–conceived state of wellness; they may in fact facilitate a wholesale alteration of the very operative notion of "wellness" in such contexts. This is why I favor Gallimore's description of psychedelics as reality switch technologies, beyond serving as tools that aid in securing determinate "solutions" to preconceived "problems" (even important ones like depression). Understood thus, they can more fundamentally serve to alter our conception of the problem space itself, including that problem space's very ontological status writ large: they are, again in Gallimore's terms, "world-building."

The history of philosophy shows that seemingly intractable problems are not so much "solved" as eventually abandoned for new problems; in a sense, for whatever reasons, what was once preoccupying ceases to appear as a "real" problem, losing its sense of urgency—like the apocryphal medieval scholastic "problem" of how many angels can dance on the head of a pin. So it is with life. Often enough we eventually determine that such-and-such was not a "real problem" after all. I see what I take to be termites in the basement and on that observational basis determine I have "a termite problem." I worry a lot about the assumed infestation and the catastrophically expensive repairs that will be needed. But then the experts from pest control determine that what I have been seeing are just ants, not the dreaded termites. My "termite problem" was therefore not real and the new information about ants has demoted it ontologically from "real" to "imaginary." The point here is that the "reality" of a given problem is not written into the fabric of the universe; "problems" always arise out of human involvements, and so their ontological status is fluid and depends on an indeterminate number of contextual factors. Psychedelics as reality switch technologies are powerful tools for rearranging these contextual factors in ways that change not only the problem space but potentially also the reality of "the problem" altogether. This is how powerful disclosive technologies function.

Like novel research instruments in the history of science, they can transfigure previous ways of seeing, not so much by directly refuting the old ways, but by going beyond the limitations that had been previously assumed, thereby opening irresistible vistas for further exploration; it is perhaps more that we are seduced by the new possibilities and feel a necessity for moving ourselves toward them than we directly confront and refute the stifling status quo ante. Once "business as usual" or "normal science," to use the Kuhnian phrase, finally allows opportunities for the epistemic levers to be deployed, the emergent puzzles and problems they create simply become too interesting to ignore and emit a siren call to the most original philosophical minds.[12] Richard Rorty (1931–2007) perfectly summarizes this indirectness of philosophical change: "Interesting philosophy is rarely an examination of the pros and cons of a thesis. Usually it is, implicitly or explicitly, a contest between an entrenched vocabulary which has become a nuisance and a half-formed new vocabulary which vaguely promises great things."[13]

Philosophical Pathway #1: Heidegger

Technology is a mode of revealing.

—Martin Heidegger, "The Question Concerning Technology," 13

Psychedelics as Technologies

Although, as they say, results may vary, the relative consistency of psychedelics gives them a fundamentally tool-like character. One may *decide* to use them or not and then attempt to use them pursuant to determinate purposes in whatever context. Widely utilized to effect outcomes in this manner, psychedelics must therefore be considered fundamentally as technologies and, as I shall illustrate below, very "pure" ones at that. This is why in the western lexicon they are experienced largely as pharmacological tools, that is, *drugs*—and this is a perfectly appropriate word for them—a state of affairs that implies no disrespect for traditional cultures apt to characterize psychedelic compounds more holistically and/or in more personalized terms as divine gifts and/or plant teachers.[14] This basic assumption about their instrumental nature entails that *the epistemic looseness achieved via psychedelics is a technological effect*, just as surely as is the hammered-in nail. To be sure, a nail can get embedded in a wooden board in other ways than having been hammered, just as epistemic looseness might be achieved by any number of non-psychedelic means. But hammers and psychedelics are empirically reliable for achieving their effects on nails and minds.

But there is much more to it. To better illustrate, I'll import insights from German philosopher Martin Heidegger's (1889–1976) famous analysis of technology, from his magnum opus *Being and Time* and other works. This philosophical excursus will render psychedelics' technological nature more vivid pursuant to how they might be conceived as *educational* mechanisms.

In line with Gallimore's reality switch characterization, Heidegger regards technology as, at bottom, *revelatory* of the world around us, what I will call a "mode of disclosure." Not only can various technologies help us see things that we may not have seen without them, but they can alter the very way we see things in general. A famous literal example from the history of science is the invention of the microscope. With this new technology, the Dutch founder of microbiology, Antonie van Leeuwenhoek (1632–1723), famously perceived a heretofore unknown world of "wee beasties," as he named the protozoa he duly magnified and examined in pond water. Psychedelics seem to reveal new worlds in this sense too, as their action at the neuronal level on our brains is capable, in Gallimore's words, of "altering the structure and dynamics of the experienced world."[15] For Gallimore, the resultant psychedelic perceptual alterations are not just "hallucinations" in the sense of mirages or distortive departures from reality. Instead, they are "world space switches" that, in a way congruent with each psychedelic's peculiar composition and capability, "alter the brain's model of reality in its own particular manner."[16] This is why the phrase "mode of disclosure" is apt. Not only can psychedelics suggest to us novel insights that "X might be real" or "Y might be real" but they are potentially able to alter our very conception of what is real in general and to occasion second-order reflection on the matter; they make us more forthrightly consider the implicit ontological frameworks by which we grant the status "real" and "not real" to various elements within what William James called "one great blooming, buzzing confusion" with which our senses constantly assail us.[17] This analysis captures the deeper, more comprehensive, metacognitive sense of epistemic loosening that differentiates it from isolated instances of perceptual distortion that do not normally engender the kind of philosophical questioning as previously described.

In sufficient dosage and after due consideration, psychedelics can cause us to appreciate that there are different experiential modes in which world spaces are disclosed to us. This insight need not necessarily be conceived in ineffably mystical or obscurantist terms. Integrating different modes of disclosure is part of our basic *modus operandi* as animals with sense organs and a nervous system. Unless there is synesthesia (sometimes reported with certain psychedelics), sight and sound may be thought of as distinguishable modes of disclosure that our brains coordinate and integrate in order to provide us with basic functionality in the world. There may be a degree of translatability—one may describe a sound through vision with visible words, say—but under normal conditions no one is going to confuse the subjective experience of hearing with that of seeing; they occur within readily distinguishable disclosive frameworks in which sight and sound appear to us as, in turn, *distinctively* seen sights and *distinctively* heard sounds. By extrapolation, especially in their more comprehensive varieties, such as the reported high-dosage "breakthrough" DMT journeys, psychedelics are tools that disclose bizarre and unanticipated worlds that are almost always reported to contain elements that, try as one might, defy articulation in terms of the experiential worlds to which we are accustomed—to at least some significant extent. Our ordinary modes of disclosure do not quite seem to be able to grasp what is going on. Gallimore beautifully elaborates:

> psychedelics reveal in a most startling manner that the familiar world of daily life is but one amongst countless others. . . . These worlds are not to be found on neighboring star systems or distant galaxies reachable only by directed pulses of electromagnetic radiation or in a promised future of interstellar travel, but are ever present, right here, waiting to be discovered and explored. It's all too easy to drift through life entirely unaware of their existence. But you are in possession of an exquisite machine motionlessly buoyant in in the softly circulating fluids of your skull. . . . A world-building machine. Your brain is the most complex structure in the known universe, and the world-building machine *ne plus ultra*. And *psychedelic molecules are the tools for tuning and operating this machine*. [emphasis added][18]

Just like with van Leeuwenhoek's microscope disclosing the wee beasties, "psychedelic molecules" animate their corresponding brain receptors and networks to disclose new worlds. As if one were to tumble down a mineshaft into a dark cavern (or like Alice down the rabbit hole), it may take some time to grope around while one's senses adjust in order to make any sense at all of one's new surroundings. And when some light is finally shed, the cavern might look entirely different from what one first thought it would be. Again, like the world of microbiology discovered by van Leeuwenhoek, indigenous traditions often hold that, although they are normally invisible, these alternate worlds are adjacent to us at all times; close, yet so far away and most of the time veiled. In fact, according to such traditions, the brief glimpses afforded by psychedelics may be showing us normally inaccessible worlds that have been with us all along, in the terminology of the Hindu tradition, penetrating the Veil of Maya.[19] Noting this possibility does not entail a flight into any supernatural realm. It represents in fact a respect for empiricism via an epistemic humility that holds open the possibility of *supra*-natural realms beyond the limits our current *limited* sensory capabilities. The history of western science itself copiously illustrates the need for maintaining this openness—lest one fall into the company of the contemporaries who confidently scoffed at now-proven realities like van Leeuwenhoek's wee beasties, Copernicus's heliocentrism, or quantum entanglement's "spooky action at a distance."

Elaborating epistemic loosening along Heideggerian lines as a consequence of psychedelics' mode of disclosure illuminates some essential aspects of the phenomenon. First, it helps counter a tendency to conceive of tools and technologies exclusively in terms of their material embodiments. It is a mistake to make that identification too tight, for their particular material embodiments are rarely if ever necessary definitional conditions. A hammer is most commonly made of metal but it could be realized with any number of alternative material substrates: wood, stone, diamond, etc. It thus cannot be so easily identified in terms of its materiality, its thing-ness. Similarly, while at the molecular level classic psychedelics are of course chemical compounds, most of them tryptamines or phenethylamines, that are agonists for certain serotonergic neuronal receptors that in turn activate the central nervous system to produce the effects we label "psychedelic," like the hammer that is usually but not always made of metal, there are many, many compounds that are agonists for alternate receptors and alternate neural networks that also seem to function experientially as psychedelics. Examples would be *Salvia divinorum* (from the mint family, an agonist for kappa-opioid receptors), ketamine (a lab-synthesized agonist for NMDA receptors), and DMT (which is, interestingly, endogenous, meaning it is produced naturally in the body—probably in mammals generally—and whose pathway seems to include sigma-1 receptors in addition to the serotonin 2A receptors).[20] They are different types of chemical compounds that utilize different neural pathways but they are still by most anyone's reckoning still psychedelic in terms of their experiential effects.

Although their chemical substrates and neurological pathways are of course interesting and worthy of study, from a philosophical point of view it would be a mistake to reduce psychedelic technologies exclusively to their substrates and pathways, for the simple reason that their subjective effects are as indispensable to defining them as is their chemistry. In a way, their proof is in their experiential pudding, especially given that ex hypothesi there is no single material substrate for generating psychedelic experiences, just like there is no exclusive material substrate necessary for most any technology (though in principle there could be a material substrate so perfectly suited to purpose as to be irreplaceable). This is not to say that no substrate is needed or that it is of no consequence what that substrate is. Neither is it a point in favor of spiritualism or immateriality (i.e., a ghost in the machine). It is only to note that psychedelics and their material instantiations do not enjoy a simple one-to-one correspondence. At a minimum, there are multiple compounds and multiple pathways, and one must always keep in mind that in this field the research is only beginning and a great deal remains unknown. There are new compounds—and for that matter neural pathways—continually being discovered and created. By all accounts, the neurochemistry in this area is still in its infancy.

A little humility thus established, the most difficult point to grasp about psychedelics as technologies is also probably the most difficult philosophical point to grasp about technologies in general: their essential nature lies not in their thing-ness but in qualitative aspects of the subjective experiences they generate, what are sometimes called "qualia": that is, the first-person, *felt* experiences they engender. Consider a very simple example. In my orchard I use a stick to get at apples at the top of my trees to make them fall when they are ripe.[21] I need the stick because the highest apples are beyond my reach, even atop my ladder. Since I pick the apples in reach by hand and they are closer to me, I can feel them and see them up close—and I discard a few that are worm-eaten or unripe. With the stick for the higher ones, I can indeed extend my reach (the point of the stick as a tool) but I also lose some of the up-close qualia present for the hand-picked apples. I just have to knock all of them because I can't see and feel as well which ones are mushy and worm-eaten and/or as yet unripe. My capabilities are extended by the stick—and I am enabled to get more apples—but simultaneously I must be less discriminating about it. The apple-picking stick is a "good" tool insofar as the quantity vs. quality harvest tradeoff is worth it. Now, any number of things and any number of material substrates could function as my stick: a metal rod, a section of PVC pipe, a riding crop, etc. The "toolness" of the tool is determined not by what it is made of but by what it enables me to do, how it alters and extends my field of operation. In fact, insofar as it functions properly, all I'm really thinking about are the apples and the range of them I can get at. It reveals new contexts for me, and *that* experiential phenomenon is the real payoff of the technology. Since any number of material substrates might enable these capability alterations and result in an "objective" measure of, say, apple productivity—apples picked per hour or some such—the qualia associated with the actual use of the technology are inevitably part of understanding what it is. Likewise, one can look through catalogs featuring all kinds of hammers, but one who has never wielded a hammer will have an inadequate understanding of "a hammer." Academics are perhaps prone sometimes to neglect such pragmatics due to a bias toward cognition. The "what it feels like" sort of knowledge—or, if you like, knowing-*how* rather than knowing-*that*—is often given unjustifiably short shrift.[22]

Note also that even with the stick example it is not all "revealing" in the positive sense of only showing more and more. There is also an inevitable *concealing* aspect as well, one that goes hand in hand with the revealing. Though the stick extends my reach and thus reveals more apples than otherwise, poking at them is not the same as grasping them, and what poking gains in terms of reach it also loses in precision in terms of qualia of color, size, hardness, etc. The telephone gives another example. Obviously, it magnificently extends reach—around the whole planet—but one also loses components of face-to-face conversation like facial expressions, hand gestures, and the like. The apple stick and the telephone thus reveal and conceal *simultaneously*, and this is an often-forgotten feature of all technologies; they always both reveal *and* conceal. "Mode of disclosure" better captures this *structural ambivalence* and, as a phrase, it should be understood to be inclusive of this necessary and simultaneous reveal/conceal movement. The structural ambivalence is often neglected with psychedelics, probably because there is so much excitement involved in all the weirdness and novelty on display and their intimacy hides their technological nature (akin to how one can "forget" one's contact lenses). But it is never *all* "reveal" with any technology;

there are inevitably also concealments as well. To take a simple example: I may be breaking through on DMT and vaulting into unimagined new worlds of complexity and wonder (very revealing) but also simultaneously I'm pinned back on the couch and not noticing what is going on in the room around me (very concealing). In a way it's a complexification of focus. To focus intently on one element of one's perceptual field or, obviously, to introspect more deeply, other environmental elements normally within that perceptual field must proportionally be lost to one's focus and become dimmed and/or muted, if not temporarily eliminated altogether.

Keeping technology's structural ambivalence in mind, consider this passage from Heidegger:

> What has the essence of technology to do with revealing? The answer: everything. For every bringing-forth is grounded in revealing. Bringing-forth, indeed, gathers within itself the four modes of occasioning—causality—and rules them throughout. Within its domain belong ends and means, belongs instrumentality. Instrumentality is considered to be the fundamental characteristic of technology. If we inquire, step by step, into what technology, represented as means, actually is, then we shall arrive at revealing. The possibility of all productive manufacturing lies in revealing.
>
> Technology is therefore no mere means. Technology is a way of revealing. If we give heed to this, then another whole realm for the essence of technology will open itself up to us. It is the realm of revealing, i.e., of truth.[23]

Here Heidegger arrives at conclusions consistent with my picking stick example: when properly understood as detachable from any specific material substrate (again: this is not suggesting immateriality, only that the *specific* material form is of secondary importance), technology is what it is owing to the subjective experiential effects it has on *us*. "Technology is a way of revealing [disclosure]." As it reveals *and* conceals—*discloses—* new contexts of involvement, it alters our ideas about our possibilities and limits and therefore alters our conception of what is and is not real. Before jet air travel it was not "real" to me that I could cross the Atlantic and be in Europe from North America by tomorrow. Enjoying teatime in London tomorrow was the stuff of fantasy, something purely imaginary or speculative in the realm of science fiction. But now the "reality" of this possibility, where I could at this very moment buy the ticket and get to the airport and go, shapes in myriad ways my sense of the world I inhabit and what is real and not real for me. In the before times, while I may have stood in the same geographical location, vis-à-vis jet travel I inhabited a different world, a different configuration of lived possibilities and actualities. In Heideggerian terms, the world disclosed itself to me in a different manner due to my understanding of what was technically possible in the situation. Of course, much of this technological world-structuring is implicit and lies beneath conscious notice in our everyday attitude; it surfaces and becomes visible only occasionally.

This occasional visibility is not accidental. As per the above, not only is technology not to be reduced to whatever happens to be its material substrate, it is most itself when it has *withdrawn* completely from our direct attention. The classic account of technological withdrawal (*zurückzuziehen*) is found in Heidegger's *Being and Time*, the goal of which is to present an "existential analytic," a description of first-person experience (i.e., Dasein, in Heidegger-speak). For Heidegger, when it functions smoothly, the hammer exists for its user as pure instrumentality; it is lost within the activity of hammering pursuant to some project. In Heidegger's terminology, the hammer exists for me as I successfully hammer along as "ready-to-hand" (*Zuhandenheit*).[24] It does not become an *object* for me ("present-at-hand" [*Vorhandenheit*]) unless it malfunctions in some way or is otherwise removed from the fluidity of engagement (e.g., one might be moved to regard it aesthetically—"oh, what a pretty handle it has"), at which time I first notice it conspicuously *as a hammer*, as some-*thing* sticking out from the project that is demanding and isolating my attention, say, in order to repair something made of wood. Without delving further into the intricacies of Heidegger's description (more on this below), the point for now is that insofar as the hammer is functioning properly it actually sinks beneath the level of my reflective concern; it *withdraws* and becomes invisible as a hammer: "The peculiarity of what is proximally ready-to-hand is that, in its readiness-to-hand, it must, as it were, withdraw in order to be ready-to-hand quite authentically. That with which our everyday dealings proximally dwell is not the tools themselves. On the contrary, that with which we concern ourselves primarily is the work—that which is to be produced at the time."[25]

The hammer, or of course whatever tool, brings content to itself from the outside, from its surrounding context: fixing a leaky roof, fixing my daughter's dollhouse and wanting to make her happy, worrying about the noise I'm making bothering the neighbors, etc. Embedded in two different settings, a tool-object is the "same thing" only in the most trivial sense; and within a particular setting a tool becomes present *as an object* only insofar as it deviates from being a tool. One might term this a *"paradox of withdrawal"* in that the tool is most visible when it ceases to be a tool, that is, when its functionality has been compromised and the pragmatic veil of its withdrawal has been, well, withdrawn. As alluded to earlier, this paradox particularly afflicts psychedelics due to their intimacy of action on our qualia and their microscopic nature that renders them unseeable by the naked eye (or any other sense organs) and makes their molecular thing-ness easy to forget.

The larger point is that tools per se are nothing (much) at all, but they become something only by virtue of the larger contexts of involvement they suggest (i.e., they function as signs). As per the paradox of withdrawal, by their very (optimized) functionality, they give themselves away—literally. Although not usually associated with Heidegger, the American pragmatist philosopher John Dewey (1859–1952), in writings from the same period as Heidegger's tool analysis (1920s), holds approximately the same view. Dewey too emphasizes the *in mente* disclosive component of technological phenomena: "Objects and events figure in the world not as fulfillments, realizations, but on behalf of other things of which they are means and predictive signs. A tool is a particular thing, but it is more than a particular thing, since it is a thing in which a connection, a sequential bond of nature is embodied. Its perception as well as its actual use takes the mind to other things."[26] A tool, then, must always be relationally defined; hammering is always "hammering-for-the-sake-of-X," where X is a project or context of involvement that is being animated by a corresponding set of imagined purposes which is what I am actually experiencing as I use the hammer. Again, I do not see the hammer as an object unless something forces it outside the context of its use; hammering along excludes the appraisal of the hammer as such—unless it suddenly demands repair, becomes a source of aesthetic pleasure, or is otherwise desired for its own sake, say, by a tool collector, in which case there is no longer hammering along, and if there were, if I took the rare tool out of the museum's ancient artifacts case to fix the baseboard, then I would actually be violating its current functionality (as collected artifact). Within the original context of ordinary hammering along in order to fix something at home, what I do see is the path to the "X"; in other words, the tool is what brings the end or purpose of my activity into view. Though I do not notice the hammer itself as an object (while hammering along smoothly), it nevertheless enables me to see possibilities to which I would have been blind otherwise: the roof might finally be patched this afternoon against the oncoming storm, I could make my daughter happy with the dollhouse, or I could join in with my neighbors to build a barn and so on. If I were not, as it were, standing upon the visionary platform the tool has disclosed for me, these ends could never have come into view.

When it is viewed internally, as a functional component of my lived experience, the tool is an existential middle term that overcomes the spurious opposition between subject and object; neither a mere "subjective convenience" nor objectively "out there," at its most characteristic, the tool instantiates the living bond between finite human being and environing world. Technologies can even become "embodied" such that it is highly ambiguous as to where *I* end and the tool begins, as with devices that have been incorporated into daily living. Again consider the contact lens that withdraws via normal daily operation (in my experience of seeing) and simply becomes in lived experience "what-I-can-see" and is only (literally) visible at times of malfunction or inoperativeness. Or, more dramatically, the amputee whose prosthetic leg in time becomes as much a part of her body as the "real" one. Tools are likewise embedded—and quite firmly so—in the construction of valid knowledge. In addition to the abovementioned van Leeuwenhoek's microscope, Galileo's telescope, Newton's prism, and my own simple yardstick are each just as efficacious in altering my experience as would be an imagined "bare effect" upon the brain (whatever that could possibly mean). Or indeed, a memorable psychedelic experience integrated afterward and incorporated so strongly into my subsequent outlook that it becomes a deep and inseparable part of my perspective on life. The possibility and ubiquity of such embodiments in both the physical and mental realms exposes the tenuousness of any sharp division between them; such biotechnological fusions and mini-singularities abound.

Chemically induced epistemic looseness should be understood as a technological effect along these same lines. Insofar as it is operating as designed, a psychoactive drug discloses worlds of involvement at a greater or lesser remove from the everyday attitude and its conventional expectations. Like all other tools, it withdraws from explicit awareness as it becomes sunken into its own functional effects on the user's experience. It only becomes visible *as such* if there is some breakdown or rupture in the experience—or perhaps, one could imagine, in an outlier exceptional case like that of a research-minded psychonaut diligently recording drug effects pursuant to knowledge accumulation. It is an absurdity to conceive of LSD or DMT announcing itself *as* LSD or DMT during the pendency of the trip. One imagines chyrons repeatedly announcing "LSD! LSD!" or a tryptamine chemical compound structure dancing about in the mind's eye of the bemused user—as silly as the idea that the lived experience of being drunk is composed of images of beer, wine, or whiskey sloshing around one's visual field. That lived experience "from the inside," the qualia, revealed by the compounds, is wholly distinct from their underlying materiality; and just as surely as with the contact lens and prosthetic leg, the experiential withdrawal of their materiality is a necessary condition for their smooth functioning. As an undergone mental phenomenon, *epistemic loosening is an artifactual residue from psychedelic compounds' functionally necessary withdrawal*, like the seashells laid bare and revealed to beachcombers by the tide's withdrawal.

An educational implication follows from the Heideggerian account of the ontological linkage between technology and disclosure. Let us assume a general definitional point that education has fundamentally to do with disclosing something to someone—in whatever manner, as opposed to hiding from, fooling, or concealing something from someone. (Though this latter could well be sometimes sequenced as a pedagogical technique, for example, holding back an answer early in a lesson, where a teacher's evasiveness ultimately serves a greater disclosure for the student by promoting acquisitional skills and greater depth of understanding via a process of discovery.) Accepting this premise about education and disclosure then commits one to the proposition that, insofar as a technology discloses some-X, it may be described as educative. And, conversely, insofar as its disclosive aperture is constricted, it is less educative. This suggests a pedagogical telos for psychedelics in their normal operation, where *they count as educative insofar as they are allowed to reveal*.[27] This revelatory effect is the *sine qua non* of an educative psychedelic experience. Correlatively, if it turned out that psychedelic usage were deleterious to one's revelatory capacity, say it caused debilitating trauma or brain damage, thereby causing a diminishment of one's future capacity for engagement with the world—a net *concealment*—it would be non-, mis-, or mal-educative.

Along these lines, one might contrast a visionary psychedelic experience with getting blackout drunk on tequila shots and passing out and/or not remembering anything afterward. Sure, one might learn something retrospectively from the ordeal, like "avoid tequila shots or there will be hell to pay the next day." But that particular lesson arises less from within the tequila-induced drunkenness itself and is more an imperative arising through the subsequent debriefing to be mindful of the *aftereffects* of the ill-advised shot-taking—a lesson behaviorally reinforced by the hangover and, perhaps in the blackout scenario, post hoc revelations of regrettable behavior the night before. In whatever form it takes (e.g., therapy, discussion with friends, meditation, cringing at the videos someone took), psychedelic integration is obviously fundamentally different from this in that one is reaching into and attempting at some *later* point to remember and make sense of what occurred *during the pendency* of the actual experience and not just its aftermath. Like alcohol, though, some psychedelic experiences such as brief but intense DMT trips can be notoriously difficult to recall with much acuity. This is why ayahuasca and "extended state" DMT (via time-release injections and under development as "DMTx") are potentially preferred as a temporal elongation of the DMT journey (though, in its own way, ayahuasca already provides that). On the analogy of deep-sea diving vs. snorkeling, more time in the trip space would allow it to be explored and processed more thoroughly and then integrated better afterwards.[28] By contrast, it would be of very limited utility to contemplate the subjective qualia inhering in the blackout drunk experience (i.e., "it was black and I was out"). Such examples show that, whereas the actual experience of blackout drunkenness is poorly educative (only indirectly, via its aftereffects, as the hangover etc. is it potentially so), the psychedelic experience, insofar as it is consciously recalled and integrated *in some manner*, has more potential to become educative because it contains revelatory power *from the initial trip itself* that is deployable later in the subject's life.

There is a caveat here, however. If, as anecdotally seems to be the case, there exists a point of diminishing returns beyond a certain threshold number of assays, tripping overly many times might cease to reveal much and could even turn counterproductive. Indeed, Watts's highly quotable advice in this regard could not be more on point: "*When you get the message, hang up the phone*. For psychedelic drugs are simply instruments, like microscopes, telescopes, and telephones. The biologist does not sit with eye permanently glued to the microscope; he goes away and works on what he has seen" [emphasis added].[29] To date, such questions are still somewhat open, but commonsense lore among psychedelics enthusiasts is that there are people who have become a bit loopy because they have tripped too much. On this point, the lore could be wrong about the causation, of course, as maybe those disposed toward over-using psychedelics do so because they are like that already (whatever "that" is).[30] But it does seem that, like most everything else in life, one can overdo it.

There is much more to it, however, than merely keeping an eye toward optimizing psychedelics' revelatory capacity and minimizing the negative efficiencies associated with concealing. As is increasingly the case outside of (sadly) dwindling traditional societies, contemporary psychedelics are ineluctably part of an applied science and ultimately pharmaceutical nexus. Whatever benefits individuals derive, psychedelics' effect parameters are set by their coherence with a certain worldview that is so encompassing that it is hard for us modern types to notice—although it is regularly emphasized by indigenous voices. Heidegger, particularly in his later writings, stresses that the development of modern technology is driven by forces beyond human control. Things get dark very fast for Heidegger, as he holds that contemporary humanity lives in an "oblivion of being" (*Seinsvergessenheit*) that renders us unable even to raise the question anymore of what it means to be (as by contrast he thinks the pre-Socratics did).[31] We have become so estranged from our ability to ask this question that even when we do consider the meaning of "to be" we are able only to conceive it under the aspect of a crude instrumentalism, as of raw material that is "on call" for human purposes. In ordinary language as well as the intuitions guiding high theory, this is what "to be" now means. Much of the concealing momentum to which we are subject is a result of events that are idiosyncratic and personal to us; it may be something larger.

Heidegger's name for what he takes this larger determination to be is "*Gestell*," loosely translated from the German as "enframing": the way in which entities are posited or "stamped." It is a characterization of the most general way in which we encounter what we consider "to exist." This pragmatic *Gestell*, this way of enframing entities as entities-for-use, is extremely pervasive in our culture, from the bottom line of the corporate boardroom to Amazonian rancher deforesters to bean-counting university administrators who peg scholars' research value exclusively to measurable outcomes (yes, this one is personal). Within technological *Gestell*, entities are arranged as a "standing-reserve" (*Bestand*) in which everything in the lifeworld is perceived as malleable matter on call and waiting for human use; everything is a "resource." In the aggressive mode of disclosure that holds sway under *Gestell*, "the revealing that rules throughout modern technology has the character of a setting-upon, in the sense of a challenging-forth. That challenging happens in that energy concealed in nature is unlocked, what is unlocked transformed, what is transformed is stored up, what is stored up is, in turn, distributed, and what is distributed is switched about ever anew. Unlocking, transforming, storing, distributing, and switching about are ways of revealing. But the revealing never simply comes to an end."[32] In this way, a river like the Rhine that has carried such a rich multiplicity of varied meaning throughout humanity's long association with it now becomes dammed up for a power plant and is now encountered simply as a "water power supplier."[33] All other meanings tend to flee in the face of this overarching and imperious one.

For Heidegger, the devices and organizational genius of modern technology presupposes a more primordial ordering of our basic encounters with entities-within-the-world. Entities are indeed disclosed, but they are disclosed *as* ordered up for human projects as "calculable in advance"; "modern technology reveals the real as standing-reserve."[34] This is the main reason Heidegger holds that the essence of modern technology is not itself anything technological: machines, organizations, and such spheres of inquiry as chemistry and physics all presuppose a sort of metaphysical gestalt shift wherein the environing world—including other people and oneself—are viewed as components of a resource well that is amenable to extraction and projective manipulation. The Rhine can be become stored up energy, the motion of an arm an algorithm, and murder a statistic. For Heidegger, in fact, the propensity to see everything in this manner is definitive of modernity itself. It is also strikingly consistent with many indigenous critiques of colonialist extractivism and its rapacity regarding natural "resources."

So pervasive seems this governing *Gestell* that, properly considered, it is not really an "outlook" we may choose to have or not have—it is too deeply embedded in the modern mind to make the heroic choice to abandon it and go "back to nature" or some such. In fact, it is more accurate to say that it has *us* rather than we have it (as a mindset). And Heidegger's greatest fear is that ultimately humanity itself will be reduced to a mere resource—a dark irony considering that the Nazi regime he supported and its genocidal machinery represented perhaps the apotheosis of the technological reduction of human beings to disposable materiel. (To be fair, by 1939 he did seem to recognize—a bit little and a bit late—that he had erred in his initial enthusiasms. He also came to be regarded as ideologically unreliable by the regime due to ambivalent wartime rhetoric such as "are the Germans not rather expending themselves in mere diffusion and dispersion for the development of the highest form of the unleashing of all instituted powers of machination?"[35]) Whatever the final moral judgment of Heidegger's activities during this period (and it does not look favorable), he presents a puzzle of moral contradictions.[36] He at once points to a set of deep and disturbing tendencies within the mindset of modernity, a critique that goes some way toward lending credence to anti-colonialist critiques of the more economically developed countries' brutality and environmental destructiveness, while at the same time he seems to be outrageously inattentive to his own past embrace of a particularly horrific version of the very same tendencies.

Philosophically, his picture of an overarching *Gestell* is highly counterintuitive to conventional wisdom that tends to hold the "commonsense" instrumentalist view that individual or collective human will is always at the helm, making choices regarding tool deployments. For Heidegger, this is a superficial and hubristic picture. In his (still) unorthodox rendering, *Gestell* seems to be a quasi-autonomous meta-force that has twisted our outlook such that we can only encounter entities as standing-reserve. And there is very little we can do about it; we cannot just heroically decide to stop seeing the world this way. For most of us most of the time what it means for something to *be* is reducible to what it can *do* (for *us*) and this is not an attitude we can choose to accept or reject—it's too deeply ingrained. Consistent with this fatalism, Heidegger proffers the judgment in a notorious posthumously published interview (where, among other things, he unconvincingly tries to distance himself from his prewar Nazi affiliations) that "only a God can save us now."[37] For Heidegger, appearances to the contrary, technology at this point mostly controls us or, more precisely, the technological disclosure of entities is just how we now see the world.

Admittedly, it is hard to understand exactly what Heidegger means here. Is technology qua *Gestell* somehow its own autonomous force and possessive of an agency greater than that of human will and volition, if indeed the latter is more than illusory? Poetic license aside, Heidegger seems perilously close to positing *Gestell* as something supernatural, a kind of quasi-satanic entity over and above humanity that has us in its grips, like some Cthulhic monster out of a Lovecraftian horror. While there is potential for such an occultist reading, it may perhaps be understood in more naturalized terms as a *deep and abiding cultural mindset* that has taken hold on a large scale over the centuries; as a matter of intellectual history, it is a mentality associated with modernity writ large, analogous to Marx's more focused critique of capitalism and the ideology it brings in its wake. On this reading, though concomitant with its rise, technology, in Heidegger's sense, is more basic than "capitalism" as *radix malorum*; it premises all modernist ideologies, including socialism and communism themselves, upon an instrumentalist and anthropocentric attitude toward nature and environment. (Socialist and communist states have never been noticeably more benign vis-à-vis nature, only perhaps less efficient in their environmental depredations.) So, for example, we enclose a wild space as a "nature preserve" on the grounds that it provides human enjoyment, or we fight to save the Amazon because of "biodiversity" and the medicines (including psychedelics) yet to be discovered. It is alien to this mindset to regard something as valuable in and of itself—for example, adopting an attitude of reverence or sacredness toward, say, a mountain or a river or a grove, an attitude that is found universally in the worldviews of non-modern (indigenous) and pre-modern (ancient) peoples.

However precisely it is conceived, this all-encompassing metaphysical malaise would make hopes for a psychedelic "cure" seem highly questionable. Intensifying experience or heightening perception could hardly alter matters. Even the wildest breakthrough DMT experiences involving autonomous entities and mind-blowing vistas takes place within this larger cultural frame where we "want" something from that which we encounter. A related tantalizing fact is that DMT trip reports commonly contain accounts of encountered entities who seem to ridicule, in various ways, such grasping expectations. Though individuals apparently sometimes get what they *need* from DMT entities, they rarely seem to get what they *wanted* (or thought they wanted) going into the experience. Insofar as they seem to reject our grasping attempts at controlling matters, perhaps the DMT entities *do* have some tricks up their sleeves. At this level of metaphysical abstraction, one can only imagine Heidegger applauding the DMT tricksters. So, perhaps in routinely thwarting pragmatic expectations, aspects of the most powerful psychedelics' experiential dynamics might possibly run counter to *Gestell*. The shamanistic tradition contains elements consistent with this possibility as well, with some ayahuasca and DMT entities described under the aspect of a "trickster ontology" as containing a radically unpredictable element.[38] They also may promote modes of non-individualistic self-understanding that runs counter to the acquisitiveness implied by the *Gestell* mode of encountering entities.[39]

This complex Heideggerian outlook warrants further examination. Despite his later turn to a more esoteric style of writing, the basic outlook of Heidegger's earlier work (such as the tool analysis of *Being and Time*) might accurately be labeled "pragmatist." One of the most basic concepts of *Being and Time*, for example, "world" (*Welt*), tries to capture the idea that when we understand or "see" something *as* something, when a thing or experience has meaning for us, it always does so on the basis of a context of practical involvements. True to the insight of Heidegger's philosophical forbear, phenomenologist Edmund Husserl, that consciousness is always consciousness-*of* (some-X), Heidegger holds that primary experience always comes prepackaged with meaning: only very rarely if ever do we just plain "see"; we always are seeing *something*. The same is true of hearing, where we never just hear *simpliciter*; if we are hearing we are always hearing *something*—strictly speaking, there is never *pure* noise. Even if we were to succeed in enjoying pure sight or sound, it would be a highly refined and artificial achievement probably taking years of monk-like meditative expertise. Consider the difficulty of hearing someone speaking in your mother tongue as just bare sound. Or, more poignantly, firing a pistol at someone, like the antihero Meursault does in Albert Camus's chilling existentialist novel *The Stranger*, and being so detached that the event is registered as just a jogging of his palm.[40] Camus's description of the murder reveals what an aberration such an evacuation of meaning would be—even the *ability* to experience this seems somehow un-human, in the realm of the psychopath. This is not to say it is impossible (Camus writes fiction not fantasy), only that the attitude of reducing the killing of someone to a fleeting tactile sensation seems a derivative if not pathological state of mind.

But Heidegger's point goes even deeper. Still following Husserl, he argues that our primary experience of the world we inhabit is always structured by our practical involvements, whether we are aware of this structuring at any given time or not. Any particular human activity has its "in-order-to" which projects significance onto the activity for the one so engaged. In the earlier dollhouse example, my project is given significance by the immediate purpose I have in mind (hammering that nail into the dollhouse wall) along with intermediate and longer-range purposes (the smile on her face when I present it to her, the fun she's going to have with it, the relationship I hope to cultivate with her, etc.). At the moment I am mentally lost in a miniature ideational world of functional relations with which I have semantically christened the activity, all of it connected by the "in-order-to's" that give meaning to the hammering for me.[41]

This world is dynamic and is ever expanding and contracting depending on the scope of my awareness of these functional relations, this "totality of involvements." I strive to make my daughter happy in part because my being a father demands it, as does my place within the family. Perhaps as I hammer along I am driven by guilt for having forgotten her birthday last week and/or by fear that my wife will castigate me for the lapse. Ultimately, according to Heidegger, if a resolute questioning pursues these in-order-to's far enough, they will lead to a deeper understanding of one's own nature as a finite being by highlighting what one cares about most deeply. Were one actually to chase down this chain of in-order-to's and keep asking "why?" at every turn—the philosophical affliction discussed at the outset of this chapter—like an existential detective one would discover one's "ownmost possibilities for Being."[42] However far down this road I may travel, though, the activity of hammering along (or whatever I do, from arranging the furniture to contemplating my own death) is necessarily ensconced in a web of involvements whose significance is limited only by my capacity and courage for wonder and self-reflection. Even supposedly disinterested or objective scientific research is grounded in some network of human involvements, always taking place within, to use Husserl's more felicitous phrase, a "lifeworld" (*Lebenswelt*). The point of the term "Being-in-the-world," arguably the central concept in *Being and Time*, is to convey this existential sense of involvement as it is experienced from the inside, as opposed to a more objectifying or aerial stance wherein my hammering is understood as a physiological activity, an exercise in value-added labor and consumerism or an example of kinship relations under late capitalism.

Not that these more abstract, thematized forms of understanding are necessarily absent from one's projects. This mode of understanding has its place: Heidegger regards as a (and perhaps *the*) decisive contribution to modern thought the Cartesian project of formalizing experience, quantifying it in physics and mapping it onto spatial grids (Heidegger was also a mathematician).[43] But it is decisive for pragmatic reasons—it is "successful" because it discloses whole new vistas in which experience can be made available, or instrumentalized for thought; quantification allows for a refined and almost unlimited usability. If one can divvy the world up into discrete quanta, one can better do things with it intelligently. But whatever utility these formulae have derives from just that, the *services* they perform in some human endeavor, and not some inherent pre-existing essence. For the Heidegger of *Being and Time*, then, a pragmatic attitude, or what he calls the stance of the "ready-to-hand" (*Zuhandenheit*) toward things as equipment, is the most basic way in which experience is structured. Other modes of experience, such as the disinterested contemplation of scientific observation or even aesthetic appreciation, are derivatives from it.

Aesthetic Openings

After what Heidegger scholars call his philosophical "turn," however, it is no longer appropriate to call Heidegger a pragmatist. In fact, his later writings take on an increasingly anti-pragmatist cast, and for three basic reasons.

First, though it is widely regarded as his magnum opus, Heidegger was dissatisfied with *Being and Time* (which was to be the first part of a much larger work) because it seemed, despite his best efforts to purge it, committed to a residual subjectivism. The very notion of Dasein, so easily misunderstood as *the* human being in the sense of an empirical entity, seems to presuppose, although covertly, a metaphysics of the individual subject; the "relays" (those ubiquitous in-order-to's) that make up the referential totality of the world seem to propose a vantage point, or at least some node or locus to whom the references have significance. His notion of authenticity (*Eigentlichkeit*), so often mistaken, from Heidegger's point of view, by Sartre and other existentialists for an ethical imperative to be "true to oneself," only redoubles the confusion. Heidegger came to feel that, despite his aims to the contrary, his earlier writings had merely reinscribed a dualism wherein an imperious self-regarding human subject oversees an objective world composed of its own purposes and projects. From the point of view of his announced grand goal of overthrowing traditional metaphysics, he may have only made things worse by erecting but a finer-grained narcissistic anthropocentrism.

Second, consistent with his ongoing efforts to expel this kind of subjectivism from his early thought, Heidegger became increasingly convinced of the extent to which language pre-forms human thought. Consequently, it has a kind of priority over the beliefs that pass in and out of our heads, a point Rorty encapsulates as "The world can, once we have programmed ourselves with a language, cause us to hold beliefs."[44] Its priority thus evident, Heidegger comes to believe that it is language and not Dasein that provides the condition of possibility for the instrumentalist ontology undergirding *Being and Time*. Less the master of all we survey, as individuals we are more like passive exchange nodes in a larger linguistic system. In an odd AI-like Frankensteinian reversal, the words think through us rather than the other way around. In effect, Heidegger tries to take the *linguistic* perspective rather than the human one, at least if the latter is taken through the first-person perspective of an individual subject—Dasein or otherwise—presiding over events. Once large-scale linguistic formations are set in motion, individual human beings must be content to be merely along for the ride. (There is the possible exception that a few extraordinarily creative types—artist, poets, scientists—might truly innovate and achieve real novelty, but this so rare as to be a non-factor in everyday life.) In this way, Heidegger respectfully rebels against his iconic predecessor Kant, who held that premising our sense perceptions and mental operations are basic "transcendental categories of the understanding" (e.g., space and time) and that the real essence of a hypothesized "thing in itself" behind our perceptions was inaccessible and unknowable.[45] Heidegger thought he could overcome this Kantian problem of the unknowability of essences by deflating the status of the human subject from being an entity on the outside trying (hopelessly) to decipher appearances to an entity who, as being-in-the-world, was never anywhere other than "inside" among them. As Kant himself agreed, the search for an unqualified reality behind all appearances—the "thing in itself"—should be abandoned for more productive forms of inquiry. Regardless of the merits of Heidegger's critique of Kant, most salient for present purposes is his contention that individuals are not as agentic in our thinking processes as we think we are; the distortions we are regularly subject to—so intensely under psychedelics—are exceedingly unlikely to be remedied by us in the sense of deciphering a hidden a priori truth behind them. For both Heidegger and Kant, such a quest is ultimately doomed. Likewise, those seeking "deeper truths" from *within* their psychedelic trips will likely emerge disappointed, as those truths must always be constructed, at least in part, by the mental apparatus we already have going into the experience and with which we will still emerge after. (There will be much more on this point in later chapters.)

On the brighter side, if one adopts a Heideggerian perspective, the characteristic perceptual "distortions" that ex hypothesi predicate epistemic loosening (despite the bias of our language in calling them "distortions") are not necessarily *less real*. Though it may seem natural to grant primacy to the world of practical involvements comprising our everyday attitude, there is no ultimately justifiable philosophical warrant for the ontological demotion. Today's distortion may be tomorrow's clarity of insight. An analogy might be with the feeling of pain: while it could be said that there is pain that isn't "real" in the sense that it is hard to locate a physical cause (e.g., psychosomatic pain or phantom limb pain), this fact doesn't matter very much for assessing whether or not the qualia of pain *itself* is present. If one feels it, ipso facto it is present because the subjective feeling of pain is simply part of what pain *is*; pain *is* a feeling. Pain's physiopathology is interesting and important. But since, whatever else it is, it is also an inherently subjective phenomenon; its raw physiology can never tell the whole story.

Relatedly, Letheby provides wider support for this contention with his provocative notion of psychedelic therapy's "epistemic innocence."[46] In his tightly argued philosophical analysis of psychedelic therapeutics, Letheby posits that legitimate knowledge acquisition may occur in these sessions even when the epistemological origins of that knowledge may be flawed (or at least without empirical justification). In some of the most profound therapeutic situations, such as Griffiths's Johns Hopkins psilocybin trials with terminally ill cancer patients, subjects feel they have achieved life-altering and even "mystical" insights. For Letheby, these insights arise from "profound changes to the sense of self," and since they are demonstrably available to individuals of a diverse range of religious and non-religious backgrounds of belief, the new perspectives and self-understandings they bring do not uniquely depend on those prior beliefs, many of which would be hard to justify independently, namely, faith-based or other metaphysically supernatural convictions.[47] More, such therapy involves little "epistemic risk" because it does not really promote any supernatural convictions (usually) and only provides the ensuing salutary gains in self-understanding. The proof is in the pudding. As in the Rortyan indirect bypass of intractable philosophical problems, Letheby is little bothered by the question of psychedelic distortions or, as he calls it, "veridicality." This is because, although psychedelics can be understood by individuals in some pretty far-out ways—DMT elves, space aliens, faeries, Jesus, Gaia, Quetzalcoatl, and so on—they can also be understood in a wholly "demystified" manner as "agents of knowledge gain and spiritual experience in a wholly materialistic world."[48] Like pain that is, regardless of its provenance, ipso facto real when it is felt as such, psychedelics-based therapeutics can generate real and salutary gains in self-knowledge regardless of a patient's operant worldview premises. They are pluripotent in this pragmatic way as well.

Letheby's diminution of psychedelics' veridicality problem is a recognition that the distortedness psychedelics occasion does not from a subjective point of view necessarily lessen the reality of any insights gained. No matter how weird and unprecedented some of these experiences may be to the individual experiencing them, the fact that they are being experienced means that they have a reality to them qua those specific experiences (more on this with Descartes in the next chapter). No matter how weird, that the perceptions are at all possible dovetails with the Heideggerian emphasis on human beings' insuperable connectedness to the world—even human beings undergoing confusing altered states; to be confused is still to be *something*. This inherent subject-object connectedness, which Heidegger later more poetically recasts as an "openness" or "clearing" (*Lichtung*), is experienced by human beings not as a stand-alone subject over against a separate world, but as an event or "happening" (*Ereignis*) that is itself made possible by language. In the jargon of analytic philosophy, language is that which makes possible our lived experience of the separation of figure (doorknob) from (back)ground (door, wall, room, building, ad infinitum). This disengagement of figure from ground is a general and necessary condition for any experience at all. Without such disengagements, we would be beset with a formless and debilitating chaos of unorganized sense impressions. This is why Heidegger reconceptualizes language as prior to Dasein's (i.e., the experiencing human being's) referential network described in *Being and Time*; before we even notice our own experiences as such, our pre-existing immersion in language has formed the molds through which experience must flow. We can't assimilate and understand anything that happens to us apart from this; it is in our hardwiring.

The discovery that the world of language is prior to the world of practical involvements marks a major shift from the pragmatic orientation of Heidegger's earlier thought. Consequently, he moves away from the project overseer implications of Dasein in favor of a series of increasingly opaque or, if you like, poetic metaphors such as the abovementioned "clearing."

Notably, though, premising an understanding of human experience on language carries an intersubjective emphasis, since language makes no sense as a private affair of individuals; it rather belongs to peoples, cultures, traditions, etc. So, for later Heidegger, "world" denotes, much more decisively than before, the intersubjectively shared network of meanings belonging to a culture. This is a key and often overlooked point with regard to psychedelics. The trips themselves seem so intensely intimate and personal—like our own nighttime dreams that are shared by nobody else—that we forget that, like every other experience, the very categories with which we make sense of what is happening (at the time or later during integration) are not our own personal inventions. However novel or mind-blowing or ineffable they may seem, the Husserl-Heidegger point is that there is never any "pure" experience, even under the influence of psychedelics; there is always conceptual and cultural baggage to be unpacked, including prejudices and biases of various sorts. These are not prejudices in the sense of racial injustice or some such, but prejudices in the literal sense of pre-judgments that as such are not necessarily value-laden one way or the other, they are simply a necessary aspect of how understanding itself works and not something always to avoid—to be completely unbiased is probably also to be unable to understand anything at all, as one would have no pre-existing ideas by which to understand something *as* something or other. (This theme is explored in more depth later in the chapter on envelopment.) But in order to avoid an overly naïve analysis, it is always something to watch out for.

A common example in psychedelia would be how, like internet memes *avant la lettre*, certain descriptions become influential such that people then begin to start "seeing" them on their own, a case in point being McKenna's famous description of ludic DMT entities as prankish "machine elves" or "self-dribbling basketballs."[49] These descriptors have entered the mainstream of the psychedelic lexicon—something "everybody knows about"—and so many DMT users are primed to see them and report about machine elves in ways they might not have absent McKenna's poetics. More powerfully, in traditional envelopments, long-established cultural lifeways create strong expectations for certain mythic figures to be present, such as the jungle animal motifs reported to be frequently present in ayahuasca journeys.[50] More subtly, with several psychedelics, closed-eye visuals of geometric patterns and similar are among the most common hallucinations (they often provide something like the decorative wallpaper of DMT trips) and precisely how one takes these is in part a function of one's background knowledge and interests: do they come across as high-tech fractals? ancient Egyptian or Aztec designs? natural phenomena like brachiating root branches? networks of mechanical equipment like circuitry or ducts and tubes? etc. From the Heideggerian point of view, all these experiences are necessarily dependent on the systems of prior linguistic (in the broad sense) categories by which we process everything we encounter. Even our illusions are prefigured in this way.

This leads to the sobering third reason for Heidegger's abandonment of pragmatism. There is a tension in Heidegger's analysis: he attempts to uncover essential aspects of human existence (Dasein) while at the same time he holds that existence to be finite and historically grounded. As per the above, all interpretation is contingent on the situation of the interpreter (linguistically, culturally, etc.), as the radical conception of human finitude seems to require. By definition, then, no interpretation—whatever its revelatory capabilities—may lay claim to ahistorical truth: the search for *a priori yet historical* structures of human existence represents a contradiction. Transposed into psychedelia, this problem represents a caveat against the kinds of grand universalizing truth claims sometimes made by those emerging from powerful psychedelic experiences, those approaching "breakthrough" and/or "mystical" levels. Given how mind-sets and settings are so deeply shaped by language and culture, anyone announcing a post-session capital-T Truth, one meant to apply beyond that individual (or at best her intimate associates), should be looked at with skepticism. Even as we ingest them, we are perhaps more like the mushrooms themselves than we care to acknowledge in that what one sees on the surface, the fruit of the mushroom cap, is just the tip emerging from a vast underground mycelial network branching out much farther than is apparent from the surface. The statements we utter—the way we make sense of the very experiences we undergo—are likely rooted in a similarly vast dark and tangled subconscious realm. This rootedness is a source of power, as one of course draws sustenance from one's culture and history etc., but also, in the spirit of the above contradiction, that same rootedness requires one to temper one's ambitions to speak for all of humanity; although everyone is rooted, by virtue of individual biographies and life experiences, everyone is also *differently* rooted. It can be a challenge owing to their subjective intensity, but the epistemic loosening engendered by psychedelic experiences should always be accompanied by a matching epistemic humility as well. It is important not to confuse intensity with insight; insight can also be subtle and fleeting and sometimes it can be disturbed by the heavy machinery of drugs and strong emotions.

Finally, Heidegger takes his convictions about finitude much more seriously than most. One of his best-known statements, after all, is that what is "ontically distinctive" about human beings is that we are ontological, i.e., we are self-consciously aware of our own mortality.[51] Heidegger is not really a gloomy thinker, but he does possess a kind of fatalistic attitude tied to this unavoidability of death-awareness and how this awareness of finitude spills over into other areas. In this regard, *Gestell* sets a special trap for mortal, limited, and temporary beings like us. For any striving to remove it would itself be participating in the very "can do" technological mindset of problem-solving that is characteristic of *Gestell* in the first place. He is rather opaque about what if anything can be done about this all-encompassing danger, as per his lamentation, cited earlier, about only a God being able to save us now. However, he does make some suggestions that are, I think, curiously compatible with telltale aspects of psychedelic experience.

Offering only a few gnomic utterances on the subject of what to do in the face of this all-encompassing yet (for him) disastrous *Gestell*, Heidegger turned to aesthetics. If active measures and problem-solving play right into the hands of *Gestell*—even if the purpose is to devise means, *per impossible*, to "oppose" it—perhaps an alternate strategy might be worthwhile. This he calls *Gelassenheit* or "releasement" (yet another imperfect translation). It has been compared to a Zen koan, a contemplative paradox whose depth must be fully plumbed before it can be "solved." The following passage is Heidegger's most direct attempt to solve the quasi koan:

> We can indeed use technological objects, and yet at the same time with all correct use keep ourselves free from them, so that we can let go of them at any time. We can thus take technological objects into use as they must be taken. But we can at the same time let these objects remain with themselves as something that does not concern us in the innermost and authentic [ways]. We can say "yes" to the unavoidable use of technological objects, and we can at the same time say "no," insofar as we do not permit them to claim us exclusively and thus to warp, confuse, and finally lay waste to our essence [*Wesen*].[52]

This "letting go" of technological objects seems mostly associated with artistic experience. In certain artworks, one glimpses a distinctively non-instrumental way of experiencing objects, even the most "technological ones." He notes approvingly, for instance, of van Gogh's "Peasant's Shoes" and Cézanne's ability in his still lifes to reveal the uncommon and the passed over in the most everyday objects. In a late essay, "The Thing," Heidegger meditates upon the potential "world-gathering" role of a simple drinking vessel, a brown jug that typically subsists withdrawn into its "invisible" functional state. This world-gathering allows the withdrawn and functionally invisible tool-object to arise as an entity that can *itself* order a world around it. (In a separate essay he provides a similar analysis concerning the ruins of an ancient Greek temple.)[53] This shift in perspective gestures toward a more authentic form of producing and experiencing than *Gestell* normally permits, a way in which one can indeed say "yes," while at the same time—to invert the Nietzschean aphorism—uttering in one's depths a sacred "no."[54] A certain way of experiencing art may be an intimation of how a "saving power" might grow from within modern technology itself, to reference a line from German poet Friedrich Hölderlin (1770–1843) that Heidegger quotes appreciatively: "where the danger threatens, the saving power also grows."[55] This hint seems to indicate an imperative toward the cultivation of a mental attitude capable of "releasing" ourselves or "letting go"—the idea of *Gelassenheit*—from the quasi-predatory attitude of viewing everything as a resource for our own consumption or in terms of how it can be utilized in some project or other. "To let be—that is, to let beings be as the beings which they are," as Heidegger puts it in one of his most orphic pronouncements.[56]

But how might one cultivate this attitude of *Gelassenheit*? Might there be a cultural practice that can alter a person's outlook and worldview? Something a person decides to do intentionally but is also widely acknowledged more profoundly to be something into which one must "release" or "let go" of oneself? This should sound familiar, as in the "trust, let go, be open" of psychedelic guidance.

I propose, then, that these difficult-to-interpret quasi-poetic passages about *Gelassenheit* are strikingly consistent with the role played by epistemic loosening in psychedelics. As suggested in Heidegger's remarks above, Cézanne and the idea of the still life genre provides a telling example, not just of pretty pictures but of a deep and weird ontological transformation. In the still life, normally unnoticed everyday objects, through the existence of the painting itself, gather an attention to themselves—a "world" in Heideggerian lingo—that, because of their typical below-the-radar unnoticed-ness, they would not have been capable of sustaining otherwise. Pushing matters still further, the readymades of Marcel Duchamp offer a more recent example, his 1917 *Fountain* (a urinal) being the most famous. Here, an intentional ontological hybridity is not just depicted but *enacted* by the artist where ordinary functional objects are, literally, placed by the artist on a pedestal and thereby transmogrified into an object of attention for public view. All these museumgoers now gawking at a urinal, perhaps exactly like one they just used moments before but didn't "see." In getting their moment, so to speak, these objects are allowed to shine forth and disclose worlds of their own, no mere objects of use dissolved into invisibility by the everyday attitude of ready-to-hand; the urinal à la Duchamp makes me consider it for the first time as a *presence* in its own right, as it has now become detached from its customary institutional-functional restroom setting.

Something like this perspectival shift is *very* familiar to most psychedelics users and is a ubiquitous component of the epistemic loosening experience. One's attention gets durably fixed on some humble random object, a feature of one's physical setting that is normally insignificant: the wallpaper, a tree, the buzzing bees, a random cloud, the weave of the rug, ad infinitum. In his inimitable style, Aldous Huxley relates just such an episode during his mescaline trip: "I looked down by chance and went on passionately staring by choice, at my own crossed legs. Those folds in the trousers—what a labyrinth of endlessly significant complexity! And the texture of the grey flannel—how rich, how deeply mysteriously sumptuous!"[57] Huxley is recounting here how everyday objects, normally withdrawn qua ready-to-hand, are now being surfaced via psychedelic tools and brought into a state of present-at-hand; they are *noticed* and become their own foci such that they can, once focally laser-painted like this, start gathering their *own* world about them, even the lowliest brown jug or pair of pants. Under such conditions, as an astonished Huxley observes, even his unremarkable gray trouser folds can become well-nigh luminescent, capable of captivating his attention comprehensively and for an indefinite period of time.

Just about everyone who has taken even a minimal threshold dose of psychedelics has been similarly mesmerized by random objects; it is an almost stereotypical trait of someone who is tripping: "whoa dude check out the ceiling fan!" "that bee in the yard," etc. I suggest that, properly considered, in such induced "fascinations," the psychedelics are actually generating a bona fide philosophical experience, in this case an epistemological pirouette long explored by artists in still lifes and ready-mades, where objects are taken out of their normal pragmatic contexts and playfully showered with world-building attention. Along with the perceptual befuddlements, this perspectival attention shifting represents a key form of epistemic loosening: a dramatization of the lived experience of a perceived object shifting back and forth from ready-to-hand to present-at-hand (a pragmatic spin on the figure-ground distinction). *Epistemic loosening thus understood opens infinite worlds, not in distant galaxies or subatomic realms, but right in front of us*, as selected items from among the teeming multitude in our environment to which we do not normally pay much attention (a slit of sunlight on the wall, the stray paperclip on the desk, how the back of my knee feels, the hum of the ceiling light, the floating dust particles, and so on ad infinitum) are illuminated and considered on something more akin to their own terms. The world thus becomes ontologically *laden* in a way that it is not normally or, perhaps, the ontological valences are deconstructed and begin to be built up again out of "novelties" that have actually been right there with us the whole time. We learn—by *feeling* it—that, although it is almost never questioned, our normal focus and "commonsense" pragmatic attitude actually conceals a great deal from us.

At the hands of an iconoclastic artist or via psychedelics there could be a point where these epistemic movements and loosenings coalesce to become outright epistemic subversions that pose an odd yet subtle threat to vested interests. Within today's "attention economy" that wages constant warfare for possession of our eyeballs and online clicks, this epistemic fluidity threatens a kind of *sub rosa* rebellion. Like the medieval Feast of Fools festivals throughout Europe, where established social order was temporarily inverted and ridiculed, epistemic loosening gone beyond a certain point can catalyze an attention inversion (one type of reality switch) where the humblest object might suddenly become the ontological peer—or superior—of whatever it is that has been predetermined as *supposed* to be holding our attention.[58] This is surely why the Nixonians instinctively so feared psychedelics and their destabilizing propensities vis-à-vis officialdom. They may have been right in their own way. A chemical Feast of Fools, psychedelics can make it hard to keep a straight face in front of those in power (e.g., the hippies, yippies, et al.); they can scramble priorities up and down the social ladder. As Pollan describes it, "Whether by their very nature or the way that first generation of researchers happened to construct the experience, psychedelics introduced something deeply subversive to the West that the various establishments had little choice but to repulse. LSD truly was an acid, dissolving almost everything with which it came into contact, beginning with the hierarchies of the mind . . . and going on from there to society's various structures of authority and then to lines of every imaginable kind."[59] No specific outcome is guaranteed, but epistemic loosening has at times aided countercultural departures from hegemonic preference schedules and landed people in unknown territories of intentionality that are less identifiable and less controllable. People's attention can be hijacked from sanctioned pathways and onto a Pandora's Box of myriad distractions. I *might* attend again to what I'm supposed to—just as soon as I spend a *bit* more time with that roaring little dandelion by the back fence that has with great courtesy just invited me to go inside it. Like the still life can do with such subtlety, psychedelics can disclose infinities right in front of us.

Psychedelics as *Umwelt* Expansion Technologies

> LSD was an incredible experience. Not that I'm recommending it for anybody else; but for me it kind of—it hammered home to me that reality was not a fixed thing. That the reality that we saw about us every day was one reality, and a valid one—but that there were others, different perspectives where different things have meaning that were just as valid. That had a profound effect on me.
>
> —Alan Moore, quoted in George Khoury,
> *The Extraordinary Works of Alan Moore*, 24–25

What in the end does epistemic loosening accomplish? First, it is a harbinger of possibilities. Research seems to support that an augmented plasticity of mind can in many instances unstick individuals from neural ruts and open new pathways around old problems. Though this is not necessarily an end in itself, psychedelics like psilocybin and LSD seem able to promote neural growth by increasing the branching density of neural pathways.[60] Relatedly, though it has not been definitively established, psychedelics have been widely reported—including copious anecdotal accounts by generations of intellectuals—to promote creativity and "divergent thinking" across different fields and in a variety of ways.[61] (A caveat: psychedelics can do the opposite of this too, as discussed in later chapters.) If epistemic loosening has the effect of diminishing— if only temporarily—the hold of one's accumulated network of prior assumptions and background beliefs, it is unsurprising that this could clear the way for innovative insights and out-of-left-field inspirations made possible by this augmentation of what neuroscientists have labeled "brain entropy."[62] Another aspect of plasticity is highlighted in a small (n=19) but interesting study finding that LSD "increased learning rates" and "exploratory behavior" and that "LSD increased the speed at which value representations were updated following prediction error (the mismatch between expectations and experience)."[63] LSD seemed to help learners depart from what was expected and augmented their ability to ascertain novel patterns. Such phenomena would certainly count toward the revelatory power of psychedelic technologies. They would function as a kind of ground-prep raking tool, a mental harrow that can loosen clumps in the psychic soil to increase its fertility. In these instances, epistemic loosening is less an end in itself than a preparation for something else.

It should be noted that, for these exact reasons, epistemic loosening can have unsettling and frightening effects too. Individuals have different levels of tolerance for psychological destabilization. Just as with amusement park roller coasters, some are exhilarated while others are traumatized. In recognition of the latter, candidates with a history of psychosis are routinely screened from psychedelic drug trials. It could be said that psychedelics are not for some people all of the time and not for all people some of the time. Set and setting are contextually dynamic, a function of individual life circumstances; even experienced psychonauts sometimes slip up and trip unwisely under inadvisable conditions. A friend, a psychedelic veteran who should have known better, once took a high dose of LSD right after returning from a loved one's funeral. Matters unfolded with predictable horror. (As the trip came on, he began seeing the walls of his bedroom start to ooze red with blood.) To drop acid under these circumstances was a poor decision, of course; people make mistakes. The point here is that epistemic loosening is not always happy and fun and "safe"; depending on the individual, and at different times for the same individual, the manifestations of epistemic loosening can vary wildly. This curious bivalence that invites both exhilaration and terror—as well as both healing and trauma—is one of the factors that can place psychedelics among individuals' peak experiences right along with sex, childbirth, undergoing danger and violence, etc.[64] While epistemic loosening is often positive and pleasant—a sunny mushroom-aided literal walk in the park—these powerful drugs always need to be handled with care and, given all the variables involved in their use, an abiding respect for their inherent unpredictability. While psychedelic trips usually follow pretty predictable routes, major deviations are always possible and one will likely come for you if you keep at it.

Epistemic loosening's specifically *educational* capability involves optimizing its world-building disclosive capabilities. Here, for the purposes of analysis, the emotional valence of a given trip can be laid aside. This is because, as is universally acknowledged, a "bad" trip (i.e., one that feels bad at the time) can be just as educationally meaningful and ultimately beneficial as a "good" one—and sometimes more so; as psychologist and "psychedelic elder" Richard Louis Miller emphasizes, "a bad trip can be the best possible trip, because it's the biggest opportunity for learning."[65] People sometimes describe revisiting wrenching memories from childhood or communicating with deceased loved ones in ways that are not at all enjoyable to relive in the moment, but when integrated afterwards these intense experiences can be quite salutary. Writer Graham Hancock describes a particularly poignant ibogaine session where, over an extended period of time (ibogaine trips are lengthy, around twenty hours), he was led to conduct some emotionally difficult unfinished business with his deceased father that was awful at the time but he regarded as salutary in the long run to have done.[66] A striking example of the putatively bad, but maybe not-so-bad-in-retrospect, trip is commonly found with 5-MeO-DMT, usually inhaled via smoking the dried venom of the Sonoran Desert toad (or lab-synthesized equivalent). Many have described it as a complete "whiteout" of consciousness, so ego-dissociative that is beyond terrifying to go through it. Yet as they come back to themselves afterwards, many users report powerful feelings of enveloping serenity and a profound gratitude for existence.[67] Given accounts such as these, any strict bad trip/good trip dichotomy seems facile, particularly from a pedagogical point of view; as in life generally, it seems clear one can learn from both ostensibly good and bad experiences.[68]

So how are we to understand epistemic loosening from a wider lens, putting aside the qualia it generates? How might it provide genuinely *durable* insights? By way of an answer, I suggest an importation into the analysis of psychedelics an idea from the philosophy of biology:

the concept of the *Umwelt*, literally translated from the German as "environment," but with much deeper connotations than mere physical surroundings. The progenitor of the idea is the Estonian biologist Jakob von Uexküll (1864–1944), who holds that not only humans but also non-human animals have a perceptual lifeworld that is constructed for each category of animals in a correspondingly distinctive way as a function of their anatomically differing sensory apparatuses. Bees, ticks, octopuses, and all others inhabit what Uexküll describes as "unknown worlds" that are also "invisible" to us and to one another.[69] Contra the traditional Cartesian conviction that non-human animals should be conceived exclusively as machine-like objects, Uexküll emphasizes that, like humans, they are also inevitably "machine operators" as well, in that they have *their own* kinds of subjective experiences created and bounded by *their own* senses. And some of these we literally cannot even imagine, such as bats' and dolphins' echolocation. Science writer Ed Yong supplies a variety of examples:

> We cannot sense the faint electric fields that sharks and platypuses can. We are not privy to the magnetic fields that robins and sea turtles detect. We can't trace the invisible trail of a swimming fish the way a seal can. We can't feel the air currents created by a buzzing fly the way a wandering spider does. Our ears cannot hear the ultrasonic calls of rodents and hummingbirds or the infrasonic calls of elephants and whales. Our eyes cannot see the infrared radiation that rattlesnakes detect or the ultraviolet light that the birds and the bees can sense.[70]

Constructed through natural selection to suit them and their distinctive features, these are "worlds" in precisely Heidegger's sense: the life-worlds, or *Umwelten*, that they inhabit.

There is a kind of tragedy in this conception as well. Not only are these worlds proliferative in numbers commensurate with speciation itself, but they are always to a degree incommensurable. We share a sense of smell with our dogs, but theirs is so many times more powerful that, from the perspective of what canine olfactory qualia are like actually to experience, even our wildest extrapolations yield very little clue. It has been theorized that, astonishingly enough, dogs can tell time through their sense of smell by being able to detect subtle deteriorations in the scent trails left by others in their environment, such as knowing a caretaker's afternoon return is imminent due to how her scent has diminished since morning.[71] We may live in parallel alongside one another, but we do not share the same experienced world with our cohabitant creatures; the same landscape may house many animals simultaneously, but they are—we are—also always enclosed in our appropriate *Umwelten*. As Uexküll beautifully describes it,

> The environments, which are as diverse as the animals themselves, offer every nature lover new lands of such richness and beauty that a stroll through them will surely be rewarding, even though they are revealed only to our mind's eye and not to our body's.
>
> We begin such a stroll on a sunny day before a flowering meadow in which insects buzz and butterflies flutter, and we make a bubble around each of the animals living in the meadow. The bubble represents each animal's environment and contains all the features accessible to the subject. As soon as we enter one such bubble, the previous surroundings of the subject are completely reconfigured. Many qualities of the colorful meadow vanish completely, others lose their coherence with one another, and new connections are created. A new world arises in each bubble.[72]

It is as if all sentient beings carry along with them these "bubbles"—reality bubbles perhaps—in which their perceptual apparatus generates an *Umwelt* that is subjectively accessible to them and not necessarily to any other creatures not similarly equipped. Only the most unjustified anthropocentrism would hold that humans alone of all animals have no *Umwelten* and do not also slog along always ensconced within *our* own reality bubbles. Granted, ours *might* be more complex than most, given our bubbles' structuration by language, but who really knows even about this? The honeybee's elaborate "waggle dances" and chemical exchanges might contain complexities we cannot remotely fathom, their pheromonal communications turning out to be just as rich as our linguistic ones. Our ignorance regarding other creatures' points of view is vast.

What we humans have that *may* be distinctive, though, is that our brains are highly flexible and possess relatively formidable *extrapolative* abilities. Even though we may not, with our inborn senses, be able to perceive echolocation or ultraviolet light first-person, we can, by learning about those phenomena, obtain knowledge about what they are by analyzing them from the outside. Technologies may enhance and even add to our sense perception with new sensory peripherals and neuroprosthetics—and these have already achieved stunning successes across a range of inputs.[73] (My father, neurosurgeon H. Martin Blacker [1933–2019], was a pioneer in this kind of research at Baylor College of Medicine [Houston], utilizing biofeedback machines in a clinical setting to help patients learn to manage chronic pain.)[74] We can learn to utilize such new sensory peripherals by translating them into our existing range of perceptions (in the sense that we can "see" radio waves with the assistance of radar detection devices), but we cannot understand something like echolocation from the first-person point of view of what it directly *feels* like internally to navigate with it. We can, however, construct cognitive models based on investigations of its nature and upon that basis then wonder by extrapolation "what it is like to be a bat," to reference Thomas Nagel's famous philosophical essay.[75] Nagel's main point in that essay is quite pertinent: we can take the bat's point of view as best we can but we can never actually know what it feels like to be a bat *to the bat*. Though it is a staple of fantasy novels featuring shapeshifters and, admittedly, it is also a feature of many shamanistic traditions that have now grown inaccessible to us moderns, the option of truly finding out by "getting inside" another creature has not yet been documented by science. Nagel's counsel of epistemic humility is thus wholly warranted. At the same time, though, it is nothing to be scoffed at, and is kind of exciting, that we are equipped to try to imagine—albeit necessarily on our own terms—what the bat's world might be like. Through informed imaginative exercises of this type, we can strain up against the limits of our circumscribing *Umwelt* and try, despite inevitable cross-*Umwelten* opacity, to glimpse what might be going on in others', perhaps opening what one study of ayahuasca shamanism suggestively dubbed a "non-local intuitive channel."[76] Such a putative inter-*Umwelt* channel might be described as a meta-educational enterprise: not only is it educational in the sense of disclosing or revealing worlds of involvement, but it is attempting, via a synthesis of both empirical and imaginative means, to glimpse other and *alien* worlds.

This then is the connection with psychedelics: I propose they should be conceived as *Umwelt expansion technologies*, at least in their epistemic loosening phase. Psychedelics are able in effect to shake things up within that *Umwelt* sensory bubble that we port around with us; or better yet, allow glimpses of worlds that are, if not outside that bubble altogether (it is impossible to know), at least denizens of its far reaches—farther than we are accustomed to reaching in the everyday attitude. That some sort of *Umwelt* bubble expansion is being reached is attested by how common, even ubiquitous, is the declaration by psychedelics users that their experiences are ineffable and inarticulable in familiar images. Words fail. While certain creative types have gone farther than most in detailing their psychedelic journeys, it is at the very least a challenge. This difficulty is not surprising, for as McKenna said, "psychedelics propel you through your local language and into this unimaginable realm."[77] As language is so basic to thought itself, and maybe a necessary constituent component of it, this means that, as they catalyze us to reach and perhaps exceed the bounds of linguistic expressibility, psychedelics also get us to reach and perhaps exceed the bounds of our previous subjective experience of thinking itself in order to take us somewhere else. We don't yet know *where* else, only that it is *some*-where else.

Akin to the philosopher's hard problem of consciousness (viz., qualia), we can map all the relevant molecules, locate all the brain receptors, and trace all the neuronal pathways.[78] And this will be enormously interesting and helpful in so many ways. Even if this physical knowledge were to be complete, however, it will never fully account for what it actually feels like from the inside to travel via psychedelics to another realm, any more than a full model of a bat's brain will fully account for what it actually feels like to be that bat. We forget sometimes that, as semiotician Alfred Korzybski (1879–1950) famously said, "A map is *not* the territory it represents, but, if correct, it has a *similar structure* to the territory, which accounts for its usefulness."[79]

A commitment to naturalistic explanation—as opposed to resorting to supernatural explanations involving deities or other transcendent entities—would require that the *Umwelt* expansion be hypothesized as composed of introspective glimpses into deeper recesses of one's own mind or, indeed, as an additive (and temporary) technological enhancement of our operative sensory equipment that is allowing for the expansion of parameters. The bubble becomes more capacious, if perhaps only for the fifteen minutes of a DMT or 5-MeO DMT trip or the four to six hours of mushrooms and ayahuasca or the twelve-plus hours of LSD and ibogaine. Through various processes of integration, though, the duration of the *Umwelt* expansion brought about by the careful use of psychedelic tools might be elongated and made more durably part of a person's life. Built as they have been over vast stretches of time through evolutionary processes, *Umwelten* are not of course static; they are dynamic and have by definition altered along with innovations of whatever type, from the growth and development of sense organs to the invention of language to capability-extending technologies like hammers and microscopes and, yes, psychedelics. I have no specific arguments against religious or mystical explanations of the ontological status of the worlds glimpsed via psychedelics except, with respect, to suggest that it is premature at present to resort to such explanations. By the same token, however, the very hypothesis of creatures' necessary enclosure within *Umwelt* bubbles also suggests that complete confidence in exclusively naturalistic explanations—those that happen to resonate within our current *Umwelt* configuration—would also be unwarranted; we simply know too little. The same lightning flashes of *Umwelt* expansion that excite our imagination to go above and beyond should at the same time also humble us regarding our inevitable boundedness and finitude.

Chapter 3

Hypertrophic Identification

> Never stop regarding the universe as a single living being, with one substance and one soul, and pondering how everything is taken in by the single consciousness of this living being, how by a single impulse it does everything, how all things are jointly responsible for all that comes to pass, and what sort of interlacing and interconnection this implies.
>
> —Marcus Aurelius, *Meditations*, 4.40

Life after (Ego) Death

> The universe for those who are awake is single and common, while in sleep each person turns aside into a private universe.
>
> —Heraclitus, T1 DK 22B89

So, you've been epistemically loosened. Then what?

The first thing to say is that there is no way to know for sure. As emphasized previously, psychedelics possess an inherent unpredictability as a function of the almost infinite variability of physiology, mindset, setting, and envelopment; the card deck can be shuffled and reshuffled and the game itself changed ad infinitum. There are, however, patterns that can be detected from available sources: accumulating bodies of academic studies, crowdsourced trip reports, personal and third-person anecdotes. Since we are dealing with the qualitative side of psychedelic phenomena, it must always be stressed, though, that individual experiences will necessarily vary.

Second, my strong suspicion is that most psychedelic journeys begin *and end* as a limited visit to the epistemic loosening funhouse; largely due to dosage levels, not too many pass "Go" and move beyond this stage. Yet some do, and characteristics of those onward and upward journeys are the subject of this chapter. A quick caveat: as indicated earlier, there are important non-cognitive aspects to psychedelic journeys like mood and emotion, and these are often underemphasized; psychedelics even in low doses are not just a screen with visuals but a somatic experience as well. Indeed, as Letheby remarks, "Despite the salience of perceptual changes, the popular conception of psychedelic experience as primary perceptual, associated with the term 'hallucinogen,' is an oversimplification at best."[1] But as far as discerning what is specifically *educative* and durably disclosive in psychedelic journeys, the more cognitive happenings actually are the appropriate focus.[2] This is not because the affective dimension is less important; there is no warrant for this bias at all. It is because event-located mood states and emotional dynamics are bound to be, from an educational point of view, *pedagogically bivalent*. It is uncontroversial that one can generate learning experiences in association with just about any emotional state. Though they may be "hard" ones, negative emotions like anxiety and fear can facilitate lessons just as easily as they can be debilitating. This is what I mean by "bivalent" here: they can go either way pedagogically; there is no bright-line border between "good" and "bad" trips in terms of what one might have gained from them—especially if one considers short-, medium-, and long-term time frames.

Empirical data from the therapeutic context seems to bolster this point. A senior researcher in a large Ohio State and Johns Hopkins University study (n=985) on "subtypes" of psychedelic experience (e.g., mystical, challenging) explains that "Sometimes the challenge arises because it's an intensely mystical and insightful experience that can, in and of itself, be challenging. . . . In the clinical research setting, folks are doing everything they can to create a safe and supportive environment. But when challenges do come up, it's important to better understand that challenging experiences can actually be related to positive outcomes."[3] One certainly doesn't need psychedelics to appreciate this point, however. It is like that harsh middle school algebra teacher, who stressed everybody out and was so unpleasant in the moment, but then ends up in the fullness of time to be retrospectively appreciated for her pedagogical effectiveness. Likewise, the negative and positive emotions attendant upon a trip can wend any which way as they unfold temporally vis-à-vis educational effects. Within extreme limits (e.g., an experience debilitating enough to cause injury or trauma), they are too fluid and bivalent to say anything definitive about them. As Nietzsche explains, there is learning available at the suffering end of life, too, maybe there most of all: "There is as much wisdom in pain as in pleasure: like pleasure, pain is one of the prime species-preserving forces. If it weren't, it would have perished long ago: that it hurts is no argument against it—it is its essence."[4]

More telling are the *durable* insights some claim, much more so than the moods and emotions they have temporarily been through *en route*—as intense as these may have been. These are *post*-experience, occurrent *thoughts* of significance, alterations of perspective and/or self-understanding (or one's "self-model"). However elusive of description such realizations may be, these gestalt-like shifts in mentality reportedly are associated with changes in general outlook, if they can be well integrated as a revision of a subject's ongoing worldview.

It is uncontroversial within the psychedelic community that first and foremost among these more intense, life-altering "transpersonal" experiences is what is commonly termed "ego dissolution" or, more dramatically, "ego death." Ego dissolution has been described in many different ways but, in a nutshell, it is the sensation that the borders of the self have dissolved or collapsed in some manner; the everyday attitude of being an "I" over and against other people and the world at large is compromised and one no longer feels oneself to exist as a separate and bounded entity. This feeling typically subsides after the peak period of a trip, but it can produce an intense "afterglow" that may eventually diminish but also may not *ever* completely leave. Such an "unselfing" can be joyous for some and very frightening for others—or some admixture of both.[5] Notably, this double-edgedness appears to be a state important to therapeutic gains associated with psychedelics, in Heideggerian terminology, by promoting not only a cognitive but an emotional "releasement" from, among others, anxiety and depression associated with excessive introspective and anomic tendencies emphasizing self-relevance. Letheby and Gerrans explain that, under the influence of psychedelics, a "very common experience is to see one's own dysfunctional emotional or behavioural patterns, and the possibility of alternatives, with striking clarity. There is a tendency towards decentring and the objectification of self-related phenomena which ordinarily are taken very personally and evoke strong emotional re-activity."[6] One may gain a salutary kind of distance, cognitively as well as emotionally, from preoccupation with self, assisting in a process of "unbinding" or, literally, getting over oneself.

This kind of self-dissociative experience is hardly unique to psychedelics. It has long been present as a theme in mainstream as well as mystical branches of all the major world religions and cultural traditions, and very copiously represented among more idiosyncratic unaffiliated spiritualists and meditators—and also quite a few secular intellectuals in schools of thought as varied as Stoicism and Spinozism. Reviewing the literature, psychologist David Yaden and colleagues have cataloged these mystical experiences under the label "self-transcendent experiences" (STEs), which they define as "transient mental states marked by decreased self-salience and increased feelings of connectedness."[7] For Yaden et al., "Mystical experiences are a particularly intense variety of STE," where "the sense of self can fall away entirely, creating a distinction-less sense of unity with one's surroundings."[8] Referencing Ronald Griffiths's landmark psilocybin trials with terminal cancer patients, they also note that the participants' accounts seem to mirror the tenor of reports of mystical experience in general.[9] These ego dissolutive and, relatedly, connectedness sorts of ideations are near-ubiquitous among serious psychedelic enthusiasts, to the extent that "ego death" is a common psychonautical *goal* where there is disappointment if it is not reached on a given assay. It is like—and according to the literature on mystical experiences *precisely* like—a chemically catalyzed DIY hit-or-miss mysticism potentially available to the masses through the graces of plants and chemistry.

The psychedelic folk convention of labeling it "ego death" is hyperbolic, however, and potentially misleading. The more cautious "ego dissolution" is probably more accurate, and the Yaden et al. "STE," while not exactly poetic, is more accurate still. The most obvious problem with "ego death" is that it is incoherent as a description of experience. If the ego "died"—that is, it ceased to exist during, say, a breakthrough DMT trip—then why are there first-person accounts *of any type* to report afterwards? True ego death would seem to require a blackout gap during the pendency of the "death"—otherwise there would be no psychic locus to which the memories of the event could adhere. This conception thus suffers from a version of what philosopher Ned Block calls "the Refrigerator Light illusion," where I think the light is always on because it's always on when I open the door and look.[10] Accordingly, anyone claiming to describe their "ego death experience" (a contradiction in terms, really) would by definition be capable of describing only the bits *around* that purported ego death; like with the astronomical observation of a black hole, one never sees the black hole directly, one only infers its presence via its effects on its surroundings. It is true, though, that intense psychedelic trips *are* often forgotten, and simple lapses of memory could sometimes be mistaken for instances of oblivion. This is why it is highly recommended to write down or record the experiences immediately afterwards—much like with the analysis of dreams. However, these alleged ego death experiences are usually described or depicted in *some* manner or, at the very least, it is indicated that the subject *was* in some important sense present; one was going through something that, even though imperfectly articulable, was definitely first-person experienced. So, it is inaccurate to call this "ego death" and incoherent to say one has gone through it. *Where* were you during the alleged ego death? If you weren't there then you didn't experience it (because there was no "you" present) and if you were there your "you" was present and so didn't "die." In form, this recalls Epicurus's (341–270 BCE) often-referenced argument against fearing death: "the most frightful of evils, death, is nothing to us, seeing that when we exist death is not present, and when death is present we do not exist."[11] There are grounds to quarrel with Epicurus here. One might hold that there is nothing irrational about fearing the unknown, as in this case, where the qualia of passing into nonexistence is the unknown—and who is really going to say that this eventuality cannot be scary? The argument is more convincing with regard to first-person reports of *ego* death, however, due to the contradictory logic by the claimant to have both been and not been there (on site at the alleged ego death). I will concede that it can be a useful hyperbolic shorthand, a bit of poetic license, although the rhetoric of "death" may frighten people off of psychedelics for no good reason; such a key component of the psychedelic experience can surely be marketed more effectively.

"Ego dissolution" and "self-transcendence" are better and seem more consistent with mystical and other relevant traditions. They raise a key question, though: if the ego dissolves or transcends itself, what then becomes of it? As the dissolution metaphor suggests, does the ego mix with some surrounding solvent like salt in water? If ex hypothesi it doesn't really go away—it's not *actual* mortality and it doesn't cause permanent psychosis where we might say one has "lost one's mind" permanently (a major fear inhibiting psychedelic experimentation for many)—then it must be something like this. The ego is still "there" but the borders have eroded such that it has become diluted and, perhaps, diffused out into the larger world somehow and in that sense "transcends" itself. But what then does this new diffuse ego become? If the *status quo ante* self/ego is non-transcendent at Point A and subsequently transcends to Point B, then presumably some alteration of it has taken place (rather than its obliteration). "Dissolution" and "transcendence" are thus very different metaphors from "death" and they raise more questions than they provide answers.

First among these is the nature of the new extended entity. I say "extended" because of the spatiotemporal enlargement suggested by the metaphor. Since we are dealing with the mind, there is likely no actual physical enlargement involving one's self-concept—it would be silly to suggest that "big ideas" in someone's mind are *physically* bigger than their "little ideas"—but there does seem to be a physicalist component to the enlarged self-concept's *referent*, that is, that to which it attaches. The mystic-psychedelic "unitive" picture, as it is usually rendered, tends to go upward and outward like widening concentric circles: from the narrowness of the ego/self to greater circles of connectedness to, as noted, others, nature, cosmos, etc. It is perhaps a coincidental circumscription of imagination, having to do with the built-in limitations of the human *Umwelt*, that the connections and identifications rarely seem to go downward and inward as, one would think, they just as easily could, toward the strange and improbable convergences of purpose represented by one's organs and bodily systems, then down into one's composite molecules, atoms, subatomic particles, and so on. Certain psychedelics such as mescaline may actually do something more like this, as they seem to cause heavy concentration on particulars.

It might be that we simply lack as vivid a working picture of microcosmic infinities as we (think) we have of macroscopic infinities; it's easier to imagine a galaxy than a quark. Regardless, it does seem very clearly that we are dealing not with *lateral* alterations, say, shapeshifting into adjacent and roughly equal-sized other people or animals or whatever (though shamanistic traditions do indeed sometimes involve these kinds of metamorphoses), but rather with transformations toward more encompassing and unambiguously "greater" entities, a specific example being cognitive psychologist Benny Shanon's observation that "an orientation towards the general is typical with ayahuasca ideations."[12] I am not sure why this is. Maybe there is evolutionary efficiency in creating a framework for coherent action that an identification with some relatively predictable and shared narrative arc—an archetype—might provide. On the whole, archaic obsessive introspectors probably had greater difficulties achieving survival-positive social coordination—and gaining practical competencies—than those focused on larger elements in their surroundings: herd, mountain, forest, children, sky, sunset, etc. Whatever the reason, though, it does seem that the envisioned transformation of the self-model has the ego *expanding* in some *hypertrophic* manner.

Following Letheby and Gerrans, this means that the implied picture of the self-model in these transformations is that of an "enduring substance," unsurprisingly derived, probably, from the underlying and immortal soul as conceived the biblical tradition. When, by whatever mechanism, the borders of this enduring self are diminished, it then diffuses out and attaches to some hypertrophic substitute as the new locus of identity. One feels that one becomes connected up as belonging holistically to "Nature" or "Love" or "God," etc.[13] Poet Robinson Jeffers (1887–1962) evokes the sentiment of this larger identification with more force: "Integrity is wholeness, the greatest beauty is organic wholeness, the wholeness of life and things, the divine beauty of the universe."[14] It is important to remember, with Jeffers, that these powerful moments of insight are multidimensional; they are not mere cognitive realizations along quantitative lines (e.g., I realize I am now greater than or equal to n+1, where n was my former self). They may—and usually do—have moral, aesthetic, emotional and spiritual aspects as well—for these are some of the most powerful ideations known to human beings. From the ancient Eleusinian Mysteries to Griffith's terminal cancer patients at Johns Hopkins, identity fusions such as these are capable of alleviating our very fear of death, of assuaging our inherent ontologizing tendencies.

As with morality, identity transmogrifications such as these also provide strong motivational force. If as a parent I now emotionally identify so completely with my child that I would without hesitation give my life for her, the problem of altruism is solved in that instance. (For altruism to be a problem requires at least two distinct entities, where one acts on behalf of another. In this case, from the subjective *felt* perspective, there are no longer two distinct entities, ipso facto no altruism and no problem of altruism.) This motivational force can be salutary, as in parenting, environmentalism, or finding purpose in serving others. However, it can also turn decidedly dark as well, depending on what exactly the hypertrophic growth attaches itself to. History shows all too well how it could be a wicked nation, ideology, fanatical religion, cult leader, or some other corrupt and/or malicious person. While inspiring rhetoric about connectedness and Oneness from spiritually benevolent psychonauts abounds, it is necessary to acknowledge these darker possibilities; fooling around with identity alterations this potent, while perhaps hugely salutary for many in therapeutic settings or wherever, is definitely also playing with fire. Admittedly, since *Homo erectus* first utilized fire a million or so years ago (precisely when is unknown), human beings have, it seems, *needed* to play with fire.[15] And for that reason, we also urgently need to know when it can burn and kill, too. I turn to these darker—and often curiously overlooked—possibilities later in the chapter.

Since it more accurately reflects the notion of identifying/transcending/dissolving into something larger and more encompassing, the subsequent modeling of the self on whatever is that larger-X is more accurately described as "hypertrophy," a growth or enlargement, in this case, of self-conception. This seems consistent with the common narrative arc of high-dosage breakthroughs: one is led beyond a narrow self-understanding and out of an abiding restrictedness about which one might not have been aware previously. This freeing move in turn leads toward some larger, unitive identification, often expressed as hard-to-articulate realizations like "all is one," "we are all connected," "it's all about love," etc. Exemplifying such sentiments at the age of 101, Albert Hofmann wrote that "psychedelic experiences in a safe setting can help our consciousness open up to this sensation of connection and of being one with nature."[16] The obverse of the isolated self, this theme of connectedness, according to Robin Carhart-Harris et al., is "pervasive" across psychedelic experience reports and is almost always described in beneficent terms—the feeling of disconnectedness being at the root of many psychiatric disorders.[17] It also seems far more comprehensive than just an acknowledgment of an intellectual thesis about the structure of the physical universe. The arrived-at feeling of connectedness is in a sense a pedagogical journey that is not just intellectual but also emotional, aesthetic and moral in that it is definitely seen as *progress*, an advance to some better or "higher" state of consciousness. From its vantage point, the world now appears more beautiful and one looks out on it as if from a normative promontory vis-à-vis other people, nature, cosmos, etc.

Thus this unitive realization is not typically regarded as a value-neutral state of affairs. It is not just another interesting perspective alongside others and is assumed to enjoy preeminence. While one might suggest that a bird's-eye view *above* a forest and walking around *in* a forest both offer valuable vantage points, the larger view, that of the forest for the trees, as it were, is to be preferred. (This is related to what is sometimes termed an "overview effect," as when the first pictures of Earth were transmitted from outer space, that, while vertiginous, can have the feel of experiencing a truer perspective from which it is hard to go back once seen.)[18] It is assumed to be, literally and figuratively, an elevated state of mind. It is a holistic gestalt differentiable from a mere aggregative cognitive information processing, however complete the data inputs. The unitive insight—and accompanying revision to one's self-model—where one now sees oneself in hypertrophic terms (i.e., as grown outward into or connecting with some larger-X) is a preferable and altogether *better* state of affairs. Conversely, the old narrow ego is typically described in comparatively disparaging terms as a debilitation or obstacle to the putative wider connective attachment; through its diminution, the ego has been overcome, freeing one for the salutary new attachment. Granted, the temporal axis along which these ipseity fluctuations proceed is varied. They are often quite temporary, limited to the pendency of the trip or, even if more durable than that, wearing off at some point shortly thereafter. As Huxley dryly relates his come-down from mescaline, "we were back at home, and I had returned to that reassuring but profoundly unsatisfactory state known as 'being in one's right mind.'"[19] On the other hand, several clinical follow-up studies of psilocybin patients have documented that most patients actually sustain the sense of "increased well-being" and other benefits generated from these intense experiences up to a year afterwards (and counting).[20] (Interestingly, "compared with low-dose, high-dose psilocybin produced greater acute and persisting effects.")[21] As Grob and Griffiths and colleagues and other researchers have shown, this follow-up prowess is also exhibited in the reductions in death anxiety enjoyed by terminal cancer patients.[22] If the insights are sometimes fleeting as per Huxley, they just as often seem very durable, too, particularly in the therapeutic context.

With regard to ego dissolution in particular, survey research conducted by Matthew Nour and colleagues with the Psychedelic Imaging Group at Imperial College, London, crowdsourced data vaults such as Erowid.org, and the valuable online archival compilation Subjective Effects Index (SEI) created by psychedelics researcher Josie Kins strongly suggest that these effects can last for *years* afterwards.[23] Nour et al. have created an "Ego-Dissolution Inventory (EDI)," with which they have been documenting, via online survey research, the experience of a "compromised sense of 'self,'" confirming through respondents the hypothesis that psychedelics produce ego-dissolution experiences, concluding that "ego-dissolution positively correlates with drug dose and experience intensity specifically for psychedelic drugs."[24] This is to be contrasted with the "ego inflation" observed with control subjects using cocaine. It should be noted that this sense of "ego inflation" should not be confused with the notion of hypertrophic identification I have been advancing here. Cocaine users' ego inflation is reported to manifest as aggressiveness and "self-centeredness" to the extent that "experiences occasioned by cocaine are in some sense antithetical to the psychedelic experience," the latter being associated more with "selflessness."[25] In contrast, hypertrophic identification has to do with a fundamental alteration in self-identity via ideational fusion with some larger entity or process, rather than a puffing-up of one's extant self-identity into an imperious posture vis-à-vis others; it is more "my cup runneth over" (Psalm 23:5) than "my cup is bigger than yours." Like the more general studies cited above, Nour et al. find that, *specifically* with regard to the ego dissolution phenomenon, those in the EDI study "reported that on average their reported experiences with psychedelic drugs had a positive and lasting impact on their well-being, which correlated positively with the degree of ego-dissolution experienced."[26]

Also based on online self-reports, Kins's online SEI compilation goes into further helpful detail, providing a more nuanced typology of reported ego-dissolution experiences.[27] SEI is "a resource containing formalised documentation of the vast number of distinct subjective states that may occur under the influence of hallucinogens" whose purpose is "to comprehensively document and describe the wide variety of potential hallucinogenic experiences."[28] Ego dissolution is just one of many categories represented in the SEI, which includes copious examples of perceptual distortions, bodily effects, psychological states, suppressions, amplifications, types of geometric patterns perceived, transpersonal states, and many others (each with several subcategories.).

For present purposes, the most relevant are two subcategories of "transpersonal states": "ego death" and "unity and connectedness." Through careful cataloging of relevant reports, important nuances emerge. Under "ego death" there are three subcategories or "types": "absent selfhood," "objectified selfhood," and "expanded selfhood." Absent selfhood ("Type

1") would be the starkest and possibly most questionable form of ego death, as highlighted earlier. Here there is "just awareness of sensory input as it is and by itself without a conscious agent to comment on or think about what is happening to it." One thinks of the dissociative 5-MeO-DMT whiteout events and also, possibly, very-high-dose psilocybin trips (and a few others). Here, one's consciousness is reduced to the barest processing of sensory input, a kind of lived impressionism where meaning-making capabilities, normally operative in the flow of ordinary experience, are short-circuited and one is subject to a disjointed and (literally) meaning-less bombardment of sensations. One is "aware" of it but unable to ascribe meaning to it, let alone articulate it afterwards—almost a belly-up catatonia. This state holds little philosophical or educational interest, I think, although one is mindful of the 5-MeO-DMT users who relate intense positive generalized emotions like being grateful for existence, etc., post hoc. In all honesty, though, it seems as if one might just as well sniff glue until one passes out or knock oneself unconscious for approximately the same effect. To be fair, not having myself experienced this extreme of a dissociative drug, my assessment here may be off. However, it is hard to conceptualize what one could really take from it educationally, as outlined above, given that, by definition, "oneself" was not truly there while it happened. Being grateful for no longer being unconscious is understandable, but that seems as far as it would go.

The second SEI ego death category ("Type 2") is "objectified selfhood." Here, the awareness of self becomes detached from the everyday lived experience of self. One's "awareness feels entirely separate from its own identity, as if this selfhood is now the object of experience instead of the subject." The nearest analogy that comes to mind is probably that of near-death experience (NDE) reports, where individuals describe having seen themselves from a distance, say, on an operating table while they were supposed to be clinically dead. Without delving into the veracity of these kinds of stories (who knows?), they seem structurally similar to Type 2 ego death. From some kind of achieved (and one guesses superior) post-NDE vantage point, one is able to look upon oneself from this new and exterior perspective. Perhaps a more prosaic version of this phenomenon is the realization, related often enough by serious meditators, that one can become capable of examining one's emotion more objectively, noticing in a distanced manner that "I am feeling anger right now . . . how interesting that I am feeling this" and the like. This would count as a kind of "transpersonal" (or I might say "rationally ecstatic") experience in that one has in a sense grown an additional observer-self, namely, the one that is now capable of turning around and examining itself, thus exhibiting an extended self-reflective capability. This does not sound much like "ego death," however, though perhaps it is an ego diminution in the sense that the old non-reflective ego is put in its place a bit.

Type 3 ego death is labeled "expanded selfhood" and it is roughly synonymous with what I am calling hypertrophic identification. Here, the sense of self expands "to include a wider array of concepts than it previously did" and, particularly on point with previous discussion, "results in intense and inextricable feelings of unity or interconnectedness between the self and varying arrays of previously 'external' systems." Of note is that it is described as inherently connective. This is consistent with the account rendered previously and is only logical: if one's self-conception expands to include things that were previously considered separate and distinct (if they were noticed at all) then this implies some intimate *in mente* connection—with more combinatory valence it could be described as "absorption by" or "absorption of"—with that larger entity or set of entities (or processes or "systems," as the SEI terms them).

No doubt one can learn a lot from Type 1 and Type 2 ego death, but Type 3/hypertrophic identification seems by far the most pedagogically fecund. It would also seem to be the most likely candidate for the more durable effects also registered in the EDI and the other studies. It also seems most consistent with the ancient enthusiasm for deep psychedelic transformation as hinted at in the Eleusinian Mysteries and other ceremonials. From a forensics point of view, it would have to be a highly significant realization that would generate the ancient inscription Brian Muraresku highlights in *The Immortality Key* that "If you die before you die, you won't die when you die."[29] It is among the most ancient of what sociologist Zygmunt Bauman called "immortality strategies" whereby, puny and mortal as we are, if we can somehow attach ourselves to that which is large enough and, ideally, imperishable, we ourselves can "participate" in that imperishability and, literally by association, overcome death.[30] Something like this may be the original form of hypertrophic identification, its motivation obvious.

Along with Muraresku and Bauman, it is possible to assert an ancient lineage for this expanded-self model because it is a core theme in one of the most documented of all ancient sources: Plato. Plato was a lifelong devotee of Pythagoras (born c. 600 BCE) who led an esoteric cult with all the trappings, including initiation rites and proto-Masonic "degrees" of advancement. It was all based on the sanctity of mathematics, on the grounds that mathematical relations, because they are themselves unchanging and imperishable, present rare glimpses of reality subsisting behind the flux of ordinary perception. Pythagoras is reputed to have been the first person to call himself a "philosopher" and he was, in the western tradition, arguably the original expositor of the notion of Oneness, that ultimately, in some deep metaphysical sense, human beings, Nature, God, etc. all belong to an organic whole where separateness and division is illusory.[31] Similarly, a core element in Platonism is the conviction that reality lies behind appearances and surface distinctions are ultimately shadows of a unified perfection.[32] This ultimate reality (God?) is understood as including, bundled within it, a unity of the True, the Beautiful, and the Good.[33]

Plato repeatedly emphasizes how enlightenment about what he called the Forms, that is, the metaphysically "pure" realities behind—and in some sense generative of—our imperfect sense impressions, could bring one into a participatory immortality with those larger entities that were, in his metaphysics, *literally* more real than everyday reality. (Note that this assertion of "more real than everyday reality" is a familiar psychedelics refrain, especially in DMT trip reports.) In Plato's most esoteric dialogue, the *Timaeus* (among other occultisms, it discusses the lost civilization of Atlantis), he outlines a version of immortality qua SEI Type 3 ego extension:

> But anyone who has devoted himself to learning and has genuinely applied his intelligence—which is to say, anyone who has primarily exercised his intellect—cannot fail to attain immortal, divine wisdom, if the truth should come within his grasp. *He achieves the full measure of immortality that is possible for a human being,* and because he always takes care of the divine part of himself and maintains the orderly beauty of his companion deity, he is bound to be exceptionally blessed. [emphasis added][34]

He further elaborates that the pedagogical project of this kind of immortality is to establish a dynamic isomorphism between the order of one's mind and the order of the cosmos. By doing so, we will find our true self:

> So, since the movements that are naturally akin to our divine part are the thoughts and revolutions of the universe, these are what each of us should be guided by *as we attempt to reverse the corruption of the circuits in our heads*, that happened around the time of our birth, by studying the harmonies and revolutions of the universe. In this way, *we will restore our nature to its original condition by assimilating our intellect to what it is studying* and, with such assimilation, we will achieve our goal: to live now and in the future, the best life that the gods have placed within human reach. [emphasis added][35]

Beyond his educational recommendations, Plato does not elaborate on this experience where we, in his striking image, "reverse the corruption of the circuits in our heads." But one has to wonder, given his explicit veneration of the Eleusinian Mysteries—and this is speculation on my part—whether the experiential qualia associated with "assimilating our intellect to what it is studying," combined with his specific linking of that assimilation to immortality, might hearken back in some way to what was learned at that ceremony, where participants claim to have overcome their fear of death. Could these passages be describing Plato's intellectualized version of those rites?

Whatever the answer to this question, Platonism provides one of the earliest and most influential western historical examples of ego dissolution as a normative ideal. These themes become even more pronounced later with Neo-Platonist thinkers such as Plotinus (ca. 204–270 CE). Centuries after Plato, Plotinus held that "the divine is not expressible" and it was therefore erroneous to say that one "sees" the ego-dissolving vision of Oneness. He explains that "the man who saw was identical with what he saw. Hence, *he did not 'see' it but rather was 'oned' with it*. . . . In that state he had attained unity" [emphasis added]. Plotinus strongly emphasizes the transformative nature of the Oneness experience (being "oned"): "The man who obtains the vision becomes, as it were, another being. He ceases to be himself, retains nothing of himself. *Absorbed in the beyond he is one with it*, like a center coincident with another center" [emphasis added].[36] Needless to say, this is strikingly anticipatory both of the ineffability and ego dissolution claims with which high-dosage trip reports are replete. Edited and modernized and coded with the tag "ego death," Plotinus's testimony would fit comfortably in the Erowid vaults and EDI reports. Shanon explicitly notes the specific affinities between these aspects of Plotinus and ayahuasca visions: "Plotinus and his followers in the neo-Platonic school also present a worldview exhibiting interesting resemblance to that associated with ayahuasca."[37]

As Plato and Plotinus make vivid, ego diminution or dissolution—or whatever terms express the fading of the "normal" boundaries of the self—is clearly not a stand-alone phenomenon. As long as *some* awareness is maintained and matters do not simply lapse into an unconscious self-oblivion (a state of mind of little interest, from the subjective point of view, except perhaps the phases of slipping into and out of it), it is, literally, inextricably linked with some form of connectedness. As per Plotinus, the self "ones" and becomes transmogrified hypertrophically into a unitive communion with some larger and concentrically greater X. (Again, it is interesting to note how it is almost always a *larger* rather than a smaller X.) As noted, in terms of fluctuations in ipseity, the psychedelic momentum seems usually to be more "onward and upward," though there are prominent counter-movements, such as Grof's analysis of a patterned perinatal regression with LSD through birth trauma, and individuals are sometimes confronted with figures having to do with intimate past relationships like deceased loved ones.[38] The progression to "the One" is jagged, not smooth. But my strong impression (from both clinical and crowdsourced data) is that the unitive and connective self-expansions—those happening to seem roughly consistent with signal elements of mystical traditions and mystery religions—are by far the most common significant insights that individuals obtain; they are also widely regarded by those who have undergone them as the major spiritual "payoff" from their psychedelic experience. At the very least, it is incontestable that unity and connection are among the leading self-conception altering experiences to be had with high-dose psychedelics.

This fact naturally leads to questions concerning precisely *what* it is that is being connected to. Back to the SEI once again for some helpful nuance. As per the foregoing discussion, the SEI wisely links Type 3 ego death directly to the categories having to do with states of "unity and interconnectedness."[39] Here there are four "levels," the first two having to do with *specific* connections one might make, for example, to a particular object or animal or another person. In this context, it is interesting to note that therianthropic attachment to animals is a signature component of shamanistic traditions, all the way back to cave and rock art.[40] Perhaps because of this ancient association within the psychedelic realm, Shanon found in his landmark Amazonian studies that therianthropes, broadly considered, are among the most frequent motifs and objects of identification in ayahuasca journeys—especially serpents and serpent-like creatures.[41] These kinds of attachments could also involve, for example, deepened romantic entanglements through erotic means, or other interactions or identifications with larger groups, as in "bonding" with a group of friends or, on a larger scale, feeling fused with a crowd at a music festival.[42] By any measure, these are extremely common psychedelic experiences. Levels 3 and 4, however, gesture toward the more mystical-type situations, where the connections are conceived to be with "external systems" of various types: the environment around one (e.g., the mountain where one is hiking, the clouds and sky) and, ultimately, at the highest level, connections with more generalizable ecological, cosmological and theological systems. These latter are the largest self-expansions. Notably, they are also the most associated with overcoming the fear of death in approximately the Platonist sense, as they represent the immortality strategy of attaching oneself with that which is enduring—or at least much more so than that which ceases with bodily death, "When we have shuffled off this mortal coil."[43] Not just with psychedelics, of course, but great solace may be derived from these large-scale attachments, as they catalyze corresponding alterations in self-understanding and therefore new perspectives on life and death. This kind of communion is a major theme in all western pagan and biblical traditions (and worldwide). Although it may seem like a "cheating" spiritual short-cut, to some, the available evidence suggests that high-dose psychedelics seem very capable of forging such life-changing macro-identifications—and that they have been doing so for thousands of years. Still, the nature of what precisely all these connects are *to* is another matter and is the subject of the next chapter.

Philosophical Pathway #2: Descartes

Withdraw into yourself and look.

—Plotinus, *Enneads*, "Beauty," sec. 9

Psychedelics as First Philosophy

However large or small the self-conception or toward whatever it eventually contracts or expands, an informed decision to take a psychedelic is a decision to engage in self-exploration. Before looking further outward into the larger contexts of connections and settings, an examination of this inward dive into the self is warranted, as this is what generates the reactive catapulting outward into the expansive concentricity of hypertrophic identification. It is like a buildup of spring tension, where the energy is eventually released via a dramatic reversal at a certain point; as in the initial phase of Plato's allegory of the cave, what one realizes about the inside powerfully turns one around and up toward the outside.[44] It may be also that ultimately, as stands to reason, the inward/outward distinction *itself* erodes right along with the self that initiates the process; perhaps it has to. This dynamic is arguably a core element in the human experience writ large. Analogous to the workings of initiation rites throughout human history, explorative knowledge is gained from within and/or without via some personal journey, after which the initiate *ritually returns* to share the new knowledge with the community. Drawing from the founder of analytic psychology, Carl Jung (1875–1961), and his influential concept of "archetypes," the deep collective narratives that continually operate sub rosa to motivate human beings, folklorist Joseph Campbell (1904–1987) describes how a "hero ventures forth from the world of common day into a region of supernatural wonder: fabulous forces are there encountered and a decisive victory is won: the hero comes back from this mysterious adventure with the power to bestow boons on his fellow man."[45] Undergone with a seriousness of purpose and an imperative to communicate about it afterwards (either for therapeutic integration or intersubjective fellowship), psychedelic explorations can certainly also take this shape where the inward journey turns outward. Further muddying any easy inward/outward distinction, McKenna postulates that "I think what's really happening is that a dialogue opens up between the ego and these larger, more integrated parts of the psyche that are normally hidden from view."[46] Sticking with naturalistic default assumptions and refraining (until evidence shows otherwise) from hypostasizing the systems and entities encountered within trip spaces, McKenna's perspective seems warranted. Like flashlights in a sunless cave, psychedelic tools help us to grope around our dark interiors and vast inner spaces for items worth taking back with us—an attitude that is wholly consistent with shamanistic attitudes and practices.[47] What we perceive down there is, in an important sense, and as DMT entities' very existence regularly implies, *waiting there* for us to learn from it.

Assuming the dose is not so high as to be wholly incapacitating, psychedelics, particularly those with hours-long durations (e.g., LSD, ibogaine, ayahuasca, psilocybin, mescaline, in contrast with quicker-acting and usually more physically incapacitating compounds like smoked DMT and 5-MeO-DMT), can be utilized in an open-facing manner that engages with one's external environment. This might mean a communal setting, perhaps a ceremony or a concert or rave or, most common, with a small group of friends going through it together, communicating and sharing it all throughout. If you're Hunter S. Thompson, maybe it is a road trip with your lawyer (not recommended). Or it might be characterized by an open-eyed engagement with nature: in a park, a mountain meadow, on a hike in the woods. If you're Albert Hofmann, maybe a bicycle ride home after work (also not recommended). Or, if you're Aldous Huxley, maybe the little things around you in your immediate environment will open up and reveal multitudes. These settings all invite lively external inputs and one's psychedelic experience will, of course, contour itself along with their influence. Depending on how one is attitudinally disposed, this communal and/or open-facing mode may be the *only* way to go about it.

However, there is another option. One might choose a more deliberately introspective path. Logistically, this would likely involve some relatively controlled setting where sensory inputs are much diminished and/or under greater control: a closed-eyes setting such as a blindfold so one has a blank visual screen (or relatively blank, as there are always entoptic visual stimuli behind the eyelids), a dark room with the blinds drawn or, in the extreme, a sensory deprivation tank. (Psychedelic therapists usually use closed-eyes methods due to this introspective directness, as it lowers the likelihood for patients to be distracted from therapeutic goals.) To be sure, there is no bright-line distinction between external- and internal-facing psychedelics experiences and it would be misleading to suggest there are. But there are trajectories, where some are more externally oriented in the above ways and some are more solo and introspective, and trip settings can be arranged to maximize one or the other. Also, of course, a trip of any length can and often does involve both orientations: one might be laughing and dancing with friends in the moonlight and then go inside and withdraw into oneself for a time. So, these are not neat categorizations, only tendencies across trips, and often serially within them—possibly even cycling in rapid succession. Amidst a communal activity, one might suddenly feel a pang of introspection. It might then blossom into a joyous realization or plunge one into a terrifying dark hole—or anything in between. From a psychological perspective, being alone with oneself can be healing and self-improving or it can be a literal torture, as in solitary confinement, considered to be a "torture method" by the United Nations and restricted by many jurisdictions worldwide.[48] Given this wide range of possibilities, the psychonautical stakes can be high. All the same, introspection is an almost inevitable part of the psychedelic experience. It might be considered the most direct approach to oneself, charging the castle head on as it were, and it is definitely not strategically advisable in all circumstances for all people (consult your local psychedelic guide). All the same, assuming it doesn't descend into pathological narcissism or some such, someone who *never* introspects—psychedelics or not—seems not to be fully human. This may seem harsh but think about it: *never* introspecting means never giving a thought to one's motives or identity, scrutinizing one's conscience, or being self-aware. It might be pathological to do too much of it, but it definitely seems pathological not to do it at all.

This focus on introspection is important because if the ego is to dis-solve and then re-solve itself into some altered identity, it must go through some kind of temporally extended pedagogical process. The insight may be felt as in a flash but, like the gestalt "aha!" moment in learning, that flash is the conscious tip of the iceberg, beneath which lies a process of development. If we take McKenna's thought seriously, that via psychedelics we are able to engage heretofore hidden and "more integrated parts" of our own interiority, those introspective moments are the *felt qualia* of the interconnective process, to use an overused phrase, when we are "doing the work." It is therefore worth pausing to consider the subjective experience of the *process* of hypertrophic identification, that is, how it is first-person experienced, before moving on to the *product*, that is, the describable nature of the newly expanded identity. What one finds is a core insight shared by the world's wisdom traditions: the journey inward, if followed through, springboards one into a journey outward. Or, more properly perhaps, collapses the inward/outward mental binary itself.

But first thing first. Though his reputation has recently fallen on hard times, there is no better guide to adventurous introspection than its most famous philosophical exemplar, René Descartes (1590–1650).

Descartes's *Meditations on First Philosophy* (1641) is probably the most influential book on introspection ever written (with apologies to Gautama Buddha, who did not write down his teachings). More, although it is highly unlikely Descartes did anything like psychedelics—though a contemporary biographer boldly (probably overly boldly) claims "of course Descartes smoked pot"—this singular philosophical work can be read, uncannily enough, as if it were an extended highbrow trip report.[49]

Though it is as canonical as it could be in the philosophy, the *Meditations* subversively seems to exemplify the psychonaut's sensibility of venturesome self-discovery. Philosopher Matthew Segall argues that Descartes's approach to seeking "clear and distinct" ideas through his own lived experience, what I have been designating as first-person qualia, makes the *Meditations* "in this way more like spiritual exercises than logical arguments."[50] Segall then adds the playful suggestion that it is

> natural to analogize not only his own meditative experience, but also the reader's experience of his textual account to the ingestion of a psychedelic catalyst: Descartes's text is an invitation to bracket our assumptions and follow him on a transformative journey beyond the edges of consensus reality. . . . [Descartes did not] have access to LSD-25, psilocybin, 5-MeO-DMT, ayahuasca or mescaline. In Descartes's case, wrapping himself in a warm winter gown and lounging in a comfortable armchair by the fire seems to have done the trick. The set and setting of his epistemological method thus provisioned, Descartes counsels us to let go of our long-held habits of thought so that we may plunge into the depths of the soul to there discover the unshakeable foundation upon which the entire edifice of scientific knowledge might be built.[51]

Given its animating desire for self-knowledge and its method of self-examination, one might think of the *Meditations* along the lines of a psychedelic trip. And why not? Like many, Segall makes clear his opinion that, although Descartes's project is admirable in some ways, it is ultimately a "bad trip" because it "helped lay much of the groundwork for the last several hundred years of modern techno-scientific thinking about external Nature and its relationships, or lack thereof, to a disembodied rational mind."[52] This is the specter of the philosophically dreaded "Cartesian dualism," concerning which nearly all contemporary schools of thought are condemnatory. It is thought to be the *fons et origo* of a host of evils, most notably a subject-object ontological split that has come to characterize western science that has, among other things, disenchanted the world by promoting a non-holistic, mechanized view of it and thereby deeply alienating us from one another and the natural environment, what Karl Marx called a catastrophic "metabolic rift" responsible for today's ecological imbalances.[53] This is certainly a lot to lay at Descartes's feet. Admittedly, though, given his massive interdisciplinary influence during the intervening centuries, as a matter of intellectual history, there may be some truth to it.

Be that as it may, to pursue the psychedelic aspects of the *Meditations*, it is necessary to give the devil its due. For this is literally the thought experiment that launches the whole enterprise: Descartes asks the reader to imagine that a "malicious demon of the utmost power and cunning has employed all his energies to deceive me"—perhaps the ultimate DMT trickster entity—empowered to warp and twist one's sense impressions and ideas such that they can no longer be trusted (VI 32–33).[54] For reference purposes, the pop culture "everything is false" analogous thought experiment would be the movie *The Matrix*, and the higher-brow philosophical version would be the influential simulation argument advanced by philosopher Nick Bostrom, who holds that "we are almost certainly living in a computer simulation."[55] However baleful might be the subsequent ramifications of Cartesian metaphysics, one must admit that this grand conceit of comprehensive sensory deception is philosophically irresistible. In the spirit of the Presocratics and their learned mistrust of the senses, Descartes goes one step farther with the paranoid vision that, not just a few sense impressions here and there, but the *totality* of our perceptions could all be wrong. For how would we ever know? What could we judge them against? Other sense impressions, one might suggest. But these too could be wrong, and so on *ad infinitum*. If we are truly and completely out to sea with only this chaotic storm of dubious perceptions, how can we ever say we truly *know* anything at all? If one is epistemically loosened enough to have really "broken through," then afterwards what perceptions can ever be fully trusted? Hyperbolic doubt descends.

Descartes's confrontation with this problem is still unrivaled. Of particular interest is his conception of how doubt and knowledge are inextricably intertwined, how the latter needs the former in order to become what it is. Ostensible appearance would have it that doubt and knowledge are opposed—to have knowledge is precisely to banish doubt, it would seem—but Descartes shows that true knowledge must be preceded and in a certain way accompanied by doubt ever after. One may in the end gain knowledge, but if and only if one first somehow becomes *hyperbolically* dissatisfied with what one had always taken to be the truth of one's experiences; if epistemic loosening starts the process, Cartesian hyperbolic doubt is its apotheosis. It all begins with that ancient, nagging, and still-mysterious presocratic epistemological hypochondria that pulls one out of the ordinariness of immersion in everyday life and "consensus reality," makes one worry whether what one has been assuming one "knows" is in fact *really* true, where there is perceived to be a novel and urgent "oomph" to the *"really"* qualifying the "true." I wonder anew—or for the first time—if "perhaps what I take for gold and diamonds is nothing but a bit of copper and glass" (VI 3). Frustratingly, this epistemological crisis does not seem to be ameliorated by teaching and learning in the formal sense; even the finest schooling lies helpless to stop this hemorrhage of epistemic confidence. It may even help precipitate and/or exacerbate the situation. As Descartes relates, "For I found myself beset with so many doubts and errors that I came to think I had gained noting from my attempts to become educated but increasing recognition of my ignorance. And yet I was at one of the most famous schools in Europe, where I thought there must be learned men if they existed anywhere on earth" (VI 5). Descartes was of course extremely learned, but it is unclear whether anything about being highly educated either assuages or precipitates hyperbolic doubt. It seems just to descend on him like depression. Probably, it is multi-causal. Formal learning might occasion such doubts when one may learn something that "blows one's mind" or some assumed lifelong verity is challenged. Yet it seems equally clear that hyperbolic doubt may be occasioned by agencies outside formal learning as well: a life-altering stroke of fortune or misfortune, a bizarre coincidence, or simply an undifferentiated feeling of unease. Also, of course, a psychedelic experience of sufficient potency to engender serious doubts concerning prior assumptions about life and the universe. In fact, compared to the alternatives, psychedelics and their neuroplasticity-inducing qualities may be one of the most effective—and risky precisely *because* of its effectiveness—pedagogical means reliably to generate that hyperbolic doubt breakthrough.

Descartes himself is unclear on the provenance of his generative doubting. At times it seems as if the doubt is merely an extension of the same sorts of curiosity arising in the course of everyday life when common sense is proven wrong. Sometimes it seems a mere rearrangement of common sense. It is possible that Descartes would, if pressed for an explanation, avail himself of the same *deus ex machina* that serves as the final epistemological guarantor of the *Meditations*, where hyperbolic doubt is simply falling into sinful error and is ultimately to be overcome via simple assertive faith "that God is not a deceiver" (VII 90). The question of the doubt's origins is mostly passed over in silence, though, eclipsed by Descartes's enthusiasm for what the doubt, once acquired, might achieve when prudently deployed: a gift from *somewhere*, it is instantly instrumentalized in the service of building reliable knowledge. Significantly, from the moment of its being announced in the preceding "Synopsis" of the *Meditations*, the occasion of Cartesian doubt is conceived as a fundamentally *constructive* event: "Although the usefulness of such extensive doubt is not apparent at first sight, its greatest benefit lies in freeing us from all our preconceived opinions, and providing the easiest route by which the mind may be led away from the senses. The eventual result of this doubt is to make it impossible for us to have any further doubts about what we subsequently discover to be true" (VII 12). It may be a temporary demolition of received opinion and the personal convictions we "have begun to store up since childhood," but the point of the enterprise is unequivocally to accomplish something positive, viz., a sound foundation for science.[56] In this light, Descartes wasn't really a skeptic at all, no matter how much we speak of "Cartesian skepticism" and the like. He was simply using it as an epistemological tool, an intuition pump primer. Descartes scholar Gail Fine relates a telling episode in the *Seventh Replies*: when Boudin mistakenly views Descartes as a patient suffering from the disease of skepticism, Descartes replies that he is "the doctor with the first sure cure."[57] What did this "cure" involve?

Descartes provides another memorable image in the *Seventh Replies*, where the doubting process is likened to someone attempting to select unblemished produce:

> Suppose he had a basket of full of apples and, being worried that some of the apples were rotten, wanted to take out the rotten ones to prevent the rot spreading. How would he proceed? Would he not begin by tipping the whole lot out of the basket? And would not the next step be to cast his eye over each apple in turn, and pick up and put back in the basket

only those he knew to be sound, leaving the others? (VI 481)

In the service of separating false from true beliefs, it is best for those concerned with getting at the truth "to reject all their beliefs together in one go, as if they were uncertain and false. They can then go over each belief in turn and re-adopt only those which they recognize as true and indubitable" (VI 481). This then is the reason for rejecting all of one's beliefs via hyperbolic doubt: not a mere gesture of refusal where one clears out one's mind in order to remain empty and free from outside influences, like some romantic visions of "authenticity" would have us believe, but rather a cognitive clearing out that is preparatory to a potentially unlimited cognitive putting back (the harrowing effect of epistemic loosening related in the previous chapter). As Descartes writes in his earliest published work, "there is no need to impose any restrictions on our mental powers; for the knowledge of one truth does not, like skill in one art, hinder us from discovering another; on the contrary it helps us" (X 360). In the sense used above, I therefore provisionally "hold back my assent" in order that I should be able truly to provide it; the propositions I accept, the small and large assumptions under which I operate, are thereby given the volitional stamp that "criticality" requires. "Regarding the opinions to which I had hitherto given credence, I thought that I could not to better than undertake to get rid of them, all at one go, in order to replace them afterwards with better ones, or with the same ones once I had squared them with the standards of reason" (VI 13–14).

Examining, rejecting, revising, or readopting in part or whole are the kinds of mental house-framing that need to be done. But it is the doubting that clears and grades the lot, even before the building's foundations can be erected.[58] Such is the (temporarily) destructive Cartesian skepticism that individuals exercise not merely vis-à-vis governmental and other authoritative claims but also, and perhaps most importantly, with regard to their *own* operant truth claims, the "paths" they have determined for themselves to follow (VI 10).

Notable Features of Cartesian Psychedelics

> To philosophize, therefore, is to invert the habitual direction of the work of thought.
>
> —Henri Bergson, *An Introduction to Metaphysics*, 52

The apotheosis of this skepticism, the famous hyperbolic doubt of the *Meditations*, has at least three features that present significant parallels with important aspects of psychedelic experience.

First is its *episodic* nature. Psychedelic experiences are obviously bounded temporally, with a general range of thirty minutes to eighteen hours. (Note: the length of action is significant for the knowledge base of these substances. The four- to six-hour window of psilocybin fits much better with clinical trials and business hours at a researcher's office than the much longer-acting LSD or ibogaine, with the result that recent clinical studies are much more likely to involve psilocybin.) There are rare outliers to the normal duration expectations, though, including a very small percentage of unfortunates who appear to suffer from "hallucinogen persisting perception disorder" (HPPD) where their trip simply does not end, or not for an unusually long time. Little is known about HPPD, but clinical research is ongoing. It seems mostly to consist of residual perceptual distortions: "flashbacks" (Type 1) or more persistent disturbances (Type 2).[59] And, interestingly, very few of those experiencing it considered it distressing—so the jury is still out concerning what this phenomenon actually is.[60] Apart from the possibility of chronic HPPD, then, psychedelic trips can be said to be reliably episodic in nature. Just like Cartesian doubt, they are not supposed to be persistent states of mind; the entropy settles and one comes back from them.

Descartes often emphasizes this aspect of the activity and, just as tellingly, does *not* emphasize it in others. The polymath's intellectual corpus itself testifies to this; the philosophical part of his writings is but a small fraction of the whole. As Descartes scholar Janet Broughton observes, "Descartes gave many more pages, and much more time, to describing methods of inquiry that did *not* begin with radical skeptical doubt, than to describing one that did."[61] It is clearly not the only or even the most likely productive method of inquiry that situations might dictate one should use; there is something special and singular about hyperbolic doubt over and against what one does in the course of ordinary investigations or in the course of more ordinary choices confronted in life. One does not engage in either hyperbolic doubt or psychonautical investigation in order to ascertain what to have for dinner tomorrow. This is apparent from the dramatic descriptive context with which the *Meditations* opens: "I realized that it was necessary, *once in the course of my life*, to demolish everything completely" [emphasis added] (VII 17). As if to dispel any ambiguity on this point, in his later *Principles of Philosophy* (1644), Descartes proffers as his first "principle of human knowledge" that the "*seeker of truth must, once in the course of his life, doubt everything as far as possible*" [emphasis in the original] (VIIIA 5). Though imperative for a "seeker of truth," engaging in hyperbolic doubt "once in the course of life" would thus seem to place the hyperbolic doubting operation alongside other things one does but once or rarely: birth, death, a bar or bat mitzvah, graduating high school, undertaking the Hajj pilgrimage to Mecca, a baptism, having a religious conversion, losing one's virginity, etc. In short, it is constructed by Descartes to be an *event*, something bounded temporally with a beginning and an end, as opposed to an occurrent situation, some state of being or ongoing quality characterizing one's existence, character, or both. Though it is likely to have consequences once it is initiated, Cartesian-style doubting is something one might be found doing at Time A, but then decidedly *not* doing at Times B, C, or D. It *begins* and *ends*. Insofar as a psychedelic trip is undertaken for the purpose of understanding, the Cartesian approach raises interesting questions. Along the lines of the Alan Watts aphorism about hanging up the phone once you get the message, and also consistent with its ceremonial envelopment in traditional cultures (more on this in the next chapter), because of their radically destabilizing potential, perhaps more care should be taken by viewing psychedelic experiences more as *episodic* occasions, where excessive returns, just because an individual may "feel like it," should be viewed warily. Though there are exceptions, particularly with ayahuasca, most indigenous and pre-modern psychedelic usage implies the importance of this episodicity, emphasized by various means such as calendrical specificity (e.g., something for holidays or prescribed dates only) or prior purification requirements such as fasting and/or purging. Such customs de facto raise the bar of entry, so to speak, as well as regulate frequency and thereby, it reasonable to presume, help to discourage overdoing it.

This leads to a *second* and related aspect that touches on one of the most pressing issues with psychedelics: what it really means to "integrate" these experiences post-trip. There are many conscientious trip sitters and knowledgeable guides with a great deal of expertise in this area in the context of therapy.[62] At back of these efforts, though, is a persisting philosophical question about how and to what extent an insight gained in such an odd and relatively anomalous context can be "brought back" and inform the actual living of one's life. What does this mean exactly? In the context of the *Meditations*, this question is pursued in the form of wondering about the practical normative force of the skeptical episode of hyperbolic doubt once it has passed. What's it like the next morning?

This connection needs some explaining. Largely out of common sense, I follow most commentators in viewing Cartesian doubt as decidedly non-Pyrrhonian. The adjective "Pyrrhonian" refers to the ancient branch of skepticism named after Pyrrho of Ellis (c. 360–270 BCE) and associated with his pupil Timon (c. 320–230 BCE) and, much later and most importantly, Sextus Empiricus (c. 160–210 CE) and his *Outlines of Pyrrhonism*, the most influential Pyrrhonian Skeptical treatise.[63] (Not to be confused with Pyrrhus, the Hellenistic King of Epius [c. 319–272 BCE], who won battles over the Romans but at a disastrous cost, originating the saying "Pyrrhic victory.") The eponymous Pyrrho's name has become an adjective owing to how he is reputed to have actually *lived* his skeptical convictions, which amounted essentially to attempting to live a life precisely *without* convictions. There are many tales of the life of Pyrrho, which may or may not be true. But that the stories were told reveals something of the Pyrrhonian skeptic's mindset. For example, the great philosophical gossip Diogenes Laertius writes that when Pyrrho's fellow skeptic "Anaxarchus fell into a slough, Pyrrho passed him by without helping him; and while others blamed him, Anaxarchus himself praised his indifference and his freedom from emotion."[64] Though "calm and gentle" as a man liberated from convention and other dogmas, Pyrrho could also be found engaged in truly shocking activities (for a free Greek male of his time) such as house cleaning, grocery shopping, and pig washing.[65] As is the case with other ancient philosophical schools such Stoicism, the goal of the Pyrrhonian Skeptic is *ataraxia* (Gk. "tranquility," "lack of disturbance"), and the "procedures" advanced by Pyrrhonians such as Sextus consist largely of philosophical "modes" or arguments of a point-counterpoint form designed to deliver the Pyrrhonian aspirant to the doxastic state of *ataraxia* via liberation from too strongly held beliefs.[66]

For the present purpose of contrasting Pyrrhonian and Cartesian skepticism, this idea of "life-guiding" is the key point, that is, the expectation that one will live one's life consistent with one's philosophical beliefs. The Pyrrhonian skeptics really meant it. They wanted to purge themselves of life-guiding beliefs in order to achieve *ataraxia* (bad news for life coaches: they produce too much stress). It has frequently been questioned, as David Hume (1711–1776) has, whether it is possible really to live such a life and to dismiss the possibility out of hand.[67] Hume has it that nature is always too strong for principle. And though a Pyrrhonian may throw himself or others into a momentary amazement and confusion by his profound reasonings; the first and most trivial event in life will put to flight all his doubts and scruples, and leave him the same, in every point of action and speculation, with philosophers of every other sect, or with those who never concerned themselves in any philosophical researches. When he awakes from his dream, he will be the first to join in the laugh against himself, and to confess, that all his objections were mere amusement, and can have no other tendency than to show the whimsical condition of mankind, who must act and reason and believe.[68]

Hume and others have long thought it impossible to *live* Pyrrhonian Skepticism, as per the above quotation, and "the Skeptic" in the history of philosophy therefore largely exists as a literary device, a polemical foil. There is, for all that, little scholarly dispute—at least following the eventful rediscovery of the work of Sextus made possible by its Latin translation in 1562—that skepticism exercised a real attraction for many of Descartes's contemporaries and near-predecessors, even among those with pious intent (who often saw greater threats from rationalist theologies) including, surprisingly, the faith-besotted Florentine fanatic Savonarola, of "bonfire of the vanities" fame.[69] As did the Church in confronting this Sextus-induced "*crise pyrrhonienne*" of the early seventeenth century, Descartes himself saw skepticism as something more than just an imaginary philosophical position. In the *Seventh Replies* he writes, "Neither must we think of that sect of skeptics as long extinct. It flourishes today as much as ever, and nearly all who think that they have some ability beyond that rest of mankind, finding nothing satisfies them in the common Philosophy, and seeing no other truth, take refuge in Scepticism" (VII 548–549). This, combined with the availability of biographical information about the ancient Pyrrhonians themselves, underscores how vivid this school of thought must have been to those of Descartes's era. For despite its initial implausibility as a realistic worldview, as classicist Miles Burnyeat explains, "Pyrrhonism is the only serious attempt in western thought to carry skepticism to its further limits and to live by the result."[70] So, given the contemporaneous fad for it, along with its being rooted in ancient sources, it seems that Descartes actually considered it a live option and therefore a real threat; he thought people could actually choose to try to live their lives according to it.

That he was capable of taking something as outlandish as Pyrrhonism so seriously underscores how his own hyperbolic doubt is most definitely *not* to be taken on similar terms (and possibly also his concern not to be seen as a heretic). Descartes *does* anticipate it to be an important event in one's life. He even acknowledges how it gave him "such great satisfaction that I thought one could not have any sweeter or purer enjoyment in this life" (VII 27). A very good trip indeed. However, he is explicit that doubting is not to be thought of as a guide for how to live one's life. Those who see skepticism in this way should be corrected. Descartes distances himself from his contemporary layabout skeptics who, in stark contrast to the more ridiculous but also more authentic ancient types, "doubt only for the sake of doubting," "reached no certain conclusions from their doubts," and did not understand "how to make use of such doubts" (VI 29; II 38, 39). Even more pointedly, he considers it a cardinal normative principle, number three, in fact, of his *Principles of Philosophy*, that the "*doubt should not meanwhile be applied to ordinary life. This doubt, while it continues, should be kept in check and employed solely in connection with the contemplation of truth. As far as ordinary life is concerned, the chance for action would frequently pass us by if we waited until we could free ourselves from our doubts*" (VIIIA 5). Amidst the doubting process of the very First Meditation, he avers that "the task now in hand does not involve action but merely the acquisition of knowledge" (VII 22). For Descartes, there may be a life of faith, a life or many other "lives." But, *pace* Pyrrho of Elis himself, there should be no "life of doubting" as such.

Despite his protests against skepticism, Descartes was still playing with fire in his milieu, and his method of doubt was considered by some to be too much of a close call. Like Milton's notoriously alluring description of Satan in *Paradise Lost* or the contemporary stock character of the FBI profiler who must perilously try to "think like the killer" in order to catch him, Descartes's deep appreciation for the gravity of the skeptical challenge necessitates his imagining it so vividly that the doubting villain ends up inadvertently stealing the show. Descartes's and his contemporaries' clear awareness of this danger helps make still more understandable his concern to distinguish his own skepticism from the Pyrrhonian life-guiding type; they were to be in effect "insulated" from ordinary life.[71] As Broughton rightly puts it, "people are to use it only when they want to discover and establish various fundamental truths. Good cognitive life goes on outside the practice of methodic doubt."[72] The question then becomes whether or not the insulation can be maintained; the corrosive acid of critique needs some barrier to stop its spread.

So can Descartes's meditator really remain, to use Hume's descriptor, non-"actional" and thus non-Pyrrhonian?[73] There is a compelling line of interpretation that in effect says "no," primarily by emphasizing the literary form and long tradition of "meditations" as spiritual exercises aimed at self-improvement. Philosopher Pierre Hadot suggests that "it was no accident that Descartes entitled one of his works *Meditations*. They are indeed meditations—*meditatio* in the sense of exercise—according to the spirit of the Christian philosophy of St. Augustine and Descartes recommends that they be practiced over a certain period of time."[74] And further: "Each *Meditation* is a spiritual exercise—that is, work by oneself and upon oneself which must be finished before one can move to the next stage. . . . For although Descartes speaks in the first person (evoking the fire before which he is sitting, the robe he is wearing, and the paper in front of him), and although he escribes the feelings he is experiencing, what he really wishes is that his reader should traverse the stages of the inner evolution he describes."[75]

This seems reasonable to me. As a prudent principle of interpretation, when dealing with an author of Descartes's genius, one should assume that both the content and the form of the text in question are deliberate. Can this experiential aspect of the *Meditations* then square with the anti-Pyrrhonian aspiration to keep the radical doubt insulated? My answer is that it can, if we wed it with the account of the episodic, event-like nature of the doubt rendered above. In short, it is a lived experience, yes, but it also must be conceived as a *special occasion*. It does not guide life in the sense that one constantly has it in mind, striving to live up to it qua perfectionist ideal, but it is to be practiced only episodically every once in a while, perhaps a *long* while.

Needless to say, this *special occasion conception* (i.e., episodic but also integrated into the rhythm of a person's life) dovetails with much informed opinion about psychedelics' optimal frequency of use: most recommend essentially once in a good long while (putting the evolving practice of microdosing aside). Of course, these things vary from person to person and depend on a host of individualized factors. One individual might constitutionally be able to withstand rather regular use, while for another once in a lifetime is all that is needed or desired. Clinical studies generally recommend an interval of at least three to four weeks for psilocybin.[76] But it depends on the compound itself and the social context. Members of indigenous ayahuasca churches report taking ayahuasca over long periods and very regularly without discernible harm.[77] An adventurous philosophy professor (retired), Christopher Bache, in his well-received book *LSD and the Mind of the Universe: Diamonds From Heaven* (2019), documents having taken high doses of LSD seventy-three times over a period of twenty years.[78] This is an area of uncertainty and, because of the number of variables involved, it may be inherently so. While psychedelics are not thought to be *physically* harmful or *physically* addicting, and with all due respect for the frequent flyers and committed psychonauts, most everyone would agree it is possible for someone to be tripping too often and it could be a sign that there are underlying problems. This is less than anecdotal, but I have had on two separate occasions earnest college-aged kids tell me they have tripped nearly a hundred times. This raised immediate red flags of concern—and I would maintain that any sensible adult should share that alarm. A commonsense "rule of thumb" from psychedelics researcher James Fadiman, in his influential *The Psychedelic Explorer's Guide: Safe, Therapeutic, and Sacred Journeys* (2011), is "the more profound the experience, the longer you should wait before doing it again."[79] He also notes that the Guild of [Psychedelic] Guides recommends at least a six-month interval because "it takes at least that long for the learning and insights to be integrated and absorbed into your life."[80]

While more research is certainly needed in this area of psychedelics, lessons can be drawn from this investigation into Descartes. Fadiman's rule of thumb recommendation belies a sensibility wholly analogous with the Cartesian approach to hyperbolic doubt: *it can be highly salutary, and for some even necessary, but it is best treated episodically as a special occasion, with plenty of care taken afterwards during the intervals for how the experience is integrated into one's overall life*. Like hyperbolic doubt, it is extremely strong medicine and so carries promise but also danger. Additionally, also like Cartesian doubt in its original historical setting, and as the Nixon period and lingering prohibitionist attitudes attest, it can be demonstrably threatening to regnant ideological orthodoxies and societal authorities. Technically speaking, like hallucinogens in most places today, practicing Cartesian doubt out loud was also highly illegal in most jurisdictions in seventeenth-century Europe, this being the age of reformation and counter-reformation, interminable religious wars, and widespread witch hysteria. Though its stigma is decreasing and its decriminalization and legalization are currently on the rise, again in parallel with the radical questioning of hyperbolic doubt, history shows that tolerance for such challenging eccentricities waxes and wanes. Given the potency of both the drugs and the doubts, future backlashes against them are always possible—and maybe inevitable.

This leads to a *third* aspect of the Cartesian project that is instructive for thinking about psychedelics: though ostensibly negative as a comprehensive rejection, it is ultimately oriented toward *construction*. As I have been stressing, when Descartes slumped into his armchair—or climbed into his cold stove, as he elsewhere suggests—though potent and worrisome, he appears to have meant his method of doubt to be something like a strategic strike: quickly infiltrate, execute the mission, and then exfiltrate rapidly.[81] The reader's experience—certainly the seventeenth-century reader's—is one of sudden dramatic suspense followed by an equally sudden deliverance from "the inexorable darkness of the problems I have raised" (VII 23). In important respects, the initial energies released via this cathartic situation are reflective of Descartes's more general purpose of *utilizing* doubt to fuel his and others' scientific inquiries more efficiently; this is a restive sort of doubt that leads not to Pyrrhonist indifference to reality but instead to discovering, creating, building, and so on. It's like an epistemological itch that one scratches and then, relieved, goes about one's business. The Cartesian conception is that, like the ancient Stoics, that business is conducted through inquiry into the nature of things.[82] After all, the "eventual result of this doubt is to make it impossible for us to have any further doubts about what we subsequently discover to be true" (VII 12). Ironically, given his vilification at the hands of pragmatist philosophers for the last hundred years, Descartes in this respect reveals himself to be a kind of pragmatist *avant la lettre*. It's all about what you can *do* with the doubt, and it is Descartes's special merit to recognize that sunny can-do-optimism and confidence may lead less well to meaningful inquiry than the disorienting fright of that apparently "inextricable darkness." I'm scared, therefore I think.

Though hyperbolic doubt is not designed as a guide to our lives, our *reaction* to the doubt may indeed supply one; life is to be lived on the *rebound* from the moment of doubt. So what is truly interesting in the Cartesian scheme is the meditator's *response* to the undergone doubt. The constructive stance provoked by methodical doubt leads, perhaps counterintuitively, to an appreciation of the ineluctably individuating and otherwise personal nature of the enterprise. A caveat must preface this claim, however. Despite the meditator's intimate voice, the *Meditations* is not simply autobiographical. It is clear from his other writings, including his correspondence, that Descartes did not himself undergo radical doubt in the same manner as is represented in the text.[83] (This is the main reason why it is prudent when discussing the *Meditations* to refer to "the meditator" rather than unproblematically to "Descartes.") But that does not mean authorial intimacy is lost. On the contrary. Released from the strictures of autobiography, Descartes constructs a persona closer to that of an "everyman," perhaps the person of "common sense," akin to how jurisprudence often has recourse to a construct of a "reasonable and prudent" person. More precisely, it is bound to be someone who has *not* yet undergone hyperbolic doubt; Descartes of course, as the author of the book, is by definition no longer himself such a person. Though the text is written in the first-person singular, strongly implied by the trappings of the *meditatio* context is a didactic second person "you, dear reader" who ought to be doing the prescribed workbook. One is therefore reading more than a collection of epistemological arguments; that would have been a very different book. One has in hand a playbook to follow, that one *has to follow* in order to understand three-dimensionally the plays that are sketched two-dimensionally in the writing. The point is to *do* the meditation for oneself; the *Meditations* is an instruction manual—if, that is, one desires to overcome unclear thinking. It actually is akin to a high-level trip report in this respect.

A fascinating update in the twentieth century is provided in Edmund Husserl's inauguration of the phenomenology school of philosophy in his aptly titled *Cartesian Meditations*. In doing so, he advocates an update of hyperbolic doubt as the starting point: "And so we make a new beginning, each for himself and, in himself, with the decision of philosophers who begin radically: that at first we shall put out of action all the convictions we have been accepting up to now, including all our sciences."[84] Husserl's bold programmatic statement well captures something of the universality of the Cartesian doubting operation, the sense that not only *can* we—you and I—engage in it, but in some unspecified yet compelling way we *should* do it, we should think for ourselves and "make a new beginning." This is a re-appreciation of the voice of the Descartes-inspired Enlightenment itself and the later Kantian motto *Sapere aude!* (Lat. "dare to be wise"), containing an imperative for any inquisitive person to shuck off prior assumptions and make a go of it *herself*: "Accordingly the *Cartesian Meditations* are not intended to be a merely private concern of the philosopher Descartes, to say nothing of their being merely an impressive literary form in which to present the foundations of his philosophy. Rather, they draw the prototype for any beginning philosopher's necessary meditations, the meditations out of which alone a philosophy can grow originally."[85] One should give due honor to the wisdom of the past, but this is not a substitute of thinking things through by one's *own* lights. Husserl dramatizes this by imaging Descartes replying to a tradition-minded critic of his newfangled—and threatening—radical doubt: "Descartes's answer might well be: I, the solitary individual philosopher, owe much to others; but what they accept is true, what they offer me as allegedly established by their insight is for me at first only something they claim. If I am to accept it, I just justify it by a perfect insight on my own part. Therein consists my autonomy—mine and that of every genuine scientist."[86] Via this reappropriation of Descartes, Husserl reinscribes the necessity of the first-person *experiential* component to philosophy, one that cannot be replaced by even the most complete account of the physical sciences. Anticipating the hard problem of consciousness that so bedevils today's philosophers, Husserl bases his phenomenological initiative on the insight that a complete account of the world must not ignore its unavoidably first-person aspects, the *Umwelt*-bounded qualia that a person *undergoes* rather than merely charts at a distance. Regarding psychedelics, this functions as a potent reminder that we may one day possess a complete neural mapping of psychedelics' action on the brain: the chemical compounds, the brain receptors, the neural networks and pathways, the interactions among networks, etc.[87] And undoubtedly this information will be hugely interesting and helpful. But there is still going to be something that it *feels* like to be on psilocybin or DMT. It may be wholly identified and mapped by a physicalist account, but it cannot be *reduced* to it. Again, the map is not the territory. Nor can it ever be, for the perfect map is no longer a map; if it were a perfect 1:1 correspondence with the territory, it would no longer be a map, but the territory itself.

Husserl's account illustrates three germane points concerning Cartesian doubt:

(1) It has a deliberately constructive nature, which for Husserl (following Descartes) does not mean mere destruction and "therefore does not leave us confronting nothing."[88] In the Cartesian manner, doubting

what it is possible to doubt, what Husserl calls the "phenomenological *epoché*," or simply "bracketing," rather "lays open (to me, the meditating philosopher) *an infinite realm of being of a new kind*" [emphasis in the original].[89] Sound inquiry begins when, during an appropriately structured episode or session or, shall we say, trip, as much as possible assent is removed from the pack of assumptions embodied in some object of inquiry—including when that object consists of oneself and one's *own* set of experiences, there being no license "to restrict the method to any particular subject matter" (VI 21).

(2) As outlined above, it is ineluctably personal in the existential sense that no one can experience it for me, however much the surrounding natural, cultural, and interpersonal environments may enable it. It is an event *I* must undergo, precisely in the psychological sense that I feel a *gestalt* "aha!" on figuring something out. Learning is one of those experiences that you have to go through for yourself and that nobody else can do for you, just as you have to die your own death (*pace* certain classical myths, no substitutes are allowed) and, yes, trip your own trip. No one can have those experiences on behalf of someone else. There is evocative writing and magnificent artworks and digital replicas, but even the best of these taken together still do not equal the holism of actually doing it oneself. All the mechanisms of the world may lead us horses to water but we still have to drink.

(3) To a surprising extent, the above points (1) and (2) are linked. Following Husserl's Cartesian reduction where we bracket assumptions as much as possible, a certain clarity arises. Just like for Descartes in his own *Meditations*, since all but one tag-end of the world is dubitable for me, namely, that doubting is being experienced, the perceptual world shrinks to a very manageable circumference: that same experience of doubting. (Try and doubt it without experiencing doubting!) "You cannot deny that you have such doubts; rather it is . . . true that you who are doubting exist; this is so true that you can no longer have any doubts about it" (X 51–55). There is no greater epistemological austerity. Here, stripped down to nothing but my own raw experience of doubting is where the meditator finds salvation and can then be built back up. This is of course the famous *cogito ergo sum* (I think therefore I am) that is the punch line of this part of the *Meditations*. It is a truly wonderful and underappreciated idea: even if I *am* comprehensively deceived, there is still something—*me*—that is experiencing that very deception; questions of accuracy aside, that *some* flow of experience is occurring for me

cannot be doubted. The Cartesian meditator ultimately finds salvation in scientific investigations whose objects' existence is metaphysically inexplicable but God-guaranteed and based on faith. The Husserlian meditator finds a secular salvation in the ensuing disciplined study of perception (phenomenology), where the indubitability of the *appearance* of my appearance provides a confident epistemological departure point. Both philosophers thus employ their introspective insights in the pursuit of their programmatic goal "to direct the study of the mind with a view to forming true and sound judgments about whatever comes before it" (X 360).

Questions and Cautions

> One way we respond to death or disappointment or the break-up of a significant relation, to ending or separation or betrayal, is with furious identification.
>
> —Jonathan Lear, *Imagining the End*, 62

With regard to higher-dose psychedelics, there are three major Cartesian takeaways:

(1) As noted, though commonly filed under "rationalism," if followed through, Cartesian inwardness is meant to be experienced as a powerful springboard toward outwardness, in a sense compatible with what I have been calling hypertrophic identification. Though introspection and hypertrophic identification seem ostensibly to be opposite movements, when conceived along Cartesian lines, they ultimately form a pedagogical whole that is ironically—given the rationalist label—wholly consistent with a common element in world mystical traditions, where spiritual self-practice (e.g., various forms of meditation and contemplation) experientially dissolves inside/outside boundaries. As in Plotinus, one looks inward and, finding the self in isolation to be fleeting and unreal, rebounds toward union in the direction of the One, or some suitable external alternative; there is nowhere else to go. In a sense the self is revealed as empty, a "nothing," or, more poetically as in the Christian tradition, a waiting vessel that needs to be filled by God. Here there is admittedly a soul underneath, but that soul is conceived as insubstantial in the sense that it cannot stand alone and is therefore radically dependent

on God's grace; salvation is not DIY. This is the point of the "jars of clay" imagery persisting throughout both Old and New Testaments (e.g., Isaiah 64:8, Jeremiah 18:6, 2 Corinthians 4:7, Romans 9:21). Similarly, many who have undergone high-dosage psychedelics attest to having experienced this emptiness-then-fullness dynamic where the feeling is that one is pulled down deeply inside oneself into a new interiority, but by that very process simultaneously ushered into an outside realm of larger images, patterns, systems, etc. that can be beautiful and/or terrifying (and, as highlighted previously, are commonly felt as vertiginous and inarticulable). The point here is that being taken *inside* oneself with sufficient force has the rebound effect of then taking one *outside* of oneself—often with a breakthrough vengeance. When made sufficiently aware of our emptiness, we jars of clay want very badly to be filled. As will be addressed below, this phenomenon can be glorious in a way that is comparable to religious ecstasy, but it is also carries contextual dangers.

(2) Like the Cartesian and Husserlian varieties of radical doubt, the *lived* component of high-dose psychedelics is multidimensional (e.g., perception, mood, etc.) and irreplaceable in the sense that it cannot be fully replicated or outsourced to a third party. One can understand a lot about it from the outside but, like learning itself, with both hyperbolic doubt and psychedelics, ultimately one is going to have to go through it for *oneself* in order to understand it. It is fundamentally an experiential and first-person phenomenon.

(3) While there is obviously a high level of entropic intensity to the trip episode during its pendency, as Descartes emphasizes, the point is not to become stuck in it forever but to rebound out of it relatively quickly with some form of constructive agenda. (For Descartes this agenda was associated with scientific inquiry, the *Meditations*' main function being to ground science in something certain.) In the clinical context of psychedelics, this usually means "setting an intention" beforehand regarding some ailment or problem and afterwards working with the therapist to integrate the experience into one's default mindset so that something salutary and durable is achieved. Outside the therapeutic context, the rebound and *post hoc* constructive phase can mean many other things and take many different forms (as discussed in the next chapter); it is pluripotent.

In relation to this third point, it is important to acknowledge a certain pragmatist bias in the Descartes-Husserl and, I would add, therapeutic stances. My own analysis is guilty of a degree of this as well, as it embraces the spirit of Cartesian constructivism in the form of suggesting the desirability of an educative rebound. Yet these pragmatic stances, if taken too far, may miss something significant by leaving little room for a *purely* aesthetic appreciation of the experience. As was mentioned, for Descartes it is to be akin to a surgical strike: do what you came to do and get out quickly. A serious question thus arises as to whether the Cartesian model pays insufficient attention to the experience's *inherent* qualities. Would it be so destructive to linger with that radical doubt a little longer, with perhaps a bit less of his disposition to flee it so quickly and with such alacrity start building things in the good old solid "real" world?

An analogous question: With psychedelics, particularly in the burgeoning therapeutic context (but in others too), might we be too quick to instrumentalize the experience, too intent to find something "useful" from it? It sounds a little heretical even to suggest this, but is it possible that psychedelics won't *necessarily* cure you of anything or cause more creativity or make you the life of the party? Maybe they are simply *also* valuable as human experiences in and of themselves, akin to other intense experiences we *sometimes* seek for the sheer qualia of them, like lovemaking, prayer, athletics, art, and learning. There may be plenty of ancillary benefits to such activities—prayer might lower blood pressure, learning might land a job, sex can lead to children, etc.—but one can also acknowledge the paradox that engaging in these things deliberately for the *sole* purpose of those ancillary benefits likely misses the mark. It is not conducive to romance to inform your beloved that your amorousness is not out of love and desire but in order to fulfill a requirement of your wellness regimen. In his massively influential account of the good life for a human being (*eudaimonia*), Aristotle famously typologizes goods according to whether they are 1) good *only* instrumentally, 2) good instrumentally *and* for their own sake, or 3) good *only* for their own sake.[90] Descartes seems eager to place his methodical doubting in Category 1, but this may be due to his wariness of religious critics who would be unenthused by a making too much of a celebration out of attempting to doubt everything. *We* on the other hand are certainly free to value it in Category 2, under whatever modernized label like "critical thinking" or "creativity." Likewise, I think, with psychedelics. If one acknowledges *both* the promise of the emergent scientific research and *at the same time* the legions of individuals who have simply enjoyed themselves one sunny afternoon, psychedelics are best placed into Category 2: (often) beneficial and also (often) valuable on their own terms.

Composer Aaron Copland, in his gem of a book *What to Listen for in Music* (1937), raises this possibility regarding classical music. He argues that, even though "most listeners are not sufficiently conscious" of it, there is a "sheerly musical plane" upon which music can be appreciated not just for "expressive" reasons, for example that it makes one feel happy or sad—or for any other instrumental reason.[91] It can be appreciated for itself alone, too; one can have *purely musical* emotions and experiences, and that is that and that is okay. Copland is very conscious that there are different ways to listen to music and that we can derive various benefits from doing so, but the "sheerly musical plane" should not be lost in the shuffle of the other "planes" on which it is usually appreciated. "Besides the pleasurable sound of music and the expressive feeling it gives off, music does exist in terms of the notes themselves and their manipulation."[92] Copland does not suggest that the sheerly musical plane is the *best* way to listen to music, only that it should be recognized as among them. In fact, he chides musicians for sometimes giving it *too* much weight. Analogously, one cannot help but think of the therapist who, understandably (out of a desire to help patients), gets wholly wrapped up in questions of clinical efficacy or the psychonaut who is perhaps too well used to "talking shop" with other psychonauts and gets lost in the arcana of her many trips and their aesthetic detail. From Copland's complexified perspective, there is room for all of these planes, but they should not become overly imbalanced. In the current third wave of psychedelia, the money and academic prestige attached to the medical-therapeutic paradigm tends to dominate discussion and may obscure the fact that there is also a "purely psychedelic plane," where there exists *inherent* value apart from healing potential. This is a somewhat radical perspective because it is less immediately pragmatic; modern people are oriented toward an instrumentalist conception of value, always wanting a payoff. It also might be still explicable as a residual aversion to second-wave attempts at non-instrumental conceptions as epitomized in Leary's now distrusted slogan "turn on, tune in, drop out." But maybe Leary didn't have it *all* wrong. Maybe it can be constructive to be un-constructive at times; *pace* Cartesian and modern pragmatic attitudes, there may be wisdom in "irresponsibly" just wanting to have fun with it sometimes. Shanon describes this very phenomenon in his participant-observer studies of indigenous ayahuasca consumption where, as "one progresses along the ayahuasca path, one acquires mastery in an involvement that may be a genuine source of pleasure and beauty in its own right."[93]

However, at the same time, a strong sense of ethical responsibility needs to be reinscribed pretty forcefully if the third wave is to continue to build. For its part, the research ethos emanating from Johns Hopkins and other research centers has by all appearances been admirably diligent in adherence to scholarly norms and protocols. This academic respectability is one of the leading characteristics of the third wave and it has premised psychedelics' increasing mainstream acceptance. There are further agents of legitimation as well, particularly social media, popular journalism, and the entrepreneurial capital flowing to psychedelic startups. But these are mostly downstream of the academic research: online influencers and journalists are for the most part reporting on the academic discoveries while the entrepreneurs in the space are monetizing them. As discussed elsewhere in this book, there is also an indirect force for legitimation arising from a different direction, especially in the US, relatively independently of these other trends, involving First Amendment law. There is now a discernible trend in constitutional law favoring religious freedom claims from indigenous groups and their entheogenic use of peyote and ayahuasca, though these settlements also regularly intersect with academic research, as when empirical "safety" questions arise.

However, this now multi-dimensional progress could be impaired due to insufficient attention to ethical dimensions of the *connective* and *hypertrophic* aspects of psychedelics in the senses discussed earlier in this chapter. In fact, an under-the-radar "hard problem" of psychedelics, I would suggest, is assessing in more detail what precisely can occur in high-dose situations resulting in ego dissolution and its aftermath. This is because ego dissolution and the resultant feelings of connectivity are not always limited to the serene, anodyne, and frankly "nice" spiritual sentiments that they are usually portrayed as being. At the neurological level, the dendritic connections are growing, but so too is connective activity at the experiential level. By all accounts, this results in an augmented neural plasticity, which in turn translates into a psychological plasticity where, to paraphrase Marx and Engel's famous words, matters that seemed previously solid are capable of melting into air.[94] Unless someone in such a condition has not just a personal "support network" of family and friends but a strong ideational support structure—that is, some existing worldview or larger framework of meaning, some meta-narrative within which to make sense of the belief alterations that have just happened—the stripped-down, weirded-out, and wobbly self that struggles to reconstitute itself post-trip is likely to be highly suggestible and vulnerable as it seeks a stable new narrative.[95] The jars of clay cannot stay empty for long and are going to get filled by *something*. Most people simply cannot sustain what Bauman called "liquid modernity" at its chaotic peak intensity for long periods, where, akin to Cartesian doubt, cherished prior assumptions—and even whole identities—are thrown into question and legacy narratives may no longer provide much psychic sustenance.

Post-discombobulation, people and their egos need to reestablish mental order by resolving the situation in favor of some successor state of mind and conception of self and place.[96] In short, every Cartesian hyperbolic doubt-like episode of ego dis-connection will be succeeded by a re-connection, every un-selfing by a re-selfing. The interregnum disconnective period—in a word, nihilism—cannot last too long and the survivors are those who can make the reconnections. The question becomes: connections to *what*?

Answering this question is complicated by the observed fact that rarely does one make good sense of a psychedelic journey from *within* the journey itself. Integration seems usually to come, sometimes with expert assistance, via interpretation afterwards. Like the Boston area theology students in Pahnke's "Good Friday Experiment," many will interpret their experiences—"mystical" or otherwise—within the frame of their own cultural and religious traditions and emerge with renewed vigor toward their prior commitments. Jesus or a jaguar or Santa Muerte will speak to them. (I say this in all humility, having actually, myself, witnessed a rather dynamic Jesus once on DMT, though I would categorize it—for me—as an aesthetic rather than mystical experience—long story.)[97] Strictly speaking, we can *only* ever interpret events within our own (psychological mind)set and (environmental and cultural) setting, broadly construed because, of course, there is no alternative—none that would fit within a naturalistic mode of explanation, that is. For whatever reason, perhaps because their prior ideologies have an especially weak hold on them, in other words they are more *impressionable*, some people in high-dosage psychedelic experiences will become *highly* dissociated, not only during the ego diminution in its immediacy, but also, more protractedly, from what they thought they believed beforehand. In the indeterminate time between the destabilization and later reconstitution of a meta-narrative—it could be minutes or days or years or never—some might feel a joy of liberation from, say, excessive material attachments that had been weighing them down, while others might feel chronically isolated, lonely, and adrift without purpose. Worse, they might as a self-soothing balm attach themselves to opportunistic bad actors and/or harmful and/or sinister systems of belief.

Third-wave psychedelia tends, I think, to downplay this dark side potential. It should be remembered, though, that this, along with aggressive legal prohibition, is exactly what invited prohibition and brought the second wave to a dead halt. Let us call this "the cult problem," the indelible icon of which is the acid-fueled "Manson Family" of the 1960s. (Considered a pejorative, "cult" has become a dirty word in religious studies, but I see no need to be so decorous about the Manson Family.) Like charismatic manipulators from time immemorial, "the smiling, dancing music man" Charles Manson was only too happy to step in and provide "answers" and narrative focus to the vulnerable people around him. As a jailhouse *Rolling Stone* interview from 1970 commented, "that a number of lost children seem to believe him is indeed a disturbing sign of the times."[98] Along with sex and music, LSD was one of the main tools in Manson's arsenal for binding his "family," mostly young women, to him.[99] They were disenchanted with life wherever in the country they traveled from to find him, and Manson was able to use all the tools at his disposal to disconnect his followers from their former lives and ways of thinking and to reconnect them to his own strange but ostensibly appealing worldview that ultimately seemed to have more to do with worship of Manson himself than anything else.

It should also be noted that the Manson group is not the only sinister cult-like grouping that has used psychedelics for recruitment and group cohesion and whatever else. Consider a couple of chilling contemporaneous examples:

> In Australia at around the same time, Anne Hamilton-Byrne, a yoga instructor and wealthy suburbanite, operated a New Age cult in secrecy for over two decades. She claimed she was a reincarnation of Jesus Christ and preached a "hodgepodge of world religions and miscellaneous esoterica (including UFOs)." A disciple, psychiatrist Howard Whitaker, helped take over a private psychiatric hospital in Kew, where he and other disci-

ples recruited patients to join the cult and administered LSD to cult members. LSD played a pivotal role in the cult—in both recruitment and maintenance. Hamilton-Byrne, under suspicious circumstances, adopted almost 30 children, who she would dose with psychiatric drugs to ensure compliance and perform initiation rituals involving LSD on. For adult followers, Hamilton-Byrne would personally provide LSD blotters and guide them through their trips, thereby "ensuring their acceptance of her divinity."[100]

Another charismatic figure was the faux-anthropological fabulist Carlos Castaneda, whose popular hallucinogenic "Don Juan" novels (which I confess to having loved as a kid) funded a bleak and depressing suicidal death cult among his coterie of southern California followers.[101]

And there are even darker examples to be found through thousands of years of history and prehistory whose details are necessarily murky, but involved a wide range of both psychoactive substances and cultures through the centuries, the best known being those of Mesoamerica.[102] To name just a few examples: Aztec (Nahua) and Maya human sacrifices seem to have featured psychedelics like magic mushrooms and morning glory seeds ("ololiuqui," which is lysergic acid–based like LSD), among other substances, and the Jivaro people (Ecuador) reportedly use ayahuasca in their ceremonial headhunting practices.[103] A macabre recent archaeological discovery from the early Nazca period (100 BCE–450 CE) on the coast of southern Peru was the physical evidence unearthed of ritual child sacrifice (and the ornamental trophy-keeping of the child corpses). Participants in these ceremonies appear to have been under the influence of powerful psychedelics, including mescaline and a proto-ayahuasca beverage.[104] (This grisly scene is the oldest known archaeological evidence of the consumption of these plants.) Considering these types of examples, especially the emerging ancient record, where it is reasonable to guess that we have only scratched the surface of psychedelics' deep past, it is exceedingly naïve to think that psychedelics are bound automatically to result in harmony, sweetness, and light.[105] There are just too many troubling counterexamples. Even a dedicated support group cannot fix everything because a given group and its animating cultural practices might *themselves* be morally problematic—in *any* cultural context. Of course, this in no way suggests psychedelics are inherently malevolent, as some religious fundamentalists have argued, only that the commonness of ethically troubling uses gives little warrant for considering them to be inherently benign either.[106]

Boosters should take heed and not sweep this dark legacy under the rug; the third wave needs to mature into an ability to take in the whole range of possibilities and not just the uplifting bits. The cult problem is too dangerous to ignore. Given that, as research confirms, "individuals on psychedelics are hyper-suggestible," it is clear that the vulnerabilities created and/or enhanced by psychedelic-induced ego diminishment can make vulnerable people easy prey for unscrupulous actors and, on group scale, greatly augment a charismatic leader's power.[107]

There is a second and related problem having to do with more intimate abuses. This we might call "the exploitation problem" and it is generated out of a similar dynamic to the cult problem. In recent years, a major issue has arisen in the psychedelic community having to do with, again, unscrupulous actors, this time in the form of self-appointed gurus and unregulated guides (in the US and abroad) who have clearly been preying on vulnerable "clients," often in the form of sexual exploitation. One pattern seems to be a function of the well-known "transference" phenomenon in psychology and psychiatry, originally described by Sigmund Freud, where patients unwittingly "transfer" their feelings for persons in their lives and/or their past onto their therapist.[108] The ego-dissociative effects of psychedelics seem to generate this phenomenon in some people vis-à-vis their sitter, guide, or therapist and, unfortunately—but predictably—there are sometimes morally twisted types in those authority positions who take advantage. In 2021–2022, a popular investigative podcast by *New York Magazine*, "Cover Story," ran a series called "Power Trip," in which Lily Kay Ross documented in wrenching detail sexual abuses allegedly perpetrated against her, then a young psychedelics enthusiast, by unscrupulous guides and assorted others both at home in the US and abroad in South America.[109] The series then went on to explore additional alleged abusive incidents, including accusations that some in the psychedelics world were ignoring them or, even worse, actively covering them up. (Two episodes also hinted at research malfeasance in MDMA clinical trials, claiming adverse effects on participants were downplayed.)[110] While legal due process must be rendered and trial by journalism is insufficient for proving anyone's guilt, this—and other parallel problems that have been raised, some concerning financial exploitation—is certainly a lot of smoke and it strongly suggests some fire.[111] The outrageous ethical breaches described in these allegations are morally indefensible and self-sabotaging for the third-wave movement. And they illustrate the extreme danger of ignoring the psychological vulnerabilities inherent in reconnective processes. In this connection, one of the leading exponents of psychedelic safety guidelines, Johns Hopkins experimental psychologist Matthew Johnson, wisely cautions against what he calls "psychedelic exceptionalism," which is "the inclination to believe that the nature of the experiences people have on psychedelics are so sacred or important that the normal rules do not apply, whether they be the rules governing clinical boundaries, the practice of clinical psychology or medicine, sound philosophy of science, or ethics. This psychedelic exceptionalism was one of the mistakes made by a subset of investigators in the earlier era of psychedelic research in the 1960s."[112] At a minimum, as Johnson also advocates, given inherent patient vulnerabilities, psychedelic practitioners will need to develop and enforce strong codes of professional ethics in the manner of therapists and social workers. The current illegal status of psychedelics in most jurisdictions hampers the development—and certainly the enforcement—of such norms, making it rather like trying to enforce ID requirements on street-level drug dealers. There is never a silver bullet, but it is safe to say that the legalization of psychedelics would do much to bring such abuses to light, regularize the relevant practices of guides and caregivers, provide greater recourse for victims, and ultimately reduce the likelihood and overall number of these exploitative harms.

Third-wave psychedelics proponents cannot just blame prohibition, though. There still persists a strong second-wave libertarian ethos that tends toward aestheticization, a tacit assumption that psychedelics' "mind-blowing" and consciousness-altering capabilities are inherently benign such that the ethics will take care of itself; the beauty of the insights alone is sufficient and somehow self-protective—"All You Need is Love," as in the Beatles' 1967 Summer of Love anthem.[113] But, as most would admit, when articulated in generic terms, the major insights that arise tend toward extreme vagueness, the kinds of mantra-like sentiments that are poignant in the moment but not durably contentful. As Michael Pollan puts it, "Platitudes that wouldn't seem out of place on a Hallmark card flow with the force of revealed truth. Love is everything. Okay, but what else did you learn? No—you must not have heard me; it's everything!"[114] This is not to dispute that important insights—and maybe the *most* important ones—may remain to a degree ineffable; language can be quite limited. Philosophers have certainly recognized this, the most famous example probably being William James's classic account of "the ineffable" in his lectures on mysticism in *The Varieties of Religious Experience*.[115] Another influential example is Ludwig Wittgenstein's summary and oft-repeated last line of his first great philosophical treatise, *Tractatus Logico-Philosophicus*: "What we cannot speak about we must pass over in silence."[116] (Interestingly for the present discussion, Wittgenstein had no reluctance labeling those "things that cannot be put into words" as "mystical.")[117] Along these lines, it could well be that, ultimately, the highest insights gained from psychedelics (should) leave us only with platitudes or silence if we attempt to articulate them in a conventional manner (admittedly, a conclusion that would challenge this book's main line of inquiry).

All the same, the very magnitude of this power of high-dose psychedelics that is capable of rendering us so mute also demonstrably influences intersubjective behavior. As such, it does not escape considerations concerning how we treat one another—the realm of ethics—no matter how personally cathartic or consciousness-altering its associated qualia may be. By definition, nobody is "beyond" ethics, and if the leader of your group starts making such assertions, it is probably time to run very far away. But a strong ethical framework for curbing abuses does not grow out of nothing. Ultimately, it must be embedded as a component part of the psychedelic "setting" in the broadest possible sense. This includes much more than just psychedelic usage's immediate surroundings; it stretches out toward the encompassing ideational milieu within which it occurs and which supplies its animating emotions, trophic forms, behavioral patterns, and archetypal imagery. In short, *a complete understanding of setting must include the institutional, cultural, and worldview contexts that supply the template and telos upon which hypertrophic identifications are projected.* These larger contexts are varied and multidimensional and, it turns out, just as important as the compounds themselves. Maybe it is not surprising, because they are both educational contexts, but just as it takes a village to raise a child, it also takes a village—and then some—to integrate a psychedelic. This wider contextual milieu is the subject of the next chapter.

Chapter 4

Psychedelic Envelopment

> Every tribe has their own cosmology, and they travel within their cosmology.
>
> —Luis Eduardo Luna, "On Encounters with Entities," 23

The Set-Setting Continuum

"Set and setting" is probably the most common phrase in all of psychedelia—so much so that it has now achieved the status of conventional wisdom, the one thing many would say they "know" about psychedelics. Though coined earlier, possibly by Al Hubbard, a.k.a. "Captain Trips," the curious 1950s second-wave "Johnny Appleseed" distributor of LSD, it was later popularized by Timothy Leary and colleagues. As Leary explains, the "nature of the experience depends almost entirely on set and setting. Set denotes the preparation of the individual, including his personality structure and his mood at the time. Setting is physical—the weather, the room's atmosphere; social—feelings of persons present towards one another; and cultural—prevailing views as to what is real."[1] For those inclined to partake in these compounds, it is helpful—even necessary—to have at least some grasp on these basic concepts. Though the chemistry may be the same, experience quickly reveals that psychedelic experiences can vary greatly among individuals and for an individual under different circumstances.

In terms of set (really an abbreviation of "mindset"), it was common knowledge among my group in college that one should do mushrooms or acid only if one felt generally "okay" about one's life, meaning that if one were undergoing a personal difficulty, suffering from anxiety or trauma, or beset for whatever reason with negativity (e.g., a bad mood, fear of the drug), it was best not to go through with it. (I have found no reason ever to doubt this advice.) In terms of setting, it was also common knowledge that the optimal conditions were as relaxed as possible, with a group of amiable friends in some secure and stress-free location (e.g., a farm or ranch in the countryside, somewhere capacious enough to buffer the outside world), as physically comfortable as possible and, ideally, with ready access to beauty and nature. On a nice day. With a good sound system. (Again, I have found no reason ever to doubt this advice either.) Set and setting are of course relevant to the experience of any psychoactive drug—or anything really: imagine a fine burgundy from the bottle by a dumpster in a back alley after having stolen it versus in an artisanal wine glass accompanying an elegant meal and light conversation in a Parisian restaurant. Set and setting are relevant to just about any human qualia past a certain threshold of intensity, sex or exercise being classic examples where the right or wrong impingements from either category could make or break the experience. A negative attitude combined with a very hot day are unlikely to result in a good 10K run, etc.

The preceding two chapters have dealt mostly with the realm of set, at least as it evolves during the pendency of a trip experience: implications of the gateway perceptual alterations and cognitive confusions that arise, along with intenser high-dosage changes that may then occur in one's deeper interiors, to one's self-model and the enlarging of one's identifications. Any account would be woefully incomplete, however, without a sustained examination of setting in the maximally inclusive sense. I say "maximally inclusive" for two reasons: 1) though not meant this way ordinarily, "setting" is an inherently elastic concept that can expand indefinitely; as a notion of generalized exteriority, in principle it can encompass everything from one's living room to one's culture to the universe as a whole; and 2) upon even cursory examination, it becomes clear that no bright lines of separation can be drawn between these infinite contexts of setting and an individual's mindset—and not just in the ordinary sense that the setting qua immediate surroundings can influence one's attitude, emotions and mood, etc., but in the phenomenological sense that, while they may be distinguishable conceptually, set and setting are really not separable at all in terms of lived experience. My "bad mood" or "positive outlook" will *in some sense* be related to environing factors that are larger than my own ego or narrow self-conception. Maybe my mood is due to a problem with a relationship, which in turn is because of some family dynamic, which in turn is given rise to by a complex of cultural expectations, which are in turn a function of human evolution, and in turn of the natural environment, ad infinitum. Or I feel upbeat about myself at the moment because I perceive myself as efficacious and successful regarding some accomplishment, the latter shaped by, say, masculine expectations about winning resources that are, in turn, also defined by cultural norms, also a function of human evolution, also of the natural environment, also ad infinitum.

When one reflects upon the categories in this way, it is clear that *set and setting are thoroughly permeable* and are only separable *in mente* as an artificial intellectual distinction, just like "individual and society," "human being and nature," "space and time," and so on. Not that the categories are useless and should be abandoned. All language is like this, as Socrates never tired of demonstrating. It is only that, if they are probed with sufficient acuity, all distinctions and definitions always fall apart in the long run. We often pretend the opposite, though: that we understand something when we have named it. But, as Nietzsche pointed out, just as often—and maybe even always—"we set up a word at the point at which our ignorance begins, at which we can see no further."[2] The relationship between language and reality is one of those inexhaustible philosophical rabbit holes that is best to avoid if one wants to talk about anything else, so I will tip-toe around it here. The point for now is that "set" and "setting" cannot neatly be delineated from one another and, although they are perfectly useful in psychedelic safety guidelines and the like, the dualism is not serviceable for very long philosophically.

This is why I am modestly proposing to supplement "setting" with "envelopment." Like any word, "envelopment" falls apart eventually, too, but it does so, I think, at a later point. "Setting" carries with it too many connotations of separateness (from the experiencer) and is, as per the above, usually taken to refer to factors taken as external, like one's physical surroundings and social milieu. "Envelopment," I think, emphasizes externality less while still maintaining it; the term has more of the needed sense of permeability: to be "enveloped" by something sounds closer and more intimate—like the thing is more part of one—than "setting" or "context," which both seem more separable and bird's-eye. As such, it seems to me that the word "envelopment" is preferable to "setting" from an experiential point of view, especially with psychedelics, whose signal feature is perhaps an intense feeling of manifold boundary dissolution. "Set and setting" is perfectly good for most circumstances, though, and I'm not campaigning against it. It's just that if we are gearing up to analyze the many contexts of psychedelics, I think "envelopment" is truer to the phenomenon. It is helpful to recognize these experiences as more nestled within, sustained and *permeated* by envelopments, than it is to describe them more banally as inserted "in" a setting or context. In terms of the present analysis, it is also much closer to the implications of both Heidegger's qualia-oriented conception of the human being, as not just anatomical but also Dasein (being-there), and the grand realization of Descartes's *cogito ergo sum* (I think therefore I am), that my only indubitable thought is that I am a connected part of *some* world by virtue of the fact that I am having *some* experience. In both cases it is concluded that we are so thoroughly enveloped by the world that it is experientially undecidable where "world" begins and "I" end, and vice-versa.

The substantive point is that set and setting are not so separable and that the contents "inside" the mind are there because they seeped into it—at various times and in various ways—from its enveloping "outside" surroundings. This is true even when the experience is one of deep interiority and/or introspection, for that enveloping outside is not only, so to speak, *spatial*, that is, having to do with ongoing occurrent contexts such as one's contemporaneous sociocultural milieu; it is also *temporal*, encompassing past contexts along a broad spectrum that includes the deep past of biological and cultural evolution (e.g., brain architecture, psychological patterns and archetypes, language), history (e.g., millennia of passed-on tradition), individual physiological and psychological development (e.g., congenital factors), and personal biography and memory (e.g., acquired habits, education, and past traumas). Pertaining to the latter two categories, for example, Grof makes the "perinatal matrices" we pass through during the birthing process (three intrauterine stages, then birth separation) central features of his analysis of how high-dosage LSD is experienced by patients in psychotherapy.[3] (In his later work, Grof goes even further back temporally, verging on supernaturalism by entertaining the possibility of extra-temporal influences allegedly felt during psychedelic sessions, such as communications with the dead and memories from past lives and reincarnation.)[4] It is in no way clear how to establish where one's set or setting "starts" either phylogenetically or ontogenetically: with the genesis of anatomically modern humans? Hominins generally? Amoebas? The birth process? Somewhere in embryonic development? Fertilization? Farther back even than all of these, into the formation of life itself? Or still further into deep time and our celestial provenance? From the grandest perspectives, it is impossible to pinpoint precisely the beginning of one's "outside" influences. Even within an individual lifetime, *lived* temporality is further complexified by the fact that there is no easy division in the flow of conscious experience between past and present, the "now" being ever elusive and receding, akin to observer effects in quantum mechanics, where the very act of noticing a phenomenon alters it; once one thinks "*now!*" the moment has already passed. "Ego dissolution" thus marks much more the *beginning* of a discussion than it provides a satisfying explanation for anything; as both an undergone state of mind and a macro- or microcosmic state of affairs, it tracks across several different dimensions.

Qualia having to do with the passage of time can be greatly altered in psychedelic journeys as well, usually slowing it down. Twenty minutes on DMT is commonly reported as having *felt* to have been of much longer duration, for example.[5] Suffice it to say that, from the point of view of the experiencer, the felt durations of psychedelic trips are very fluid and hard to pin down; the ordinary (ostensible) distinguishability of past from present and relative regularity of time flow cannot be counted upon. This multi-axis and intense blurring of boundaries is a core characteristic of psychedelics. Across the board, dichotomies and distinctions that appear so stark in everyday life—so "obvious" as to be considered commonsensical—deconstruct themselves to reveal manifold unexpected continuities and integralities. The ensuing hypertrophic identifications that then arise from these sundry boundary collapses are experienced as flashes of insight (the reality switches or *Umwelt* expansions) that alter one's self-model for an indeterminate period or possibly even permanently. That this can occur at all *itself* shows how set and setting are on a continuum rather than neatly separable, as one's personal "set" of mind now fuses with what was heretofore considered to be part of the extra-personal "setting," thoroughly and inseparably entangling the two. That set and setting are actually a continuum means that what goes on "inside" one's mind during a psychedelic reality switch must always be understood as a function of what is "outside" of one's mind too. This is also why, incidentally, much of the debate about whether the psychedelic experiences going on "in one's head" are "real" or not misses the point. If there is a single lesson from Descartes it is that yes, of course the DMT entities (or whatever) are real. The interesting question is "what does that *mean?*"

All of this premises an important hypothesis that Grof proposes: psychedelics are "pluripotent," in that they function as "non-specific amplifiers and catalysts of the psyche."[6] Consistent with this thesis, Grof further holds that these substances "increase the cathexis (energetic change) associated with the deep unconscious contents of the psyche and make them available for conscious processing."[7] These phenomena are best understood not only "objectively," as pharmacological processes (though of course they have those aspects), but also "subjectively," *as reality switches that direct our qualia in an indeterminate manner*. (A *fortiori*, this would include psychedelics' "political pluripotency" as well; history is replete with political exotics of diverse descriptions who were enthused about these substances, a crowded and ancient rogues' gallery of saint and sinners, as per one's political tastes.)[8] I provided a few examples in my preceding discussion of the cult and exploitation problems and, in addition, compelling histories of psychedelics have supplied overwhelming empirical proof of Grof's pluripotency hypothesis.[9] The wildly different uses to which psychedelics have been put and the radically divergent ideologies they have serviced—from benign to malignant, wonderful to sinister, conventional to "high weirdness"—should make this hypothesis axiomatic.[10] It is in fact the natural social correlate of the plasticity they augment at the neural level; as in Platonic philosophy, there seems to be a "structural isomorphism" between mind and society where, in this case, epistemic loosening on the subjective plane mirrors a matching loosening and malleability on the *inter-subjective* plane.[11] As reality switch tools, it seems that psychedelics not only reveal worlds, but can reveal indeterminately many of them.

Four Psychedelic Envelopments

The pluripotency hypothesis entails that the ideational envelopments within which psychedelics are necessarily experienced greatly determine the nature of those experiences and, even more importantly, the meanings that are afterwards ascribed to them. As outlined at the outset, I propose four basic envelopment categories, with major subcategories within each, as the basic channels through which psychedelic experience flows. These channels dramatically shape and direct the experience. What I am calling envelopments are not neatly separable by bright lines, though. There is plenty of overlapping, crisscrossing, and instances where the borderlines recede; this is not set theory, but hopelessly untidy and human. Nonetheless, placing matters in a larger frame than mere "setting" helps better illuminate how psychedelics are encountered by individuals and their surrounding communities. This sociocultural dimension is crucial to any account of their educational potential. Although a psychedelic trip always has the feel of something that is happening intimately to *me* personally, matters are not nearly so simple.

1. The Medical Envelopment (Therapeutic, Clinical)

Telos: patient care, trauma recovery, wellness

Platforms: clinical trials, hospitals, wellness centers (where legal)

First and currently most prominent, particularly among the credentialed and degreed in the modernist west, is the medical envelopment. In the more economically developed countries, there have been variations of the medical-therapeutic context for psychedelics across all three modern waves, shaped mostly by the disciplines of psychiatry and psychology. There are more somatic medical potentialities for psychedelics—for example, LSD may alleviate cluster headaches—but the mental realm has always been by far the main focus.[12] As discussed earlier, first and second wave forms of this envelopment were mostly a small coterie of mavericks within psychiatric institutions, broadly defined, including figures such as Grof, in the former Soviet-bloc countries in the immediate postwar decades (and also, in a twisted manner, bad actors subverting Hippocratic norms like the CIA did with MK-ULTRA). The focus here tended to be mental illness and substance abuse, particularly alcohol addiction. In the US, these activities continued into the early 1970s, when the generalized shutdown of research and clinical activity with psychedelics took hold. After almost a quarter century hiatus, the third wave commenced with the likes of Strassman, Grob, and Griffiths, who set the early template for further work that garnered federal research funding for clinical trials (ironically, much of it from "war on drugs" funding), most notably with DMT (Strassman) and psilocybin (Grob and Griffiths). This research has been the motor of the current psychedelic "renaissance" and has strongly captured the attention of policymakers and the general public.

(MDMA research funded by MAPS has been a leading edge of these developments as well in terms of seeking regulatory approval.) It is hard to deny the potential therapeutic promise of psychedelics, given the standing of the leading institutions worldwide conducting this research and their impressive initial results in a number of areas such as MDMA with veterans with PTSD and psilocybin with terminal cancer patients. Additionally, there appear to be ongoing successes with psychedelics, particularly psilocybin, and a range of treatment-resistant conditions like anxiety, depression, drug addiction, smoking cessation, anorexia, and childhood trauma.[13] Given this emerging record of documented achievement, it is understandable that the medical envelopment has dominated contemporary public discourse about psychedelics and is undoubtedly the main impetus behind the increasing public acceptance of these drugs. Backlashes will undoubtedly emerge, but the demonstrable therapeutic promise of psychedelics has released a host of powerful political, legal, and financial genies that will be hard to put back in their bottles. If the first wave was characterized by avant-garde coteries of dabblers, and the second wave by a concentrically wider, though still culturally delimited, creative outpouring in the arts and music (1960s culture), the third wave may well, in retrospect, be characterized by institutional prestige-driven social acceptance pursuant to a deeper societal integration of psychedelics—a mainstreaming even.

Adjacent to this sphere and, in some sense, parasitic upon it is an emergent wellness industry, heavily associated with recent fads for microdosing for productivity and creativity among Silicon Valley and other information industry types. There are also burgeoning sectors, both above- and underground, of psychedelic counselors and guides, some of them self-credentialed and some of them "accredited" through unaffiliated organizations like the Guild of Guides in the Netherlands. These efforts also belong to the medical envelopment because their telos is client/patient welfare, helping individuals overcome obstacles in the way of maximizing their psychedelic journeys or simply providing practical knowledge and/or tips on safety practices about how to go about it. As analogs of the caring professions like teaching, social work, and nursing, and like therapists with psychiatric and psychological credentials, wellness mentors and guides are (ideally) focused on the personal wellbeing of the concrete individuals in their charge. This focus on patient/client welfare is what places them in the medical envelopment along with their more formally credentialed peers.

If one undergoes therapy with psychedelics, either legally, as part of an authorized clinical trial at a research facility, or extra-legally (underground), with a knowledgeable guide in a private residence, one is experiencing the situation—before, during, and after—in a certain way. There are expectations of healing and/or personal betterment, a layer of comfort (for most people) that one is "in the hands" of an expert, and, particularly in the clinical trial situation, an obligation to provide data regarding the experience to those conducting the trial. Also, if one is trying psychedelics as a curative, then by definition there is some background of suffering or other sub-optimal personal history leading up to the treatment attempt. These factors are bound to influence the trip and its aftermath—in fact, to frame the whole trajectory from start to finish. How exactly such envelopment influences manifest themselves is an important question, one implicitly acknowledged by researchers concerned about possible distorting effects from an overly medicalized setting—analogous to a "white coat syndrome" concern, where patients might suffer anxiety or other symptoms simply from being in a hospital environment. This concern is at the forefront for psychedelics researchers, who usually try to make their subjects' surroundings less "clinical" with a more comfortable and homelike "living room-like environment . . . free of unnecessary medical or research equipment."[14] (As part of such efforts, in their psilocybin trials, Johns Hopkins carefully curates musical playlists to promote salutary atmospherics, versions of which have become popular on streaming platforms. These are mostly of a soothing "easy listening" type, which itself also reflects researchers' attitudes and priorities.)[15] All trips have some setting/context/envelopment and so the argument here is not that the medical envelopment is inherently distorting; this could be said about any envelopment—and there is always *some* envelopment. It is just that it is important to be mindful that the medical-therapeutic setting comes with a significant amount of cultural baggage and a set of expectations toward recovery and wellness that are not as central to other envelopments.

One of the largest of the cultural baggage items is money. In the US, at least, hospitals make many non-wealthy people nervous, not because of white coat syndrome, but because they associate hospital and other medical settings with financial difficulties and expect a bill to arrive eventually—even if they are participants in a free research trial.[16] This is just part of the health system in the US; everyone has heard the lore—with enough actual news items to bolster the stories—about someone getting a gigantic "surprise bill" from a hospital stay (e.g., one in five Americans report actually having received such a bill).[17] If one were worried about money (as many of course are), and even mildly paranoid about hospitals and their billing practices (as many rightly are), this could definitely affect a person's trip experience.

The bigger issue in this arena, however, lies at the institutional level, where corporate interests in pharmaceuticals and mental health are becoming infused with start-up venture capital and are poised to enter the emerging psychedelics industry around the delivery of psychological services. Particularly if psychedelics become widely used as treatment for widespread (and lucrative) maladies like depression and substance abuse, there will be a lot of money to be made. This financialization would of course parallel the American health care system generally, from the drugs themselves (there is a torrent of new psychedelic patents) and, perhaps even more profitably, on the delivery of therapy surrounding their administration. This profit-driven momentum is definitely a novel aspect of the third wave. LSD psychotherapy was big for a time in the 1950s and 1960s (especially in England and Eastern Europe) and Albert Hofmann's Sandoz Ltd. was a for-profit corporation, certainly.[18] But LSD was never a big moneymaker for them or anyone else. It was too illegal and too cheap to manufacture—and many of the major early underground LSD chemists did not seem to be highly motivated by profits.[19] But the currently emerging model of allying "respectable" psychiatric research with venture capital might be different and, if the market proves big enough, could develop into a powerful force unto itself—as we have seen in many other areas of the pharmaceutical industrial complex, popularly known as Big Pharma.

Given the potency and mental invasiveness of psychedelic compounds and the fact that, as mentioned earlier, industry is now turning its attention toward synthesizing and patenting new ones, the growing corporate wing of the medical envelopment could be cause for serious future concern. One left-wing commentator rather apocalyptically warns,

> With the emergence of a legal market for psychedelics, capital will invade human consciousness to a depth unimaginable even to the evilest geniuses at Facebook, seeking to link the production of dopamine in the consumer's brain to the number of push notifications. The proximity of the psychedelic industry to Silicon Valley tech giants—and the influx

of capital from there—would make this penetration so rapid that the next decade would forever go down in history as the "psychedelic twenties."[20]

Time will tell if this corporate involvement will be so impactful and if it will be as nefarious as some fear. But if the nexus of Big Pharma and psychiatry is able to create a plausible revenue stream, perhaps on the prescription model of antidepressants and anxiety medications, the financialization of psychedelics will become an enormous part of the medical envelopment. For one thing, whereas the medical envelopment in quantitative terms is currently minuscule (only a tiny percentage of psychedelics users have participated in a clinical trial), a legalized prescription model would bring psychedelics to the general public on an unprecedented scale. As a result, many individuals' first and only experiences with psychedelics would be as treatment seekers "under the care" of a doctor or therapist, and perhaps physically undergone in hospitals, clinics, or designated centers (where patients would, one can be sure, "need" to stay a few days at great cost). Under scaled-up, for-profit conditions such as these, the medical envelopment of psychedelics would proceed along significantly different lines from the non-profit discovery-driven research ethos that has animated the area thus far.

There are a few additional considerations to mention. Anthropologically, the origin of the medical envelopment arises within the practices of indigenous cultures worldwide (still ongoing), where psychoactive plants have long been central to healing practices involving shamans, *curanderos*, *ayahuasqueros*, *brujas*, or others in native healer roles under their many appellations. In the long span of human history and prehistory, these *shamanic envelopments* are by far the most ubiquitous of envelopments. The shamanic envelopment also defies to a large extent the present envelopment typology altogether, which is, admittedly, constructed through a western and modernist cultural frame (my own inevitable frame). These traditional envelopments—indigenous and otherwise—however, do not by and large separate medicine from religion and spirituality. There is perhaps a touch of this in contemporary wellness regimes with a New Age "self-care" aspect, where supernatural agencies or "energies" are implicated in healing processes, such as crystals and the like, but these practices are fly-by-night outliers compared to the deeply rooted and culturally integrated psychedelia of worldwide shamanic traditions.[21] From within a western modernist frame, medicine and spirituality do not mix and calling upon divine intervention or prayer for healing purposes has long since fallen out of favor with educated opinion. People still pray for recovery, of course, but this is vestigial and not considered a serious medical intervention. But religion and healing are typically not easily separable in traditional societies; on the contrary, the two tend to be wholly integrated to the point that it would not be possible to make sense of medical practices within those cultures otherwise.

I would also suggest, however, that it is inaccurate wholly to exclude western traditions from this hybrid sub-category. This is evident in two arenas: 1) Europe's prehistoric past, e.g., ancient cave and rock art with hallucinogenic themes worldwide, including Europe, and the prevalence of proto-psychedelia in European folklore and folk motifs such as the ubiquitous psychoactive mushroom *Amanita muscaria*; and also 2) hidden and often actively suppressed currents *within* the stream of European culture itself, e.g., folk herbalist practitioners, often persecuted and associated with witchcraft and the remnants of druidism, as well as distinct subcultures with their own fraught positions vis-à-vis the mainstream, such as the herbal "brews" of the *chovihanos* ("Gypsy shamans") of the Romani people (Roma).[22] While it is true that western medicine has until very recently lost touch with ancient psychedelics like magic mushrooms and other herbal concoctions, it is demonstrably incorrect to assert that the ancient lineages of these substances are exclusively non-western. (This is even truer when one considers larger-scale and more "purely" entheogenic settings such as the Eleusinian Mysteries of ancient Greece.) It seems clear that the further and more carefully we peer into the past, psychedelics (and other consciousness-altering substances) emerge as a common *global* inheritance, a human universal even, albeit one based on many different biochemical substrates and folded into many cultural pathways.

As observed in contemporary indigenous cultures, however, the shamanic psychedelic envelopment has distinctive characteristics that both fit and do not fit modern western expectations about the nature of medicine and healing. As noted previously, it is commonplace for psychoactive plants in traditional societies worldwide to be encountered as "plant healers," "the tree of life" (iboga), and "plant medicines."[23] In shamanic traditions this is arguably their central role, in terms of both *direct* administration as a cure and also *indirect* administration in the sense that the shaman him or herself undertakes the psychedelic journey to diagnose and/or prescribe a cure on behalf of the patient.[24]

As anthropologist Michael Harner summarizes in his classic book on the subject, "Through journeys of exploration, the shaman gains spirit helpers . . . and knowledge of how to treat different kinds of illnesses."[25] Sometimes it is conceived that the spirits of the plant themselves, in some form, provide the relevant answers that, say, a *curandero* might then take back for performing whatever healing is needed. Anthropologist Jeremy Narby vividly relates how Amazonian Yanomami shamans conceive a certain type of challenging spirit called the *xapiri*: "When you see the xapiri spirits they arrive dancing and singing. They can't not sing. Their melodies are infinite, and what they bring, first and foremost, is knowledge about healing. What the shamans do is put themselves in the presence of these entities, listen to their songs, and learn them."[26] Likewise, *kayiglu* spirits among the Piro people, also Amazonian,

> see inside plants and animals and are like people—what they do is, they sing. That is their characteristic—when you take ayahuasca, you see these powerful entities, they are like people, and they sing. And what the shaman does is listen in to these songs and sings along with them, and by singing with these powerful entities the shaman then attains the subject position of these powerful beings and sees as they do and then knows as they know. The point is to sing with them so as to see like them and having seen like them to then do something about it. And doing something about it often involves healing.[27]

The main telos of the activity is still healing, but in this case the psychedelic journey is a vicarious one; unlike in the medical-therapeutic setting where the patient *herself* undergoes the psychedelic trip pursuant to healing whatever psychological ailment, here the *shaman* is the one undergoing the experience with the goal of bringing information back about what is needed. The ayahuasca is a conveyance to bring the healer into proximity with a spirit realm where answers to the pressing question reside. As Narby summarizes, "the shaman is the person who by profession and *in the name of the community* entertains an intermittent commerce with the spirits of nature."[28] "Medicine" is thus framed entirely differently in these traditions as essentially a spiritual gift, one that cannot be understood apart from a particular cosmology and worldview.

2. The Entheogenic Envelopment (Religious, Spiritual)

Telos: salvation, community, eudaimonia

Platforms: houses of worship, sacred spaces, individualized introspection

This leads to the next major envelopment, the *entheogenic*, by far the most ancient envelopment. Here, psychedelics are consumed pursuant to religious insight and/or as a component of a religious sacrament, most commonly shamanic or theological (see this book's introduction). Traditional entheogenic envelopments, of both western and non-western settings and provenance, are almost always *communal* in nature. They are most often characterized by ceremonial and ritual repetition in situations such as holidays, major life cycle events (e.g., birth, death, marriage, rites of passage), and ongoing community needs (e.g., healing, locating lost items, miscellaneous guidance, and consultation for important decisions). These enhanced rituals are important for effectively transmitting social groups' belief systems.[29]

The iconic example in western history is the Eleusinian Mysteries (through its possible evolution into the early Christian Eucharist), where psychedelics seem to have been imbibed via the mysterious *kykeon* wine cocktail. The Mysteries were deeply enshrined in Greek law and custom— it was a capital offense publicly to reveal their content—for nearly one thousand years.[30] A further strange type of entheogenic envelopment bears noting: an *inadvertent* though highly influential psychedelic episode in European history involves the probable ergot poisoning (with an LSD-like profile) that sprang up from the mold on damp grain crops, throughout the medieval and early modern periods, and led to outbreaks of witch hysteria. If this sounds counterintuitive as an example of entheogenic use, there are two points to consider: 1) not all entheogenic envelopments are intentional and perhaps, in certain ways, most are not; and 2) there is also no warrant for assuming them automatically to be benign by any stretch. Those suffering from ergot underwent entheogenic experiences because from start to finish their visions were replete with their communities' pre-existing biblical imagery and otherwise wholly framed by the then-dominant religious narratives, e.g., hell, Satan, damnation, angels, heaven, salvation, demons, witches, etc. These ergot outbreaks appear to have been nightmarish torments with very bad outcomes and high mortality rates, but they were no less entheogenic for that reason.

As previously discussed, leading non-western theological examples include the large-scale officiated ceremonies of prehistoric Mesoamerica, including those of the Aztec, Maya, and other peoples. Such examples may extend even deeper into the human past if, as some suggest, rock and cave art in various locations worldwide evidences psychedelic usage and sensibilities, both in direct depictions of mushrooms and drug paraphernalia (e.g., pipes and pouches) and, perhaps more importantly, in the striking psychedelic-seeming visionary depictions in the art itself.[31] There is no way to tell for sure, but the drawings are very suggestive. If true, this could push entheogenic drug use back to tens of thousands of years ago—and even if it is not, it is at a minimum several thousand years old. (As suggested in chapter 1, the ubiquity of animal usage—including primates—would seem to make early human use all the more plausible.)[32] In more recent times, akin to the medical envelopment, the classic entheogenic envelopment is communal and centered around the many worldwide shamanic traditions. Some of these are probably spiritual legatees of imperial predecessors, e.g., New World native cultures vis-à-vis their distant Aztec and Maya ancestors (though the religions of the successors are characterized by interwoven syncretisms of the older gods with Catholicism).[33] Neither their age nor their cultural "purity" (an incoherent notion), however, determines their status as entheogenic. Even if they are relatively recent start-ups, like the Native American Church in North America, if their telos is spiritual and/or religious, that would be sufficient for the classification.

Another noteworthy feature of the communal form of entheogenic envelopment is that it is decidedly *not* counter-cultural. While psychedelics are typically styled as *outré* and rebellious, thanks largely to their association with first-wave avant-garde and second-wave hippie subcultures, serving as agents of intracultural challenge is not at all their traditional role. The prohibitionist Nixonians of the early '70s might be surprised to consider how in non-modern traditional societies, far from being cultural antagonists, *psychedelics have almost always served in a culturally integrative manner that reminds, renews, and reinforces community and religious ties*, rather than alienating and separating psychedelicized individuals from their own established customs. In fact, it seems entirely a modernist western innovation for psychedelics to become associated with distance and disenchantment from an individual's cultural mainstream. On the contrary, the most likely outcome of a psychedelics-infused traditional ritual seems actually to be more along the lines of a *re-enchantment* and *re-commitment* to shared cultural norms.[34] At a meta-level, though, psychedelics may also function as cultural reinforcers in the modernized west, despite appearances. A culture that places such high formal value on personal autonomy and individual freedom (viz., the legal emphasis on human/civil rights and strong expectations having to do with self-expression and "following your bliss," etc.) may find that, while psychedelics do not necessarily reinforce conformity to *surface* norms, the "nonconformity" that they seem to promote may actually represent a *deeper* conformity to the culture's dominant individualist ethos. This may be a bit of a paradox: conforming to a culture of nonconformity. But it may be a paradox that accurately reflects the nature of psychedelics themselves. As we have seen with the phenomena of epistemic loosening and hypertrophic identification, they are protean in that they can simultaneously serve, at the personal and cultural levels, as causes of *both* disintegration *and* integration.

This capability, I think, should be recognized as yet another way—a very deep one—in which psychedelics are pluripotent à la Grof. Not only are they nonsectarian, in the sense that they might be harnessed to a diversity of religions, cultures, and worldviews, but also, *within* a particular culture or worldview, they can provide both centrifugal (outward) *and* centripetal (inward) force; these exquisite tools and their attendant visions can, like the many-faceted Hindu god Shiva, function as both builders and destroyers of worlds. They can engender Gallimorean reality switches—or what neuroscientist Mona Sobhani calls "worldview flips"—toward some new-X, but they can also deepen and consolidate extant worldviews, supplying an intense *experiential* component to what may previously have been a less full-bodied mere propositional assent to dry theological tenets.[35] This mirrors what is regularly described by psychedelics users who report "spiritual" and/or "breakthrough" events, where they are led to a deeper appreciation of the simple unitive propositions, the variations on the theme of Oneness, as previously discussed.[36] Modern educated people know in the abstract that "everything is connected" and would give cognitive assent to such a proposition in the sense of a scientific statement about the laws of physics or some such. But undergoing an emotional and/or spiritual catharsis where one also strongly *feels* that connectedness is another matter altogether. Shared metanarratives that are not only known but deeply felt—to the point of reflexive recall and adherence—may well also provide evolutionary advantages: more deeply internalized metanarratives might greatly enhance in-group solidarity (we are all in this together) while simultaneously augmenting the efficiency of everyday strategic communications and facilitating the intergenerational transmission of culture generally, which is to say, education writ large.[37]

Consonant with its strong individualism, the westernized world has also seen the rise of a more DIY entheogenic envelopment characterized by a Protestant-rooted "seeker" ethos that "emerged in the wake of liberal Protestantism's nineteenth-century turn towards demythologized Christianity and religious pluralism."[38] This ethos is in many ways at the heart of historical Protestantism itself, as a rebellion against Roman Catholicism's institutionalization and formalism, in favor of a more direct communion with the divine, where priestly intermediaries are cast as obstacles to a personal experience of God. (It is tempting to see the early modern heretical fervor as a championing of subjective qualia against an institutional Catholic Church grown overly formalistic and distant from the immediate "feel" of spirituality.) This emphasis on personal experience is key. By the 1970s, this seeker mentality would eventually result in the fragmentation of what Davis calls "a diverse and exploding spiritual marketplace," where the "distrust of authority that characterized the sixties shifted towards a new caste of experts offering new and more marketable forms of positive thinking, exotic religions, and the psychologized 'Self-spirituality' that would initiate the New Age."[39] Davis labels this California-inflected phenomenon "consciousness culture," which he characterizes as "a largely psychological current of empirical mysticism and proto-New Age self-care."[40] In contrast to the more collective and communal posture of traditional envelopments—both indigenous and non-indigenous—the seeker phenomenon represents the individualistic entheogenic envelopment that is very heavily present in much online and popular discussion of psychedelics. Intersecting somewhat with therapeutic and wellness communities, it is common to find a strong emphasis on personal spiritual development and self-care and a desire to "find one's own truth." Psychedelics are often cast in this light as, essentially, spiritual tools for individual seekers that lend themselves to a relatively laissez-faire and nondogmatic experimentalist mentality of "I'm okay, you're okay" and "this may work for you or it may not and either is fine."

The seeker mentality is largely libertarian and certainly sees itself as anti-authoritarian, for example being strongly anti-prohibitionist regarding drug laws. Nonetheless, despite this live-and-let-live self-image, there may be some inconsistencies on this matter within the psychedelic community. A leading drug libertarian, Carl Hart, has strongly criticized a "psychedelic exceptionalism" that he identifies as symptomatic of a race- and class-oriented (and frankly snobbish) bias in favor of supposedly higher-minded entheogens vis-à-vis other more "somatic," "dangerous," and "criminal" drugs like opioids.[41] (Hart gained a great deal of public notoriety by "coming out of the closet" and frankly disclosing his own recreational heroin use—a shocking thing for the chair of Columbia University's Psychology Department to admit.)[42] At its most extreme, this prohibitionist inconsistency recapitulates some of the worst racial tropes and policies of past centuries, where minority groups were regularly associated with "lower" and more animalistic enthusiasms and pleasures.[43] These attitudes have resulted in real-world consequences concerning racial disparities in the enforcement of crimes like cannabis possession and, perhaps most famously, differential sentencing regarding crack cocaine (more prevalent among poor people of color) and powder cocaine (more prevalent among wealthier whites).[44] There are legitimate debates to be had on the merits of drug policy if they are conducted on a sound empirical basis concerning harms. And all drugs are simply not the same in terms of their social consequences. We do not see urban and rural communities devastated by mushrooms or DMT, for example. And the individualist aspect of the seeker mentality certainly does not *inherently* comport with the prejudices of previous eras. But Hart's argument that these old and sinister prejudiced patterns of thought still persist is another reminder that humility is always in order, even when it comes to an intensely felt spiritual journey; ideas that appear so innocent and so unrelated to injustice—like the praiseworthiness of psychedelic spirituality—sometimes are not so innocent. Hart himself implies that his argument should be taken this way, that is, as a helpful caveat rather than a knock-down argument against psychedelic individualism, as his overwhelming focus is very much in line with seeker individualism. His main argument is a defense of "cognitive liberty" based, as Hart indicates, on the very American individualist ethos of "the pursuit of happiness" as stated in the Declaration of Independence: "Simply put, it is my birthright to use substances in my pursuit of happiness. The point is that whether I use a drug or not is my decision; it is not the government's decision. Further, my responsible drug use should not be subjected to punishment by authorities. These ideas are central to our notions of liberty and personal freedom. The current punitive approach to dealing with recreational drug users is wholly un-American."[45] Such libertarian sentiments are very much in line with the seeker ethos.

Whatever the inconsistencies, taking psychedelics as an individual spiritual seeker is an important category within the contemporary entheogenic landscape. I know of no survey research on this topic, but it surely comprises a significant percentage of users. Proof of this is that whole economic sectors catering to this mindset have arisen, perhaps most notably from various psychedelic guide services and the emerging trend of outfitters and resort-style operations catering to psychedelic tourism—usually in countries where such activity is legal.[46] To be sure, some of these tourists are more purely recreational in orientation and there are copious therapeutic and wellness overtones present, too. But it is clear, from promotional materials and personal testimony, that a significant subset of individuals using such services would style themselves as spiritual seekers who are approaching the substances as entheogens.[47] The shaman-led (they are often advertised in this manner) ayahuasca retreats in Peru and other Amazonian locations seem particularly to emphasize these aspects, as they purport to offer an "safe, authentic and compassionate environment" for indigenous ceremonial setting structured for gringos in search of enlightenment.[48] By all accounts, these retreats vary widely in quality, fidelity to native custom, and sensitivity to local concerns such as fair wages and equitable distribution of profits, environmental damage, and safeguards against potential abuse against all parties, of the type discussed at the end of the previous chapter. Buyer beware.

Despite these difficulties to which the individual seeker is prone, some sympathetic perspective is also in order. In modern western societies, worldview fragmentation and anomie are the order of the day, with increasingly large percentages: between a quarter and a third of the population describing themselves as "spiritual but not religious," meaning precisely that they are unaffiliated with any official church or organized religious practice.[49] Additionally, within this group, there is a growing number of what religious scholars call the "faithful Nones"—particularly among the rising generation—who are, in addition, actively seeking for "something bigger."[50] Some eventually band together and join into newer collectivities, sometimes under the aegis of ancient (though hard to delineate historically) traditions such as Wicca and druidism, but most simply remain DIY and individualistic in their search for a sustaining meta-narrative and meaning. It is probably unprecedented in human history to have so many people spiritually wandering alone and largely bereft of what political philosophers call "a comprehensive conception of the good" (secular or religious).[51] It remains to be seen how sustainable this level of disconnectedness is for society as a whole, but there are increasing signs that it is not so for individuals, as rising rates of anxiety and depression seem commonsensically tied to the system's ideational liquidity. (I have made this argument at length in a previous book.)[52] At the very least, it seems to me that the figure of the individualized entheogenic seeker should be viewed as a *symptom* of modernity for which there is no known cure, only hints and suggestions—such as my halting attempts in this very book. Wandering on a Quixote-like quest for meaning is a fate to which any modern person can be subject and, *pace* many traditionalist religious revivalists, there is no easy path out of it. Because by definition they are unmoored from history and tradition, solitary spiritual quests are bound to be unsure and seem ridiculous at times, prone to idiosyncrasies and a clumsy trampling of others' toes; they are all too human. Still, seekers deserve empathy because their efforts strive toward what *all* human beings desire perhaps above all else: the development of a sustaining sense of the meaning and worthwhileness of our lives.

In the US, a special feature of the entheogenic envelopment is highly prominent due to the religion clauses of the First Amendment to the Constitution's Bill of Rights. Norms of nonestablishment (the Establishment Clause) and especially of free exercise of religion (the Free Exercise Clause) have been interpreted by the US Supreme Court in recent decades to provide a surprising degree of latitude for religious groups sincere in their use of psychedelics as entheogens, *especially* both domestic and immigrant indigenous communities who are practicing historically continuous religious traditions. By far the oldest legal accommodation in this regard is for the Native American Church, founded about a century ago in response to the desperate straits caused by the cultural eliminationism faced by native peoples. As mentioned previously, based on traditional practices, a peyote religion grew up as a synthesis of Indian traditions in reaction to the despair engendered by current conditions as a means of cultural survival.[53] After many years of government persecution as part of a broader cultural eliminationism, federal law finally began to relent and make accommodations, first as a de facto memorandum of nonenforcement of applicable federal drug laws on reservations and later as a more federally codified religious exemption specific to Native Americans.[54] These peyote exemptions have become so well ensconced that the Native American Church has opposed a universal legalization of peyote (mescaline) on the environmental grounds that it would further endanger the peyote cactus and possibly jeopardize their own access to it.[55] This is an interesting circumstance, as American law is formally based on the civil rights of individuals and very rarely recognizes group rights, though there are rare exceptions, like Federal Indian Law (and its recognition of aspects of tribal law) and a few non-precedential accommodations such as the "Amish exceptionalism" regarding compulsory education.[56]

More recently, the most dramatic developments have occurred with Amazonian ayahuasca churches who have won blockbuster victories at the federal level, including a unanimous decision in their favor by the US Supreme Court. In *Gonzales v. O Centro Espírita Beneficente União do Vegetal* (2005), the eponymous Peruvian ayahuasca church, "UDV," sought relief from federal drug enforcement under the Religious Freedom Restoration Act of 1993 (RFRA), a federal statute that was enacted in response to a previous Court decision, *Employment Division v. Smith* (1990), an Oregon case that found against Native American state employees (who were using peyote in a sacramental context) and therefore allowed the state to prohibit their peyote use.[57] *Smith*'s rationale was that Free Exercise rights did not justify a special exemption from "generally applicable" drug laws; the governmental interest in controlling (allegedly) dangerous drugs trumped individual free exercise rights. The point of the RFRA was to augment free exercise rights in order to correct this, mostly by requiring the government to adhere to "strict scrutiny," a very high constitutional bar requiring it to establish a compelling state interest *and* that the law or policy in question is narrowly tailored to achieve that end. In addition to generating many attestations of Rastafarianism from federal prisoners wanting access to cannabis (some of them sincere, some of them not), the RFRA ended up resoundingly protecting the ayahuasca churches. From a pro-psychedelics point of view, this ended up as a happy example of the often unanticipated consequences of legislation: in part because it did not seem "dangerous" and presented a low risk of "diversion" (i.e., a leakage of the ayahuasca into the surrounding community), the UDV Church won the case and is now allowed to hold its sacraments in peace.[58] The *UDV* ruling was quickly followed by a lower federal court case, *Church of Holy Light of Queen v. Mukasey* (2008), involving another ayahuasca church, the Brazilian Santo Daime Church, a syncretistic blend of Christian and indigenous Amazonian religions. Here, on the basis of the *UDV* decision, the Church also allowed the Santo Daime congregants an exemption from federal drug laws for sacramental use. Combined with the peyote exemptions, there is now a clear federal legal trend in favor of indigenous groups' religious free exercise regarding traditional plant-based entheogens. There are intriguing stirrings at the state level as well that could bear watching, as exemplified in a 2020 New Hampshire State Supreme Court case allowing hallucinogenic mushroom use on indigenous religious freedom grounds.[59]

Matters could get even more interesting on this front. Philosophically, the way is wide open for further free exercise concessions in the direction of sincere entheogenic use to be extended to the non-indigenous. That an argument is philosophically attractive is, admittedly, no guarantee that it will be adopted by judges. Hardly. But it is possible. First, as partially noted, and like most indigenous religious traditions, both the Santo Daime and UDV Churches are syntheses of indigenous *and* Christian beliefs. And the guarantees of the Free Exercise Clause are in theory not supposed to be contingent upon a judgment concerning the truth or falsity of a religious claim. This is associated with a broad reading of the Constitution's Article VI Religious Test Clause that prohibits religious requirements or "tests" for public office.[60] Relevantly, the Supreme Court has interpreted this to mean that, while courts can decide on the *sincerity* of a religious belief, they must refrain from passing judgment on its *validity*, reasoning that "it is not for the Court to say that the religious beliefs of the plaintiffs are mistaken or unreasonable."[61] The government is thus constitutionally prohibited from making a substantive determination on the truth of religious doctrine, no matter how outlandish it may seem to non-adherents. This is only reasonable, as on their face and shorn of convention and familiarity, most mainstream religious doctrines are objectively outlandish as well, and all of them started out at some point as minority, even heretical, doctrines at odds with contemporaneous societal norms. The prohibition on making truth determinations about religious claims is obviously important for psychedelics-using religionists because of how "weird" they are bound to seem to the mainstream. This degree of judicial deference represents a very significant legal concession and a major potential shelter for emergent belief systems.

Despite validity judgments being off the juridical table, however, much can fall under the "sincerity" determination. Even if one is wholly opposed to drug prohibitions in general, it is understandable why some sincerity criterion is necessary, for this is an area of law encompassing much more than just entheogen use. Religion is listed as a "suspect class" in civil rights law, for example, right alongside race, ethnicity, and national origin (meaning it is singled out by federal statute as a group of special legal concern because of a history of discrimination).[62] And, even apart from civil rights law, there is a long jurisprudential history concerning religious accommodations across a wide of range of issues: from exemptions to having to say the Pledge of Allegiance, to the "expressive association" rights of religious groups to control their own message, to the aforementioned Amish exemption from compulsory education, to the conferring of conscientious objector status vis-à-vis military service, to certain contexts of parental rights—and many others.[63] It is not just about drug possessors claiming that cannabis is their religion to get out of a pot bust or 1960s hippies claiming LSD is sacred to them (though it has been that, too, as in scores of cases of psychedelic "outlaw churches" since the 1960s).[64] There are many pressing legal contexts where it is important to be able to determine if a religious claim is sincerely held and, by extension, whether the collective claim of a putative "church" represents an actual religion.

But how can "religion" be defined for legal purposes? Obviously, it is difficult. And our courts have a history of stumbling when attempting to arrive at defensible definitions of key contested concepts, perhaps most notoriously emblematized in Justice Potter Stewart's quip about pornography that "I know it when I see it," a statement Stewart himself meant to be tantamount to giving up on a definition.[65]

Unlike Stewart on pornography, though, there is a game attempt on the federal record regarding "religion." Having represented entheogenic churches in litigation, attorney George Lake argues that the fullest operative legal definition of a bona fide "religion" is found in a lower federal court case from Wyoming, *United States v. Meyers* (1995), where a defendant's idiosyncratic "Church of Marijuana" was ruled not to rise to the level of a religion under the RFRA.[66] What is interesting about *Meyers* is not so much the judgment against the church as it is the criteria the court used in determining whether or not the church was sincerely religious. (David Meyers and his cohort lost the case on the grounds that they were deemed a "philosophy or a way of life" rather than an actual religion.)[67] These criteria are known as the "*Meyers* factors," which, as Lake indicates, should be considered as "guideposts" rather than a "bright-line" test. They comprise a long self-explanatory qualifying list regarding a would-be religion's belief system, including the presence of ultimate ideas, metaphysical beliefs, a moral or ethical system, and the belief system's comprehensiveness.[68] There is also a broad category outlining the "accoutrements of religion" that queries the presence of such items as a "founder, prophet or teacher," "important writings," "gathering places," keepers of knowledge," "ceremonies and rituals," "holidays," "appearance and clothing," and several more.[69] The *Meyers* court also makes clear that none of these factors is dispositive and there is no set threshold for inclusion; it is a judgment call where the threshold to validate a religious claim under the RFRA seems to be the presence of at least several and perhaps most of these items.[70] The *Meyers* criteria are meant to exclude "purely personal, political, ideological or secular beliefs" such as political ideologies (e.g., communism, fascism) or philosophical schools of moral thought (e.g., Kantianism, utilitarianism) or other belief systems that do not typically share many of the looked-for attributes. Lake also cautions that overly ludic presentations whose *raison d'être* seems mostly to consist of mocking established religions and mores are also unlikely to be looked upon favorably as bona fide religions: "I have seen instances where certain organizations which use psychedelic or entheogenic sacraments and claiming to be religious, go out of their way to mock other religious institutions and it never bodes well for them in court."[71] One should note that the US Supreme Court has not to date endorsed the *Meyers* framework, but it is currently being used elsewhere in the system for adjudicating RFRA claims. It stands as probably the most comprehensive attempt thus far legally to define "religion" and distinguish it from other belief formations.

The legal realities are important because they often powerfully shape religious adherents' beliefs. There is nothing "fake" about this; all religious traditions represent complex cultural inheritances that reflect particular histories and societal battles—theological, martial, legal, etc.—over their respective contents and definitions. "Purity" with any kind of tradition is an illusion. "Creationism," for example, is a doctrine claiming scientific support for the biblical account of the origins of human beings and the universe from the Old Testament's book of Genesis. And it certainly exists as a doctrine with adherents. But the label "creationism" was created as a legal strategy in the twentieth century to challenge the dominance of Darwinian evolution in American school science curricula; it was in a sense a legal fiction.[72] Yet many fundamentalist Christians in the 1970s and beyond came to see themselves as fervent "creationists" in a way that was strongly intertwined with their faith. Though they staunchly believed in the Genesis creation account, nobody in medieval times identified as a "creationist." In a very different context, the Native American Church also arose in part as a cultural, political, and legal project to open a protected space for indigenous people to be able to revive their ancient traditions and simultaneously pursue DEA exemptions for their sacramental use of peyote.[73] The peyote use thus needed to "fit"—and continue to fit—into the relevant legal status quo (viz., Free Exercise Clause jurisprudence, federal statutes like the RFRA) in order for it to continue to be practiced freely. If it were to need to go underground, like it had in the past (and many other religions have done in history), that necessity would shape its religious practices as well.

With contemporary psychedelics, the legal landscape seems to be tilting toward greater regulatory permissiveness, in terms of both research approvals and outright legalization (within a regulatory regime) in certain jurisdictions. This combines with the already existing entheogenic rights for indigenous religious groups I have been describing with the NAC and UDV et al. This religious avenue toward legalization, I think, has a high potential to be expanded in the US, given its religion clause jurisprudence, and it is likely to play a major role in shaping the entheogenic envelopment for a very long time. Particularly significant is that, as noted, *both* of the legally victorious ayahuasca churches, UDV and Santo Daime, present syntheses of indigenous *and Christian* beliefs. Along with the courts' reluctance to judge the truth of religious beliefs, to refrain from functioning as "oracles of theological verity," this would seem, in theory at least, to leave the door ajar for sincere religious formations *of whatever tradition* who have genuinely integrated entheogens.[74] This would be the case particularly for those with the "look" and trappings of traditional religions, along lines suggested by the *Meyers* factors. Despite organized religion's demise in the modern world, the entheogenic envelopment may yet have a bright above-ground future.

3. The Intellectual Envelopment (Academic, Artistic, Psychonautical)

> Telos: scientific knowledge, intellectual discovery, artistic expression
>
> Platforms: laboratory, studio, miscellaneous individualized venues

Distinguishable from the therapeutic and entheogenic, the next major category of envelopment contains a congeries of sub-categories where intellective and aesthetic endeavors are center stage. Particularly if one considers the long span of human history, this is, as far as numbers of individuals involved, quantitatively by far the rarest envelopment of them all. But it has been disproportionately influential, particularly in recent times, as the last century has seen robust engagement with psychedelics from within a range of disciplinary perspectives. (As noted earlier, there was a long previous tradition of self-experimentation with psychoactive substances, exemplified by William James and nitrous oxide.) Though intellectuals, particularly scientists, sometimes work in groups, the psychedelic explorations in this envelopment tend to be highly individualized and, at the higher end, result in scientific studies and other academic (e.g., philosophical) as well as popular publications, including those of journalists and unaffiliated psychonauts such as Michael Pollan and Terence McKenna.

Although not often considered as part of the modern psychedelia pantheon, included in this group is perhaps the contemporary period's purest exemplar of the intellectual envelopment: the bestselling author, neuroscientist, and clinician Oliver Sacks. It is difficult to think of anyone in history with his combined skillset of scientific knowledge, clinical experience, writerly talent, and, most germane for present purposes, psychonautical zeal for self-experimentation (and, frankly, ready access to drugs). For decades, as documented in the autobiographical chapter on "Altered States" in his 2012 book *Hallucinations*, Sacks self-dosed with a vast range of substances, from classic psychedelics like LSD and mescaline to opioids, chloral hydrate (or, more precisely, the delirium tremens associated with its withdrawal), amphetamines, a range of Parkinson's drugs, and many others.[75] Sacks's own trip reports—often with drugs not often thought of as "psychedelics" such as morphine that are nonetheless potentially highly psychedelic—makes much of the reading from Erowid and the other dedicated repositories seem positively tame by comparison. In one among many wild examples, Sacks decides to try a high dose of Artane, a deliriant associated with belladonna and used to treat Parkinson's. In the truest psychonautical spirit of the intellectual envelopment he asks himself, "But would a delirium be fun? Or informative? Would one be in a position to observe the aberrant functioning of one's brain—to appreciate its wonder?"[76] The result? After a series of extreme "true hallucinations" (i.e., wherein, unlike most classic psychedelic trips, one does not "know" at some level that one is hallucinating), in veritable *Alice in Wonderland* fashion, he is greeted with a verbal "Hello!" by a spider on his kitchen wall: "I said, 'Hello, yourself,' and with this we started a conversation, mostly on rather technical matters of analytic philosophy. Perhaps this direction was suggested by the spider's opening comment: did I think that Bertrand Russell had exploded Frege's paradox?"[77] Sacks admits he eventually sought therapy for his raging drug use, so there are additional issues at play for him personally, but he relates that his main motivation for self-experimenting with such a wide range of powerful substances was his intellectual curiosity about their qualia *as* a scientist and clinician, to understand what is going on in the mind and to help his patients. Although, as a physician, his professional duties are officially within the medical frame, Sacks's zeal for self-experimentation makes him a perfect exemplar of the driving impetus of the intellectual envelopment: pure curiosity.

Sacks and his ilk are very rare, though. By far the most copious instances of this category are of the envelopment's aesthetic branch and are to be found the art and music worlds. Music especially should be stressed. It is an important component of just about all trip experiences across all envelopments (except perhaps those of very short duration like inhaled DMT) and, from the Grateful Dead onward, have undoubtedly furnished the most culturally recognized symbols of psychedelia. Modern psychedelia would be unrecognizable without the musical currents that have flowed in and among its every facet. As mentioned previously, even Johns Hopkins has its suggested trip accompaniment playlists, and there is clinical evidence emerging, as one would expect from overwhelming popular experience on this matter, that psychedelics and music are mutually reinforcing.[78] Many artists might see their psychedelic forays as simultaneously spiritual or recreational, if not therapeutic as well. But, to the extent that there is something distinctive about their enterprises as aesthetic endeavors—from the "concept albums" of Pink Floyd or the Beatles to the more direct explorations of psychedelic states in psychotrance and the paintings of Alex and Allyson Grey—their skilled innovativeness within their artform places them also in the intellectual sphere. In fact, the Greys, probably the best-known psychedelic artists, are in addition a perfect illustration of an intentional melding of artistic and entheogenic envelopments with their founding of the Chapel of Sacred Mirrors in upstate New York, a nonprofit museum and gallery that features their "visionary art" and "combines elements of a cultural institution and interfaith church."[79] Such hybrid artists' inclusion in the intellectual envelopment is a reminder that the qualifier "intellectual" should not be reduced to the cognitive focus of scientists of philosophers and must also include aesthetic forms of discovery that are more emotive and embodied, and easily graftable onto entheogenic and other projects.

Most of this book's introduction consists of accounts of denizens of the intellectual envelopment. To avoid repetition, I will refer the reader back to that section for its canvas of significant figures across the three psychedelia waves of writers, artists, scientists, psychonauts, and others.

A few clarifying remarks are in order, though.

First, in identifying individuals as, in a way, *intellectual* seekers, that is, those whose tendency is predominantly along those lines, as previously indicated, I do not mean to suggest that they might not simultaneously experience psychedelics across other envelopments as well, crossing envelopment lines like the Greys. For example, Rick Strassman, the pioneering DMT research psychiatrist at the University of New Mexico, clearly has a place in the therapeutic envelopment as a clinician exploring psychedelics for patient welfare, the more purely intellectual envelopment in his research on the nature of DMT. But Strassman also has an entheogenic stress, especially in his later work regarding his personal spiritual journey, as documented in his studies of psychedelics and the Jewish prophetic tradition of the Old Testament.[80] Envelopments are not bright-line delineations so much as they are denotations of *telic tendencies* characterizing psychedelic usage. And since they are reflective of the width of the settings in which psychedelics are experienced, the subjective experience of most psychedelic trips is unlikely to be wholly single-minded. Though the conventional wisdom that set and setting are crucial is certainly correct, psychedelic experience is multivariant and dynamic and unfolds in ways that are always to a degree unpredictable. (This unpredictability is true about their predictability, too; along with all the trips that veer off course, it is also the case that plenty of them *are* predictable and do indeed unfold according to expectations, particularly for psychedelic veterans.) A lot can happen during an LSD trip of a dozen hours. There is more than ample time for the trip to differentiate itself along multiple envelopment axes.

Bache's intensive self-study of his seventy trips, *LSD and the Mind of the Universe*, is a good example of this. Across these many journeys, there are wellness aspects, like in his trip reports, where he describes his own personal experiences of the Grofian "perinatal domain" and discusses LSD's "healing energy" quite a bit.[81] Bache also shares spiritual insights connected to quasi-religious sentiments, as when he relates that his "original project was spiritual awakening" and when larger themes of "creation" and such are addressed as major themes.[82] And throughout, he wrestles with philosophical problems as an academic philosopher with the intent of writing a philosophical book that is conversant with canonical philosophers. Bache goes as far as to credit LSD with enabling him to "let go of my conventional academic training and embrace psychedelics as a new method of philosophical inquiry."[83] Like the Greys, Bache's autobiographical panorama illustrates how it is possible to be thoroughly interpellated across several envelopments simultaneously. Though the predominant envelopment is clearly identifiable in most cases, envelopments should be conceived as *tendencies* rather than fixed regions with sharp borders; there is no reason for it to be all-or-nothing. In fact, as mentioned earlier, it would probably be best to describe discrete instances of psychedelic experience as having an *envelopment profile*, where envelopment proportions could be identified comparatively. So, one might describe a trip as set primarily in a therapeutic envelopment but with religious or spiritual elements, or, like Bache's LSD series, a philosophical envelopment with strong entheogenic (individual seeker) aspects.

General qualifications and hedges aside, within the intellectual envelopment there are many illustrative archetypes from which to choose for heuristic purposes. With regard to scientific inquiry, beginning with chemists, there is a fairly obvious trio of "patron scientific saints" of psychedelia across the three waves: Albert Hofmann, Alexander Shulgin, and David Nichols. Hofmann's famous 1943 bicycle ride home from his lab—celebrated on April 19 as "Bicycle Day"—is still the most enduring icon of intellectual envelopment in this disciplinary sphere. Aside from its obvious discovery aspects, what makes Hofmann emblematic is that the setting of the original LSD trip is conducted in the venerable tradition of scientific self-experimentation; Hofmann wasn't just observing other people take LSD, he was conducting the inquiry on *himself*.[84] Shulgin, too, is candid on this matter regarding MDMA and many other substances.[85] (Though he speaks of having tried mescaline, Nichols, who has been described as "the greatest living psychedelic chemist," is tight-lipped on this point, however, as his pharmacological research at Purdue was conducted according to far stricter Institutional Review Board protocols where investigator self-experimentation with pharmaceuticals would be considered outside the norm.)[86] These figures represent, of course, the highest echelons of the intellectual/scientific envelopment, as their products are groundbreaking and historically significant research. Most intellectual envelopments are proportionately more modest but, in essence, if the primary telos of a trip is the discovery of knowledge about the world (as opposed to, say, a vaguer desire for personal "self-knowledge" in a therapeutic or wellness vein), then it is distinguishable as its own unique envelopment setting.

Along with chemists, there are academicians of other "hard" scientific disciplines, including research by brain scientists across a range of sub-disciplines attempting to understand the nature of psychedelics at the molecular level and map the neural receptors, mechanisms, and pathways of their action. If first-wave psychedelic scientific research was strongly characterized by psychiatry within the therapeutic envelopment (e.g., psychiatrists Stanislav Grof and Humphrey Osmond, the coiner of the term "psychedelic"), the third-wave psychedelic "renaissance," while strongly powered by clinical research as well (e.g., psychiatrist Roland Griffiths), has also seen an explosion of research productivity in neuroscience proper. A National Public Radio story about the annual meeting of the Society of Neuroscience, Neuroscience 2022, reported that "the appetite for psychedelic research permeated the sessions, discussions, and even after-hours barroom talk—drawing in researchers, neuroscientists, companies, reporters, and advocates alike."[87] A great deal of basic knowledge is now being amassed concerning the physical nature and mechanisms of psychedelics, and while it is presumably comparatively rarer actually to ingest psychedelics for insight in this area, it is clearly among the desiderata of certain scientists to understand them at the molecular level—quite apart from whatever may be their curative capabilities for specific maladies. To understand more about the hard science of psychedelics is to understand more about our brains and bodies *simpliciter*. Adjacent inquires in the biological sciences should not be forgotten either, as figures like the earlier-mentioned ethnobotanist Dennis McKenna and mycologist Paul Stamets (both of whom have publicly discussed having taken psychedelics, at least in part in order to enhance their knowledge about them) have played outsized roles in enriching the knowledge base of psychedelics and helping to foster vibrant and multidisciplinary contexts of inquiry around them.

In addition to scientific work, psychedelics as an area of study admits of an indeterminate number of additional disciplines, and there are now strong research programs across the social sciences and humanities as well. (This book itself attempts a contribution in the fields of philosophy and education.) Basic research is of course highly relevant to the medical-therapeutic and even the entheogenic envelopments but, ultimately, the intellectual envelopment is to a much greater extent driven by a telos of "knowledge for its own sake" than it is by the practical goal of healing or, certainly, making pharmaceutical profits or catalyzing non-naturalistic spiritual encounters.

With regard to the structuration of the intellectual envelopment, a "reality check" sort of consideration is in order at this point, as well. As in the medical-therapeutic envelopment, in the intellectual envelopment, particularly in the hard sciences which requires costly labs and research teams to function, financial interests of various kinds inevitably also shape this area, from government research grants to a range of private grants and investments (some from for-profit corporations). The attachment of financial stakes and the distributive realities of capital have a way of altering mentalities (think how the vast sums and market exigencies associated with alcohol and tobacco shape those experiences), and one of the great questions for the third wave is how it will be shaped by the mainstreaming of psychedelics and their entrance into legal markets. Primarily a non-profit research and education outfit, MAPS currently exemplifies this ambivalence, as it seems poised to morph into something more like a commercial corporate structure dealing with expected revenue streams in the wake of an anticipated FDA approval for MDMA therapy.[88]

Further aspects of aesthetic production are worth attention. It is common for artists, musicians, writers, and creative types of all kinds to engage with psychedelics as part of their creative process, perhaps to get themselves out of mental ruts, disturb conventional patterns of thinking, or simply find new sources of inspiration. Psychedelics seem always to have had a special appeal for intensely creative types and there are countless instances where they have been so acknowledged. Entering into a psychedelic trip with an intention to enhance one's artistic insight and perspective is very different from doing so mainly to seek a cure for a specific problem or for a religious or devotional purpose (though these all can intertwine). In addition to the artists themselves, art and music are universally appreciated as integral aspects of psychedelia. During the pendency of a trip, it is very common—to the point of expected—for music to provide a background and/or focus and, quite commonly, an emotional ballast throughout. I have always felt this latter to be one of the reasons for the Grateful Dead's enduring popularity in the psychedelic world. From the outside, their music is pretty ordinary—an inventive synthesis of elements and charismatic performers, but nothing startling or groundbreaking from a musical perspective. But from the inside point of view of the tripper (this is something one may need to experience directly), the Grateful Dead have a soothing "yes, you're tripping, but just relax and everything's going to be alright" vibe that is demonstrably capable of bringing people together and helping individuals through difficult moments. Music is obviously a matter of taste and some have negative reactions to the Grateful Dead—and some enjoy them for reasons having nothing to do with psychedelics. But their undeniably *psychedelic* appeal has been evident to millions. There are of course many other popular musicians very heavily associated with psychedelia (e.g., Jimi Hendrix, Donovan, The Beatles, Pink Floyd, Led Zeppelin, Tool), and their output was a major hallmark of second-wave culture. But psychedelic music is not just an artifact of the past; it is still a popular musical category that shows no signs of slowing. To take just one example, there are many contemporary playlists for "psytrance," a subgenre of psychedelic music that diverges sharply from the Grateful Dead and the big rock bands of the '60s and '70s. Originating in Goa, India, psytrance and its variations are specifically designed to heighten psychedelic experience, with its weird, otherworldly ambiances floating alongside driving quasi-tribal rhythms and fast repetitive beats. With celebrating psychedelia forthrightly as its *raison d'être*, psytrance anchors large, dedicated festivals and "gatherings" worldwide that advertise themselves as offering "an immersive and transformative experience for all those who attend."[89] Psytrance is very far from one's parents' (or grandparents') second-wave nostalgia, well illustrating that psychedelic music is not just old-time "acid rock" and that it can dramatically change and adapt like other musical styles. And its very clear purpose to its devotees is the enhancing of psychedelic trips in a communal setting.

Also fitting within the intellectual envelopment in the aesthetic mode are many visual artists. This category would include painters, in addition to the Greys, such as Amanda Sage, Martina Hoffmann, Robert Venosa, Barbara Takenaga, and many others, whose works seem clearly to have drawn inspiration from psychedelic mindscapes.[90] With even farther public reach than traditional media and artistic venues (e.g., galleries, museums), there also now exists an artistic community of replicators whose ingenious digital art convincingly simulates the visual aspects of psychedelic trips with uncanny verisimilitude, including highly informative comparative presentations—that is, what it looks like to be on lower and higher doses of different compounds. Examples may be found on YouTube channels like @LokaVision, @hypnagogist-art, @SymmetricVision, and @dmtenlightenment. As far as visuals go, these are just about the closest one could get to tripping without actually ingesting a drug. (For a sober glimpse of what a psychedelic trip looks like, these channels are the place to go.) As previously observed, visual art has long had a special pedagogical place in psychedelia, not only because most psychedelics are highly visual, but because the medium helps preserve elements of the psychedelic experience through time, potentially aiding the durability of any lessons learned. This is sometimes true of writing and, of course, music, but there is an instantaneousness to visual art—in both its still and its cinematographic forms—that can, at a glance, more directly call to mind an often elusive and fleeting past vision, particularly one originally encountered in the course of a short-acting substances like DMT; the visual representations function to elongate the psychedelic experience temporally by providing periodic mementos that one may encounter at planned or random moments. (This very temporal extension is why longer-duration ayahuasca is often thought to be superior for providing insight than inhaled DMT, as it gives more time for an experiencer to learn and process trip information—and also why there is high current interest in extended-state "DMTx" drip injections.)[91] Ready reminders like these can be highly significant to psychedelically inclined individuals, who may adorn their living spaces with such artworks, owing to how easily trip details can be forgotten, a commonly reported regretful refrain. One wonders if a similar function was performed by ancient indigenous art, as far back as visionary cave art at places like Chauvet in southeastern France, and the even older rock art of South Africa, with its psychedelic-seeming entoptic designs.[92] But one need not go so far back for examples. There are also inventive and riveting psychedelic visions depicted in contemporary indigenous art, such as the intricate and colorful "yarn paintings" of the Huichol people of central Mexico, that present psychedelic panoramas of local nature and everyday life, interwoven (literally) with religious imagery.[93]

In addition to the musicians and artists, there are scores of writers who have looked specifically to psychedelics for inspiration and integrated their experiences into their work, such as Aldous Huxley, William S. Burroughs, Hunter S. Thompson, Allen Ginsberg, and the contemporary Taiwanese American novelist Tao Lin, to name just a few. Lin happens to be an effusive admirer of perhaps the most iconic nonfiction writer within the intellectual envelopment, Terence McKenna (also discussed in the introduction and elsewhere), who is hard to categorize but might best be labeled as "psychonautical," because he exudes such zeal for interior exploration and reflection on what it all might mean. For Lin, McKenna's "language was a mix of idiomatic, literary, poetic, popular, obscure, crass, ventriloquial, scientific and academic."[94] McKenna is also just plain funny, and audience laughter is a constant presence in his recorded lectures. McKenna exemplifies the intellectual envelopment because, across his voluminous books and recorded talks, he does not much emphasize specific healing or wellness outcomes or religious and spiritual realizations, as those terms are conventionally understood. He is more a psychedelic *raconteur*, displaying, as Davis puts it, a "curious blend of occult anti-rationalism and rational technophilia."[95] In a word, I would call McKenna a *speculative* thinker who utilizes insights from a range of academic disciplines (and much else) in order to explore his many flashes of psychedelic insight. The particular views for which he is most known—for example, the stoned ape theory (also mentioned earlier)—are, in my view, less important than what his body of work represents overall: a testament to how, in the best case, curiosity and psychedelics can combine to fire the imagination, engender wonder, and promote a zeal for learning and discovery—all with a light touch and plenty of humor. Along with the other key figures mentioned, Terence McKenna is definitely a patron saint of the intellectual envelopment and almost certainly its most prominent modern influencer.

4. The Recreational Envelopment (Individuals, Friend Groups, Festivals, Raves)

> Telos: curiosity, participatory cohesion, love and friendship, fun
>
> Venues: everyday private or public spaces, event spaces, nature

This leaves modern times' most common psychedelic envelopment: recreational or informal. Here, there may certainly be intellectual and aesthetic inspiration, spiritual insight, and therapeutic/wellness effects, but the primary motivational expectations are not fixed on these. Distinguishable from the tendency of the other envelopments toward an aura of self-importance concerning their healing mission and/or depth of insight, there persists an entirely different world in which psychedelics are enjoyed without all the portentousness. A percentage of "bad trips" and anxious individuals aside, amid the dominance of medical and spiritual discourse, it is easy to forget that *one of the best-kept secrets about psychedelics is simply that they can be great fun.* A group of friends might find themselves beset with constant laughter during an evening on mushrooms or LSD; in the right situation it can all be highly amusing. Some might just sit around watching TV or playing a video game, activities that might seem wasteful and superficial to those inclined to scold. But who is to say that the amusing and diverting qualities of psychedelics are necessarily morally suspect? It would be a bit like saying laughter should be forbidden because there is suffering in the world. Individuals lead different lives at different paces and maybe, sometimes, there can be too much "meaning" and heaviness, to the point that a cheap and colorful respite from the weight of the world is welcome. As Hart emphasizes, there is a deeply ingrained belief in the American psyche that the Declaration of Independence's "pursuit of happiness" is not just about grudgingly tolerating others, but it expresses a basic and universal *right* to such pursuit (subject to other pursuers' identical rights), particularly concerning the choice to alter one's own consciousness.[96] In the overall scheme of one's life, perhaps exploring different ways to make vivid memories with friends is as inherently valuable as anything else in our search for what Aristotle terms *eudaimonia* ("the good life"), which he recognizes as a human being's highest purpose and the animator of any sense of ethics. If psychedelics can play a part by amplifying a portion of humanity's quest for *eudaimonia* through fostering good times and intersubjective connection, who is to say that is a misuse of them? Obviously, this is not to suggest that there are neither ill-advised uses of psychedelics nor risks inherent in ingesting these powerful drugs. It is just that an individual's risk-reward calculations are always a function of what one considers the "reward," a determination that cannot *itself* be made rationally. (More on this in the next chapter on Hume's notion of rationality.) In fact, as previously discussed, one special quality of psychedelics as tools is that they do not so simply aid in the straight-line achievement of predetermined goals; they are capable sometimes of helping to alter and reorder the goals *themselves*. Trip reports are replete with people claiming that they emerged with a greater understanding of what was really valuable and what was not, separating the wheat of life from its chaff, and providing greater clarity about general priorities.

Most take psychedelics not in clinical trials, labs, churches, or studios, but at home by themselves or with a few friends. (If they are safety-minded, maybe someone is designated as a "trip sitter," much as conscientious drinkers will include a designated driver for a night out.) They are doing it out of curiosity and a sense of adventure or just to add some needed weirdness or edge to a day or night out. They might be a couple looking for intense intimacy. Or they may be headed to a "scene" venue where it is an expected part of a full experience. Decades ago, this might have meant an acid test in a San Francisco warehouse, as famously depicted in Tom Wolfe's *The Electric Kool-Aid Acid Test*, or on the road for all the festivities surrounding a Grateful Dead concert, or a few days at a giant outdoor festival like Woodstock.[97] More recently, it might mean a glam mega-event like the (now) upscale Burning Man festival in the Nevada desert, an all-night dance party or maybe an excursion into nature at a planned wilderness retreat. In the recreational envelopment, the world is one's oyster and there are about as many settings as there are individual trippers.

That voluntary collectivities have such persistence as psychedelic settings is an interesting phenomenon that likely speaks to deep intersubjective needs that can be enhanced by psychedelics (the very same needs that are dangerously divertible into the cult problem). To use the analytic language of Sartre, a group that does psychedelics together often seems ontologically "fused" in the sense that they adopt an especially strong collective sense of identity—they become a "we"—in a more thoroughgoing way than if they were more casually inhabiting the same physical space (under normal conditions where individual minds wander this way and that); it is a way to have an intensely focused *shared* experience with others, including sometimes large gatherings, where individuals are no longer identifiable as such and "the crowd" becomes felt as a first-person "we."[98] Consider the mindset reportedly developed among Ken Kesey and the Merry Pranksters, among the most influential progenitors of sixties acid culture: "In 1964, after their first run across the States in their famous psychedelic bus, the Pranksters began to feel the effects of their daily diet of LSD. They felt they were acquiring strange powers and developing a group mind. . . . As other alternative groups in the sixties would experience, a weird gestalt began to evolve among the Pranksters: they began to feel their separate psyches were fusing into a single collective consciousness with superhuman powers."[99] The Pranksters and others may certainly have been delusional about their "powers," but the point about their envelopment is that they *thought* and *felt* it to be so; their subjective experiences were powerfully shaped by their conviction that they had grown together into a larger fused "we."

Psychedelics are not the *only* catalysts that can coalesce an assemblage into a fused group, and Sartre's primary examples are drawn from political contexts like the shared purpose animating the stormers of the Bastille during the French Revolution.[100] Sufficient intersubjective intensity can sometimes also be observed during religious revivals, a recent example provided by the 2023 spontaneous "outpouring" of religious fervor among college students and visitors at Asbury Theological Seminary in Kentucky, where many participants claimed to feel a divine spirit moving among them for days on end.[101] Rationalists may be quick to dismiss religious revivalisms like this—despite their regular occurrence and influence in history—as mere mass delusions. But this would be to miss the point: the particularities of their theological trappings vary, but, parallel with the deep first-person meaning of the Cartesian cogito, they are indubitably powerful experiences that are actually being undergone by the participants (however those experiences might be described subsequently) rather than staged deceptions. Someone actually drunk is different from someone acting drunk, regardless of the eventual epistemological verdict of the former's at-the-time sodden claims and self-image. One also sees degrees of group fusion in many other social contexts: music concerts, sporting events, military operations, etc. In their own way, psychedelics do seem to be able to function as relatively rapid catalysts for group fusions like these. This may be one reason raves and similar events remain popular, with accoutrements like glow sticks enhancing participants' feeling that they are—for a few shining hours of ecstatic communion—part of something larger and more fulfilling than their isolated selves.[102] (Plus, glow sticks look cool.) In these cases, hypertrophic identification finds its tether, on the above terms, in a Sartrean group fusion. Yes, when this occurs in the recreational realm it appears to be "merely" fun and frivolous. But those surface appearances do not lessen the fact that they are also deeply human. Although designed as an outlet for youthful exuberance, in their communal nature, "awe-inspiring" and "prosocial" raves are probably closer than most contemporary settings to the oldest known contexts of large-scale ceremonial psychedelic use, from Eleusis to Mesoamerica.[103] Psychedelics' ludic and social aspects should not be underestimated; profundity need not always come wrapped in "seriousness" and hushed tones.

Philosophical Pathway #3: Gadamer

> Every experience worthy of the name thwarts an expectation.
> —Hans-Georg Gadamer, *Truth and Method*, 356

The REBUS Model

The notion of envelopment gives greater specification to the concept of setting or context. It is premised on the assumption that, although—like other brain phenomena—they obviously possess material mechanisms of action, the most important aspects of psychedelics are how they are *experienced* via the subjective qualia they induce. This is not penicillin, where the subjective experience is largely irrelevant. Psychedelics definitely have a range of somatic effects (e.g., LSD can cause blood pressure to rise, ayahuasca can induce vomiting) and perhaps neural plasticity might someday be perfectly mapped in terms of its physiological manifestations.[104] It is also possible that non-experiential, non-hallucinatory "psychedelics" could be developed, although it remains an open question whether these would actually *be* psychedelics and remain useful in therapeutic contexts (where patient qualia associated with actually undergoing a psychedelic trip may well be integral to recovery process).[105] There remains disagreement about precisely how context-dependent is psychedelic experience—there may be instances of context independence in this respect, such as a tendency toward the promotion of certain holistic metaphysical views about interconnectedness and the weird commonalities among DMT entities reported across users, though this latter is much contested—it may be that chimeras like McKenna's "machine elves" have permeated the zeitgeist to the point that they are conjured out of tripper expectations. Despite debates about particulars, though, as Timmermann et al. suggest, the proposition "that context may have an enduring influence" on both the quality of psychedelic experiences and their aftereffects is not really in doubt.[106]

As an ineluctable component of "context," the particular envelopment *matters* for the nature of the experience, just as does history, culture, socioeconomic status, setting in the traditional sense (viz., immediate surroundings), an individual's psychological makeup and life circumstances, etc. Because of their differing *teloi*, expectations, and other social determinants, undergoing psychedelic treatment as part of therapy, as a moment in a communal religious ceremony, out of curiosity about the human brain, or at a summer psytrance festival are almost guaranteed to yield different experiential results from the same drug.[107] This is obvious in one respect because the settings are so different. But the notion of envelopment incorporates the deeper point about psychedelics that, especially at high doses, the conventional borders of the self almost always—at the very least—begin to blur. Via the hypertrophic identification process, in the first-person experiential sense, one melts into and/or merges into one's larger context such that one is more holistically *enveloped* in it; the ordinary separability of subject/object, figure/ground, unconscious/conscious, self/nature—and a host of other default dichotomies—start to appear as contingent, their assumed ontological status newly questionable. One's *Umwelt* horizons can be profoundly altered in a way that would be impossible if set and setting were neatly distinguishable. The idea of envelopment, then, represents psychedelics' own subjective tendency to meld set and setting into one another in a kind of Hegelian psychedelic dialectic where two ostensibly separable concepts are "raised up" (*aufgehoben*) into an incorporative third term that encompasses them both. Sometimes this Hegelian "logic" is taken in overly simple terms as "thesis-antithesis-synthesis," and it can be explained in highly obsfucatory terms (including by Hegel himself). Hegel's own more metaphorical explanation is far superior: "The bud disappears in the bursting-forth of the blossom, and one might say that the former is refuted by the latter; similarly, when the fruit appears, the blossom is shown up in its turn as a false manifestation of the plant, and the fruit now emerges as the truth of it instead. . . . Their fluid nature makes them moments of an organic unity in which they not only do not conflict, but in which each is as necessary as the other."[108] "Envelopment" captures this sense perfectly, I think; it is not a "refutation" of "set and setting," but grows out of the two terms as we come to see them as not exactly opposites but as living "moments" of a dynamic unity.

Heavy Hegelian weather aside, I would emphasize that "set and setting" remains a helpful construct for commonsense public messaging about how to optimize psychedelics and to use them safely. Theoretically, though, it is unsatisfying because it implies that mind and world are separable entities. This default dualistic conceit probably evolved because of its practical utility in everyday life, for example, enabling the realization of mistaken response to stimuli (i.e., reality-testing)—the sound over there was *not* in fact what I thought it was—and the recognition of the distinctiveness of individuals and their mental states within one's group, thus facilitating learning by trial and error as well as undergirding sociality—undoubtably it is a survival-positive metacognitive ability to be able to discern others' mental states such as potential aggression. However, one of the hallmarks of the classic psychedelics is that they promote connective and unitive states of mind that precisely *collapse* these everyday distinctions and assumptions into a smoother flow that, while disorienting, confusing, and sometimes scary, reveal that we are not, after all, so separable from others, nature, cosmos, and so on. Probably, moments of vision like this—whether they are labeled "mystical" or not—are survival positive too in that they can occasionally correct the default modes of experience—perhaps *literally*, in part by temporarily suppressing the brain's overseeing Default Mode Network (DMN)—and injecting a greater degree of situationally salutary flexibility. One might speculate that this is why many animals are commonly observed *intentionally* to "drug themselves" with psychoactive plants, not so much as a mental escape from unpleasant realities (this would seem rather survival negative; if a prey animal were woozy from eating magic mushrooms the ensuing temporary episode of incapacity would seem to invite predation) but as an enhancer of adaptability to environmental alterations ("environmental" in the broad sense of anything going on around them).[109] It would seem that, in principle, a highly dynamic brain system that, while not chaotic, is capable of both constructing *and* deconstructing experiential channels would be optimal. This is especially so given that the long span of history always sees massive environmental change for any category of creature and therefore the inability to adapt over time by definition entails extinction. *Umwelt* bubbles arise and are maintained but also, like actual bubbles, need a level of flexibility to expand, contract, reshape, etc., lest they pop.

This protean plasticity underwrites a cortical dynamism described as "entropic" by neuroscientists, in a usage of this term drawn from information theory concerning levels of uncertainty in packets of information, "the effect of noise in the channel" (itself conceived analogously to the second law of thermodynamics).[110] In the account given by Carhart-Harris et al., the "entropic brain" represents a state of "high disorder" when neural kinetic activity spikes from a baseline of normal everyday consciousness into an "elevated" state characterized by a blossoming of interconnectivity; established patterns of brain activity are disrupted and neural networks are reanimated and altered into new patterns.[111] Psychedelics are agents of brain entropy due to their ability to "disrupt stereotyped patterns of thought and behavior by disintegrating the patterns of activity upon which they rest," which is thought to be the basis for their therapeutic potential—given that many debilitating mental conditions have to do with stubborn rigidities of thought (e.g., PTSD, OCD, various self-image dysphorias).[112] Elsewhere, Carhart-Harris and K. J. Friston liken this entropic process to the annealing of metal (and other substrates) where heat is used to soften it into a more pliable state—a "hot state"—which represents a "window of plasticity" where it can be worked and then afterwards cooled back to its former rigidity.[113] As they put it: "As the acute drug effects begin to subside, the system (brain) will settle back into its default regimen of efficient free-energy minimization, mirrored by a renewed subjective sense of familiarity and assuredness, but may not return entirely as before."[114] Psychedelics thus create a kind of limited and temporary chaos in the brain, in the best case a salutary one, where mental ruts can be gotten out of, encrusted patterns altered, and new potential pathways forged.

But there is more. In an influential 2019 paper, Carhart-Harris and Friston describe what they call the "REBUS" model for how psychedelics work. "REBUS" is an acronym for "RElaxed Beliefs Under pSychedelics," designating their general theory of how psychedelics act on the brain. In a nutshell, they suppress or "relax" what neuroscientists call "high-level priors," meaning the basic and/or longstanding beliefs and assumptions that underlie one's worldview and outlook on life and the persistent habits and patterns of thinking and behavior that an individual has developed.[115] Psychedelics can act as if cracking up an ice jam made up of these high-level priors that then has the consequence of "liberating bottom-up information flow," that is, allowing for a new consideration of an upswell of neglected information and/or experiences.[116] With one's ordinarily governing assumptions quieted for a time, one is able to enjoy "at the subjective level . . . an increase in the richness of conscious experience."[117] One thinks of the common phenomenon on psychedelics of becoming fascinated with something previously not much noticed, as in Huxley's pants creases or a bee buzzing about the backyard. With the normal prejudices and prioritizations concerning what is significant and what is not suspended, one may indeed become less functional operationally (don't drive!), but one is simultaneously rendered more alive to a range of inputs than in one's normal state. (This is, by the way, a classic example of the Heideggerian reveal/conceal structural ambivalence of technology discussed in chapter 2.) The REBUS model is, I believe, fully consistent with my previous analysis (some of which is also drawn from Carhart-Harris's work) concerning epistemic loosening and hypertrophic identification, for example the emotional lability and psychic fragility that can be expected from going through the entropic hot state, which, of course, can be felt as exhilarating or as an ordeal, or both. Furthermore, something like the REBUS situation is clearly central to any meaningful learning and insight that may take place under psychedelics, not just for therapy patients but for *anyone*. As discussed, Socratic questioning functions in a highly analogous manner: in his unsettling quest for definitions, the old Drug Fish (as Socrates is described in the *Meno*) was in his own way aiming at "relaxing high-level priors" among his fellow Athenians to allow for an upsurge of new ideas, "and in so doing, promote an open, inquiring state of mind," "thereby enabling fresh perspectives to be entertained" where a certain mental "canalization" can be overcome.[118] That Socrates considered this gadfly task his life's sacred mission—and that he was executed for it—only shows how high the stakes can be.

For both the REBUS model and the Socratic method to induce learning, though, there is a silent partner that too often goes unacknowledged. Whatever metaphors one employs—entropy, annealing, plasticity, torpedo fish numbing, etc.—to create insight out of one's basic assumptions or high-level priors by altering them, adjusting their weight, discarding them, or whatever, *it is necessary for those prior assumptions to be there in the first place*. Socrates's challenges to conventional wisdom only function to the extent that his interlocutors possess a rich and accessible font of that very conventional wisdom from which they can draw. Otherwise, there would be nothing to challenge and no background knowledge out of which to grow and define insight. Insight is novelty, the new, and there is no "new" without juxtaposition with whatever might be the "old"; there could be no "out with the old and in with the new" if there were no "old" to throw out. Similarly, with the REBUS model and psychedelics, the relaxation of high-level priors presupposes a pre-existing and operant network of priors that can be relaxed. Though, ex hypothesi, they can become "overweighted" and hopefully slated for alteration or elimination, they also, overall, must provide a relatively stable and functional basis for organismic functionality. As Carhart-Harris and Friston well recognize, over-fluidity is just as much a problem as over-rigidity; some goldilocks level of plasticity is optimal and decidedly *not* one of the extremes; the problem with priors is that they can be *over*-weighted, not that they are weighted at all (which also implies that priors could sometimes be *under*-weighted too). So, a healthy nest of high-level priors would seem necessary to serve as a broad epistemological platform from which psychedelic-induced insights could launch. But how might such a platform of priors and its generative capacity be conceived?

Philosophical Hermeneutics Complements REBUS

I suggest that just such a conception is found in the tradition of philosophical hermeneutics associated with German philosopher Hans-Georg Gadamer (1900–2002). Hermeneutics has its roots in theological methodologies for interpreting sacred texts. Allegories are a common rhetorical device in the Old and New Testament and, since they are obviously (to most) not to be taken merely literally—which would bear very meager pedagogical fruit—there arises a need for understanding how to interpret such passages. Religious authorities thus have long used biblical hermeneutics to provide methods of justifiable interpretation of otherwise unclear texts and an authorized manner of using potentially "dangerous" contextualizing information (admittedly, with a side benefit of legitimating the stamping out of any heresies that might arise). Consider the parable of the Good Samaritan found in Luke 10:25–37. A theologian might use a layered hermeneutical approach that draws on wider sources for interpreting the passage. Salient considerations would include 1) historical and cultural context: examining the parable's contemporaneous Jewish and Roman milieu, including the socio-political and religious climate of the time; 2) literary context: the parable's placement within the larger narrative of Luke's Gospel, the other Gospels, and the New Testament as a whole; 3) its placement within a genre: considering the parable as an allegory that explains the symbolism behind its characters and actions; and 4) a close textual reading: attention to specific language and imagery used in the parable to help uncover deeper meanings and themes. Putting it all together, the parable might then be interpreted from within the Judaic moral tradition as a call to care for others, even strangers, even if they share no religious or cultural affiliation.[119]

Perhaps an even more significant hermeneutical tradition is found in common law jurisprudence, an accumulative historical tradition developed to interpret case law. A bedrock methodological principle of common law is *stare decisis* (the decision stands), where judges are obligated to respect prior decisions by justifying their rulings in light of them. Competing considerations may cause the occasional overturning of an established precedent—a famous example is *Brown v. Board of Education*'s (1954) reversal of *Plessy v. Ferguson* (1896) on racial segregation—and so it is not inviolable. Even so, precedent is still considered to have independent weight and is not to be removed lightly. In this tradition, for a judge, due to *stare decisis* it is quite consistent to resolve a dispute against personal inclination in favor of an established precedent that compels a decision in the opposite direction.

What unites these different hermeneutical traditions is their operating assumption that the meaning of a text (or event) is not *sui generis* nor in any sense self-interpreting; it is always a function of *constructing* that meaning out of a passage's larger context. The main forerunner of this kind of generalized version of hermeneutics in philosophy, Friedrich Schleiermacher (1768–1834), was especially concerned with how to approach the work of an author or artist long removed from its original historical context. Arguing that immediate inspiration by the observer is insufficient—as Gadamer later stresses, "understanding is not a psychic transposition"[120]—Schleiermacher holds that a reconstruction of the original context should be attempted and that it is possible as a result that an understanding of the text or artwork might be achieved that is actually superior to its creator's own.[121] In transferring and generalizing this contextualizing approach from biblical hermeneutics, Schleiermacher advances the proposition that a hermeneutics of some sort is necessary for understanding *anything*; human understanding is always contextual and therefore there is no interpretation-free access to knowledge.

The inescapability of interpretation in this sense is Gadamer's starting point. For Gadamer, all understanding—whether of a text or artwork or another person—is interpretive. In general terms, human understanding moves in what Heidegger called a "hermeneutic circle." This is not, however, the "vicious circle" reviled in logic, where one assumes what one has set out to prove, but it is a precondition for any understanding whatsoever; this kind of circle is necessary for the production of meaning. To generate meaning from a text, for example, one must always move around from whole to part and back again, continually circling until clarity is achieved. The "whole" may be the language in which the text was written, the literary tradition to which it belongs, its historical period, the biographical circumstances of its author, and so on. This whole then provides the backdrop against which one gives significance to the "part," which could be the particular words comprising the text, the individual work in question, or the specific period of the author's life. So, I might ascertain facts about the author's political context or family life and these informational items might shed light on a given theme or passage in one of her novels. At a smaller scale, another analog would be elucidating the meaning of an ambiguous word within a sentence. If the meaning of the word is not obvious, one must seek its larger context. The newly appreciated meaning of the part (the word) then alters to a degree the meaning of the whole (the sentence)—even though the surrounding sentence is what first "gave" the word its meaning. Understanding works by continually traversing whole-part circuits like this, as we always must "fit" novelty into our existing prior frameworks and assumptions. Epistemologically, one never escapes to an imagined "outside" of this whole-part circuit; even an authoritative dictionary only relates words to other words.

Gadamer appropriates the older hermeneutics of biblical exegesis and follows Schleiermacher in taking it beyond the narrow confines of sacred texts. Like his predecessor, he claims a universality for hermeneutics, as its circle characterizes any attempt to understand. An important normative element in Gadamer's approach is his recommendation to grant a kind of provisional truth to the text/phenomenon/person, similar to a "principle of charity" in argument where one maintains an initial attitude that grants truth to what one is attempting to understand. Here one takes on a humble posture that what may at first glance appear to be deficiencies in the text are more likely to be deficiencies in one's own comprehension. One may grow more critical eventually, but it is more fruitful to adopt this operating assumption *before* entering a more destructive mode in order to identify weaknesses and errors. I teach my students this approach with canonical texts. It is a kind of humility, really, where you assume the genius of a time-tested canonical author and further assume that if at first you (who are likely not a genius) identify what looks like an obvious problem, the author must have already thought of that and so you must not be understanding the text properly. It is amazing how much this approach yields because it forces very careful and attentive reading. Of course, even the genius author might be making a dumb mistake, and you were the one who caught it, but this is unlikely to happen without putting in the time to ascertain the author's actual meaning.[122]

For Gadamer, this openness to the possible truth value of the thing to be understood is crucial because a hubristic I-know-the-answer attitude blocks the hermeneutic circle from being able to move, and in so doing prevents understanding; it is one side of the old Socratic Meno's paradox, where if one already knows, one has no need to learn. In such a case, one's own presumption of falsehood—a prejudice—is what drives the encounter. If one desires truly to understand, one must try to bracket one's prejudices as much as possible in order to try to maintain an attitude of "openness" regarding the case at hand. It is a delicate balance, though. It does not mean that one should strive to eliminate one's prejudices and biases completely—this would be a fool's errand. On the contrary, even as we try to minimize them upon an initial encounter with the unfamiliar, Gadamer strongly argues against the possibility or desirability of adopting a neutral, non-prejudicial standpoint (a "view from nowhere" in Nagel's phrase) from which we can make our evaluations.[123] Understanding in Gadamer's sense does not involve being "swept up" as by a charismatic orator. The interpretive challenge is to maintain the attitude of openness, while *also* permitting, as best one can, one's own prejudices to rise so the surface so as to "put them at play."

But how are we to understand this delicate and demanding balancing act where one is both open to experience and yet not forgetful or silent about one's prejudices? Gadamer compares this interpretive situation to a dialogue in which "a spirit rules, a bad one or a good one, a spirit of obdurateness and hesitancy or a spirit of communication and of easy exchange between I and Thou."[124] The spirit emerging from the dialogue is in turn likened to a game, whose normative authority (i.e., the rules and customs to which participants adhere insofar as they are *playing*, e.g., the chess king has to move a certain way and one cannot, by definition, defy that rule without quitting) has a priority over the individual players. Insofar as they enter the world of the game, no matter how violent or competitive it might become, players cede to a degree their private concerns to something larger than themselves, namely, the game *itself*. "The very fascination of the game for the playing consciousness roots precisely in its being taken up into a movement that has its own dynamic. The game is underway when the individual player participates in full earnest, that is, when he no longer holds himself back as one who is merely playing, for whom it is not serious. Those who cannot do this we call men who are unable to play."[125] It might even be said that the game "takes over," becoming the master of the players, while at the same time, perhaps paradoxically, its very being depends on those same players to play it. One does not give oneself *completely* over to "the game," though, for this would commit the error of assuming that one is "no one" and "nowhere," and can simply take on the identity of the game without *importing* any of one's own situational baggage. We are never so pure. I cannot kid myself into thinking that I am just going to go selflessly with the flow of what Toni Morrison writes in the novel because, even though I feel swept up into the narrative, I am still *me*, prejudices and all, and so that feeling of simple communion with the authorial narrative is bound to be at least partly illusory; one can't leave one's own mind behind so easily. From Gadamer's hermeneutical point of view, the trick for winning understanding is tiptoeing on a tightrope where one is simultaneously open to the "call" of the other, that is, charitably anticipating the substantive truth claim that *must*, ex hypothesi, be lying *somewhere* therein, while simultaneously maintaining a steady awareness of one's own perspectives and peculiarities.

Under these exacting conditions, Gadamer argues, the phenomenon of play may provide a "clue to ontological explanation": in the interpretive dialogue hermeneutic understanding establishes with its object, something comes about that is to a degree independent of both of them. (Again, this could apply to human dialogue partners or the "dialogue" I establish with a text or whatever else I am trying to apprehend.) In other words, the (inevitable) prejudices of the interpreting consciousness are *put into play* with the object and, as their "horizons" are "fused," a third entity emerges that is not exactly either of them alone but something novel.[126] Hegel has a grand notion of this process writ large that he labels *Bildung* (culture, development), where "Spirit" comes to know itself through unfolding historically (analogous to theological traditions where creation itself is a process of divine self-knowledge.) Philosopher David Ingram describes the process:

> Gadamer compares *Bildung* to a progressive fusion of horizons in which interpreter and tradition are elevated to participation in a higher universality. This fusion is at once the cancellation of both the parochial prejudices of the interpreter which impede access to the unique message of the tradition and the dead anachronisms implicit in the latter as well as the preservation and extension of what is common to both of them. The moment of cancellation results in a dual negation whereby both the being of the interpreter and the being of the tradition are altered.[127]

Unlike Hegel, however, Gadamer does not posit an end-state of absolute knowledge in which Spirit come into complete knowledge of itself. His concept of experience is much more open-ended than Hegel's; it does not "progress" by undergoing of stages of history, but rather renders itself ever more open to new experiences. This is the true meaning of education for Gadamer; *Bildung* is a never-ending process of openness and a perpetual fusion of horizons (with tradition, other people, nature, etc.) in which the ideal is never to stop learning.

It is thus a very process-oriented vision, in that the learning that is enabled is not conceived instrumentally as a means to some higher end, as in one *utilizing* the learning to gain some Great Insight and then kicking the ladder away when it is no longer needed. Instead, it is the learning *itself* that is the thing: a Nietzschean "eternal recurrence" of unceasing learning that provides not torment but purpose and pleasure as we undergo it.[128] As Gadamer concludes the "Afterword" to his magnum opus *Truth and Method* (after some 579 pages): "the ongoing dialogue permits no final conclusion. It would be a poor hermeneuticist who thought he could have, or had to have, the last word."[129] The truly educated person—true "hermeneuticist"—then, is "radically undogmatic" and ever open to the "experience that is made possible by experience itself."[130] Such a person is open for education through intercourse with others as she undergoes a "continually recurring temptation to engage oneself in something or to become involved with someone."[131] Ideally, the hermeneutically educated person becomes so "dialogically sensitive" that the mere *presence* of another person or novel situation can help break up her biases and enlarge her vision.

Ultimately, these smaller ongoing and occasional dialogues we continually undergo with the many worlds that are always surrounding us are taken up in a kind of invisible symphony of *Bildung* with a far wider range than any of us have on our own. Gadamer recasts *Bildung* as a grand dialogue between interpreter and tradition in which the former is made capable through education of approaching the latter as a Thou. It is not an authoritarian vision where one is expected to approach tradition on one's knees, so to speak; Gadamerian hermeneutics is too dynamic to be described as mere isomorphic reproduction of a static past. His eyes are on the larger prize of *facilitating* individuals' engagement in larger-scale dialogues with their own (and perhaps others') traditions. Gadamer is not a "back to nature" pedagogue à la Rousseau or, necessarily, an advocate of child-centered learning in the manner of Montessori or Summerhill schooling movements. He is too staunchly traditionalist to be placed in those camps. His normative vision of education is less individualistic: teaching and learning places individuals into interaction with tradition, and from that interaction arises a third term, *Bildung*, that is not reducible to its individual participants; in terms of intellectual history, Gadamer thus presents an updated vision of Hegelian "Spirit" continually conversing with itself (through each of us).[132] In a Spinozan vein, this grand conversation of *Bildung* could be conceived in religious terms as God or, equally valid, as Nature, unfolding itself in a process of deepening self-awareness. Thus, one attraction of this view is that there is no need to "choose sides" between reason and religion, science and art, nature and culture, etc.; these become seen as superficial and partisan labels for a mysterious-yet-knowable larger process that encompasses all such binaries.

With regard to psychedelics, Gadamer's account is strikingly consistent with—and complementary to—the REBUS model.

First, the relaxing of beliefs, including high-level priors, is almost identical to the hermeneutical gateway attitude of charity toward the Other, whether this be cast as another person or as new information. In both conceptions, the key precursor for allowing insight is depressing one's a priori orienting assumptions, whether this be conceived neurologically, perhaps in part as a relaxing of the brain's DMN (though the jury is still out on this explanation), or subjectively, as an effortful awareness of one's prejudices.[133] This temporary suspension (of beliefs and/or disbeliefs) allows "the new" to be seen more comprehensively than it would be otherwise. As in Husserlian phenomenology, there is never "pure" consciousness per se at the experiential level but always consciousness-*of* (some-X). However, on both the REBUS and hermeneutical models, by chemical and/or educational means, we can mitigate our consciousness's prior attachments to a degree, such that our potential for learning and insight is augmented—and perhaps dramatically so in the therapeutic context, where certain prior attachments have come to be debilitating.

Second, as the next part of the two-step process with the relaxation of priors, bottom-up information flow is then increased as obstacles are removed; the logjam is broken up. Unlike hermeneutics, the REBUS model provides a physiological mechanism for how this may happen under psychedelics: as previously discussed, via the appropriate receptors, the compound acts as a catalyst for increasing brain entropy and hence foments a temporary plasticity, on an analogy with how annealing temporarily makes a metal more malleable and forgeable. Previously inhibited information flows are then free to filter into conscious awareness, where these newly formed ideational ensembles can be reconsidered and reconfigured via subsequent integration with extant beliefs and perspectives, in which we subjectively see things anew, re-appreciate simple truths, spark new curiosity, etc.

Third, the hermeneutical model goes beyond REBUS in that it posits a large-scale telos for the process; it is normative in that it, qua philosophy, goes beyond the *how* and extends into the *why* of it all. Interestingly, the Gadamerian account can be taken both naturalistically and non-naturalistically in that it presents a macro-vision of an unfolding process of self-understanding that is not reducible to individuals, but rather knits them together into a collective enterprise that admits of varying descriptions. Inflected with the appropriate perspectival idioms, it constitutes a vision that can be added onto and is capable, I think, of inspiring religionists and scientists alike.

As a broader educational approach, the hermeneutical model diverges somewhat from the medical/therapeutic envelopment within which the REBUS model operates. REBUS is fundamentally a therapeutic model that provides a physiological explanation for how patients can achieve breakthrough insights with psychedelics toward ridding them of pathologies. It is certainly *suggestive* of broader applications, but one would have to be cautious. This is because, like all medicalized approaches, it carries within it a priori normative baseline assumptions about what constitutes proper mental health, etc. There must always be "success" criteria for assessing patient recovery. Usually, these are wholly uncontroversial, of course—nobody reasonable is going to argue about the undesirability of severe PTSD, for example, as its debilitations clearly manifest in everyday life. But, at a more general level, the therapeutic envelopment necessarily requires the wholesale assumption of a neutral and objective vantage point from which mental health can be assessed—otherwise there are no criteria for assessing the improvement or deterioration of a condition under treatment. This telic requirement is wholly appropriate and necessary for clinicians, and research ethics demands it.

As much as it enables, though, it is also limiting. Gadamer associates this medico-scientific research-based approach to other people with a drive for a "knowledge of human nature." It is the guiding ideal of psychology and social science, in which one tries to "discover typical behavior in one's fellowmen and make predictions about others on the basis of experience."[134] The projects of abstraction and typification in psychology are exemplary. Their guiding assumption is that behavior can be regulated and manipulated (which is certainly correct). But since that founding assumption takes the other person as calculable and manipulable in advance, it potentially runs grave ethical risks by treating other persons as mere means rather than as ends in themselves, as "objects of attention" reducible to material that is processable in various ways, including via "the research" itself. (There is no Panglossian reason that legitimate scientific knowledge could never be gained from ethical horrors like the MK-ULTRA program and the sinister experiments by Nazi "doctors.") Under established human subjects protocols, patients formally give consent, of course, but ex hypothesi, there can be no full preparation for the dramatic alterations that may ensue from a high-dosage psychedelic experience, as has been explicitly recognized, to their credit, by conscientious psychedelics researchers concerning potential ethical problems with the alteration of patients' "metaphysical beliefs," as, for example, Timmermann et al.'s conclusion that psychedelic use has the potential "to alter some of the most deep-seated and influential human beliefs."[135] From the perspective of philosophical hermeneutics, the objectifying elements of the medical envelopment are not "wrong" in some abstract deontological sense (hermeneutics is not a fleshed-out moral theory in that regard). Rather, the hermeneutical problem is that their productivity will likely be limited due to a flattening of the hermeneutical circle; objectification impoverishes the abovementioned edifying dialogue by recognizing "only what is typical and regular in human behavior."[136] The overall goal of hermeneutics is to enable a larger dialogue among all interlocutors that is not reducible to any one of them—not simply an amplification of the researcher's voice. As an educational theory, hermeneutics cannot adopt the therapeutic goal of bringing patients into alignment with an a priori conception of where they should be, the *eidos* already in the mind of the therapist.

This is where therapy and education ultimately diverge; what is appropriate in one sphere of activity is not always appropriate in the other. Though it inevitably has therapeutic aspects (just as therapy inevitably has educational aspects), education must preserve a much greater degree of open-endedness in its interactions, lest it devolve into an indoctrinatory mode where the goal is the control of human subjects via conformity to some static and "official" body of knowledge. (Those who do not recognize this distinction are not educators but manipulators and commissars.) By extension, recognizing this teleological difference (often elided due to the power and prestige of medicine) implies that *there are important normative differences between the therapeutic and educational contexts of psychedelic use*. At a minimum, educational psychedelics are much more of a co-creation among individuals and between individuals and their traditions and culture, whereas therapeutic psychedelics are an alignment of individuals with received notions. This is not for a moment to denigrate the latter, even slightly; it is only to emphasize the distinctness of the envelopments and that, despite appearances, they are not at all the same. In this respect, good fences indeed make good neighbors; things tend to go very wrong when the therapeutic and the educational are run together. For one thing, as the past century has shown all too well, such conflation is the road to ideological "re-education" and the punishment of dissent.

Additionally, as outlined earlier, hermeneutics emphasizes something very important that is taken for granted in the REBUS model: the very existence of networks of prior beliefs in the first place. When priors are invoked in the REBUS account, they tend to be negatively characterized as part of the pathology meant to be overcome. They appear as "overweighted" or "canalized," and in need of "pruning," "inhibiting," "constraining," "restricting," etc. This is understandable in the psychiatric context where the point is to make beneficial changes in a patient's mentality having to do with persistent debilitating beliefs. Hermeneutics, by contrast, stresses the *positive* role played by high-level priors in human understanding, namely, that there is no understanding without them, however much it may be salutary to alter them in certain circumstances. Gadamer famously argues for a "rehabilitation" of the notion of prejudice (*Vorurteil*, sometime translated as "fore-meanings"), not, obviously, in the sense of promoting injustice, but in the literal sense of the pre-judgments we make all the time and without which everyday life would be impossible.[137] From one angle, as neuroscientist Anil Seth suggests, the brain is essentially a "prediction machine" wired to make Bayesian-like "best guesses," and most of its probabilistic predicting is based on prior assumptions about the world.[138] (Seth also provocatively argues that normal experience is none other than a "controlled hallucination" in which the "control" is simply the feedback loop provided by the input received via our sensory peripherals; our actual brain matter is dark and silent, even as it manufactures the manifold sights and sounds that we undergo.)[139] This means that without those prior assumptions there would be nothing for therapy to adjust; the only thing worse than overweighted priors would be the lack of priors altogether. Where there is no initial understanding, there can be no emendation of that understanding.

For Gadamer, since understanding is a process that represents a fusion of horizons of self/other, self/tradition, self/nature, etc., then without the perspectival horizons, understanding would not be possible. This strongly implies an educational imperative toward erecting and maintaining a robust network of initial priors, even though in doing so we simultaneously also sometimes (and perhaps inevitably) accrue counterproductive priors that need occasional revision or recission. This entails an important positive role for adequate socialization and education as backdrops for an individual to maximize insight from psychedelics. It once again brings to mind Broudy's notion of the allusionary base, that "store of images and concepts" (and much else) that every person carries around with them and enables them to see the world *as* something.[140] It stands to reason that the richer one's allusionary base, the more grist one has for making meaning out of any experience, including the non-ordinary. A snobbish take on the role of the allusionary base would miss the point, as it is not about credentialism and fine phrases; what is important is a rich store of life experiences and dialogical encounters allied with a predisposition to reflect upon them, out of which one has built some ideational ensemble or worldview, however incomplete. One's worldview provides a temporally stable orientation through which to channel and assimilate bottom-up information and to make "higher" meaning out of it, to see it *as* something; as Gadamer puts it, "Only when an idea is placed in relation to another does it display itself as something."[141] For most people—and maybe all people—this is not a DIY affair, however much one may admire the ideal Enlightenment figure of the "self-made" individual who operates wholly rationally and without prejudice and superstition (and, presumably, without socialization and enculturation). But most—and probably all—of us are far too socially embedded in language and culture and too temporally determined by history and our own life cycle to achieve this fabled ideal of autonomous criticality. Even if one styles oneself a rebel against it, one needs to be enveloped in a tradition—*some* tradition—against which to rebel in the first place. Otherwise, one is lost, a lonesome fool, adrift. As in Aristotle's dictum, "The individual, when isolated, is not self-sufficing; and therefore, he is like a part in relation to the whole. But he who is unable to live in society or has no need because he is sufficient for himself, must be either a beast or a god."[142] Gods among us being exceedingly rare, it is axiomatic that a project of extreme resection from inherited tradition will reduce one's chances for insight through psychedelics or any other method. As is generally true with a psychedelic trip itself, to use the Frostian line, "the best way out is always through."[143]

In short, the REBUS model and something like Gadamerian hermeneutics should be married in order to steady imbalances in either model if taken alone. This echoes Gadamer's own convictions that the "basic task" of hermeneutics is not at all "anti-science" but to "reconnect the objective world of technology, which the sciences place at our disposal and discretion, with the fundamental orders of our being that are neither arbitrary nor manipulable by us, but simply demand our respect."[144] Furthermore, "the transmission of scientific knowledge [is] monological in form," and it needs "the counterbalance of hermeneutical appropriation, which works in the form of dialogue."[145] Broadly, characteristic of the medical envelopment, REBUS partakes of a curative paradigm geared toward remedying deficiencies in patients, based on scientific research of relevant "cases." (Again, there is nothing per se wrong with this, but that is what it entails, no matter how much the assumption of "deficiency" might be sugar-coated.) Coming from its own angle, hermeneutics emphasizes that the background "horizons" someone brings to the table are never just deficiencies but are also always potentially productive of meaning and insight—and in fact they are *necessary* in order for understanding and learning to be generated and integrated out of an experience. For its part, hermeneutics is also potentially subject to a corrupted counterpart, as it can tend toward an "I'm okay, you're okay" relativism that can be oblivious to destructive ignorance and limiting pathologies and, in general, to the reality that horizons can indeed contain priors that can be severely debilitating and in need of repair. Knitting REBUS and hermeneutics together yields a more nuanced equilibrium where grounded scientific research may be deployed while also centering the uniqueness and dignity of individual human beings (and their potential for unanticipated insights beyond the scope of researchers' own initial assumptions)—an intellectual and moral synthesis that has long been the stock-in-trade of sensitive clinicians.

As indicated, given its provenance in psychiatry, it is understandable that REBUS assumes pathology in the direction of overweighted priors, given the wide range of mental illnesses with which over-weighting is associated. One sees this in certain optimistic assumptions about the salutariness of plasticity-yielding entropy. For patients *in extremis* with PTSD, OCD, agoraphobia, etc. this seems easily justifiable, because why not try something? This is a sensible stance to take, particularly for a medical practitioner.

For a more complete educational account, I would raise two last sets of considerations:

(1) Is it *always* the case that a period of augmented brain entropy is necessarily beneficial? Certainly, it is widely acknowledged that certain individuals, such as those suffering from schizophrenia, should be excluded from psychedelic trials. Apart from these rarities, though, what about the vast majority who do *not* possess major pathologies associated with over-weighting? If psychedelics can relax priors, are there circumstances where the *wrong* priors could be relaxed and/or *overly* relaxed? (Also, developmental concerns would be relevant here as well.) As previously discussed, Carhart-Harris and colleagues very explicitly recognize these issues in terms of children and other vulnerable types regarding the dangers inherent in the "hyper-suggestibility" etc. of the hot entropic states so, from a scholarly point of view, it is a matter of more clearly integrating this work together.[146] This is therefore more a concern about how the REBUS model could be misappropriated if conceived in isolation. Along the same lines, a larger point is that there are dangers inherent in any assumption of universal validity for a model appropriate to pathological conditions. An analogy in education would be the 1990s "reading wars" over instructional methods. Here, a "whole language" model, emphasizing the context of words over a "phonics" approach, focused on the decoding of letters and sounds, was exported from a special education method for children with severe reading disabilities, and then inflated into being advocated as a universal model for *all* reading instruction. The resulting over-correction and one-sidedness in reading pedagogy may have damaged a generation of rising readers in the United States.[147] Perhaps a similar dynamic applies to psychedelics: for some, the induced plasticity is lifesaving, but for others not so much; it might well be the opposite of what certain individuals need. It is axiomatic that across different contexts medicines can become poisons and vice-versa. Psychedelics for well persons seeking educational insight might need to look very different from what is counseled for those seeking to alleviate trauma and illness.

(2) With regard to plasticity, is it always the case that it lessens rather than strengthens high-level priors? It seems it could go either way.

Remember that, in the Pahnke Good Friday psilocybin study, almost all of the Christian theology student research subjects indeed had mystical experiences, but these were all in their accustomed Christian idiom.[148] Nobody had Mazatec or pagan visions. This might suggest that their Christian framework was *validated*, *extended*, and *strengthened* rather than "relaxed" in any appreciable sense. Even if we stipulate, as per REBUS, that the relaxation of high-level priors can elevate plasticity and subsequently alter entrenched beliefs, perhaps it can also entrench beliefs even *more thoroughly* by adding a visceral experiential dimension to them (e.g., actually "seeing" Jesus rather than the usual more sober imagination of him). It seems that it could go either way, an important aspect of the Grofian thesis of the pluripotency of psychedelics. Under the right conditions and in the right company, psychedelics might actually *enhance* one's previous convictions and *reinforce* one's prior worldview. This in fact seems to be the typical way in which psychedelics function with ancient and contemporary indigenous peoples, where they appear to augment group cohesion and solidarity along pre-existing cultural templates.

To wit, there could just as plausibly be an *under-weighting* of high-level priors that is perhaps manifest in the feelings of anomie and dissociation that are widespread in our culture. People suffering from an under-weighting of priors may feel it as an existential malaise, manifest as a nihilism where it is hard to feel that much of anything matters. Writ large, this is, to a tee, the "post-modern" condition, first characterized by philosopher Jean-Francois Lyotard (1924–1998) as an "incredulity toward metanarratives" where, for whatever historical reasons, we have lost faith in the stories that have guided human beings for millennia.[149] I am sure there are psychiatric labels (some kind of collective dissociative state?), but this is clearly more a philosophical problem symptomatic of modernity itself, where we have been very proficient at destroying old idols but less successful at replacing them with anything—in short, the problem of nihilism. If psychedelics could correct for under-weighting, too, they might well be relevant to this larger problem. In addition to liberating new information and unleashing curiosity, they could also function to revivify, restore, and reintegrate older beliefs that may have been too hastily discarded.

Chapter 5

Doxastic Enhancement

> Funny, I'd forgotten that what comes to you when you take psychedelics is not always a revelation of something new and startling; you're more liable to find yourself reminded of simple things you know and forgot you knew—seeing them freshly—old, basic truths that long ago became clichés so you stopped paying attention to them.
>
> —Alexander Shulgin, *PIHKAL*, 262

Psychedelic Integration Movements

Probably the second-most-used word or phrase in psychedelics is "integration," a somewhat vague and catch-all term for the process of making sense of the experience afterwards. The expectation is that the psychedelic happenings will be placed into some sort of coherence with one's overall life and framework of existing beliefs. This may be done with the aid of an expert, a therapist or "integration specialist," or less formally with friends or simply by oneself. When under the REBUS model someone has had important prior assumptions relaxed or, less technically, one has been numbed by a Socrates or Socratic process, disabused of one's conceit to knowledge, and rendered ready to learn, the question of what comes next becomes pressing. As a supplement to the REBUS account, Gadamerian hermeneutics suggests a broadly Socratic direction, where the information welling up through the cracks in the affected high-level priors was in an important sense "within" one the entire time. It is not novel empirical information in the sense of new inputs of data; as

McKenna said, "it's very hard with psychedelic compounds to bring back information."[1] Claims of LSD superpowers by the Merry Pranksters and a few other eccentrics aside, psychedelics do not seem to act as perceptual peripherals that directly augment one's normal vision, hearing, or other senses.[2] The perceptual aid they render is of a different order having more to do with the reconceptualization and rearrangement of extant material; it is a higher-order redesign with existing elements rather than a complete tear-down followed by a *de novo* reconstruction.

Carhart-Harris and Friston explain that these "mechanics of insight" include two key forms of learning: "structure" and "fact-free."[3] Structure learning has to do with how large data sets can be seen anew by the detection of previously unnoticed larger patterns and structural relations. This is associated with the familiar psychedelic refrain of feeling as if one has glimpsed a "bigger picture," as in appreciating the forest for the trees or realizations along the lines of the neo-Platonic Oneness, mentioned earlier as a prototypical example of hypertrophic identification. The allied notion of data-free learning "refers to learning without necessarily accumulating new information or facts, i.e., because a fresh perspective or frame of reference, rather than more new data per se, may be more valuable for advancing understanding."[4] This brings to mind Wittgenstein's observation that many non-empirical problems "are solved, not by giving new information, but by arranging what we have already known."[5] By contrast, indigenous shamans commonly conceive of themselves as, in fact, bringing back beneficial new information, often in the context of healing. But within the modernist western frame, although there have been attempts (e.g., asking DMT entities complex math problems), so far there are no credible instances of new empirical information being imparted.[6] Psychedelics enthusiasts sometimes veer into occult territory and claim to have experienced telepathy, astral projection, speaking to the dead, and the like, but this too is so far unsubstantiated. As Shanon relates regarding his extensive participant-observer studies *in situ* with ayahuasca,

> Personally, I do not believe in ayahuasca providing or enabling any such non-ordinary factual knowledge at all. This categorical stance of mine is a corollary of my disbelief in the paranormal and the parapsychological in general. In the specific context of ayahuasca, despite many attestations by many drinkers of paranormal experiences, more careful inspection on my

part revealed no actual substantiation for such claims. In particular, let me comment on telepathy. It is often claimed that ayahuasca elicits telepathic communication. Indeed, an earlier name of one of its active chemical constituents was "telepatina." I have experienced the feeling of telepathy too. Yet, it is crucial to distinguish between experiences in which a person feels telepathic and actual occurrences of such paranormal information transfer.[7]

Again, from within the modernist western frame, at least, it seems far more likely, therefore, that psychedelic insights are of the structural, fact-free, and Wittgensteinian "rearrangement" type.

Say, on a moderate dose of psilocybin mushrooms, I fixate on a honeybee in the yard, enclosed in its *Umwelt* and buzzing about its business as usual. Bees are not new to me; I have seen many of them previously and on many occasions. I "know" all about bees. What I am doing now is *noticing* them in a certain way, seeing them with "new eyes," as it were: I see several of them all at once in a way that I hadn't before, I zero in on the vibratory motion of their wings, the sonic layer their buzzing provides to the scene's ambience, their determined motion as they traverse from plant to plant, how a strong breeze buffets them from their beeline until back on course, etc. This then leads me to "deeper" thoughts about the backyard interdependencies on display before me, how crowded and interconnected are all those plants and insects with each other and their habitats, and how the larger animals need them, how the earth, sky, and sun underwrite the whole affair, as does the planet itself nestled in its space-time orbital niche, etc.—all this on an afternoon when "nothing" was happening outside. There is little newsworthy in such realizations (in fact it sounds like a satirical newspaper headline, "Man on Mushrooms Realizes Cosmic Interconnections in Backyard") and they don't really contain new data. So, exactly what high-level prior is being relaxed here in favor of exactly what bottom-up information flow? It seems that what is being released from my everyday operating assumptions and involvements is something less determinate: my *attention*, my *notice*, my *care*—a heightened fluidity and focus vis-à-vis my experience flow. Where hermeneutics comes into play is how, in the course of these "new" realizations, they so largely depend on the "old" status quo ante of my *existing* pieces of knowledge and larger sets of assumptions, like my bias toward naturalistic explanations (others might be biased toward supernatural ones, like marveling at God's handiwork), normative-ethical impulses, aesthetic proclivities—all of these tied into some sort of operative worldview. I would not be seeing the bees *as* much of anything at all without all this *in mente* doxastic background that regularizes and narrativizes the incoming data, thus making possible whatever ecological realization I take to be significant. This means that an insight gained while on psychedelics is not just a matter of eroding the grip of prior assumptions; *it is also a matter of which among those priors are left standing and amplified.* Unless one is clear-cutting, when one weeds a garden, one is also allowing whatever one has chosen as non-weeds to remain and grow.

This is not just an epistemological point. Take the important ethical questions around abuse and exploitation with psychedelics touched on earlier. As both contemporary researchers and the historical record make clear, hyper-suggestibility, peer-conformity, "feelings of collective belonging," and related vulnerabilities arising from psychedelic sessions create real psychological dangers.[8] Adding to this concern is the suggestion, in a recent LSD study, "that what is newly or recently learnt through reinforcement under LSD is more 'stamped in', and thus may subsequently be harder to update."[9] This potential potency heightens the stakes of there being no automaticity to the *beneficial* nature of either the plasticity as such or the post-trip integrative interactions, and it is unacceptably naïve to assume as much. And, whereas it may be uncontroversial what counts as beneficial in the medical-therapeutic envelopment when dealing with severe mental debilities like PTSD or depression, it is unclear by what criteria we establish the normative valences for (relatively) well persons, the vast majority of psychedelics takers. Again, apart from people overcoming severe trauma where what constitutes improvement is relatively clear, someone reporting they are "better off" or on a "higher level" after psychedelic intake begs the question of the normative criteria for making such comparative judgments. It is undoubtedly possible for someone to be *worse off* after psychedelics, and many have seen this occur in themselves or others (as have I myself). These general normative questions are unlikely to be answered by recourse to criteria internal to psychedelic experience itself; though there may be inspirations and insights here and there, nobody has come back, in the manner of a Moses, Jesus, or Mohammed, with a moral code or framework with any level of elaboration. The closest examples are probably the cosmologies and outlook of many indigenous peoples that are clearly enhanced by psychedelic visions, but these are products of already integrated worldviews where the substances are clearly *extending* and *enlivening*—rather than *creating* on their own—a pre-existing meta-narrative or worldview that incorporates the major areas of life: religion, healing, food production, ethics, life cycle events, etc. In these already integrated traditions, psychedelic use is neither meaningful nor, really, even conceivable to insiders apart from their encompassing cultural lifeways and worldview.

By contrast, with the grip of traditional metanarratives having historically waned, the modernist West is largely bereft of a widely shared normative framework for establishing what "better" or "worse" might mean—apart from very shallow and nonspecific medicalized norms of "health" and "wellness." Our public relativism is so pervasive that we can only agree on that bare minimum (if that). So, in the situation of a well person ("well" defined as not currently suffering from an identifiable trauma) seeking insight via psychedelics, what then provides the ethical guardrails for both the experiencer *and* whoever sits in the integrationist role? What prevents the cults and the abuse? An occupational code of professional ethics may help, as it has in other caring fields, from teaching to psychiatry, but the principles undergirding such codes are *themselves* dependent upon some deeper moral understandings and agreements. And this is precisely what the modernist West now lacks. In a "thick" traditionalist culture (or, possibly, subculture—more on this later), a high level of shared norms and practices serves this role. But in a "thin" modernist culture that is more relativistic and *modus vivendi* (essentially nonjudgmental and "going along to get along") like our own, things are not so easy.[10] In a normatively disintegrative situation such as this, we are left with what philosopher Alasdair MacIntyre calls mere "emotivism": "the doctrine that all evaluative judgments and more specifically all moral judgments are *nothing but* expressions of preference, expressions of attitude or feeling, insofar as they are moral or evaluative in character."[11] After a psychedelic experience, if I *feel* that it is "beneficial," then ipso fact it is—whether I am Charles Manson or John Lennon or my twentysomething self. Current moral intuitions may still be vestigially operative off the fumes of the past cultural norms (e.g., the moral system of Christianity that underwrites principles of human equality), but mostly the justificatory anchor is simply in what *feels* "good" or "right," with almost no ability to provide any deeper rationale for the authorizing emotion. Perhaps fittingly at present, emotivism represents a widespread consumerist mentality regarding morality where "the customer is always right"—no more questions need be asked—and, aside from a few atavistic intuitions lingering from legacy worldviews, it is impossible to have any kind of rational discussion about what is right and wrong; you just *feel* it, and it is seen as unattractively judgmental and moralistic to assert otherwise. Conversely, if you just don't "feel it" in accord with social convention, you are also, for unknown reasons, designated a "bad person," an all-purpose disapprobation that is itself also inexplicable on any other than a superficial emotivist level.

Within the psychedelic realm, one possible response to the charge of emotivism is that, if one is properly attuned, contentful answers will be found from *within* the trip itself. Commentators sometimes speak this way: DMT entities gave one a lesson in humility, or "the mushrooms," "the toad," or the "plant teachers" *themselves* yielded a profound answer of some sort, etc. Though comparatively rare, such instances of intra-trip sensemaking should not be discounted (and they are, as noted previously, a huge and intricate aspect of the psychedelic usage of shamanic systems).[12] However, even in such cases of intra-trip insight, one still cannot escape the hermeneutic circle because the lessons are nonetheless always *interpreted* in some manner post hoc; that is, they are viewed as meaningful against a backdrop of whatever are the still-standing high-level priors that remain operative in the integration process—whatever form that process takes. This means that *one's pre-existing doxastic network is always implicated in psychedelic insight*. It cannot be otherwise. With regard to the ethical questions about potential abuse, my view is that only a strong and, as they say, *based* set of ethical intuitions—not free-floating impulses, but embedded in a persistent worldview—will do this job. Absent any comprehensive conception of the good, all that can hold sway for an individual is an immediately gratifying but ultimately unjustifiable consumer-based emotivism. Serious insight requires that intuitions be encased in a more accessible and durable ideational superstructure.

Under the therapeutic envelopment, if one is unwell, the optimism among clinicians regarding the necessarily *beneficial* nature of epistemic loosening or relaxing priors may well be warranted. As stated earlier, patients *in extremis* may reason that something—*anything*—is worth trying because, from their point of view, the status quo is intolerable. This desperate logic does not necessarily apply to the well, those who, at least for the time being, enjoy equanimity within a range that should reasonably be characterized as "well." (Some would of course say that *everyone* in the modernist West is unwell, but this is figurative hyperbole in the present context and, among other things, it trivializes the situations of those in real crisis.) The problem, then, with the REBUS assumption of the benignity of relaxing priors is that for those who are not unwell, there could be priors that are relaxed that *should not* be relaxed. For how would we know? Surely, as per the hermeneutical conviction that one's horizon of priors is a necessary condition for any human understanding at all, it would be unreasonable to suggest that it is desirable to relax *all* of one's priors. What would this even mean? Coma? Some sort of amnesia wholly bereft of memory or personal identity? There is therefore an inevitable task of *discernment*, that is, of distinguishing the priors to retain from the priors to discard. It seems to me the only way to accomplish this task—including the maintenance of the aforementioned ethical guiderails—is to operate from the basis of some stable traditional intersubjective base. Otherwise, there would be no criteria by which to assess the normative status of said priors and thus by default that assessment would be done on the basis of ad hoc and "intuitive" gut-level responses—in other words, MacIntyrean emotivism. Typically, the discerning job is in fact being done, but under the table; what is obscured is the set of criteria by which it is operating.

Sometimes the underlying norm-yielding worldview rises to the surface and is made more explicit. Within its Amazonian context, Shanon concludes that ayahuasca promotes "a comprehensive metaphysical view of things" that he characterizes as "an idealistic monism with pantheistic overtones" (IMPO):

> By this view, reality is conceived as constituted by one, non-material substance which is identified as Cosmic Consciousness, the Godhead, the ground of all Being, or the Fountain of Life. Coupled with this is the assessment that all things are interconnected and that in their totality they constitute one harmonious whole. This, in turn, entails an experienced realization that there is sense and reason to all things and that reality is invested with deep, heretofore unappreciated, meaningfulness. By and large, it seems that the metaphysical perspective induced by Ayahuasca is most similar to the views entertained in classical Hindu philosophy . . . as well as by Plato, Plotinus and Hegel.[13]

As Shanon further suggests, this general outlook also seems consistent with what is reported regarding the other major psychedelics as well (although, as discussed below, non-ayahuasca DMT might be an exception). At any rate, while almost universally hailed as compelling and salutary, this IMPO worldview should be considered as available for analysis and interrogation on the same basis as any other worldview or set of religious beliefs. "Connectedness" has a strong intuitive appeal, as we are social beings. It seems less lonely and sad. But "separateness" may need to have its day in court as well; as metaphysical abstractions, it may not be defensible—or even coherent—to make an ultimate choice between "One" and "Many." Heraclitus and Hegel, for their parts, would both seem to balk at the choice as a false one that misses the point that the ultimate reality of flux and change encompasses *both* of these moments.

Relatedly, some argue that psychedelics could straightforwardly involve what Letheby and Mattu call "moral enhancement"; that is, they "may be a viable way to improve individuals' moral character and cognition."[14] In line with IMPO, philosopher Virginia Ballesteros goes so far as to assert that the changes wrought by psychedelics can be "morally desirable" because, as potentially mystical experiences, they augment the personality trait of openness and a wider outlook of nature-relatedness. For Ballesteros, this signals "the emergence of a morally improved agent."[15] This may be so. But as an evaluative judgment, the moral worth of "enhancement" or "diminishment" must always be indexed against a set of contextual criteria—whether these are explicit or implicit. For a Gaian-oriented pagan, openness and nature-relatedness will tend to be prized far more highly than for a fundamentalist Christian who may question nature-relatedness as God-obscuring and neglectful of an individual's non-natural soul. The Gaian and the Christian are of course operating from different overarching moral narratives. There is no view from nowhere from which to assess their respective moral enhancement claims; any attempt to do so must acknowledge the evaluator's dependency on some prior criterion-giving worldview meta-narrative. Otherwise, matters devolve into the relativistic emotivism of which MacIntyre warned, where there is no justifiable basis for preferring one impulse or intuition over another and therefore no normative ordinates by which to assess either improvement or deterioration. Popular psychedelia can be overly facile in this regard. It is often simply assumed, mostly along emphatic IMPO lines, that unitivity, connectedness, oneness, etc. represent a self-evidently "higher" level of consciousness and no further justification is needed. It seems, however, that if this is indeed an enhancement (and it may well be), it is an enhancement of a particular latent worldview on the part of those advancing it. Where is nothing wrong per se with advancing this worldview, philosophical expectations require this to be done explicitly rather than under a cryptonormative fog that conceals its major premises by assuming them to be self-evident.

Psychedelics sidestep this problem if, however, ex hypothesi, they function as non-specific amplifiers. Under this conception, it is not possible for them to be morally enhancing *as such*, because 1) there is no "as such" in this context (normativity always needs criteria) and, correlatively, 2) if they *are* enhancing, it is always an enhancement of a worldview within which the experiencer is, at least in part and at some level, already enveloped. Though an intense psychedelic trip may seem like a completely novel experience, ultimately, when all is said and done and the integrative smoke has cleared, even psychedelics can never grant us escape from our own *Umwelt* bubbles, horizons, and projections; they may be expansive but they are not *deus ex machina*.

Psychedelics are thus viewed more defensibly not as bearers of a particular worldview (i.e., context-independent), but rather as *worldview accelerants* that *re*-vivify, *re*-enchant, and *re*-animate worldviews that were, in a Platonic recollective sense, always already there all along. Interestingly, as per the foregoing, the learning and insight they produce seem to provide neither new factual information nor rational argumentation—one does not see trip reports from those emerging with formal proofs or rigorous chains of reasoning. (Maybe this has happened somewhere, but I have yet to see it reported.) Parallel to the model of Cartesian doubt, what they seem to do is provide *occasional* flashes of fact-free illumination, an image that, if accurate, presupposes something that was latently present beforehand in the inward darkness; the metaphor of illumination implies a prior something to be illuminated. As in the Husserlian phenomenology of consciousness, there is no illumination *as such*, only illumination-*of* some-X. As hermeneutics would have it, psychedelic insight and its subsequent integration seem very much to do with how we are appropriating something that is *already there*, in the exact sense of the Shulgin quote that is the epigraph for this section. But this remains puzzling philosophically. How might such a process be conceived?

Philosophical Pathway #4: Hume

> At the foundation of well-founded belief lies belief that is not founded.
> —Ludwig Wittgenstein, *On Certainty*, §253

Reason, Passion, and Psychedelic Integration

What are we to make of a kind of learning that is episodic, functions as a non-specific amplifier, but is based on no new information or rational argumentation? What exactly is being amplified? And how does one gain deep insight from amplification? As I have been arguing, psychedelics clearly operate on the vast existing doxastic network each of us carries with us—most of it normally beneath explicit awareness—and provide us with a vast allusionary base of previous learnings, assumptions, miscellaneous beliefs, evolved and habitual patterns of thought, cultural and historical inheritances, aesthetic imagery, and much else. Whether in the epistemic loosening-of-priors mode of the REBUS model or the more affirming-of-priors mode of hermeneutics, that allusionary base is drawn on during the psychedelic experience; elements of it are either *relaxed* to allow reframing and perspective or *augmented* to do the same. The insight does not come from an importation from an "outside" but results from a rearrangement of existing material (for an indeterminate period: from a short afterglow to a lifetime). In philosophical parlance, this presents an *internalist* model, where the given insights arise from elements that are not themselves created by the psychedelics so much as they are exposed and illuminated by them. On this view, the anarchic brain in its entropic hot state alters attention such that new connections and insights are *revealed* rather than *constructed* in a classically empirical manner. (Again, it is about not new information, but new ways of seeing "old" information.) This is not to say that information inputs and the capabilities of rationality are irrelevant—they are tightly intertwined with the big insights and how they are operationalized—it is just that information gathering and rational calculation usually come into play post hoc; they help steer the ship toward the insight, but they do not provide the destination.

But, at the same time, psychedelic insight is not *irrational* and neither is reason irrelevant to it. It would be more accurate to say that these psychedelic illuminations are *extra-rational*; the mental operations typically associated with reason and rationality *supervene* on the deeper orienting insights and their more holistic subjective qualia—these are changes that one *feels* along with whatever intellective processes accompany them. It is no wonder that mystical experience provides such an influential model for the alterations produced by high-dosage psychedelics: it parallels conversion, "born again," and other faith-based intensities that for religious adherents are not reducible to the acquisition of new information or cognitive assent to a proposition; the cognitive stuff doesn't hurt, but it is more important to let Jesus into your heart than into your brain.

As he is one of the western tradition's most famous atheists, it is ironic that a venerable philosophical model for how this doxastic dynamic might be conceived is found in the moral psychology of David Hume. Parallel to the above discussion of the internalist thesis that psychedelics work on existing priors, Hume famously presents his own, more general internalist account of reason and what he calls "the passions" or "sentiments." Though reason shapes, structures, and "disciplines" the passions, it is not responsible for either their original generation or their elimination; passions come and go without reason—literally. They are deeply interrelated, though: Hume's overall picture is that reason is subservient to the passions yet at the same time it is an instrument for altering them. With psychedelics, an example of such interrelation would be an attempt at post-trip integration, where the rational faculties are deployed to "make sense of it all" by placing the psychedelic experience as it was undergone retrospectively into some sort of coherent relation with one's ongoing life concerns, outlook, and worldview. Reason is crucial in such a process, but it is never a motivational force; it cannot set our basic aims in life, but it is consigned to scheme over and deploy the means toward achieving them. Hume thus disputes the received rationalist picture (a tradition including Plato and Descartes) that morality involves a struggle between reason and the passions, where "winning" involves ensuring that reason is firmly in control, as in Plato's image of the mind as a charioteer needing to handle the unruly steeds of passion and steer them in the proper direction. In Plato's influential metaphor, the charioteer represents reason as it struggles to control the powerful equine passions, which pull against one another and against the driver, and jerk the chariot in different directions. In a well-ordered mind and soul, reason is in control and is able to stabilize one's life by reining in the passions and then utilizing them at its discretion.[16] Though an emblematic "rationalist," Plato well recognizes the motivational power of passions and how human life is unimaginable without reason being intertwined with them. But his picture of morality is one in which reason needs to rise above the passions and assert control.

Hume rejects this. Humean moral psychology admits of no such struggle between reason and passion because the former is incapable of providing *by itself* a motivation for moral action. If reason is incapable of providing such a motivation, then *a fortiori* it cannot be party to such a motivational struggle. As philosopher John Rawls (1921–2002) explains Hume's position, "Nothing can oppose a passion except a contrary passion; and no passion, or impulse, can arise from reason alone. Thus there is no struggle between reason and the passions."[17] Human beings are moved by passions to which, ultimately, reason is instrumental and hence subordinate. Hence Hume's famous line that "Reason is and ought only to be the slave of the passions, and can never pretend to any office than to serve and obey them."[18] Reason may generate well-formed and universally applicable propositions about moral principles, but what it can never do is by itself motivate an actual human being to *care* about those principles or, indeed, the other human beings toward whom those principles are directed. Philosopher Bernard Williams vividly illustrates this point when he describes the task of talking a suicidal "amoralist" into caring about something. Williams plausibly suggests that rational argumentation in the sense of logical proofs and the like will be of little assistance in such a situation. "We might indeed 'give him a reason' in the sense of finding something that he is prepared to care about, but that is not inducing him to care by reason, and it is very doubtful whether there could be any such thing. What he needs is help, or hope, not reasonings."[19] The best one might do is *point out* that-about-which and those-for-whom the suicidal person cares—hoping against hope that some of those bonds of care are still there, however obscured they may have become. If the bonds of care are altogether absent—by definition pathologically so—then all hope of persuasion would be gone. For good or ill, premising our moral choices is always some-thing (or set of things) that is irreducibly nonrational. Hume underscores this point in another oft-quoted passage, where he explains that "the understanding can neither justify nor condemn" a passion. "'Tis not contrary to reason to prefer the destruction of the whole world to the scratching of my finger."[20]

This is the more detailed sense in which Hume's psychologistic account of moral motivation may be labeled an "internalist" one: moral motivation arises not from generally applicable laws of rationality (e.g., à la Kant, deontological principles that guide all rational creatures insofar as they are rational) but rather from the passions qua the set of already existing motivations that an individual has, from whatever ultimately naturalizable source.[21] Internalism is roughly the idea that if something is to count as a reason X for person Y, X has to "link up" with Y's already existing set of motivations. (This should sound familiar from the discussion of psychedelics.) Given Hume's assumption that our passions are necessary conditions for our being moved, his account is an internalist one.[22] Hume would not say, for example, that Y has *her own reason* X for doing Z. (Alternatively, an "externalist" analysis might hold that there is some categorical sense in which Y does or does not *have reason* X for doing Z, that is, in a putatively objective sense of having a *good* or bona fide reason.) If moral motivation is explained causally, this means that the passions are always at the final end of any chain of reasoning purporting to explain moral action; though their motivational force is not always apparent on the surface, the passions anchor the entire enterprise of reason. And given that the relevant category (viz., the passions) admits of variety, there are, among the roiling mass of those passions, irreducibly plural sources for moral motivation. As Rawls puts it, "there are many possible stopping points given by the passions. The aims of the passions are many, and there is no single end, not even that of aiming at pleasure and avoiding pain."[23] In all of their monstrous and wonderful variety, the passions provide the final "stopping points" for our furthest and deepest whys.

What is more, according to Hume, where rationalist philosophers and many others err is in confusing reason with what he calls the "calm" passions, as against those that are "violent." When, considered from my own point of view, someone reacts to a situation disproportionately, I might stress the importance of "being reasonable" in order to calm that person. Despite the colloquial use of the term "reasonable" here, Hume thinks that what is most likely being appealed to in this situation is not reason but one of the calmer passions. Say I want to shoot someone who has just insulted me. My friends implore me to be reasonable, perhaps expressing in whatever language sentiments like "it's not worth it," "you can't just kill someone like that," "you'll ruin your life," or "think of your family." Then let's imagine I do eventually "see reason" and calm down, avoiding the murder. One might be tempted to say that I stood down from the shooting because I was motivated by reason not to do it; I "saw" reason. But Hume would say that this kind of talk obscures what has really happened. A better explanation involves looking at the situation as one in which the calm passions have, happily in this case, triumphed over the more violent passions such as my reflexive aggrievement. The latter might include a sense of being disrespected, a hot desire in the moment for revenge, perhaps even sadism. The former, however, might include (corresponding to my cohort's exhortations) calmer, more durable passions such as long-term self-preservation, a "natural" benevolence toward other human beings (e.g., as the fog of the violent impulses dissipates, I begin to "remember" the humanity of my antagonist), or, even more "naturally," an abiding concern and love for my own family (e.g., my children will be fatherless if I am jailed for the crime). Hume does not see how unadulterated reason could, by itself, enter into this picture: what we have here instead are certain passions jockeying for motivational status with others. Properly understood, the more "reasonable" course of action turns out to be the one motivated, not by reason per se, but by the calmer passions, which, although they may often seem dormant in everyday situations (precisely owing to their calmness), can when called on overpower their more effervescent violent counterparts.

Reason still has a central role for Hume, however. Despite the initial impressions given by the "slave of the passions" remark, he is no simple irrationalist. Hume presents a kind of moral-developmental account in which the acquisition of morality requires not the elimination or demotion of the passions, but rather the *cultivation* of them, a "corrected sympathy," leading in the best case to what he calls a "progress of the sentiments."[24] This seems remarkably apt as a general description for the insight psychedelics can yield, where one sees things from a new angle or appreciates a previously obscured interconnectedness—and in this neutral sense perhaps the widening of one's moral lens as discussed earlier. If psychedelic insight does not arise from new information or acquisition of proof or argument, then it seems appropriate to describe it as *moving* us in a novel way, in the holistic sense of that term, as in "it was a moving experience." Plato means something like this, I think, in his famous likening of deeper learning to a "turning of the soul." "'That's what education should be,' I said, 'the art of orientation. Educators should devise the simplest and most effective methods of turning souls around. It shouldn't be the art of implanting sight in the organ [i.e., the brain or whatever it is we utilize to learn], but should proceed on the understanding that the organ already has the capacity, but is improperly aligned and isn't facing the right way.'"[25] Despite their opposing metaphysics, Hume and Plato agree that significant insight of the motivational type is more along the lines of fact-free learning; it represents an alteration of a subject's relation to her own mental contents, including how we narrativize near-infinite sensory data points and within that narrative define our self-image.

Although reason cannot *itself* provide motivational impetus, given Hume's internalism, it regularly performs crucial deliberative work on passions both calm and violent. It can work to orient or progress our sentiments in a several ways.

First, reason may *indirectly* augment, diminish, or catalyze the replacement of our passions by supplying and helping us to organize relevant information concerning them. So, for example, my craving for a dessert cheesecake may vanish and turn into revulsion once I realize it has been poisoned. This new information, placed by reason into a syllogism involving my getting sick or dying on eating it, helps reconfigure my passions accordingly.[26] My love for cheesecake (perhaps playing the role of a violent passion) is not extinguished, but is instead temporarily displaced—through information and logic—by my greater, though usually calmer, passion to avoid dying. Again, reason's assistance here is only in replacing one passion with another, not in insinuating *itself* as the motivational force.

Similarly, there may be cultivated passions that are actually instrumental to greater and more durable passions where new information and logic may in fact be effective. For example, a vegan may develop a visceral loathing for meat, even though she once loved it. One might call this a kind of asceticism but for the fact that the vegan (and I know people like this) actually does find meat repugnant now. In the Humean manner, she has over time corrected her previous passions by gradually internalizing the new convictions, owing to her rational understanding of the health effects of certain foods, moral arguments about animal suffering and environmental sustainability, etc.—even in the face of the constant and powerful countervailing forces of convention. By way of solidifying the point, one could imagine a future scenario where the correction goes in a different direction. In Woody Allen's madcap movie *Sleeper* (1973), future scientists discover that deep fat, steak, cream pies, and hot fudge are actually the healthiest things to eat (a future doctor explains to his incredulous colleague: "those were thought to be unhealthy, precisely the opposite of what we now know to be true").[27] Moral arguments aside, the (merely) health-conscious vegan in such a world might now reverse course and recalibrate those same sentiments in light of the new information. The acquired revulsion would still have to be unlearned in a new progress of the sentiments, though—presumably—a revulsion to hot fudge would be easier unlearned than learned. The point is that a passion that is instrumental *to another greater one* is vulnerable to correction by reason if it is revealed (by reason) in actuality to be ineffective or counterproductive. The premise behind cognitive behavioral therapy functions similarly to this, where a motivation can be exposed as based on mistaken information in order to diminish its hold on the patient's mind. In Humean internalism, in such cases reason is not now in "control" as in the rationalist picture, but it, in a way, is merely shifting its fickle allegiance to the new and improved successor controlling passion.

Reason may also *specify* and *sequence* the passions. My general hunger may find me looking about for fish and chips in particular, my desire to smoke may focus on a pack of Marlborough reds, my impulse to take flight when I hear a noise may be specified into a determinate desire to run up a tree to escape the menacing dogs I subsequently realize are making the noise, my desire to "have children" may be specified as a love for *this* particular child I now have, and so on. Once again, passions are corrected and refined, this time by being brought into greater focus. Reason may also aid me in *sequencing* the attempted fulfillment of my passions: a smoke after dinner, a bottle of wine after work rather than before it, erotic involvements at appropriate times and places, and so on.[28] In such instances, I am employing reason as an engine of comparison among my passions in the ensemble, where I widen and narrow the scope of my passions as the situation dictates, allowing for the range of what I value, on the solid premise that our desires are polymorphous (i.e., desires are always multiple and therefore must be adjudicated). Since I value drinking wine yet I also value the work I do during the day, I should quite rationally schedule those activities so that I can accomplish both. Remember that it is not *direct* adherence to reason that causes me not to drink wine before work; it is because I want to enjoy two passions rather than only one of them. The drunkard who loves his work but gets fired because of his drinking on the job is actually *less* of a hedonist than the rational sequencer who enables enjoyment of both work *and* drink.

Lastly and most dramatically, I will from time to time need to *weight* my passions qua final ends.[29] Though Hume certainly does think that some passions are more basic than others, he seems always to speak of even the most basic passions in the plural. He writes, for example, of the calmer set of desires (the ones so often mistaken for reason itself) that they "are of two kinds; either certain instincts originally planted in our natures, such as benevolence and resentment, the love of life, and kindness toward children; or the general appetite to good, and aversion to evil, consider'd merely as such."[30] If even our most basic set of passions admits of variety, then there is always the possibility of conflict among them. These are seen in the blessedly rare moments where we are confronted with a heart-rending hard choice between two courses of action, either of which is "backed up" by an irreducibly powerful passion. Sartre's poignant wartime example of a young man's agony over whether to stay and care for his aged mother or join the resistance against the Nazis comes to mind.[31] Hume would, I think, agree with the thesis that Sartre means to support with such an example, namely, that the objective reason cannot provide some neutral set of rules or a failsafe decision procedure through which we can solve such dilemmas. We must, in a way, make a certain leap of faith. Reason can be effective, for Hume, though, where there is some disparity between the horns of the dilemma, that is, at least some way to differentiate them by their subjectively "felt" potency. Though Hume may be somewhat optimistic on this score (for him such conflicts are largely resolvable), reason may with the aid of such dilemmas help us establish for ourselves what one might call, after the economists, a personal "preference schedule," a "motivational set," or, perhaps more poetically, what philosopher Max Scheler (1874–1928) describes as an individual's underlying *ordo amoris*, an ordering of one's loves.[32]

To engage in these kinds of moral deliberation is precisely to embark upon a progress of the sentiments, where reason facilitates the progress but never replaces the sentiments themselves. Ultimately, Hume has a much larger story to tell about how this progress leads us to embrace social conventions of justice (because of this he calls justice an "artificial virtue," by which he means, in the sense of "artifice," *avant la lettre*, that it is "socially constructed") on which all civilization depends and, ultimately, a shared sense of humanity where one's narrow sense of self yields to a larger intersubjective moral identity (i.e., Ballesteros's moral "widening" or, more generally, the process of hypertrophic identification in its benign forms): "I esteem the man whose self-love, by whatever means, is so directed as to give him a concern for others, and to render him serviceable to society."[33] As Hume scholar Annette Baier elaborates, "Hume has a famously fluid concept of the self, and the fluid ego boundaries that allows work interestingly in his moral psychology. One could say that, on a Humean version of moral development, the main task is to work to a version of oneself and one's own interests which both maximizes the richness of one's potential satisfactions and minimizes the likely opposition one will encounter between one's own and others' partially overlapping interests."[34]

This centrality of this fluidity for Hume regarding self-identity and ego boundaries, needless to say, renders his outlook surprisingly serviceable for conceiving how all those reported flashes of psychedelic insight might be integrated by a person into their perspective and worldview. This is what in essence psychedelic integration would be for Hume: a space for reason to flex and operate post hoc on the "great blooming, buzzing confusion" of sense impressions, ideas, half-ideas, images, inarticulable feelings, etc. that have been provided in a significant trip journey. In connection with one's existing worldview and convictions, as an operation of reason, integration can, in the best case, progress the psychedelically altered sentiments in an amenable direction.

All of Hume's talk of the passions and reason emphatically does not entail any simple sort of individualist egoism or moral solipsism, where I can never break out of the cage of my narrow personal interests. It might be said that in Humean moral psychology, my passions, my loves and fears, hopes and desires, are rather gateways or opportunities for me to grow toward my fellow human beings, the progress of such sentiments being motored by an inbuilt impulse toward fellow feeling, the basis of which is, fortunately according to Hume, natural to human beings as a social species (though of course this impulse varies in intensity contextually). In this way, the latter-day Humean might say, in the manner of contemporary evolutionary psychology, that the moral—the whole amalgamated reason-passion package—is continuous with the psychological; like everything else about us from a naturalistic perspective, morality is an evolved trait that has been selected for because it is, on the whole, adaptive. By whatever routes, we have evolved an ability consciously to shape and arrange the conglomeration of our inherited instincts and impulses; reason just *is* the arrangement and rearrangement of our passions, and its exercise does not place us somehow above or beyond them. Reason and rationality are not "purer" or "higher" or any kind of escape from our "baser" passions but represent our very integrative ability to make our insights and impulses cohere into something meaningful and, just as important, render them *livable* over the course of an actual human life. Hume's moral psychology is thus an attractive model for psychedelic integration writ large, in that it offers a holistic vision for how the actual undergoing of a trip and reflecting upon it afterwards can both be considered as part of a single process of potential deeper learning.

Psychedelic Revivalism

> I'm doing this wonderful study with religious professionals from different world religions. Giving them two high-dose psilocybin experiences and trying to measure how it impacts the effectiveness of their ministry. Some of them even find themselves believing what they preach on Sunday mornings.
>
> —William Richards, "Ineffability and Revelation on the Frontiers of Knowledge," 118–119

Psychedelic experiences are notoriously hard to remember, let alone integrate, so incorporating insights gained from them can be doubly so. This frustrating effervescence can be mitigated to some extent by making notes and/or talking with others immediately afterwards. And as previously discussed, art and music can play important roles in improving psychedelic recall. Most often, it seems to remain the case that the most memorable lessons reported have to do with large-scale gestalt-like shifts of general outlook that concern one or two "big ideas." In an essay on intellectual history that is often quoted because of its vivid imagery, philosopher Isaiah Berlin (1909–1997) explains that "one of the deepest differences which divides writers and thinkers" is between what he labels, drawing from ancient Greek poetry, "hedgehogs and foxes," in that the "fox knows many things, but the hedgehog knows one big thing."[35] Berlin explains further:

> there exists a great chasm between those, on one side, who relate everything to a single central vision, one system, less or more coherent or articulate, in terms of which they understand, think and feel—a single, universal, organising principle in terms of which alone all that they are and say has significance—and, on the other side, those who pursue many

ends, often unrelated and even contradictory, connected, if at all, only in some de facto way, for some psychological or physiological cause, related to no moral or aesthetic principle.[36]

In a great nerdy parlor game for humanities graduate students, it is possible—pint in hand—to place past masters in either camp. On his own list, Berlin has Plato as a hedgehog (with his focus on the world of Forms and the One), whereas Shakespeare, with his diverse panoply of close observations of human nature, counts as a fox. In the manner of many indigenous cultures, if we were to personify psychedelics (e.g., Mother Ayahuasca, Father Iboga, "the Toad"), it seems to me that, fitting its dynamic visuals, the felt experience of psychedelics would quality as *both*: it initially appears as a fox, with its dynamic and dazzling visuals and ability to render a movable focus on just about any perceptual detail, but then, in the ensemble—and very often post hoc—it settles into memory in hedgehog form, where what has been learned can be boiled down to One Big Thing—whatever that Thing may be for the experiencer. As discussed, there are copious examples: oneness, love, intersubjective connectedness, connectedness with nature and cosmos, life-as-a-continuum, temporal cyclical wholeness, and so on. Yet psychedelics might still more accurately be cast as "hedgehogs plus" in that the grand yet largely inarticulable insights are not undergone merely as a cognitive assent to a logical or empirical proposition, but rather, they are felt as robustly *moving* to individuals in a more holistic manner than mere intellectual realization. It is more than a gestalt "aha" experience—like the feeling of finally figuring out a math problem—in that it carries with it a greater level of emotion and viscerality. Ancient participants in the Eleusinian Mysteries and contemporary cancer patients in clinical psilocybin trials were not moved to their core and made less afraid of death via greater acquaintance with physiological facts about mortality or some proposition about death; separated by millennia, these disparate individuals reported similar and substantial reductions in death anxiety due to more encompassing and gut-felt sentiments about their lives as a whole. Thus, the psychedelic hedgehog is the one that endures and the one that proves to be integrable into a person's life.

If we remove transmission of information and intellective operations like logical argument as sources of psychedelic hedgehog's insight, and consider its pluripotent or nonspecific aspects, by elimination, what remains is some sort of altered relationship with one's priors. Or, in different terminology, insight comes about when one's hermeneutical horizons are marshaled toward a fusing partner, via psychedelic catalyst, to generate understanding. It is in effect a retrospective operation, where one's already existing horizon is granted more potency than it had before such that it can *project* itself in the hypertrophic identification process; psychedelics seem to be able to "reach back" into one's priors and enable one to illuminate more brightly what is already known and to resuscitate it into a state seeming more "alive" than it had been (it may even have been so far at the back of mind as to have escaped notice altogether). The kinds of examples associated with Heidegger's first-person existential analytic of Dasein provide an analogy: consider again the oncologist who deals with terminal patients daily but then one fine day receives a terminal diagnosis *herself*; in such a case, there is an existential shift that occurs from mere knowledge of mortality to a more holistic, moving experience of mortality. It is one thing to *know* X objectively, but another to *accept* and then *integrate* X subjectively, in terms of its qualia. This example shows in miniature what psychedelics can do on a broader canvas: namely, they can catalyze a reality shift whereby some portion of one's prior doxastic ensemble can be, literally, *enlivened*; beliefs that one "holds" in some sense (consciously or unconsciously) can be, as it were, given a breath of life and awakened so that one's awareness of them is now *felt* as well as known. Writ larger, this provides the possibility of a major *doxastic enhancement* of very wide belief-sets comprising one's cultural inheritances, including one's religious, moral, aesthetic, and intellectual assumptions and impulses. The entropy of the psychedelic experience during its peak pendency (the dazzlingly clever and multifarious fox) may weaken any of these tendencies (epistemic loosening), but afterwards, through the integration process, it may strengthen any of them as well, as some subset of those commitments is placed in a new light (the hedgehog who now knows Something Really Big).

Under optimal conditions, psychedelics can thus function as a *worldview accelerant*, like gasoline being poured on smoldering coals; they do not start the doxastic fire, but they can fan its flames to great effect. Latent beliefs that have become rote and formulaic, half-noticed, or unnoticed altogether can now be brought inside the ambit of first-person *lived* experience, rather than the lip-service truisms they had become. Like the clerics in this section's epigraph, one can say "everything is interconnected" and "it's all about love," etc., but actually mean it. In Humean terms, a new passion thereby assumes the throne over its previous occupant and begins its successor regime that reigns, as some passion must, over the reason-knowledge apparatus.

But for doxastic enhancement and worldview acceleration to take place, there first has to be something present to be enhanced and enlivened in the first place. As nonspecific amplifiers, psychedelics do not *themselves* supply the material that is amplified, any more than stereo speakers are the ultimate source of the music. If psychedelics mainly enliven and project what is already present, then great care must be taken concerning those beliefs and that worldview.

First, there is a quantitative concern. If we imagine someone with a very thin cultural inheritance, little accumulated lived experience, and, let us say, an anemic and/or superficial mindset, then there will not be much there even when it is enhanced. This consideration compels, I think, a kind of psychedelic educational imperative premised on a "garbage in, garbage out" maxim—again not in a snobby credentialing sense, but in the widest sense possible—where the insight produced by psychedelics is likely to be a function of the quality of the mental raw material with which it is working. If this sounds "elitist," it is. But it has nothing to do with exclusivity around the usual lines of socioeconomic status, ethnicity, race, gender, etc. (although it may contain some built-in prejudice concerning developmental status and age). Due to her superior allusionary base built up out of receptivity toward lived experience, a severely disabled and impoverished person could easily possess a goldmine of relevant mental material as compared to a far more physically and materially privileged—and formally educated—counterpart with comparatively less ability to attend to and make meaning out of the events in her own life. Anyone who thinks that deep insight is commensurate with material privilege and formal education really needs to get out more.

Second is a qualitative concern. As encountered in extreme form with the cult problem, "non-specific amplifier" means just that: *non-specific*. Many have perfectly lovely and benign insights and realizations on psychedelics about love, nature, connection, etc. Ex hypothesi, however, that *these* are their insights has mostly to do with what they possessed to begin with and are now projecting those priors through the intensity of their psychedelic journeys. Ex-hippies with an ecological bent and harboring off-the-grid fantasies are unsurprisingly prone to realizations about being one with nature and cosmos. But then again, techies awash in circuitry and computers and living in artificial urban environments might find a high-tech Tron aesthetic and gain insights about cosmic information flows. Christian theology students at Marsh Chapel saw visions of Christ but, had they been Muslim students at a madrasa, surely they would have been beset with Islamic figurations. Peoples of the Amazon have visions that are colored and articulated in terms of village life and tropes from their jungle environment. And learned classicists may see visions of the caves at Eleusis or the Eucharist as conducted in the catacombs. Even those who do not see themselves as strongly committed to any particular worldview—the religious "Nones," self-styled agnostic or the merely curious—will inevitably project via an imagination itself formed by the zeitgeist, with characteristic modernistic assumptions about, say, personal identity and basic human equality, etc. But this very same pluripotency also means, of course, that inveterate racists might see reinforcing images of demi-gods of ancestral purity, while pre-Roman Druids and ancient Mesoamericans might find their ardor for mass human sacrifice augmented. Manson Family members, too, might be made more zealous and determined to slaughter those who "Charlie" said were their enemies up in the Hollywood hills. The obvious point is that psychedelics are not going to build their insights *ab initio*. Rather, they are at one order of remove going to "reveal" them by vivifying what is already there. For this reason, it might be said that the bulk of psychedelic insight is not particularly psychedelic at all; in the Heideggerian disclosive sense, psychedelics are just the tools for access.

Keeping these two stipulations in mind, an intriguingly original and extended example of psychedelic doxastic enhancement is provided in Rick Strassman's work on DMT and the western prophetic tradition. Strassman's analysis is, I believe, wholly consistent with what I have provided here. Strassman holds in general that the DMT experience is "aesthetics-rich" and "message-poor," in that there is much breathless intensity to report and describe within these astonishing chemical journeys, but the longer-term integrative takeaways as to their overall meaning seemed regularly to disappoint.[37] The overwhelming focus was on "descriptions of the DMT state itself" and, even where there was some "message" being articulated, "it nearly always involved personal psychological issues, rather than ones of a larger social or spiritual nature."[38] Thus, on the basis of observations like these, in the course of his pioneering and extensive research with (intravenous) DMT takers—with a particular focus on participants *not* discernibly suffering from any mental debility—Strassman reaches what was for him initially a surprisingly disappointing conclusion: the vaunted unitive-mystical states of "enlightenment" were actually far scarcer than he had anticipated. "When faced with the facts of my volunteers' reports being so different than those I expected, I felt my theoretical framework begin to totter."[39] Not that the DMT experiences proved insignificant to the participants. On the contrary. It was just that what they reported did not quite fit the expected script: "the highly articulated contents of the DMT experience, its sights, sounds, feelings, and physical sensations felt more real than the highly articulated contents of everyday reality. Applying the yardstick of a unitive-mystical state was simply inapplicable."[40] Strassman then goes on to stress a "quality of relatedness" peculiar to the DMT experience as opposed to the "a-relational enlightenment-like states" that are more commonly advertised and expected with psychedelics. The purpose of Strassman's book is then to provide a "neurotheological" argument for how DMT in particular—and there may be a DMT exceptionalism vis-à-vis other classic psychedelics in this regard—because of its "interactive-relational" aspect (as opposed to the "unitive-mystical" aspect of other psychedelics), is, in his view, more consistent with the western prophetic tradition.[41]

This is because, according to Strassman, in the Hebrew Bible, "the prophetic state is interactive and relational, never mystical or unitive."[42] A quick example would be Moses communicating with God via the burning bush in Exodus 3:1–17 (an apt story to reference, as it has been speculated, rather extravagantly, that the burning bush may have been of a DMT-laden species native to the region that Moses could have inhaled).[43] In this episode, God emphasizes his separateness with such pronouncements as "'Do not come any closer,' God said" and "God said to Moses, 'I am who I am'" (note the usage of first-person singular). Also highlighting the separateness of the prophet from the deity, Moses is even afraid to look directly upon God ("Moses hid his face, because he was afraid to look at God"). As is typical in the Old Testament, in this address to Moses, God goes on to relate what *He* has done for individuals like him, his "forefathers," "the Israelites" in general, etc. It is very much *not* a unitive message of "we are all in this together" or "I am you and you are Me" or any such. For Strassman, the clear picture that emerges in this prophetic tradition is one in which God is radically separate from human beings and, in fact, that His unbreachable distinctness is a prerequisite for the veneration that is due to Him and the holiness with which He is imbued. Strassman sees this as much more parallel to the DMT experience that is commonly populated with entities who are, as is reported, perceived as very distinct from oneself and very clearly possessive of their own attributes, personalities, and agendas. The appearance of these entities is one of the hallmark aspects of the DMT "otherworld" and is one of the most intense areas of psychonautical interest. Psychologist David Lukes notes that "When described by independent and seemingly naive DMT participants the entities encountered tend to vary in detail but often belong to one of a very few similar types, with similar behavioural characteristics. For instance, mischievous shape-shifting elves, praying mantis alien brain surgeons and jewel-encrusted reptilian beings, who all seem to appear with baffling predictability."[44] These entities' ontological status is unknown, and the regularity of their intersubjective appearance is puzzling, but naturalistic explanations account for them as internal products of a subject's subconscious, maybe even a glimpsing of shared Jungian archetypes, and/or internalizations of environmental suggestions (e.g., machine elves and the mantis-like creatures are common knowledge—or common enough knowledge in DMT circles—and so breakthrough sojourners are primed to see them beforehand).

From Strassman's trip report data sets, this general "interactive-relational" aspect of the DMT experience is what emerges most prominently, in which the multifarious DMT entities typically behave in ways that imply and reinforce a sense of those entities' autonomy and otherness, e.g., "healing, harming, guiding, and most important, communicating information."[45] I would add also that they are also widely reported often to be welcoming in a "glad to see you" manner and that there is a sense that one is visiting *them* going about their business rather than being visited *by* them in the manner typical of UFO alien encounters or angelic visitations. (Strassman does note this "dropping in" phenomenon as well, although it would seem to cut against his thesis somewhat because it runs opposite to the biblical examples, where the prophets are always the visited and not the visitors.) It is not "relational," but it should be noted too that, interestingly, DMT entities sometimes are reported to appear indifferent to their "visitors" and continuing to go about their business—an attribute that may actually imply greater autonomy and distinctness from the observer. It is difficult to know what to make of all this ontologically, as figures in dreams can appear to operate autonomously, too, as do the voices heard by schizophrenics, etc. So, something *appearing* autonomous hardly seals the deal as far as its *actual* existence as something autonomous. Strassman's main point is preserved, however, because he is attending to the shared subjective *experience* of relationality in both DMT and the prophetic tradition, and then juxtaposing these with the default subjective experiences of the unitive type that are so highly prominent with other psychedelics and in the relevant literature.

Furthermore, in Strassman's view, it is the stress on the mystical-unitive aspect—and the assumption that has arisen that this is *the* archetypal psychedelic insight—that has led so many to interpret and integrate their psychedelic experiences according to themes and motifs more consonant with eastern religions and philosophies such as Buddhism (as he himself initially did).[46] He also notes the enthusiasm for importing Latin American shamanistic approaches. Although, like the prophetic orientation, the *curandero*-led ayahuasca traditions also very much stress psychedelic entities' separateness and distinctness (unsurprising, perhaps, because of the DMT basis for ayahuasca), he finds them potentially ethically problematic for modernist western sensibilities. This is due, he alleges, to their widespread focus on manipulation and control of behavior, in which "violent, often murderous, competition for power, prestige, money and sex is commonplace."[47] This may, however, overstate matters, keeping in mind—with all due respect to the religions involved—that this list of sins could easily apply to the Old Testament as well (not to mention the modernist West's cult problem), and clerics in the modernist West also have their share of what appear to be systemic ethical challenges (e.g., the widespread abuse scandals involving Catholic priests); this particular ethical concern laid out by Strassman is therefore not unique to shamanic traditions. His main point still stands, though: given how deeply ensconced we are within the cultural horizons of our upbringing, it is harder than often imagined simply to adopt and import wholesale selected core narratives and practices from other traditions, particularly when doing so will decontextualize and inevitably distort those narratives and practices.

Granted, cultural synthesis and religious syncretism are the rule rather than a "deviation" from some imagined original "purity." For example, the legally triumphant União do Vegetal and Santo Daime ayahuasca churches are, like most contemporary indigenous religions in the Americas, fully fusioned with Christianity. But, for this same reason (i.e., hybridization takes at least two parties), wholly excluding one's *own* cultural inheritance may, in an entheogenic envelopment, prevent psychedelics from resonating as deeply and durably as they could. "I believe that in order for the psychedelic drug experience to exert the greatest possible influence on western religious sensibilities, it is advantageous to present and interpret that experience in a manner consistent with religious notions already existing within those religions."[48] The predominance of eastern and Mesoamerican psychedelic motifs is understandable, given the unimaginable enormity and richness of those spiritual traditions, but attending to them *at the expense* of ignoring one's own cultural and ideational lineage seems adventitious and unnecessarily limiting. Consistent with this point, Swedish psychedelics researcher Patrick Lundborg argues that we in the modernist West need

> to develop our own psychedelic philosophy and rites, and the richer the links to our own cultural history are, the stronger they will grow. We already have an alternate spiritual history, we just need to find our way back into it. Following today's psychedelic impulse backwards, through the wild ride of the 20th century, back to the Renaissance and the Neoplatonists and the hallucinogenic initiation at Eleusis. . . . It was all there at the Great Temple at Eleusis, in the dawn of Western culture—the psychedelic affirmation of something greater than reality, and the forming of a mystery cult based on this shared experience. We've done it before, we can do it again.[49]

West, East, North, or South, psychedelics are very demonstrably an ancient *global* heritage including, as discussed earlier, and they are very strongly and copiously present within many streams of western culture as well (including, of course, Strassman's favored Judaic prophetic tradition). To be sure, the shutout of western religious lineages in modern psychedelia has by no means been complete. Far from it. Prominent borrowings can be found, not only in ancient Greece and early Christianity, but in the often underground but continuous threads of western paganism, including druidism, Wicca, and, more recently, Gaian/ecological thought.[50] Furthermore, societal conditions are now such that mainstream religious formations might also be receptive to the reigniting spark that psychedelics can provide.

Along such lines, Strassman's recommendation, one shared very enthusiastically by another prominent psychedelics researcher in the intersection of psychedelics, psychology, and religion, Johns Hopkins University clinician William Richards, is what I will term a kind of *psy-*

chedelic revivalism. On the basis of years of trials conducted with Roland Griffiths, Richards is convinced that "psilocybin and similar substances are indeed molecules that can facilitate beneficial and often sacred experiences."[51] (He simultaneously cautions that "when used irresponsibly with insufficient knowledge, these substances can facilitate experiences that may have negative consequences for some persons.")[52] Moreover, Richards finds that psychedelics seem able to catalyze a "deeper" foray into one's *own* spiritual traditions, though not in any chauvinistic or exclusivist manner: "I am finding a deeper appreciation for the person's own religious heritage. That the symbols and scriptures start to come alive in new ways, but that's coupled with increased tolerance and appreciation for other world religions, other paths up the mountain, if you will."[53] This situation where "symbols and scriptures start to come alive" is, in a nutshell, the idea of psychedelic revivalism, where dormant religious scripts that have grown lifeless and formalistic might be reanimated, functioning as a doxastic defibrillator to jump-start what will otherwise soon become a corpse. While there are of course non-chemical means by which to accomplish such a feat, as there have been repeatedly in history—consider the Protestant Reformation in its early iconoclastic stages and later outbreaks such as the American Great Awakening of the 1730s—in a modernist world grown skeptical and incredulous about prefabricated narratives, a more worldly, science- rather faith-based catalyst might prove efficacious for many, as it has demonstrably done in the Johns Hopkins and other clinical trials. It would, in fact, be to take direction and inspiration (and it is high time to do so) from the model provided by indigenous entheogenic usage, where plant teachers actually *augment* belief commitment and community cohesion, rather than signifying countercultural avant-garde gestures and acts of rebellion against society, as was the norm in the first and second psychedelic waves. As mentioned in earlier chapters, in the United States, it is not only the indigenous churches, but there is an exemplification of this general idea in emerging movement of churches and synagogues, like the Jewish reform Shefa congregation in the Bay Area and the Baptist Legare group in Savannah, Georgia—and many others besides—who are devoted to exploring the power of psychedelics within the inherited framework of their Jewish and Christian (and other) traditions.[54] Befitting this traditionalist approach, and in the Jewish traditions of both irreverence and commemoration, Shefa has even put out a psychedelic Haggadah companion for the traditional Passover seder, *The Four Cups of Consciousness.*[55]

In terms of the foregoing philosophical analysis, this represents the half of the hermeneutic circle not addressed in the REBUS model, the part where dormant high-level priors might be awakened and affirmed rather than just relaxed and weakened—in fact it is likely the case that *all* of these are happening simultaneously in the high-dosage situation (and then reinforced and made to cohere via post hoc integration). In Humean terms, this would also represent a reintroduction of the passion part of the reason-passion amalgam that is necessary for a "progress of the sentiments." Psychedelics in these entheogenic envelopments would be in the role of reanimating the religious impulse that has given purpose and direction to human beings throughout our entire anatomically modern existence and served as an antidote to social disconnection and demoralizing nihilism. In this way, they would function as magnitudinal enhancements to the traditional frameworks that the last few generations have grown up with but don't really, on the whole, believe in anymore. To be sure, in the process of their enlivening, those frameworks would necessarily be revised according to modernist cultural and ethical precepts, just as revivals have always reappropriated and reconstructed their inherited traditions; such movements are not antiquarian projects to replicate an *ancien régime* (admittedly, sometimes they *think* they are, but it never works out that way—one thinks of the disastrous restorationist nationalisms of past centuries or reactionary traditionalist movements within established churches). They would, for instance, be sure sedulously to incorporate ethical notions about equality and tolerance into the enlivened emergent synthesis in accord with modern sensibilities. (No matter the potency of the revived enthusiasms, ritual human sacrifice along archaic lines is likely to be ruled out, as it mostly has been since the dawn of the Axial Age.)[56] Such a process of cultural reappropriation, parallel to the individualized process of psychological integration, would be akin to the work Hume imagines reason to be able to effect on the passions: arranging, sequencing, forecasting their effects, balancing them against one another, etc., and in the process of all this collective pruning and shearing, growing an altogether new syncretism out of the old elements. In this Humean way, the reinforcement of a portion of the legacy priors does not entail cultural or mental stasis.

Boldly, Strassman envisions a kind of "takeover from within" strategy for entheogens inside of mainstream religions by incorporating psychedelic use alongside traditional practices. Within the Jewish frame, he suggests that we "might consider enhancing our subjective experience of performing mitzvot [sacred obligations] through the psychedelic drug state. Doing so may allow us to approach closer to prophecy, inasmuch as those who received these precepts did so through the aegis of spiritual experience."[57] He even proposes a little undercover work: "Lower doses of a psychedelic substance may allow someone to sit in a chair, read the text, associate new meanings with it, and converse with study partners and fellow congregants."[58] It is hard to ignore the potential for comedy in such suggestions (we Jews love comedy), but one must applaud Strassman for getting down to brass tacks about how actually to conduct such psychedelic infusions. For his part, Richards takes things further and forwards ideas that are even more audacious, going beyond the entheogenic envelopment and into education generally (and, to be honest, with even greater comic potential). In addition to approvingly citing Tupper's earlier-mentioned idea of an "Inward Bound" educational program for twentysomethings, Richards sees even greater psychedelic potential for academics. He imagines that future scholars, "with the assistance of psychedelics," might be able "not only to study Plato's writings in the dark carrels of libraries, even in the original Greek, but also to visit the states of consciousness that inspired Plato's writings and confirm for themselves their nature and validity."[59] He even goes so far as to envision some changes to the college curriculum:

> What if universities offered an experimental seminar, perhaps called Philosophy 599, in which qualified students could legally receive a psychedelic substance in a context that offered skilled preparation and provided for maximum safety? Probably not at all students in the seminar would experience the full mystical consciousness described by Plato in their first session. Some would find alternative states of thought and perceptions would help them understand the perspectives of other philosophers instead. But the subsequent class discussions would most likely be riveting.[60]

Indeed. (I will say, however, as a former philosophy graduate student myself, I can with great authority relate that something like this has already occurred, at certain times and places, though in an admittedly ersatz fashion.) The same kind of curricular infusion could of course be imagined elsewhere, from art to anthropology. Regardless, I am not sure such an initiative would be feasible in formal academic settings as they are currently constituted. One must always remember the one guy in

Pahnke's Good Friday experiment who ran crazed down a busy street outside the Chapel to announce the Second Coming and had to be sedated with Thorazine.[61] One must account for that possibility, especially in a group of any size (as Richards, a psychologist who runs psychedelics trials, obviously knows). Still, one can only admire the chutzpah in the suggestion. Nonetheless, the main point about the potential doxastic enhancement of students is well taken. It is only that formal educational institutions are not the best places for every educational experience.

Zooming out again to the larger panorama, as long as we in the modernist West don't expect them to yield ready-made answers to questions that are best explored carefully within developed traditions of collective inquiry—religious, scientific, artistic, philosophical, etc.—psychedelics would seem to hold exciting potential for effecting consequential changes in states of mind, reinvigorating our sense that there might still be—at this late date—mystery and meaning to it all. And that it might still be possible—at this late date—to commit to something significant. In this way, in the best case, psychedelics could help as part of an antidote to (post)modernist nihilism. Based on their neurological effects, under the right conditions, psychedelics seem able to provide a nonspecific *motivation* and *impetus* that can put to work whatever mental resources we may possess toward reanimating our outlook with a well-grounded *feeling* that things matter, a counter to the cynicism and lack of hope that has arisen amidst modernism's ruination of the metanarratives of the past; there may be life in the old stories yet.

Interestingly, we can locate this deflationary momentum within our own attitudes toward belief themselves, and among some truly high-level priors that have become so deeply embedded that they are rarely noticed as such (the Marxist political philosopher Louis Althusser calls this process "interpellation," and emphasizes how we internalize dominant ideologies subconsciously).[62] Among the most important of these is articulated by philosopher Charles Taylor in his monumental work of intellectual history, *A Secular Age* (2007). Taylor argues that we moderns are living through a centuries-long "nova effect" in which ancient notions of cosmic order have eroded and along with them any reliable sense of life's meaning and significance; and like a celestial supernova, the blast from this grand alteration in consciousness eventually radiates outward into all areas of society.[63] Whereas, in the premodern past, when belief in whatever cosmic order (and God or Gods) was unchallenged, and the sense of purpose this provided was given and assumed, the "secular shift" ushered in with modernity precipitated a situation where "belief becomes an option"; it is not that no one any longer possesses religious belief (or belief in some animating secular meta-narrative), but that "Belief in God is no longer axiomatic. There are alternatives."[64] Even fervent believers understand this to be the situation. Not only might someone *choose* to adhere to a different worldview or choose not to believe in one at all (nihilism), but even the believers themselves come to accept that their own belief is one *choice* among others, analogous to a "lifestyle" that one may decide to take up or not—they *could have* chosen otherwise. It seems very normal for us to think of religion this way. So and so *chose* to become a Buddhist, say, and this sounds perfectly right and natural in the twenty-first century.

But Taylor gets us to see that, no matter how many true believers might still be around, this widespread acceptance of belief's voluntariness means religion's status and its hold *as truth* has thereby necessarily diminished. Consider how it would sound to say that so and so chose not to accept the theory of gravity or the heliocentric solar system or, perhaps, the evolutionary origins of life on earth. To any educated person in the modernist West, this does not sound as if so and so has made a legitimate choice, *que sera, sera*; instead, it sounds *crazy* and outside the bounds of legitimacy—even that it is not possible *actually* to hold such views. One must appreciate that it would sound just about like this to a twelfth-century European peasant if you suggested that the Bible is just another book, there is no God in heaven, and the devil isn't real. You could mouth the words and the utterances would be intelligible, but they just wouldn't make any *sense*.

Our peasant's inability to comprehend such claims is the result not of a limitation set by intelligence, but of one set by the cultural and historical boundaries that every age places upon imagination (including ours), even as that same imagination sometimes simultaneously strains outward against the constraining membrane of its *Umwelt* bubble. The long acid bath of modernity and its emphasis on individualism has, in the past half-millennium, liberated and broken bonds of superstition, cruelty, and injustice, but it has also, by gradually making individual volition the locus of all value, made everything else outside the individual seem questionable and arbitrary; there is nothing larger felt to be credible enough to *believe* in as a platform for self-understanding and societal solidarity. We are thereby cut adrift, adjacent to one another, but each of us in a solitary mental confinement, each postmodern self the prisoner of a sovereign decision-maker that is none other than *itself*. Predictably, loneliness and an abiding malaise as to the worthwhileness and meaning of *any* larger narrative—and consequently, any sustainable self-model—has become far too common, especially among youth, for whom cynicism about "big picture" explanations, along with generalized anxiety and lurking depression, are now generation-defining conditions. We have, collectively, fallen into a dissociative state, whose nova effect radiates ever wider.

As doxastic enhancers, psychedelics are perhaps uniquely situated to help address a crisis of belief, where it is not a crisis of having wrong or deficient beliefs, but a problem with locating *any* strong belief as a motivational base. This is where Hume steps in: his recognition of the controlling position of the passions recommends an intervention that is capable, not of convincing us didactically of its plausibility, but of *compelling* us by surfacing and deploying our deepest sentiments. Unlike most other educational interventions, psychedelics get right at the passions in order to render them ready to be organized and directed (which is also one way to look at the demonstrable vulnerabilities they can engender). Concerning the precise coordinates of that direction, as per Hume, psychedelics will ultimately have little to contribute; firmly within the Grofian nonspecific amplifiers camp, I disagree with those who think that psychedelics come prepackaged with their own substantive worldview and will save the world with their wisdom. One often hears such views: "if only the conflicting parties would sit down and take ayahuasca together," and the like.[65] But such attitudes rest on an erroneous view of how psychedelic insight operates. Psychedelics can indeed spark insight—and even commitment—but what exactly the spark lights on fire rests on other factors, primary among them being the nature of the allusionary base a given individual brings to the psychedelic event—in hermeneutical terms, that individual's horizons. Things might go one way, they might go another, but whatever the result, it is not due to an inherent ideological directionality in the drug.

In a sense, psychedelics deliver both less and more than advertised: less, in that they do not, by themselves, provide the contents of belief, yet also more, in that they are strikingly capable of addressing deeper problems of motivation. Michael Pollan's wise and justly influential book *How to Change Your Mind* might thus be more precisely titled *How **to Care** to Change Your Mind* (though the original is admittedly more felicitous). It is a tall order, but I believe that, since psychedelics seem able to promote a deeper learning by helping to enhance the basic motivating force of belief like little else, they might just be able to play an important role in repairing what, for the modernist West, seems to have been broken within us.

Conclusion

Some Parting Thoughts

> I don't necessarily believe what the mushroom tells me; rather we have a dialogue. It is a very strange person and has many bizarre opinions.
>
> —Terence McKenna, *Archaic Revival*, 47

A Caveat

In the spirit of "good fences make good neighbors," in the modernist West, therapeutic treatments for the unwell should be left to the medical professionals and, by the same token, the vast numbers who are *not* taking psychedelics for a *specific* cure for a *specific* ailment should not be forced into the medical envelopment and its characteristic modes and assumptions. This includes, of course, the emerging pharmaceutical-regulatory model, whose logic compels a system where the only way to take psychedelics legally is as a prescription-bearing and paying customer—and that is the best case, our regulatory regimes being notoriously corruptible by politics and corporate interests. Fortunately, in the US, as we have seen, there is a powerful alternative to this corporatist paradigm in the form of a potentially even wider route to legal psychedelics via the constitutional norm of free exercise, though this avenue is currently severely limited to the few with a documentable religious and cultural "lineage."[1] At present, only a select few indigenous peoples' lineages fit the bill, though free exercise protections could prove expansive, and there are ample persuasive precedents for them to do so in adjacent legal areas (e.g., conscientious objector status and other religious accommodations, along with relevant action at the state level). Whatever the legal developments, however, absent the direct rescinding of prohibition as in Oregon and Colorado (which still involves substantial state regulation), if psychedelics are not being used under tightly monitored entheogenic or medical criteria, almost all psychedelic use within the intellectual and recreational envelopments remains illegal and officially "dangerous."

Although the reopening of medical research and the constitutional victories for indigenous entheogens should be celebrated by psychedelics advocates, the emerging situation also creates an imbalance that will shape the third wave's psychedelic legacy. These structural conditions create the conditions for the medical-therapeutic and entheogenic envelopments to take the exclusive mantle of legitimacy as far as official permissibility and what is socially considered to be appropriate use. Psychedelics users will thereby be shunted into one of these two categories, "attached" within them, and the range of their experiences inevitably shaped by the priorities of the authorizing religious or medical institutions.

There may be defensible elements to such a set of policies, but there is a telling precedent in the US for precisely this kind of societal settlement. During the Prohibition era, alcohol was also limited to "medicinal" and religious use; the federal prohibition statute, the Volstead Act of 1920, contained explicit exemptions for physician-prescribed spirits and sacramental wine.[2] Yet prohibition proved culturally and politically unsustainable and was repealed by constitutional amendment in 1933. Alcohol is, of course, far more widespread and deeply rooted in the mainstream than psychedelics. Still, the regulatory contours of the Prohibition era too precisely match those of the emerging reformed psychedelics prohibitionism to ignore: though relaxed from the Nixon era, matters are again resolving into a boon favoring medicine and religion only. Though religion and science are often at war with one another across many other fronts, in the area of mind-altering substances, both enjoy their own vast constituencies and have been able predictably to parlay that support into regulatory advantages. These legal privileges have long histories and may be defensible in given instances. Or they may not be. But either way, on the basis of the foregoing analysis, these two envelopments should never be considered the whole of the "legitimate" psychedelic universe. Under the long historical shadow of the Prohibition era, laying out the envelopment framework as I have will, I hope, raise questions about whether medicine and religion should, once again, be granted a duopoly over the management of altered states of consciousness. At their best, these two envelopments have distinctive and compelling internal logics along with powerful evolved ethical norms concerning the proper use of psychedelics. Even so, the universe of psychedelia is far wider than can be covered even by these two portfolios combined; as philosopher Osiris Sinuhé González Romero recommends, it is imperative to get past the prohibitionist logic and "move beyond the false dichotomy of hospitals and churches."[3]

The main focus of this book has been on what for many is the most important aspect of psychedelics: the significant insights they are alleged to enable. From the research data and widespread testimony, it is very clear that, judged from the point of view of the individuals having them, such insights can occur within both the medical-therapeutic and entheogenic spheres. But it is equally clear that they also occur in the intellectual and recreational envelopments—in the latter by indirection and retrospection, perhaps, as psychedelic insight is unpredictable, not necessarily immediate and not always amenable to practical "demands." Furthermore, *each* of the four envelopments has its dangers, its corrupted counterparts, if you will. As noted: 1) the medical sphere is highly vulnerable to capture by moneyed interests; 2) the religious arena is the site of some of the worst cultic and abusive scenarios; 3) the recreational sphere is subject to developmental harms and other excesses such as drug abuse; and 4) as in its other endeavors, the intellectual sphere can be prone to hubris and a self-exceptionalism (i.e., the rules don't apply to me because I'm so brilliant: see one Leary, Timothy F.).[4] But these represent potential *corruptions* of envelopments and, while they illustrate that mitigation and reasonable oversight are warranted, their mere possibility does not, by itself, justify blanket illegality and stigma. If every human area of endeavor were judged and sanctioned according to its very worst practitioners and outcomes, little liberty of any kind would remain.

It is possible, of course, that certain drug dangers are just too high, but these should be addressed ad hoc and with careful attention to contextual and causal factors. Wholesale prohibitions motored by pharmaceutical interests or unsupportable cultural prejudices—fomented, especially during the second wave, by exaggerated claims of harm in sensationalist journalism—should certainly not be tolerated.[5] Until we hear about significant numbers of families torn apart and communities devastated by mushrooms and ayahuasca, the legal and regulatory apparatus should back off and we should err, as Hart suggests, on the side of the freedom to pursue happiness, including the choice by adults to alter their own consciousness, consistent with their obligations to others around them (i.e., "cognitive liberty").[6] A main message of this book is that *each* envelopment—and each of the many hybrids thereof—constitutes a legitimate arena in which to pursue psychedelics and each is capable of serving as an enabling backdrop for profound insights.

The integration of psychedelics at the community level that is so central to many indigenous cultures—and, it must be remembered, to western culture historically as well—provides copious models for how psychedelics can rest comfortably and alongside the mainstream in a prosocial manner. In many respects, the first and second waves of psychedelics in the modernist West are, in "the long trip" of deep human history, aberrations, in that within them psychedelics were positioned as antagonistic to their host cultures, intellectually, politically, aesthetically, and spiritually; prior to the third wave, their usage was framed largely as an anti-bourgeois oppositional gesture by which to challenge society or to "drop out" of it. For the better, I think, the third wave is escaping this limiting oppositional box. Two main factors have assured this: 1) rigorous medical science from prestigious institutions illustrating health benefits (and, admittedly, the legitimacy-consolidating effect of the financial interests following in their wake) and 2) legal accommodationism, but also, intertwined with the accommodations, an increasing understanding from *within* the entheogenic sphere—along with supporting independent work from archaeologists, historians, anthropologists, ethnobotanists and others—of the ancient continuities represented by psychedelic use and practice. Crucially, these latter also highlight how the relevant lineages are not just confined to certain contemporary indigenous groups; more accurately considered in its massive variety, dating to prehistorical times, psychedelia comprises a many-threaded and universal global lineage that constitutes a shared inheritance as a cultural universal.

In this connection, a special word concerning the recreational envelopment, which is the one most likely to run a social legitimacy deficit in certain circles. As suggested in chapter 4's analogy with Copeland's postulation of specifically musical emotions, there is a radical perspective on psychedelics that is rarely discussed, even among ardent boosters. Much discourse highlights psychedelics' *instrumental* value, that is, their practical uses in healing, spiritual enlightenment, and, as I have done, learning and insight. However, given that the desire to alter consciousness is a human universal, it is worth seriously considering whether, wholly aside from its use-value, psychedelic experience could be a good unto itself; *it may be valuable also on its own terms, simply as a human experience to be had*—one not to be missed if one can help it. Sadly, some will miss out on it, including those who probably should avoid it altogether—for example, individuals with certain underlying conditions like schizophrenia.[7] But this same limited exclusivity is a feature of many worthwhile human experiences that are also valuable both for their uses *and* in their own right: childbirth, swimming, art, music, lovemaking, dancing, having a companion animal, friendship, exercise, gardening, cuisine, intellectual discovery, meditation, and on and on, ad infinitum. Not everyone can or should engage in all of these (or wants to), and each of them can be undertaken for the purpose of deriving benefits from them. Yet each of them is also recommendable as *something simply to experience* as a human being.

From the mildest small-dose epistemic loosening and onward unto the wildest high-dose hypertrophic identifications and doxastic enhancements, it seems to me entirely legitimate to conceive psychedelics under this aspect as well: as *a worthwhile human experience that needs no more justification outside itself than does being moved by a piece of music or loving someone*. To engage in it might not reveal the secrets of the universe, but nonetheless it can be valuable to experience anyway, full stop. The ancient shamanic envelopment seems on the whole to carry with it an implied acknowledgment of this intrinsicality. It is axiomatic in these traditional contexts that plant teachers and the "flesh of the gods" are *utilized* in many ways, especially for healing and other tangible benefits accruing to the seeker via the *curandero* or equivalent shamanic figure (including occasional mischievous use). But at the same time, it is evident also that there is almost always an accompanying deep and abiding sense that the ayahuasca, mushrooms, ibogaine, etc. make accessible otherwise hidden worlds, the direct experience of which is *itself* part of a life well lived, where missing out on non-ordinary states of consciousness would be considered sad and omissive. This is what, in the modernized West, the recreational or ludic sphere "knows" in its own way that the other much more purposive and "serious" spheres sometimes do not: simply going with the flow of it for its own sake—and not "asking" the psychedelic to do anything for you beyond itself—can sometimes yield the richest and most memorable journeys. This should not be too surprising, after all. Some of life's most precious moments abide in memory as if unconnected to anything else, shining by their own lights, not because of their achievement of some external purpose, but simply and purely because they just *were*, they existed, and we were there to live them—and that is enough.

Summary

To conclude, I will summarize the findings of this book as plainly as I can: Is there deeper learning and insight with psychedelics? Yes, there can be.

But it should be undertaken in a spirit of adventure and, as with any adventure worthy of the name, one should prepare well and realize that it is not possible to eliminate the possibility of something unpleasant occurring. On a high enough dosage, what one should expect is a deep dive into oneself and/or one's environing world, where anything can be up for grabs. There is also the possibility of a breakthrough that takes one far outside the boundaries of what one had previously taken that "self" and that "world" to be, so much so that one might no longer be able to distinguish the two categories from one another. One might see the world as a whole differently afterwards and feel it differently too; and this might well include the way one sees and feels about oneself as well. It is likely to be especially productive if one has a rich set of non-drug interests going into the experience; that way the integration process occurring afterwards has more to work with. It is also possible, however, that one may need to try less hard and resist the impulse to need to gain something useful out of the experience; one may need to think less deeply about it and simply enjoy it (psychonauts take heed: you should be expert in something more than drugs). It is a cliché to say that the journey itself is the thing, but sometimes one can only hat tip the cliché and try not to outsmart oneself. If insight comes, immediately, in the moments afterwards or years later, it is likely to be One Big Thing that one feels and/or realizes about oneself and/or the world, rather than anything informational or anything like a blueprint for what to do or how to think or a roadmap to any particular destination. (In fact, one should probably be wary of any "message" that is too specific, especially if it supplied by someone else in one's circle.) This limitedness does not at all diminish the insight, but actually enhances it by, in the best case, enabling a wondrous illumination of vast reaches of what each of us normally keeps buried and hidden deep inside our own minds, as we begin, in writer Ernst Jünger's (1895–1998) words, to "invoke our own absent part."[8] As these absences are filled, what dreams and nightmares arise cannot be known beforehand; there will always be mysteries there to discover for oneself—*always*. Like life itself with all its joy and suffering, this is one of those things that have to be undergone in the first person; there is no substitute for *living it* and no one else can do it for you.

Note: It is your own choice whether or not to undergo this particular educational experience and this author recommends neither for nor against it. Also, it is still illegal in most places. And: neither my university, profession, publisher, people I quote or like, family, nor any of my friends necessarily endorse anything I say here; all of it is my fault, and my fault alone.

Notes

Introduction

1. I mean "alienation" in the old Hegelian sense of the term that does not have the negative connotations of modern usage, as in feeling "alienated" from something or phobias about "aliens," etc. Later incorporated by Marx, this Hegelian sense of alienation has to do with the extending of oneself into some-X, such as an artist into her artwork or, as in Marx, a worker via labor into some object during the production process.

2. The classic paper on this subject is David E. Nichols, "Studies of the Relationship between Molecular Structure and Hallucinogenic Activity," *Pharmacology Biochemistry and Behavior* 24, no. 2 (1986): 335–340, doi.org/10.1016/0091-3057(86)90362-X.

3. Karolina E. Kolaczynska et al., "Receptor Interaction Profiles of 4-Alkoxy-3,5-Dimethoxy-Phenethylamines (Mescaline Derivatives) and Related Amphetamines," *Frontiers in Pharmacology* 12 (February 9, 2022), doi.org/10.3389/fphar.2021.794254.

4. (2S,4aR,6aR,7R,9S,10aS,10bR)-9-(acetyloxy)-2-(furan-3-yl)-6a,10b-dimethyl-4,10-dioxo-2,4a,5,6,7,8,9,10a-octahydro-1H-benzo[f]isochromene-7-carboxylic acid methyl ester.

5. Tom O'Neill, *Chaos: Charles Manson, the CIA and the Secret History of the Sixties* (New York: Little, Brown, 2019), 430. See also Matthew W. Johnson, "Consciousness, Religion, and Gurus: Pitfalls of Psychedelic Medicine," *ACS Pharmacology & Translational Science* 4, no. 2 (December 16, 2020): 578–581, doi.org/10.1021/acsptsci.0c00198. The prison experiments are discussed in Kali Holloway, "The Secret Black History of LSD," *The Nation*, March 22, 2022, www.thenation.com/article/society/lsd-acid-black-history/.

6. See Mike Jay, *Psychonauts: Drugs and the Making of the Modern Mind* (New Haven, CT: Yale University Press, 2023), 19, 103, 201.

7. See Alan Piper, "Leo Perutz and the Mystery of St. Peter's Snow," *Time and Mind* 6, no. 2 (July 2013): 175–198; and Leo Perutz, *Saint Peter's Snow* (London: Pushkin Vertigo, 2014 [1933]).

8. See Walter Sullivan, "New Study Backs Thesis on Witches," *New York Times*, August 29, 1982, which reports the findings in Mary Matossian, "Ergot and the Salem Witchcraft Affair," *American Scientist* 70, no. 4 (July–August 1982), 355–357, later published in Mary Matossian, *Poisons of the Past: Molds, Epidemics, and History* (New Haven: Yale University Press, 1991).

9. Albert Hofmann, *LSD My Problem Child: Reflections on Sacred Drugs, Mysticism and Science*, 4th ed. (Santa Cruz, CA: MAPS, 2017), 48.

10. Stanislav Grof, *Realms of the Human Unconscious: Observations from LSD Research* (London: Souvenir, 2019).

11. The definitive account of mescaline's rich history is Mike Jay, *Mescaline: A Global History of the First Psychedelic* (New Haven, CT: Yale University Press, 2019).

12. See Piper, "Leo Perutz and the Mystery of St. Peter's Snow," and Jay, *Mescaline*.

13. John Gerassi, "When Sartre Talked to Crabs (It Was Mescaline)," *New York Times*, November 14, 2009.

14. Jean-Paul Sartre, *Nausea*, trans. Lloyd Alexander (New York: New Directions, 1964 [1938]), 16–17.

15. Aldous Huxley, *The Doors of Perception and Heaven and Hell* (Harper, 2009) and *Island* (Harper, 2009).

16. See Joanna Klein, "A Mushroom Out of a Fairy Tale You Might Find in the Forest," *New York Times*, October 17, 2017; and Kat Morgenson, "Fly Agaric (*Amanita muscaria*)," *Sacred Earth*, November 11, 2020, sacredearth.com/2020/11/11/fly-agaric-amanita-muscaria/.

17. Valentina P. Wasson, "I Ate the Sacred Mushrooms," *This Week*, May 19, 1957, bibliography.maps.org/bibliography/default/resource/17683.

18. James Stephen, "R. Gordon Wasson & Maria Sabina: First Contact with Magic Mushrooms," *Truffle Report*, November 10 2020, truffle.report/maria-sabina-and-r-gordon-wasson-psychedelic-first-contact-warning/; see also R. Gordon Wasson's mea culpa, "Drugs: The Sacred Mushroom," *New York Times*, September 26, 1970: "what I have done gives me nightmares. I have unleashed on lovely Huautla a torrent of commercial exploitation of the vilest kind."

19. William S. Burroughs, "The Art of Fiction, No. 36," interview by Conrad Knickerbocker, *Paris Review* 35, Fall 1965, www.theparisreview.org/interviews/4424/the-art-of-fiction-no-36-william-s-burroughs.

20. Xan Brooks, "Cary Grant: How 100 Acid Trips in Tinseltown 'Changed My Life,'" *Guardian*, May 12, 2017.

21. Amelia Hill, "LSD Could Help Alcoholics Stop Drinking, AA Founder Believed," *Guardian*, August 23, 2012.

22. An early proponent, Cohen is an interesting figure who later became alarmed at the popular spread of psychedelics. See S. J. Novak, "LSD Before Leary: Sidney Cohen's Critique of 1950s Psychedelic Drug Research," *Isis* 88, no. 1 (March 1997): 87–110, doi.org/10.1086/383628.

23. Tom Wolfe, *The Electric Kool-Aid Acid Test* (New York: Picador, 2008 [1968]).

24. See Martin A. Lee and Bruce Shlain, *Acid Dreams: The Complete Social History of LSD: The CIA, the Sixties, and Beyond* (New York: Grove Press, 1994), 44–70.

25. Shulgin was a unique operator who developed profitable pesticides for Dow Chemical Company and then extensively consulted with the DEA, testing compounds for them, until they raided his lab in 1994. Shulgin's main books (with Ann Shulgin), which the DEA described as "cookbooks" for manufacturing illegal drugs, are *PIHKAL: A Love Story* (Berkeley, CA: Transform, 1990) and *TIHKAL: The Continuation* (Berkeley, CA: Transform, 2002). The titles of these lengthy tomes are acronyms for "Phenylethylamines I have known and loved" and "Tryptamines I have known and loved." See also Drake Bennett, "Dr. Ecstasy," *New York Times Magazine*," November 17, 2011.

26. The Beatles, *Sgt. Pepper's Lonely Hearts Club Band* (London: Parlophone, 1967). There are mountains of literature on the Beatles and this album, but for the topic at hand, see William Echard, *Psychedelic Popular Music: A History through Musical Topic Theory* (Bloomington: Indiana University Press, 2017), 160–188. For a wide-ranging description of Black Psychedelia, see Emily Lordi, "The Radical Experimentation of Black Psychedelia," *New York Times Style Magazine*, February 10, 2022.

27. This fragmentation thesis is compellingly presented in Erik Davis, *High Weirdness: Drugs, Esoterica and Visionary Experiences in the Seventies* (Cambridge, MA: MIT Press, 2019).

28. Hunter S. Thompson, *Fear and Loathing in Las Vegas: A Savage Journey to the Heart of the American Dream* (New York: Vintage Books, 2010 [1972]), 178.

29. See Patrick Lundborg's magisterial *Psychedelia: Ancient Culture, a Modern Way of Life* (Stockholm: Lysergia, 2012), 309–335.

30. My use of the "three waves" metaphor is indebted to the valuable website "Third Wave," thethirdwave.co, a source of helpful psychedelic guides and other research-based information, including an eponymous interview-format podcast.

31. Formerly at the University of Minnesota, Dennis McKenna is the founder of the McKenna Academy of Natural Philosophy, https://mckenna.academy/.

32. There are many works by and featuring Terence McKenna. A good introduction is *Food of the Gods: The Search for the Original Tree of Knowledge: A Radical History of Plants, Drugs, and Human Evolution* (New York: Bantam, 1993) and, perhaps better, sampling his lectures that are copiously available online at sites such as YouTube.

33. Brandon Bryn, "Inaugural Class of Invention Ambassadors Highlights Need for Innovation," *American Association for the Advancement of Science*, July 18, 2014, www.aaas.org/news/inaugural-class-invention-ambassadors-highlights-need-innovation.

34. Examples are Paul Stamets, *Mycelium Running: How Mushrooms Can Help Save the World* (New York: Ten Speed, 2005) and his reference books such as *Growing Gourmet and Medicinal Mushrooms* (New York: Ten Speed, 2000). Stamets is also easily found online (including his own paulstamets.com) and is featured in the popular cable television series "Fantastic Fungi" (Directed by Louie Schwartzberg. Netflix, 2019), whose companion book is Paul Stamets, ed., *Fantastic Fungi: How Mushrooms Can Heal, Shift Consciousness and Save the Planet* (San Rafael, CA: Earth Aware, 2019).

35. Melvin Sheldrake, *Entangled Life: How Fungi Make Our Worlds, Change Our Minds and Shape Our Futures* (New York: Random House, 2020), 183.

36. See Rick Strassman, *DMT: The Spirit Molecule: A Doctor's Revolutionary Research into the Biology of Near-Death and Mystical Experiences* (Rochester, VT: Park Street, 2001). For an overview of Roland Griffiths and his work at the Johns Hopkins Center for Psychedelics and Consciousness Research, see Julie Scharper, "Crash Course in the Nature of Mind: Roland Griffiths' Psilocybin Experiments Have Produced Striking Evidence for Therapeutic Uses of Hallucinogens," *Johns Hopkins Magazine*, Fall 2017, hub.jhu.edu/magazine/2017/fall/roland-griffiths-magic-mushrooms-experiment-psilocybin-depression/.

37. Stephen Szára, "Dimethyltryptamin: Its Metabolism in Man; the Relation to its Psychotic Effect to the Serotonin Metabolism," *Experientia* 12, no. 11 (November 15, 1956): 441–442.

38. See Hamilton Morris, "A Four Hour Long Conversation with Dr. David Nichols," *The Hamilton Morris Podcast*, November 23, 2022, audio, 4:02:49, hamiltonmorris.buzzsprout.com/1870388/11732744-a-four-hour-long-conversation-with-dr-david-nichols.

39. See Roland R. Griffiths and Charles C. Grob, "Hallucinogens as Medicine," *Scientific American*, December 1, 2010, www.scientificamerican.com/article/hallucinogens-as-medicine/; see also Roland R. Griffiths et al., "Psilocybin Produces Substantial and Sustained Decreases in Depression and Anxiety in Patients with Life-Threatening Cancer: A Randomized Double-Blind Trial," *Journal of Psychopharmacology* 30, no. 12 (December 2016): 1181–1197, doi.org/10.1177/0269881116675513; and Charles S. Grob et al., "Pilot Study of Psilocybin Treatment for Anxiety in Patients with Advanced-Stage Cancer," *Archives of General Psychiatry* 68, no. 1 (January 3, 2011): 71–78, doi.org/10.1001/archgenpsychiatry.2010.116. For further implications of this research for end-of-life care, see Mason Marks et al., "Introducing Psychedelics to End-of-Life Mental Healthcare," *Nature Mental Health* 1, no. 12 (November 8, 2023): 920–922, doi.org/10.1038/s44220-023-00166-1.

40. See Ryan Basen, "Academic Centers Start to Take Psychedelics Seriously," *MedPage Today*, November 24, 2021, www.medpagetoday.com/specialreports/exclusives/95865; and Sara Willa Ernst, "Psychedelic Therapy Research is

on the Horizon for Texas Veterans with PTSD," *Houston Public Media*, November 11, 2021, www.houstonpublicmedia.org/articles/news/in-depth/2021/11/11/413205/.

41. See Lauren Gravitz, "Hope that Psychedelic Drugs Can Erase Trauma," *Nature Outlook*, September 28, 2002, www.nature.com/articles/d41586-022-02870-x; and Natasha Loder, "Ketamine, Psilocybin and Ecstasy are Coming to the Medicine Cabinet," *Economist*, September 21, 2022, www.economist.com/technology-quarterly/2022/09/21.

42. See Sonari Glinton, "Big Pharma's Bet on Psychedelics," *Slate Magazine*, August 14, 2022, audio, 25:35, slate.com/podcasts/what-next-tbd/2022/08/the-corporatization-of-psychedelics ("Psychedelic drug research is increasingly being funded by pharmaceutical companies"); Betsy Reed, "Australia to Allow Prescription of MDMA and Psilocybin for Treatment-Resistant Mental Illnesses," *Guardian*, February 3, 2023; A. J. Herrington, "Alberta to Be First Canadian Province to Regulate Psychedelics for Therapeutic Use," *Forbes*, October 6, 2022, www.forbes.com/sites/ajherrington/2022/10/06/alberta-to-be-first-canadian-province-to-regulate-psychedelics-for-therapeutic-use/?sh=7ae14a5e85ea; and Deborah Samenow, Kristi Kung, and Rachel Ludwig, "State Psychedelic Regulation: Oregon and Colorado Taking the Lead," *DLA Piper*, January 11, 2023, www.dlapiper.com/en/insights/publications/2023/01/state-psychedelic-regulation-oregon-and-colorado-taking-the-lead. The Oregon Psilocybin Services Act (2021) may be found at secure.sos.state.or.us/oard/displayDivisionRules.action?selectedDivision=7102; and the Colorado Natural Medicines Act of 2022 at www.sos.state.co.us/pubs/elections/Initiatives/titleBoard/filings/2021-2022/58Final.pdf.

43. The letter to US Congresswoman Madeleine Dean (PA-04) from Miriam E. Delphin-Rittmon, Assistant Secretary for Mental Health and Substance Use, U.S. Substance Abuse and Mental Health Services Administration, may be found at www.lucid.news/wp-content/uploads/2022/09/Letter-1_SAMHSA-Response-to-Rep.-Dean-et-al.pdf; see also Representative Dean's press release on the proposed Breakthrough Therapies Act, "Reps. Dean and Mace Join Senators Booker and Paul to Introduce Bipartisan Legislation to Promote Research and Access to Potential Life Saving Drugs," Congresswoman Madeleine Dean, Press Releases, March 7, 2023, dean.house.gov/2023/3/booker-paul-mace-dean-introduce-bipartisan-legislation-to-promote-research-and-access-to-potential-life-saving-drugs.

44. A. J. Herrington, "House Lawmakers Launch Bipartisan Psychedelics Caucus," *High Times*, November 21, 2022, hightimes.com/psychedelics/house-lawmakers-launch-bipartisan-psychedelics-caucus/.

45. Will Yakowicz, "U.S. Government Will Test Ibogaine Derivative as an Addiction Treatment," *Forbes*, December 7, 2021, www.forbes.com/sites/willyakowicz/2021/12/07/us-government-will-test-ibogaine-as-an-addiction-treatment/?sh=329d426d4c4e; see also Faye Sakellardis, "How Ibogaine Emerged

as an Addiction Treatment in the West," *Lucid News*, June 1, 2022, www.lucid. news/ibogaine-addiction-treatment-in-the-west/.

46. "Younger people, those with previous recreational psychedelic experience, and those with non-religious beliefs were more likely to have favourable attitudes towards psilocybin therapy." Kate Corrigan et al., "Psychedelic Perceptions: Mental Health Service User Attitudes to Psilocybin Therapy," *Irish Journal of Medical Science* 191, no. 3 (June 15, 2022): 1385–1397, doi.org/10.1007/s11845-021-02668-2. But there is much uncertainty as well; see Gabriela Schulte, "Poll: 65 Percent of Voters say Psychedelic Substances Do Not Have Medical Use," *The Hill*, June 1, 2021, thehill.com/hilltv/what-americas-thinking/556304-poll-65-percent-of-voters-say-psychedelic-substances-do-not/. Psychedelics researcher James Fadiman (jamesfadiman.com) is an often referenced as an authority on microdosing (and psychedelics generally). See James Fadiman and Sophia Korb, "Might Microdosing Psychedelics Be Safe and Beneficial? An Initial Exploration," *Journal of Psychoactive Drugs* 51, no. 2 (April 2019): 118–122, doi.org/10.1080/02791072.2019.1593561. A popular account of microdosing is Ayelet Waldman, *A Really Good Day: How Microdosing Made a Mega Difference in My Mood, My Marriage, and My Life* (New York: Alfred A. Knopf, 2017).

47. For Tyson, see "Mike Tyson on Doing DMT/Joe Rogan [taken from "The Joe Rogan Experience #1227," *JRE Clips*, January 17, 2019, video, 6:07, www.youtube.com/watch?v=EmJsTf6hCRM; and for Rodgers, see "Aaron Rodgers's Ayahuasca Experience," *Aubrey Marcus Clips*, August 12, 2022, video, 15:16, www.youtube.com/watch?v=Wl6w8tXbJaY.

48. Carl Hart, *Drug Use for Grown-Ups: Chasing Liberty in the Land of Fear* (New York: Penguin, 2021).

49. See Richard Glenn Boire, "On Cognitive Liberty," *Journal of Cognitive Liberties* 1, no. 1 (Winter 1999–2000): 7–13, www.cognitiveliberty.org/on-cognitive-liberty-boire/.

50. Chacruna Institute for Psychedelic Plant Medicines, "Queering Psychedelics," conference, San Francisco, June 1–2, 2019, with accompanying papers and video recordings available at chacruna.net/queering-psychedelics/; and Nicolle Hodges, "How Psychedelics Help with Gender Identity and Transition," *Double Blind*, updated May 26, 2021, doubleblindmag.com/psychedelics-transgender/.

51. Brian C. Muraresku, *The Immortality Key: The Secret History of the Religion with No Name* (New York: St. Martin's, 2020), 141–151.

52. MindState Design Labs, www.mindstate.design; and *Josie Kins*, www.youtube.com/@josikinz.

53. Josie Kins, "Subjective Effect Index," *Effect Index*, accessed May 20, 2023, effectindex.com/effects/.

54. The neologism "entheogen" was coined by Carl Ruck from the Greek, literally "divine inspiration giving." The term has honorific connotations usually reserved for psychedelics in their religious, spiritual, and visionary uses. Carl A.

P. Ruck et al., "Entheogens," *Journal of Psychedelic Drugs* 11, no. 1–2 (1979): 145–146.

55. See S. C. Gwynn, *Empire of the Summer Moon: Quanah Parker and the Rise and Fall of the Comanches, the Most Powerful Indian Tribe in American History* (New York: Scribner, 2010), 303–318.

56. Gonzales v. O Centro Espírita Beneficente União do Vegetal, 546 U.S. 418 (2006); Church of Holy Light of Queen v. Mukasey, 615 F. Supp. 2d 1210 (D. Or. 2009).

57. See United States v. Meyers, 906 F. Supp. 1494 (D. Wyo. 1995) and the helpful discussion in George G. Lake, *The Law of Entheogenic Churches in the United States* (self-pub., 2021), 15–22, and John Rhodes, "Up in Smoke: The Religious Freedom Restoration Act and Federal Marijuana Prosecutions," *Oklahoma City Law Review* 38, no. 3 (Fall 2013): 337–340.

58. A critical analysis of the experiment is provided in Rick Doblin, "Walter Pahnke's 'Good Friday Experiment': A Long-Term Follow-up and Critique," *Journal of Transpersonal Psychology* 23 (January 1991), maps.org/research-archive/cluster/psilo-lsd/goodfriday.pdf.

59. See Alan Watts, *The Joyous Cosmology: Adventures in the Chemistry of Consciousness* (New York: Pantheon, 1962), and Huston Smith, *Cleansing the Doors of Perception: The Religious Significance of Entheogenic Plants and Chemicals* (New York: Tarcher/Putnam, 2000).

60. See Frederick R. Dannaway, Alan Piper, and Peter Webster, "Bread of Heaven or Wines of Light: Entheogenic Legacies and Esoteric Cosmologies," *Journal of Psychoactive Drugs* 38, no. 4 (2006): 493–503. One might include that Sufism is famous for the inducing of non-drug trance states that might aptly be described as "psychedelic." See Ala Kheir, John Burns, and Ibrahim Algrefwi, "The Psychedelic World of Sudan's Sufis—In Pictures," *Guardian*, February 5, 2016. More loosely, some have noted the curious similarities between the patterns of abstract art in the Islamic tradition and the ubiquitous geometrical designs often apparent in DMT and other psychedelic trips. An interesting speculative essay on this topic is Sam Woolfe, "The Psychedelic Nature of Islamic Art and Architecture," *Sam Woolfe*, October 1, 2018, www.samwoolfe.com/2018/10/the-psychedelic-nature-of-islamic-art-and-architecture.html ("why are people entering mosque-like spaces under the influence of DMT?").

61. Taylor Orth, "One in Four Americans Say They've Tried at Least One Psychedelic Drug," *YouGov (US)*, July 28, 2022, today.yougov.com/topics/society/articles-reports/2022/07/28/one-in-four-americans-have-tried-psychedelic-drugs.

62. "Past-year hallucinogen use had been relatively stable over the past few decades until 2020, when reports of use started to increase dramatically. In 2021, 8% of young adults reported past-year hallucinogen use, representing an all-time high since the category was first surveyed in 1988. By comparison, in 2016, 5% of young adults reported past-year hallucinogen use, and in 2011, only 3% reported

use. Types of hallucinogens reported by participants included LSD, MDMA, mescaline, peyote, 'shrooms' or psilocybin, and PCP. The only hallucinogen measured that significantly decreased in use was MDMA (also called ecstasy or Molly), showing statistically significant decreases within one year as well as the past five years—from 5% in both 2016 and 2020 to 3% in 2021." National Institutes of Health, "Marijuana and Hallucinogen Use Among Young Adults Reached All-Time High in 2021," *New Releases*, August 22, 2022, www.nih.gov/news-events/news-releases/marijuana-hallucinogen-use-among-young-adults-reached-all-time-high-2021.

63. Davis, *High Weirdness*, 4.

64. For Tupper, these peculiar tools are to be reserved for "later in education," perhaps as an Outward Bound–type experience for college-age students. See Kenneth W. Tupper, "Entheogenic Education: Psychedelics as Tools of Wonder and Awe," *MAPS Bulletin* 24, no. 1 (2014): 14–19. Tupper elaborates this theme further in a recent podcast interview, "Could Psychedelics Become a Crucial Part of Our Education?" *The Psychedelic Podcast by Third Wave*, episode 31, July 23, 2017, thethirdwave.co/podcast/episode-31-ken-tupper/. The earliest advocate for psychedelics in contemporary education appears to be Hofstra University philosopher of education Ignacio Götz, who went so far as to argue for it as part of teacher education in his *The Psychedelic Teacher* (Philadelphia: Westminster, 1972). Götz does not argue for the inclusion of psychedelics in teacher training programs, because of their narrowness, and instead advocates for a less formal though vaguer role tied to religion and spirituality: "The psychedelic teacher is one who is able to unveil the dimensions of the human soul" (102). Important books by contemporary philosophers include Chris Letheby, *Philosophy of Psychedelics* (New York: Oxford University Press, 2021), which explores psychedelics in the context of therapeutic usage, and Peter Sjöstedt-Hughes, *Modes of Sentience: Psychedelics, Panpsychism, Metaphysics* (London: Psychedelic Press, 2021), which addresses a wider range of topics; also on philosophy in psychedelic therapy, see Peter Sjöstedt-Hughes, "On the Need for Metaphysics in Psychedelic Therapy and Research," *Frontiers in Psychology* 14 (March 2023): 1–17, doi.org/10.3389/fpsyg.2023.1128589.

65. See Brian A. Pace and Neşe Devenot, "Right-Wing Psychedelia: Case Studies in Cultural Plasticity and Political Pluripotency," *Frontiers in Psychology* 12 (December 2021), doi.org/10.3389/fpsyg.2021.733185; see also Matthew W. Johnson and David B. Yaden, "There's No Good Evidence that Psychedelics Can Change Your Politics or Religion," *Scientific American*, November 5, 2020, www.scientificamerican.com/article/theres-no-good-evidence-that-psychedelics-can-change-your-politics-or-religion/.

66. Samuel Beckett, *Nohow On: Company, Ill Seen Ill Said, Worstward Ho: Three Novels* (New York: Grove, 1995), 89.

67. See Nancy Estévez Pérez, "Neuroplasticity and the Zone of Proximal Development: A Neurobiological Reflection on a Key Psychological Construct,"

IBRO/IBE-UNESCO Science of Learning Briefings, June 23, 2020, solportal. ibe-unesco.org/articles/neuroplasticity-and-the-zone-of-proximal-development-a-neurobiological-reflection-on-a-key-psychological-construct/.

68. Guang Chen et al., "A Large Dose of Methamphetamine Inhibits Drug-Evoked Synaptic Plasticity via ER Stress in the Hippocampus," *Molecular Medicine Reports* 23, no. 4 (February 11, 2021): 278, doi.org/10.3892/mmr.2021.11917; Christopher C. Giza and Mayumi L. Prins, "Is Being Plastic Fantastic? Mechanisms of Altered Plasticity after Developmental Traumatic Brain Injury," *Developmental Neuroscience* 28, no. 4–5 (August 1, 2006): 364–379, doi.org/10.1159/000094163.

69. For a review of the literature on psychedelics and neuroplasticity, see Cato H. M. de Vos, Natasha L. Mason, and Kim P.C. Kuypers, "Psychedelics and Neuroplasticity: A Systematic Review Unraveling the Biological Underpinnings of Psychedelics," *Frontiers in Psychology* 12 (September 10, 2021): 1–17, doi.org/10.3389/fpsyt.2021.724606. The Watts phrase is from the subtitle of *The Joyous Cosmology*. See also Andrew Gallimore, *Reality Switch Technologies: Psychedelics as Tools for the Discovery and Exploration of New Worlds* (Tokyo: Strange Worlds, 2022), 9–38.

70. Arthur Schopenhauer, "Psychological Remarks," in *Parerga and Paralipomena*, vol. 2, trans. and ed. Adrian Del Caro and Christopher Janaway (New York: Cambridge University Press, 2015), 520.

Chapter 1

1. Michael Pollan, *This is Your Mind on Plants* (New York: Penguin, 2021), 1.

2. See Elisa Guerra-Doce, "Psychoactive Substances in Prehistoric Times: Examining the Archaeological Evidence," *Time and Mind* 8 (2015): 11–91. For an overview, see Paul Devereux, *The Long Trip: A Prehistory of Psychedelia* (Brisbane: Daily Grail, 2008).

3. Michael James Winkelman, "Altered Consciousness and Drugs in Human Evolution," in *Entheogens and the Development of Culture: The Anthropology and Neurobiology of Ecstatic Experience*, ed. John Rush (Berkeley, CA: North Atlantic, 2012), 45.

4. Paul Devereux, *The Long Trip*, 46; and José Manuel Rodriguez Arce and Michael James Winkelman, "Psychedelics, Sociality and Human Evolution," *Frontiers in Psychology* 12 (September 2021): 1, doi.org/10.3389/fpsyg.2021.729425.

5. Ronald K. Siegel, *Intoxication: The Universal Drive for Mind-Altering Substances* (Rochester, VT: Park Street, 2005), 209. For more animal examples, see Giorgio Samorini, *Animals and Psychedelics: The Natural World and the Instinct to Alter Consciousness* (Rochester, VT: Park Street, 2002).

6. Siegel, *Intoxication*, 11, 14.

7. See Christopher Raetsch, *The Encyclopedia of Psychoactive Plants: Ethnopharmacology and Its Applications* (Rochester, VT: Park Street, 2005), 277–282. As with henbane and pigs, some plants are selectively and differentially psychoactive for certain animal species and not others; henbane can have hallucinatory effects on humans, but it is also deadly.

8. Oliver Sacks, *Hallucinations* (New York: Vintage, 2012), 90.

9. Ben Sessa, *The Psychedelic Renaissance: Reassessing the Role of Psychedelic Drugs in 21st Century Psychiatry and Society*, 2nd ed. (London: Aeon, 2019).

10. There is a plant alkaloid (a diverse group of nitrogen-containing organic compounds) closely related to LSD and found in morning glory seeds (*Turbina corymbosa* and *Ipomoea tricolor*). Sometimes called "LSA," it is known in Mesoamerica as "ololiuqui," and has been around for centuries (at least), including at the time of the Spanish conquest.

11. See R. Gordon Wasson, Albert Hofmann, and Carl A. P. Ruck, *The Road to Eleusis: Unveiling the Secrets of the Mysteries* (Berkeley, CA: North Atlantic, 2008); and Muraresku, *The Immortality Key*.

12. Carl A. P. Ruck, Blaise Daniel Staples, and Clark Heinrich, *The Apples of Apollo: Pagan and Christian Mysteries of the Eucharist* (Durham, NC: Carolina Academic Press, 2001), 14. For mushroom motifs in medieval churches, see Jerry B. Brown and Julie M. Brown, "Entheogens in Christian Art: Wasson, Allegro, and the Psychedelic Gospels," *Journal of Psychedelic Studies* 3, no. 2 (June 2019): 142–163, doi.org/10.1556/2054.2019.019. This article provides photographs of entheogenic mushroom art and defends the provocative thesis that "psychedelic traditions were not suppressed by the Church, but were rather maintained for the secret instruction of initiates and possibly for the education of the illiterate masses" (162).

13. "Inside the human body, the Soma becomes 'boundless' in the sense of producing a feeling of infinite expansion, a sensation characteristic of psychedelic drugs." In *The Rig Veda*, ed. and trans. Wendy Doniger (New York: Penguin, 2005), 136, n. 2.

14. "At the 14-month follow-up, 58% and 67%, respectively, of volunteers rated the psilocybin-occasioned experience as being among the five most personally meaningful and among the five most spiritually significant experiences of their lives." Roland Griffiths et al., "Mystical-Type Experiences Occasioned by Psilocybin Mediate the Attribution of Personal Meaning and Spiritual Significance 14 Months Later," *Journal of Psychopharmacology* 22, vol. 6 (August 2008): 621–632, doi.org/10.1177/0269881108094300; Griffiths et al., "Psilocybin Produces Substantial and Sustained Decreases in Depression and Anxiety": "When administered under psychologically supportive, double-blind conditions, a single dose of psilocybin produced substantial and enduring decreases in depressed mood and anxiety along with increases in quality of life and decreases in death anxiety in patients with a life-threatening cancer diagnosis. Ratings by

patients themselves, clinicians, and community observers suggested these effects endured at least 6 months. The overall rate of clinical response at 6 months on clinician-rated depression and anxiety was 78% and 83%, respectively." See also Roland Griffiths et al., "Survey of Subjective 'God Encounter Experiences': Comparisons among Naturally Occurring Experiences and Those Occasioned by the Classic Psychedelics Psilocybin, LSD, Ayahuasca, or DMT," *PLOS ONE* 14, no. 4 (April 2019), doi.org/10.1371/journal.pone.0214377: "Similar to mystical-type experiences, which are often defined without reference encountering a sentient other, these experiences were rated as among the most personally meaningful and spiritually significant lifetime experiences, with persisting moderate to strong positive changes in attitudes about self, life satisfaction, life purpose, and life meaning that participants attributed to these experiences."

15. "'Entheogen' is a neologism to designate psychoactive substances employed in culturally sanctioned visionary experiences in ritual or religious contexts." Carl A. P. Ruck, "Entheogens in Ancient Times: Wine and the Rituals of Dionysus," in *Toxicology in Antiquity*, 2nd ed., ed. Philip Wexler (Cambridge, MA: Academic Press, 2019), 343–352.

16. James Boswell, *The Life of Samuel Johnson* (New York: Penguin, 1979 [1791]), 122.

17. David Chalmers, "Facing Up to the Problem of Consciousness," *Journal of Consciousness Studies* 2, no. 3 (1995): 200–219.

18. Martin Heidegger, *Being and Time*, trans. John Macquarrie and Edward Robinson (New York: Harper &Row, 1962 [1927]), section 43. Subsequent references to *Being and Time* will be presented parenthetically in the text with the section number.

19. Immanuel Kant, *Critique of Judgment*, trans. J. H. Bernard (New York: Hafner, 1951 [1790]), section 241; Mircea Eliade, *Shamanism: Archaic Techniques of Ecstasy*, trans. William R. Trask (Princeton, NJ: Princeton University Press, 1964).

20. Kant, *Critique of Judgment*, section 250.

21. Plato, *Meno*, trans. Robin Waterfield (New York: Oxford University Press, 2005), 79e–80b.

22. "It is likely that those who established the mystic rites for us were not inferior persons but were speaking in riddles long ago when they said that whoever arrives in the underworld uninitiated and unsanctified will wallow in the mire, whereas he who arrives there purified and initiated will dwell with the gods." Plato, *Phaedo*, trans. G. M. A. Grube (Indianapolis: Hackett, 2002), 69c.

23. Sigmund Freud, *Civilization and Its Discontents*, trans. James Strachey (New York: Norton, 1961 [1930]), 11.

24. Some neuroscientists suggest that the brain's "default mode network" (DMN), only discovered in 2001 and still not fully understood, becomes more operational when we are in the more contemplative states rather than engaged

in the purposive involvements characterizing everydayness. There are further suggestions that psychedelics can activate this DMN and this in part explains their mechanism of action. Fernanda Palhano-Fontes et al., "The Psychedelic State Induced by Ayahuasca Modulates the Activity and Connectivity of the Default Mode Network," *PLOS ONE* 10, no. 2 (February 2015), doi.org/10.1371/journal.pone.0118143. Palhano-Fontes et al. argue, "A remarkable increase in introspection is at the core of these altered states of consciousness. Self-oriented mental activity has been consistently linked to the Default Mode Network (DMN), a set of brain regions more active during rest than during the execution of a goal-directed task. . . . Altogether, our results support the notion that the altered state of consciousness induced by Ayahuasca, like those induced by psilocybin (another serotonergic psychedelic), meditation and sleep, is linked to the modulation of the activity and the connectivity of the DMN." There are more recent counterindications about the DMN's role as well, though, and this is a rapidly evolving areas of research. See James J. Gattuso et al., "Default Mode Network Modulation by Psychedelics: A Systematic Review," *International Journal of Neuropsychopharmacology* 26, no. 3 (March 2023): 155–188, doi.org/10.1093/ijnp/pyac074: "Although the DMN is consistently implicated in psychedelic studies, it is unclear how central the DMN is to the therapeutic potential of classical psychedelic agents."

25. Muraresku, *The Immortality Key*, 291f.

26. Carl A. P. Ruck and Mark Hoffman, *Entheogens, Myth and Human Consciousness* (Oakland, CA: Ronin, 2013), 51.

27. See Deena Scolnik Weisberg et al., "Making Play Work for Education," *Phi Delta Kappan* 96, no. 8 (May 2015), 8–13; Lewis Hyde, *Trickster Makes This World: Mischief, Myth and Art* (New York: Farrar, Straus & Giroux, 2010).

28. Being merely suggestive may indeed be one of their most important functions, as reminders of the trip and by extension what may have been learned during it. Having the art around may help one be less forgetful of it all.

29. The term "psychedelic" was coined in the 1950s by the English psychiatrist Humphry Osmund (1917–2004) in correspondence with Aldous Huxley. It might also be rendered as "mind manifesting" or "mind shining forth," from the Greek *psykhē* (mind) and *dēlos* (visible, clear), from the Proto-Indo-European root *dyeu* (to shine). See "The Online Etymology Dictionary," Etymonline.com, updated January 19, 2021, www.etymonline.com/word/psychedelic. It is a perfectly good term, I think, with the acknowledgment that the *psyche-* prefix connotes the emotional as well as the cognitive.

30. Samorini, *Animals and Psychedelics*, 83.

31. Aristos Georgiou, "Depression and Grief Wrecked a Man's Life—Until He Took Magic Mushroom Ingredient," *Newsweek*, December 26, 2021, www.newsweek.com/depression-grief-wrecked-man-life-magic-mushroom-ingredient-psilocybin-therapy-trial-kirk-rutter-1660581; see also Richard E. Daws et al.,

"Increased Global Integration in the Brain after Psilocybin Therapy for Depression," *Nature Medicine* 28, no. 4 (April 2022): 844–851, doi.org/10.1038/s41591-022-01744-z; Robin von Rotz et al. "Single-Dose Psilocybin-Assisted Therapy in Major Depressive Disorder: A Placebo-Controlled, Double-blind, Randomised Clinical Trial," *eClinicalMedicine* 56 (February 2023), doi.org/10.1016/j.eclinm.2022.101809 ("results suggest that a single, moderate dose of psilocybin significantly reduces depressive symptoms compared to a placebo condition for at least two weeks. No serious adverse events were recorded. Larger, multi-centric trials with longer follow-up periods are needed to inform further optimisation of this novel treatment paradigm"); and Robin L. Carhart-Harris et al., "Psilocybin for Treatment-Resistant Depression: FMRI-Measured Brain Mechanisms," *Nature Scientific Reports* 7, 13187 (October 2017), doi.org/10.1038/s41598-017-13282-7.

32. A moving example of this is Roland Griffith's account of his own diagnosis of terminal cancer after years of working with such patients as a physician and researcher. See David Marchese, "A Psychedelics Pioneer Takes the Ultimate Trip," *New York Times Magazine*, April 7, 2023.

33. Jonathan Lear, *Imagining the End: Mourning and Ethical Life* (Cambridge, MA: Harvard University Press, 2022), 4–5.

34. Carroll, *Alice's Adventures in Wonderland* (New York: Penguin, 1998 [1865]), 10.

35. Plato, *Republic*, trans. Robin Waterfield (New York: Oxford University Press, 2008), 357a–b.

36. One such 5-MeO-DMT session is memorably presented in Hamilton Morris, "The Psychedelic Toad," *Hamilton's Pharmacopia*, season 2, episode 1, directed by Hamilton Morris, Vice TV, November 28, 2017, video, 44:05, www.vicetv.com/en_us/video/hamiltons-pharmacopeia-the-psychedelic-toad/59cd5cd7c6e1eb5725458fdc.

37. This phrase is from one of McKenna's many lectures. See Wired Staff, "Terence McKenna's Last Trip," *Wired*, May 1, 2000, www.wired.com/2000/05/mckenna/. For a helpful resource, see the crowdfunded digital archive by Kevin Whitesides, "Archiving Terence McKenna," terencemckennaarchives.com/tag/heroic-dose/.

38. See Shunryu Suzuki, *Zen Mind, Beginner's Mind: Informal Talks on Zen Meditation and Practice* (Boulder, CO: Shambhala, 1970), 78.

39. For a compelling description, see Sam Harris's account of his own heroic doses: Sam Harris, "Drugs and the Meaning of Life," *Making Sense Podcast*, July 4, 2011, www.samharris.org/podcasts/making-sense-episodes/drugs-and-the-meaning-of-life.

40. For the concept of unitive experience, see Ninian Smart, "Understanding Religious Experience," in *Mysticism and Philosophical Analysis*, ed. Steven T. Katz (New York: Oxford University Press, 1978), 10–21.

41. Lucretius, *The Nature of Things*, trans. A. E. Stallings (New York: Penguin, 2007), 1068–1076.

42. See David J. Blacker, *Dying to Teach: The Educator's Search for Immortality* (New York: Columbia University Teachers College Press, 1997), 33–36.

43. Baruch Spinoza, *Ethics*, in Michael L. Morgan, ed. and Samuel L. Shirley, trans., *Spinoza: Complete Works* (Indianapolis: Hackett, 2002 [1677]), Part V, Propositions 22–23, 374.

44. Spinoza, *Ethics*, Part V, Propositions 32–33, 377: "From this kind of knowledge, there arises pleasure accompanied by the idea of God as cause, that is, the love of God not insofar as we imagine him as present, but insofar as we understand God to be eternal. And this is what I call the intellectual love of God." (Proposition 32, Corollary.)

45. Thomas à Kempis, *The Imitation of Christ* (New York: Vintage, 1998 [c. 1420]): "*Whoever follows Me will not walk in darkness*, says the Lord. These are Christ's own words by which He exhorts us to imitate His life and His ways, if we truly desire to be enlightened and free of all blindness of heart. Let it then be our main concern to meditate upon the life of Jesus Christ. . . . Certainly when judgment day comes we will not be asked what books we have read, but what deeds we have done; we shall not be asked how well we debated, but how devoutly we have lived" (1, 7).

46. See Bill Minutaglio and Stephen L. David, *The Most Dangerous Man in America: Timothy Leary, Richard Nixon and the Hunt for the Fugitive King of LSD* (New York: Twelve, 2018).

47. "The rationale for general studies depends in no small measure on the need for a common allusionary reservoir; that an adult who has passed end-of-course examinations cannot now recall most of their details or apply their principles does not prove that the studies were useless." Harry S. Broudy, "The Humanities and Their Uses: Proper Claims and Expectations," *Journal of Aesthetic Education* 17, no. 4 (Winter 1983): 133.

48. Ruck et al., "Entheogens," 145–46.

49. Mircea Eliade, *The Myth of the Eternal Return: Or, Cosmos and History*, trans. Willard Trask (Princeton, NJ: Princeton University Press, 1957).

50. See Muraresku, *The Immortality Key*, 267–290.

51. Wasson, Hofmann, and Ruck, *The Road to Eleusis*, 142.

52. Muraresku, *The Immortality Key*, 20–21.

53. *Gonzales v. O Centro Espírita Beneficente União do Vegetal*, 546 U.S. 418 (2006).

54. Thomas C. Maroukis, *The Peyote Road: Religious Freedom and the Native American Church* (Norman: University of Oklahoma Press, 2010).

55. Maya Stringer documents the "brave new world of psychedelic wellness," including a Zoom session with her "psychedelics integration coach," in "Could the Embrace of Psychedelics Lead to a Mental-Health Revolution?" *Vogue*, February 12, 2001, www.vogue.com/article/psychededlic-wellness-mental-health. See also Maya Fern and Hannah McClane, *Trans-Affirming Care in the Psychedelic Space: A Guide*

for Therapists, Clinicians, Facilitators and Healers (Philadelphia: Sound Mind Institute, 2022), drive.google.com/file/d/1TGP9LbVZ0C7JZGKATx5JYdw2qboPMIJa/view.

56. "Despite being an industry in its early stages, the potential for psychedelic health care is growing, with the market projected to reach $10.75 billion by 2027." Sean McClintock, "Why Investors Are Turning toward Psychedelic Health Care Companies," *Forbes*, September 4, 2021, fortune.com/2021/09/04/psychedelic-industry-investment-growth-stocks-companies/.

57. William J. Brennan et al., "A Qualitative Exploration of Relational Ethical Challenges and Practices in Psychedelic Healing," *Journal of Humanistic Psychology* (September 16, 2021), doi.org/10.1177/00221678211045265.

58. See Olivia Goldhill, "Psychedelic Therapy Has a Sexual Abuse Problem," *Quartz*, May 13, 2020, qz.com/1809184/psychedelic-therapy-has-a-sexual-abuse-problem-3/; Brennan et al., "A Qualitative Exploration of Relational Ethical Challenges and Practices in Psychedelic Healing," find that "psychedelic psychotherapy is rife with unique ethical challenges that require self-awareness and practical approaches that go beyond the training of a conventional psychologist" (24). These issues are dramatized in Lilly Kay Ross, "Cover Story: Power Trip," *New York Magazine*, November 2021–February 2022, nymag.com/podcasts, an investigative series documenting the harrowing story of a sexual abuse victim and the alleged cover-up by psychedelic guides.

59. From the YouTube channel *The Acid Left*: "The Acid Left is a hub for online and in real life happenings around class consciousness. Working across platforms we aim to create a forum of a dispersed organisation that can coordinate creative opposition to the stifling practices of capitalism," www.youtube.com/@TheAcidLeft/, January 1, 2021. But see Nicholas Langlitz, "Rightist Psychedelia," *Society for Cultural Anthropology*, July 21, 2020, culanth.org/fieldsights/rightist-psychedelia; Brian Pace, "Lucy in the Sky with Nazis: Psychedelics and the Right Wing," *Psymposia*, February 3, 2020, www.psymposia.com/magazine/lucy-in-the-sky-with-nazis-psychedelics-and-the-right-wing/. See also Eric Lonergan, "Psychedelics are Pluripotent," *Mind Foundation*, April 27, 2021, mind-foundation.org/psychedelics-politically-pluripotent/: "psychedelics are politically pluripotent: they can strengthen all sorts of political movements depending on the political set and setting. Here, the 'political set' is the political orientation of the subject, and the 'political setting' is the political orientation of the environment"; and Johnson and Yaden, "There's No Good Evidence That Psychedelics Can Change Your Politics or Religion"; and Patricia Duerler et al., "LSD-Induced Increases in Social Adaptation to Opinions Similar to One's Own Are Associated with Stimulation of Serotonin Receptors," *Nature Scientific Reports* 10, 12181 (July 22, 2020), doi.org/10.1038/s41598-020-68899-y.

60. Matthew W. Johnson, "Consciousness, Religion, and Gurus," 578–581.

61. See Werner Jaeger, *Paideia: The Ideals of Greek Culture*, 3 vols, trans. Gilbert Highet (New York: Oxford University Press, 1986).

62. E. R. Dodds, *The Greeks and the Irrational* (Berkeley: University of California Press, 1951), 146.

63. For a Jamaican mushroom tourist retreat, see "MycoMeditations, psilocybin-assisted retreats," www.mycomeditations.com, accessed May 21, 2023; and for a tourism-style review of Peruvian operations, see "10 Best Ayahuasca Retreats Peru in 2023," Behold, updated January 4, 2023, www.behold-retreats.com/post/10-best-ayahuasca-retreats-peru.

64. Following Husserl, Sartre puts it as "all consciousness is consciousness of something." Jean-Paul Sartre, *Being and Nothingness*, trans. Hazel E. Barnes (New York: Philosophical Library, 1956), 11, 13.

65. Edmund Husserl, *Logical Investigations Volume II* (London: Routledge, 2001 [1921]), "Investigation V: On Intentional Experiences and their 'Contents,'" 77–125.

66. For an analysis of the temporal dimensions of hallucinogens and other altered states, see Mark Wittman, *Altered States of Consciousness: Experiences out of Time and Self* (Cambridge, MA: MIT Press, 2018): "To sum up our study with exceptionally experienced meditators, our results are in accordance with the knowledge of other psychological or pharmacological induction types of altered states of consciousness where in peak states, subjective time and self are temporarily changed, reduced, or even lost."

67. René Descartes, *Meditations on First Philosophy*, trans. Donald A. Cress (Indianapolis: Hackett, 1980), 60.

68. Tao Lin, *Trip: Psychedelics, Alienation, and Change* (New York: Vintage, 2018), 96.

69. Christopher Timmermann et al., "Psychedelics Alter Metaphysical Beliefs," *Nature Scientific Reports* 11, 22166 (November 2021), doi.org/10.1038/s41598-021-01209-2.

70. Hans-Georg Gadamer, *Truth and Method*, trans. Joel Weinsheimer and Donald G. Marshall (New York: Continuum, 1989), 306.

71. "I encounter self-transforming elf machines, which are creatures, entities perhaps, although they're not made out of matter," McKenna explains in a recorded interview. "They're made out of, as nearly as I can figure it out, syntax-driving light." Anna Wilcox, "Machine Elves or 'DMT Elves': A Journey Into The DMT Spirit World," *Double Blind*, September 4, 2020, doubleblindmag.com/machine-elves-clockwork-elves-dmt-rick-strassman-terence-mckenna/. See also Pascal Michael, David Luke, and Oliver Robinson, "An Encounter With the Other: A Thematic and Content Analysis of DMT Experiences From a Naturalistic Field Study," *Frontiers in Psychology* 12, 720717 (December 16, 2021), doi.org/10.3389/fpsyg.2021.720717; and for a catalog of DMT entities, see the online clearinghouse for DMT information, *DMT Nexus* (www.dmt-nexus.me); and, as always, the DMT experience reports at *Erowid* (erowid.org). A particularly fascinating roundup of entity reports—with a wide variety of

entities—has emerged from the extended-state "DMTx" experiments at Imperial College, London, a preliminary discussion of which is available at "DMTx Breakthrough Panel Moderated by Graham Hancock, Dr. Andrew Gallimore & Dr. Rick Strassman," *Noonautics*, May 23, 2023, video, 2:27:58, www.youtube.com/watch?v=Myq_Hc_39aI. A conclusion shared by the DMTx panel participants is that, while there are many guises and varieties of DMT entities, they are usually diminutive and present in groups (not always, though). Also: often there are interactions with these entities, but sometimes their activities are merely observed. They do seem to be welcoming on the whole, but occasionally they are indifferent to the interloper.

72. For an account of the Gaian worldview, see David J. Blacker, *What's Left of the World? Education, Identity and the Post-Work Political Imagination* (Winchester, MA: Zer0 Books, 2019), 183–203.

73. Evans, *The Art of Losing Control*, 205–211.

74. See Doblin, "Walter Pahnke's 'Good Friday Experiment,'" 1–28.

75. Analogously, in the context of theological belief, Rick Strassman, in *DMT and the Soul of Prophecy* (Rochester, VT: Park Street, 2014), stresses that there are two major possibilities regarding such visions: one that they are "neurotheological," by which he means the theological visions are generated by the neurophysiological substrate (i.e., the brain) as epiphenomena of that substrate, and, two, that they are "theoneurological," meaning that the neurophysiological substrate, suitably chemically altered by, say, elevated levels of DMT, can be temporarily transformed into a conduit for these experiences. For Strassman's theoneurology, an analogy is with radio waves, which are not "created" by the radio but merely picked up by them (3–4).

76. Gadamer, *Truth and Method*, 306.

77. Plato, *Meno*, 80e. Plato "solves" the paradox with his theory of learning as recollection.

78. Stanislav Grof, *LSD Psychotherapy: The Healing Potential of Psychedelic Medicine*, 4th ed. (Santa Cruz: MAPS, 2008), 11.

79. See Eberhard Fuchs and Gabriele Flügge, "Adult Neuroplasticity: More than 40 Years of Research," *Neural Plasticity* 2014, 541870 (May 2014), doi.org/10.1155/2014/541870. For a helpful general discussion of neuroplasticity, see Andrew Huberman, "How to Focus to Change Your Brain," *Huberman Lab*, February 8, 2021, video, 1:29:43, hubermanlab.com/how-to-focus-to-change-your-brain/.

80. See Andrew Huberman, "Dr. Matthew Johnson: Psychedelic Medicine," *Huberman Lab*, September 2021, video, 2:52:04, hubermanlab.com/dr-matthew-johnson-psychedelic-medicine; and Willy Pedersen, Heith Copes, and Liridona Gashi, "Narratives of the Mystical among Users of Psychedelics," *Acta Sociologica* 64, no. 2 (January 2021): 230–246, doi.org/10.1177/0001699320980050. Pedersen et al. suggest that within the archetypal patterns, the mystical occasions display "culturally specific storylines."

81. L. S. Vygotsky, *Mind in Society: The Development of Higher Psychological Processes* (Cambridge, MA: Harvard University Press, 1978).

82. "Handel's unbending manliness and freedom under the law." Friedrich Nietzsche, *Human, All-Too-Human, Part II: The Wanderer and His Shadow*, trans. Paul V. Cohn (New York: MacMillan, 1913 [1880]), 298, www.gutenberg.org/files/37841/37841-h/37841-h.html.

83. Kant, *Critique of Judgment*, section 241.

84. I note this is essentially the Platonic-Pythagorean strategy for immortality, as I argue in my *Dying to Teach*, 2–8.

85. See Robin L. Carhart-Harris et al., "LSD Enhances Suggestibility in Healthy Volunteers," *Psychopharmacology* 232, no. 4 (February 2015): 785–794, doi.org/10.1007/s00213-014-3714-z.

86. Stamets, *Mycelium Running*. Stamets does not literally believe this either; note his subtitle is "how mushrooms can *help* save the world"—he is being playfully hyperbolic. He also is not focused only on psychedelics; he advocates for mushrooms across the board, for example, how they might help with certain environmental problems by aiding in the cleansing of toxic waste.

87. See Matthew W. Johnson, "Consciousness, Religion, and Gurus," 571–581.

88. Kenneth W. Tupper, "Entheogens and Education: Exploring the Potential of Psychoactives as Educational Tools," *Journal of Drug Education and Awareness* 1, no. 2 (January 2003): 145–161.

89. Spinoza, *Ethics*, Part IV, Preface, 321.

90. Gadamer, *Truth and Method*, 374.

91. John Dewey, *Art as Experience* [1934], in John Dewey, *The Later Works, 1925–1953*, vol. 10, ed. Joanne Boydston (Carbondale: Southern Illinois University Press, 1989), 268.

Chapter 2

1. There is debate about Thales's traditional pole position, due to a compelling recent article by Lea Cantor, "Thales–the 'First Philosopher'? A Troubled Chapter in the Historiography of Philosophy," *British Journal for the History of Philosophy* 30, no. 5 (March 2022): 727–750, doi.org/10.1080/09608788.2022.2029347: "the view that philosophy originated with Thales (along with its misleading attribution to the Greeks in general) has roots in problematic, and in some cases manifestly racist, eighteenth-century historiography of philosophy" (727).

2. Heraclitus, F33, F34, T3, T4, in *The First Philosophers: The Presocratics and Sophists*, trans. and ed. Robin Waterfield (New York: Oxford University Press, 2000), 41.

3. Heraclitus, F25. Sometimes this is rendered more poetically as "nature loves to hide."

4. Grof, *Realms of the Human Unconscious*.

5. Michael, Luke, and Robinson, "An Encounter with the Other"; see also Terence McKenna, "DMT Elves" [lecture], accessed May 21, 2023, www.youtube.com/watch?v=XYrfMnvTy3o. McKenna reports the DMT "self-transforming machine" or "clockwork elves" as exclaiming "Hooray! Welcome! You're here!" (4:30) and adds that "my immediate impression is that they are welcoming." For further elaboration, see his *Archaic Revival: Speculations on Psychedelic Mushrooms, the Amazon, Virtual Reality, UFOs, Evolution, Shamanism, the Rebirth of the Goddess, and the End of History* (New York: HarperCollins, 1992), 16.

6. See Marco Aqil and Leor Roseman, "More Than Meets the Eye: The Role of Sensory Dimensions in Psychedelic Brain Dynamics, Experience, and Therapeutics," *Neuropharmacology* 223 (February 2023), doi.org/10.1016/j.neuropharm.2022.109300.

7. On psychedelics' "mood-enhancing effects," see Matthias Forstmann et al., "Transformative Experience and Social Connectedness Mediate the Mood-Enhancing Effects of Psychedelic Use in Naturalistic Settings," *Proceedings of the National Academy of Sciences* 117, no. 5 (February 4, 2020): 2338–2346, doi.org/10.1073/pnas.1918477117.

8. Robert Hughes, *The Shock of the New: The Hundred-Year History of Modern Art—Its Rise, Its Dazzling Achievement, Its Fall* (New York: Knopf, 1991).

9. Aqil and Roseman, "More Than Meets the Eye," 9–10.

10. Thompson, *Fear and Loathing in Las Vegas*, 89.

11. See Chelsea Tersavich, "Why the 'Trust, Let Go, Be Open' Mantra is Important in Psychedelic Healing," *Mindbloom*, August 15, 2022, www.mindbloom.com/blog/exploring-the-trust-let-go-be-open-tlo-mantra; see also Mary Cosimano, "The Role of the Guide in Psychedelic Assisted Treatment," in *Handbook of Medical Hallucinogens*, ed. Charles S. Grob and Jim Grigsby (New York: Guilford, 2021), 377–394: "on the day of the psilocybin session, the guidance is to let go of attempts to direct the session and go into the experience with an openness to whatever arises" (381).

12. Thomas S. Kuhn, *The Structure of Scientific Revolutions* (Chicago: University of Chicago Press, 2012 [1962]), 1–41.

13. Richard Rorty, *Contingency, Irony, and Solidarity* (Cambridge: Cambridge University Press, 1989), 9.

14. I qualify this remark because indigenous people often strongly resist such pharmaceutical phrasing, instead preferring more personalized descriptions such as "plant teachers" and the like. See Luis Eduardo Luna, "The Concept of Plants as Teachers among Four Mestizo Shamans of Iquitos, Northeastern Peru," *Journal of Ethnopharmacology* 11, no. 2 (July 1984): 135–156; and Robin Wall

Kimmerer, *Braiding Sweetgrass: Indigenous Wisdom, Scientific Knowledge and the Teachings of Plants* (Minneapolis: Milkweed, 2013).

15. Gallimore, *Reality Switch Technologies*, 5.

16. Gallimore, *Reality Switch Technologies*, 6.

17. William James, *Principles of Psychology* (New York: Henry Holt, 1918 [1890]), 488.

18. Gallimore, *Reality Switch Technologies*, 5.

19. See Luis Eduardo Luna, "On Encounters with Entities in the Ayahuasca Realm," in *DMT Entity Encounters: Dialogues on the Spirit Molecule*, ed. David Luke and Rory Spowers (Rochester, VT: Park Street, 2021), 3–29.

20. Dominique Fontanilla et al., "The Hallucinogen N,N-Dimethyltryptamine (DMT) Is an Endogenous Sigma-1 Receptor Regulator," *Science* 323, no. 5916 (February 13, 2009): 934–937, doi.org/10.1126/science.1166127; and Attila Szabo et al., "The Endogenous Hallucinogen and Trace Amine N,N-Dimethyltryptamine (DMT) Displays Potent Protective Effects against Hypoxia via Sigma-1 Receptor Activation in Human Primary iPSC-Derived Cortical Neurons and Microglia-Like Immune Cells," *Frontiers in Neuroscience* 10 (September 14, 2016), doi.org/10.3389/fnins.2016.00423. It should be noted that research is ongoing regarding all of these mechanisms and very little is settled; see Maxemiliano V. Vargas et al., "Psychedelics Promote Neuroplasticity Through the Activation of Intracellular 5-HT2A Receptors," *Science* 379, vol. 6633 (February 16, 2023): 700–706, doi.org/10.1126/science.adf0435: "serotonin might not be the endogenous ligand for intracellular 5-HT2ARs in the cortex."

21. See Don Ihde, *Technology and the Lifeworld: From Garden to Earth* (Bloomington: Indiana University Press, 1990), 40.

22. A beautiful rendering of this point is found in Matthew B. Crawford, *Shop Class as Soulcraft: An Inquiry into the Value of Work* (New York: Penguin, 2010).

23. Martin Heidegger, "The Question Concerning Technology," in *The Question Concerning Technology and Other Essays*, trans. William Lovitt (New York: Garland, 1977), 12.

24. Heidegger, *Being and Time*, 99.

25. Heidegger, *Being and Time*, 99.

26. John Dewey, *Experience and Nature* [1925], in *The Later Works, 1925–1953*, vol. 1, ed. Joanne Boydston (Carbondale: Southern Illinois University Press, 1981), 101.

27. I draw this notion from my account in David J. Blacker, "Allowing Educational Technologies to Reveal: A Deweyan Perspective," *Educational Theory* 43, no. 2 (Spring 1993): 181–195, doi.org/10.1111/j.1741-5446.1993.00181.x.

28. Justin Higginbottom, "The 'Psychonauts' Training to Explore Another Dimension," *New Republic*, January 3, 2023, newrepublic.com/article/169525/psychonauts-training-psychedelics-dmt-extended-state; see also Andrew R. Galli-

more and Rick J. Strassman, "A Model for the Application of Target-Controlled Intravenous Infusion for a Prolonged Immersive DMT Psychedelic Experience," *Frontiers in Pharmacology* 7 (July 14, 2016), doi.org/10.3389/fphar.2016.00211.

29. Watts, *The Joyous Cosmology*, 26.

30. See Jacob Aday et al., "Long-Term Effects of Psychedelic Drugs: A Systematic Review," *Neuroscience and Biobehavioral Reviews* 113 (June 2020): 179–189, doi.org/10.1016/j.neubiorev.2020.03.017: "limited aversive side effects were noted by study participants. Future researchers should focus on including larger and more diverse samples, lengthier longitudinal designs, stronger control conditions, and standardized dosages."

31. See Mark A. Wrathall, ed., *The Cambridge Heidegger Lexicon* (Cambridge: Cambridge University Press, 2021), 329–339, doi.org/10.1017/9780511843778.089.

32. Heidegger, "The Question Concerning Technology," 16.

33. Heidegger, "The Question Concerning Technology," 16.

34. Heidegger, "The Question Concerning Technology," 21.

35. Martin Heidegger, *Ponderings XII–XV Black Notebooks, 1939–1941*, trans. Richard Rocjewicz (Bloomington: Indiana University Press, 2017), 40.

36. Much has been written in recent decades about Heidegger's Nazism or quasi-Nazism—or whatever it was—and whether or not it is separable from his other philosophical views. For a wide-ranging summary and strong indictment, see Richard Wolin, *Heidegger in Ruins: Between Philosophy and Ideology* (New Haven, CT: Yale University Press, 2023). I see no reason to dispute Wolin's damning characterization of Heidegger's political views, but I think one must *always* be able to use one's critical faculties to disentangle a thinker's views and make distinctions. Otherwise, even an extreme case like Heidegger's initiates a slippery slope toward eliminating thinkers and obliterating our engagement with our own past, as just about every canonical thinker is guilty of grave moral sins by contemporary standards (e.g., Plato, Aristotle, Rousseau, Kant, Nietzsche, Marx, etc.).

37. The *Der Spiegel* interview, entitled "Only a God Can Save Us Now," can be found in the *Graduate Faculty Philosophy Journal* 6 (Winter 1977): 1–23.

38. See Rich Doyle, "Hyperbolic: Divining Ayahuasca," *Discourse* 27, no. 1 (Winter 2005): 30, www.jstor.org/stable/41389716. Going so far as to suggest "jester therapy," an insightful essay on this topic is Sam Woolfe, "Why Do Jesters and Tricksters Appear in the DMT Experience?" *Sam Woolfe*, September 19, 2019, www.samwoolfe.com/2019/02/jesters-tricksters-dmt-experience.html.

39. Alex K. Gearin and Oscar Calavia Sáez, "Altered Vision: Ayahuasca Shamanism and Sensory Individualism," *Current Anthropology* 62, no. 2 (April 2021): 138–163.

40. Albert Camus, *The Stranger* (New York: Vintage, 1954), 75–76.

41. Heidegger, *Being and Time*, 116.

42. Heidegger, *Being and Time*, 434.

43. See Hans-Georg Gadamer, *Philosophical Apprenticeships* (Cambridge, MA: MIT Press, 1985), 34.

44. Rorty, *Contingency, Irony, and Solidarity*, 6.

45. Immanuel Kant, *Critique of Pure Reason*, trans. Norman Kemp Smith (New York: St. Martin's, 1965 [1781]), 160f.

46. Letheby, *Philosophy of Psychedelics*, 3–4, 194–195.

47. Letheby, *Philosophy of Psychedelics*, 31.

48. Letheby, *Philosophy of Psychedelics*, 35.

49. Terence McKenna, *True Hallucinations: Being an Account of the Author's Extraordinary Adventures in the Devil's Paradise* (New York: HarperOne, 1994), 74–75 (inter alia).

50. See Benny Shanon, *The Antipodes of the Mind: Charting the Phenomenology of the Ayahuasca Experience* (New York: Oxford University Press, 2003), 120.

51. Heidegger, *Being and Time*, 31.

52. Martin Heidegger, *Discourse on Thinking*, trans. John M. Anderson and E. Hans Freund (Harper & Row, 1966), 54, as quoted in Michael Zimmerman, *Heidegger's Confrontation with Modernity* (Bloomington: Indiana University Press, 1990), 219.

53. Martin Heidegger, "On the Origin of the Work of Art," in *Martin Heidegger: Basic Writings*, ed. David Farrell Krell (New York: Harper, 2008), 162–181.

54. Friedrich Nietzsche, *Thus Spoke Zarathustra: A Book for Everyone and No One*, trans. R. J. Hollingdale (New York: Penguin, 1961), 55.

55. Friedrich Hölderlin, *Selected Poems and Fragments*, trans. Michael Hamburger (New York: Penguin, 1998), 231.

56. Martin Heidegger, "On the Essence of Truth," in *Martin Heidegger: Basic Writings* (New York: Harper, 2008), 131.

57. Aldous Huxley, *The Doors of Perception*, 30.

58. A classical source for the Feast of Fools and similar phenomena is philosopher and literary theorist Mikhail Bakhtin, *Rabelais and His World*, trans. Helene Iswolsky (Bloomington: Indiana University Press, 2009 [1940]).

59. Michael Pollan, *How to Change Your Mind: What the New Science of Psychedelics Teaches Us About Consciousness, Dying, Addiction, Depression, and Transcendence* (New York: Penguin, 2018), 214.

60. "Data thus far supports the theory that psychedelics stimulate dendritogenesis, synaptogenesis, and the upregulation of plasticity-related genes in a 5-HT 2A receptor-dependent manner, affecting the cortex in particular. The window of neuroplasticity appears to open within a few hours and may last a few days, although neuroplastic changes occurring during this time may survive for at least a month." Abigail E. Calder and George Hasler, "Towards an Understanding of Psychedelic-Induced Neuroplasticity," *Neuropsychopharmacology* 48 (2023): 104–112, doi.org/10.1038/s41386-022-01389-z. See also Jonathan W. Kanen et al., "Effect of Lysergic Acid Diethylamide (LSD) on Reinforcement Learning

in Humans," *Psychological Medicine* 53, no. 14 (October 2023), doi.org/10.1017/s0033291722002963; and S. Parker Singleton et al., "Receptor-Informed Network Control Theory links LSD and Psilocybin to a Flattening of the Brain's Control Energy Landscape," *Nature Communications* 13, 5812 (October 3, 2022), doi.org/10.1038/s41467-022-33578-1.

61. Miguel Ângelo Costa, "A Dose of Creativity: An Integrative Review of the Effects of Serotonergic Psychedelics on Creativity," *Journal of Psychoactive Drugs* 55, no. 3 (2023), doi.org/10.1080/02791072.2022.2106805.

62. Inês Hipólito et al., "Pattern Breaking: A Complex Systems Approach to Psychedelic Medicine," *PsyArXiv Preprints* (July 13, 2022), doi.org/10.31234/osf.io/ydu3h.

63. Kanen et al., "Effect of Lysergic Acid Diethylamide (LSD)," 8.

64. See Griffiths et al., "Mystical-Type Experiences Occasioned by Psilocybin."

65. Richard Louis Miller and Mariavittoria Mangini, "Psychedelics and the Social Matrix," in *Psychedelic Wisdom: The Astonishing Rewards of Mind-Altering Substances*, ed. Richard Louis Miller (Rochester, VT: Park Street, 2022), 216. The chapter is an interview with professor of nursing and psychedelic researcher Mariavittoria Mangini.

66. Graham Hancock, *Visionary: The Mysterious Origins of Human Consciousness* (Newburyport, MA: New Page Books, 2022), 7–9.

67. A forum thread of testimonials about 5-MeO "whiteout" may be found at "Whiteout Experiences From 5-MeO-DMT: Testimonials," *5Hive/5-MeO-DMT Forum*, accessed May 21, 2023, forums.5meodmt.org/index.php?topic=50719.0; for a scholarly synthesis of research, see Anna O. Ermakova et al., "A Narrative Synthesis of Research with 5-MeO-DMT," *Journal of Psychopharmacology* 36, no. 3 (March 2022): 273–294, doi.org/10.1177/02698811211050543; for more detail on the comparative intensity of 5-MeO-DMT, see Joseph Barsuglia et al., "Intensity of Mystical Experiences Occasioned by 5-MeO-DMT and Comparison with a Prior Psilocybin Study," *Frontiers in Psychology* 9 (December 6, 2018), doi.org/10.3389/fpsyg.2018.02459.

68. For an interesting philosophical initiative exploring the "bad" or "challenging" trips, see Jules Evans, "What Helps with Challenging Psychedelic Experiences?" The Psychedelic Society, accessed May 21, 2023, psychedelicsociety.org.uk/media/what-helps-with-challenging-psychedelic-experiences.

69. Jacob von Uexküll, *A Foray into the Worlds of Animals and Humans*, trans. Joseph D. O'Neill (Minneapolis: University of Minnesota Press, 2010 [1934]), 41.

70. Ed Yong, *An Immense World: How Animal Senses Reveal the Hidden Realm around Us* (New York: Random House, 2022), 6.

71. See Alexandra Horowitz, *Inside of a Dog: What Dogs See, Smell, and Know* (New York: Simon & Schuster, 2012), 77–79.

72. Uexküll, *A Foray into the Worlds of Animals and Humans*, 42–43.
73. See David Eagleman, *Livewired: The Inside Story of the Ever-Changing Brain* (New York: Vintage, 2021), 84–88.
74. See H. Martin Blacker, "Volitional Sympathetic Control," *Anesthesia and Analgesia* 59, no. 10 (October 1980): 785–788.
75. Thomas Nagel, "What Is It Like to Be a Bat?" *Philosophical Review* 83, no. 4 (October 1974): 435–450, argues for the importance of the subjective character of consciousness and against a reductively materialist account. See also Peter Sjöstedt-Hughes, *Noumenautics: Metaphysics, Meta-Ethics, Psychedelics* (Falmouth, UK: Psychedelic Press, 2015), 25.
76. Ede Frecska, Mihály Hoppál, and Luis Muñiz Luna, "Nonlocality and the Shamanic State of Consciousness," *NeuroQuantology* 14, no. 2 (May 2016): 155–165. For unclear reasons, the article has disappeared from the journal's website, but a PDF is still available at real.mtak.hu/36545/1/2016_Frecska_E_Nonlocality_and_SSC_u.pdf.
77. McKenna, *Archaic Revival*, 12.
78. Chalmers, "Facing Up to the Problem of Consciousness."
79. Alfred Korzybski, *Science and Sanity: An Introduction to Non-Aristotelian Systems and General Semantics*, 5th ed. (Lancaster, PA: International Non-Aristotelian Library, 1933), 58, available at esgs.free.fr/uk/art/sands.htm.

Chapter 3

1. Letheby, *Philosophy of Psychedelics*, 46.
2. For a literature survey of the range of effects, see Link R. Swanson, "Unifying Theories of Psychedelic Drug Effects," *Frontiers in Pharmacology* 9, no. 172 (March 2018), doi.org/10.3389/fphar.2018.00172. Swanson investigates generations of studies of psychedelics' "characteristic range of acute effects in perception, emotion, cognition, and sense of self" (1), concluding that, from the nineteenth century to the present, *all* of them "propose that psychedelic drugs inhibit neurophysiological constraints in order to produce their diverse phenomenological, psychomimetic, and therapeutic effects" (17). Swanson also notes that "weakened constraints," while key to psychedelics' therapeutic usefulness, are for that same reason not always salutary because the inhibition of "adaptive constraints" is also associated with psychosis. Interestingly, *constraint inhibition is a goldilocks phenomenon where pathologies can arise from "either too much or too little constraint"* [emphasis added] (16).
3. Ohio State University, "Breaking the Shackles of Anxiety and Depression: How Psychedelic Experiences May Improve Mental Health," *SciTech Daily*, February 25, 2023, scitechdaily.com/breaking-the-shackles-of-anxiety-and-depression-how-psychedelic-experiences-may-improve-mental-health/. The research article is Aki Nikolaidis et al., "Subtypes of the Psychedelic Experi-

ence Have Reproducible and Predictable Effects on Depression and Anxiety Symptoms," *Journal of Affective Disorders* 324 (March 1, 2023): 239–249, doi.org/10.1016/j.jad.2022.12.042.

4. Friedrich Nietzsche, *The Gay Science*, trans. Josefine Nauckhoff (New York: Cambridge University Press, 2001 [1882]), 318.

5. The term "unselfing" is from philosopher Iris Murdoch, *The Sovereignty of the Good* (New York: Routledge, 2000), 82. She first explains the notion in terms of the feeling of losing oneself in aesthetic contemplation.

6. Chris Letheby and Philip Gerrans, "Self Unbound: Ego Dissolution in Psychedelic Experience," *Neuroscience of Consciousness* 2017, no. 1 (June 30, 2017), 7, doi.org/10.1093/nc/nix016.

7. David Bryce Yaden et al., "The Varieties of Self-Transcendent Experience," *Review of General Psychology* 21, no. 2 (June 2017): 143–160, 1, doi.org/10.1037/gpr0000102.

8. Yaden et al., "The Varieties of Self-Transcendent Experience," 5.

9. Yaden et al., "The Varieties of Self-Transcendent Experience," 6. For this claim they reference the "Mystical Experience Questionnaire (MEQ)" used by Katherine A. MacLean et al., "Factor Analysis of the Mystical Experience Questionnaire: A Study of Experiences Occasioned by the Hallucinogen Psilocybin," *Journal for the Scientific Study of Religion* 51, no. 4 (December 2012): 721–737, doi.org/10.1111/j.1468-5906.2012.01685.x; and R. W. Hood Jr., "Chemically Assisted Mysticism and the Question of Veridicality," in *Seeking the Sacred with Psychoactive Substances: Chemical Paths to Spirituality and God. Volume 1: History and Practices*, ed. J. Harold Ellens (New York: Praeger, 2014), 395–410. The locus classicus for theories of mystical experiences is W. T. Stace, *Mysticism and Philosophy* (Philadelphia: Lippincott, 1960).

10. Ned Block, "Paradox and Cross Purposes in Recent Work on Consciousness," *Cognition* 79, no. 1–2 (April 2001): 197–217; updated and expanded version available at peterasaro.org/courses/MMP/Block%2C%20paradox%20consciousness.html#_ftn1.

11. Epicurus, *Letter to Menoeceus*, 124–127, in *The Hellenistic Philosophers Volume 1: Translations of the Principal Sources with Philosophical Commentary*, ed. and trans. A. A. Long and D. N. Snedley (New York: Cambridge University Press, 1987), 150.

12. Benny Shanon, "The Epistemics of Ayahuasca Visions," *Phenomenology and Cognitive Science* 9, no. 2 (June 2010): 268. For a classic work on shamanism replete with examples, see Eliade, *Shamanism*.

13. Letheby and Gerrans, "Self Unbound," 9.

14. Robinson Jeffers, "The Answer," in *Selected Poetry of Robinson Jeffers*, ed. Tim Hunt (Stanford, CA: Stanford University Press, 2002), 522.

15. Amber Dance, "Quest for Clues to Humanity's First Fires," *Scientific American*, June 19, 2017, www.scientificamerican.com/article/quest-for-clues-to-humanitys-first-fires/.

16. Albert Hofmann, *LSD and the Divine Scientist: The Final Thoughts and Reflections of Albert Hofmann* (New York: Simon & Schuster, 2013).

17. Robin L. Carhart-Harris et al., "Psychedelics and Connectedness," *Psychopharmacology* 235, no. 2 (February 2018): 547–550, doi.org/10.1007/s00213-017-4701-y.

18. See Alexander Beiner, *The Bigger Picture: How Psychedelics Can Help Us Make Sense of the World* (London: Hay House, 2023), 192–194.

19. Huxley, *The Doors of Perception*, 62.

20. See Natalie Gukasyan et al., "Efficacy and Safety of Psilocybin-Assisted Treatment for Major Depressive Disorder: Prospective 12-month Follow-up," *Journal of Psychopharmacology* 36, no. 2 (February 2022): 151–158, /doi.org/10.1177/02698811211073759.

21. Roland Griffiths et al., "Psilocybin-Occasioned Mystical-Type Experience in Combination with Meditation and Other Spiritual Practices Produces Enduring Positive Changes in Psychological Functioning and in Trait Measures of Prosocial Attitudes and Behaviors," *Journal of Psychopharmacology* 32, no. 1 (January 2018): 49–69, doi.org/10.1177/0269881117731279.

22. Charles S. Grob et al., "Pilot Study of Psilocybin Treatment for Anxiety in Patients with Advanced-Stage Cancer," *Archives of General Psychiatry*, 68, no. 1 (January 3, 2011): 71–78, doi.org/10.1001/archgenpsychiatry.2010.116; Griffiths et al., "Psilocybin Produces Substantial and Sustained Decreases in Depression and Anxiety." See also Gabrielle Agin-Liebes et al., "Long-Term Follow-Up of Psilocybin-Assisted Psychotherapy for Psychiatric and Existential Distress in Patients with Life-Threatening Cancer," *Journal of Psychopharmacology* 23, no. 2 (February 2020): 155–166, doi.org/10.1177/0269881119897615.

23. See Matthew M. Nour et al., "Ego-Dissolution and Psychedelics: Validation of the Ego-Dissolution Inventory (EDI)," *Frontiers in Human Neuroscience* 10, no. 269 (June 14, 2016): 7, doi.org/10.3389/fnhum.2016.00269.

24. Nour et al., "Ego-Dissolution and Psychedelics," 9.

25. Nour et al., "Ego-Dissolution and Psychedelics," 9.

26. Nour et al., "Ego-Dissolution and Psychedelics," 10.

27. One notes the limitations to these online questionnaire-based studies, as the researchers themselves explicitly do; e.g., the subjects are a fairly homogeneous group: mostly twentysomething white college-educated males who have previously tried psychedelics. More heterogeneity in future studies would of course strengthen any conclusions.

28. All of the quotations and information about SEI may be found at Kins, "Subjective Effect Index," effectindex.com.

29. Muraresku, *The Immortality Key*, book epigraph (from an inscription at St. Paul's Monastery on Mount Athos, northern Greece).

30. Zygmunt Bauman, *Mortality, Immortality and Other Life Strategies* (Cambridge: Polity, 2013).

31. See Manly P. Hall, *The Secret Teachings of All Ages* (New York: Penguin, 2003), 192–194.

32. Plato, *Republic*, 514a–520a.

33. See Gregory Vlastos, "The Unity of the Virtues in the "Protagoras," *Review of Metaphysics* 24, no. 3 (March 1972): 415–458.

34. Plato, *Timaeus*, trans. Robin Waterfield (New York: Oxford University Press, 2008), 90c.

35. Plato, *Timaeus*, 90d.

36. Plotinus, "The Good or the One" [from the *Enneads*], in *The Essential Plotinus*, ed. and trans. Elmer O'Brian, S.J. (Indianapolis: Hackett, 1964), 87.

37. Shanon, "The Epistemics of Ayahuasca Visions," 269.

38. Grof, *Realms of the Human Unconscious*.

39. Kins, "Subjective Effect Index," effectindex.com/effects/ego-death#ego-death-subcategories.

40. This is a big topic of research; see, e.g., Matthew Guenther, *Human-Animal Relationships in San and Hunter-Gatherer Cosmology, Volume 1: Therianthropes and Transformation* (New York: Palgrave Macmillan, 2019), and David Lewis-Williams, *A Cosmos in Stone: Interpreting Religion and Society through Rock Art* (Lanham, MD: AltaMira Press, 2002). Another aspect of this is a kind of quasi-animism that may be enhanced by psychedelics in terms of attributing consciousness to animals. See Sandeep M. Nayak and Roland R. Griffiths, "A Single Belief-Changing Psychedelic Experience Is Associated with Increased Attribution of Consciousness to Living and Non-living Entities," *Frontiers in Psychology* 13, no. 852248 (March 2022), doi.org/10.3389/fpsyg.2022.852248.

41. Benny Shanon, "A Cognitive-Psychological Study of Ayahuasca," *Newsletter of the Multidisciplinary Association for Psychedelic Studies* 7, no. 3 (Summer 1997): 13–15, available at maps.org/news-letters/v07n3/07313sha.html; and Shanon, *The Antipodes of the Mind*, 117–120.

42. Kins, "Subjective Effects Index," effectindex.com/effects/unity-and-interconnectedness.

43. William Shakespeare, *Hamlet*, 3.1.67.

44. Plato, *Republic*, 514b–516d.

45. Joseph Campbell, *The Hero with a Thousand Faces* (Princeton, NJ: Princeton University Press, 1949), 23.

46. McKenna, *Archaic Revival*, 10.

47. Often this is to "bring back" healing knowledge from "spirit helpers." See Michael Harner, *The Way of the Shaman* (New York: Harper, 1990), 76–103; see also Ralph Metzner, "Hallucinogenic Drugs and Plants in Psychotherapy and Shamanism," *Journal of Psychoactive Drugs* 30, no. 4 (October–December 1998): 333–341, doi.org/10.1080/02791072.1998.10399709.

48. See United Nations, Human Rights, Office of the High Commissioner, "Istanbul Protocol: Manual on the Effective Investigation and Docu-

mentation of Torture and Other Cruel, Inhuman or Degrading Treatment or Punishment," (2022), 187–188, www.ohchr.org/sites/default/files/documents/publications/2022-06-29/Istanbul-Protocol_Rev2_EN.pdf.

49. On the basis of a series of series of conjectures, Richard Watson then goes on to speculate that "Possibly he was even under the influence when he has his dreams." See his *Cogito Ergo Sum: The Life of René Descartes* (Boston: Godine, 2007), 77. There is no direct evidence supporting Watson's claim.

50. Matthew D. Segall, "Altered Consciousness after Descartes: Whitehead's Philosophy of Organism as Psychedelic Realism," in *Philosophy and Psychedelics: Frameworks for Exceptional Experience*, ed. Christine Hauskeller and Peter Sjöstedt-Hughes (London: Bloomsbury, 2022), 198.

51. Segall, "Altered Consciousness after Descartes," 199.

52. Segall, "Altered Consciousness after Descartes," 195.

53. See John Bellamy Foster, "Marx's Theory of Metabolic Rift: Classical Foundations for Environmental Sociology," *American Journal of Sociology* 105, no. 2 (September 1999): 366–405.

54. For reasons of economy and scholarly convention, Descartes will be cited parenthetically in the main body of the text. All citations are to "AT": Charles Adam and Paul Tannery, eds., *Oeuvres de Descartes*, rev. ed., 12 vols. (Paris: Vrin/CNRS, 1964–1976). For example, the present citation (VI 32–33) means, "Adam and Tannery, volume 6, page 10." Unless otherwise noted, I will use the standard anglophone collection: John Cottingham, Robert Stoothoff, and Dugald Murdoch, trans., *The Philosophical Writings of Descartes*, 2 vols. (Cambridge: Cambridge University Press, 1985). Portions of the next several pages are drawn, in substantially altered form, from David J. Blacker, *Democratic Education Stretched Thin: How Complexity Challenges a Liberal Ideal* (Albany: State University of New York Press, 2007), 129–138.

55. Nick Bostrom, "Are We Living in a Computer Simulation?" *Philosophical Quarterly* 53, no. 211 (2003): 243–255, available at www.simulation-argument.com.

56. See Stephen Graukroger, who provides further evidence for Descartes's motivation to provide a foundation for his science or "natural philosophy" in *Descartes: An Intellectual Biography* (New York: Oxford University Press, 1995).

57. Gail Fine, "Descartes and Ancient Skepticism," *Philosophical Review* 109 (2000): 199.

58. The building metaphor is thoroughly Cartesian. See, e.g., VII 18: "Once the foundations of a building are undermined, anything built upon them collapses on its own accord."

59. Pietr J. Vis et al., "On Perception and Consciousness in HPPD: A Systematic Review," *Frontiers in Neuroscience*, 15 (August 11, 2021), doi.org/10.3389/fnins.2021.675768.

60. See Katie Zhou et al., "Predictors of Hallucinogen Persisting Perception Disorder Symptoms, Delusional Ideation and Magical Thinking Following

Naturalistic Psychedelic Use," *PsyArXiv Preprints* (November 15, 2022), doi.org/10.31234/osf.io/txzha.

61. Janet Broughton, *Descartes's Method of Doubt* (Princeton, NJ: Princeton University Press, 2002), 2.

62. E.g., at Johns Hopkins, the Director of Guide/Facilitator Services is Mary Cosimano, LMSW, who has conducted over 450 psilocybin sessions and coauthors research at the Center; see "Mary Cosimano, LMSW," Johns Hopkins Center for Psychedelic and Consciousness Research, accessed February 25, 2023, hopkinspsychedelic.org/cosimano.

63. Neil Gascoigne, *Scepticism* (Montreal: McGill-Queen's University Press, 2002), 32.

64. Diogenes Laertius, 9.63, as quoted in Martha C. Nussbaum, *The Therapy of Desire* (Princeton, NJ: Princeton University Press, 1994), 314.

65. Nussbaum, *Therapy of Desire*, 301–307.

66. Louis E. Loeb, "Sextus, Hume and Peirce: On Securing Settled Doxastic States," *NOÛS* 32 (1998): 205–230.

67. See Miles Burnyeat, "Can the Skeptic Live His Skepticism?" in *The Skeptical Tradition*, ed. Miles Burnyeat (Berkeley: University of California Press, 1983), 117–148.

68. David Hume, *Enquiry Concerning Human Understanding* (New York: Oxford University Press, 1999 [1777]), 128. Burnyeat describes this as "Hume's Challenge," in Burnyeat, "Can the Skeptic Live His Skepticism?" 117–118.

69. Richard Popkin, *The History of Skepticism: From Savonarola to Boyle*), rev. and expanded ed. (New York: Oxford University Press, 2003), 6–7.

70. Burnyeat, "Can the Skeptic Live His Skepticism?" 118.

71. Myles Burnyeat, "The Skeptic in His Place and Time," in *The Original Skeptics: A Controversy*, ed. Miles Burnyeat and Michael Frede (Indianapolis: Hackett, 1997), 92.

72. Broughton, *Descartes's Method of Doubt*, 88.

73. Hume, *Enquiry Concerning Human Understanding*, Section XII.

74. Pierre Hadot, *Philosophy as a Way of Life*, ed. Arnold I. Davidson, trans. Michael Chase (London: Blackwell, 1995), 271.

75. Pierre Hadot, *What Is Ancient Philosophy?*, trans. Michael Chase (Cambridge, MA: Harvard University Press, 2002), 264. See also Harry G. Frankfurt, *Demons, Dreamers and Madmen: The Defense of Reason in Descartes's Meditations* (New York: Bobbs-Merrill, 1970), 4: "Religious meditations are characteristically accounts of a person seeking salvation, who begins in the darkness of sin and who is led through a conversion to spiritual illumination. While the purpose of such writing is to instruct and initiate others, the method is not essentially didactic. The author strives to teach more by example than by precept. In a broad way, the *Meditations* is a work of this sort: Descartes's aim is to guide the reader to intellectual salvation."

76. See Erika Perez, "How Often Should You Take Psilocybin Mushrooms?" *Psychedelic Passage*, June 6, 2022, www.psychedelicpassage.com/how-often-should-you-take-psilocybin-mushrooms/.

77. See Lake, *The Law of Entheogenic Churches*, 40.

78. Christopher M. Bache, *LSD and the Mind of the Universe: Diamonds from Heaven* (Rochester, VT: Park Street, 2019).

79. James Fadiman, *The Psychedelic Explorer's Guide: Safe, Therapeutic, and Sacred Journeys* (Rochester, VT: Park Street, 2011), 37.

80. Fadiman, *The Psychedelic Explorer's Guide*, 37. For the Guild of Guides (Netherlands), see "Professional Association for Facilitators of Psychedelic Experiences, Guild of Guides," accessed May 21, 2023, www.guildofguides.nl.

81. In "Altered States of Consciousness after Descartes," Matthew Segall notes that in his earlier work *Discourse on Method*, Descartes "says the experience first occurred while he spent the winter in Bavaria in 1619–1620 shut up in a 'poêle' (literally, a 'stove')" but that "most commentators agree this was just shorthand for a room heated by a tile stove" (199 n.23).

82. Pierre Hadot makes an explicit connection between the Cartesian meditator and the Stoical spiritual exercises in support of the claim that the "extent to which the ancient conception of philosophy is present in Descartes is not always adequately measured," in *What Is Ancient Philosophy?* 265.

83. See Broughton, *Descartes's Method of Doubt*, 23.

84. Edmund Husserl, *Cartesian Meditations: An Introduction to Phenomenology*, ed. Dorion Cairns (The Hague: Martinus Nijhoff, 1960), 7.

85. Husserl, *Cartesian Meditations*, 2.

86. Husserl, *Cartesian Meditations*, 2, n.2, listed as "Appended later."

87. For one such advance, see Manesh Grin et al., "A Complex Systems Perspective on Psychedelic Brain Action," *Trends in Cognitive Sciences* 27, no. 5 (May 2023): 433–445, doi.org/10.1016/j.tics.2023.01.003, arguing that complexity theory focused on the interaction of multiple brain systems is the most promising way to analyze the neurology of psychedelics.

88. Husserl, *Cartesian Meditations*, 20.

89. Husserl, *Cartesian Meditations*, 27.

90. Aristotle, *Nicomachean Ethics*, trans. Terence Irwin (Indianapolis: Hackett, 2019).

91. Aaron Copland, *What to Listen for in Music* (New York: New American Library, 2009 [1937]), 13.

92. Copland, *What to Listen for in Music*, 13.

93. Shanon, "The Epistemics of Ayahuasca Visions," 273.

94. "All that is solid melts into air" is from Karl Marx and Frederick Engels, *Manifesto of the Communist Party*, trans. Samuel Moore in cooperation with Frederick Engels, in *Marx/Engels Selected Works*, vol. 1, 98–137 (Moscow: Progress Publishers, 1969 [1848]), www.marxists.org/archive/marx/works/1848/communist-manifesto/index.htm.

95. See Carhart-Harris et al., "LSD Enhances Suggestibility in Healthy Volunteers"; and Timmermann et al., "Psychedelics Alter Metaphysical Beliefs."

96. Zygmunt Bauman, *Liquid Modernity* (London: Polity, 2000).

97. I would characterize this experience as a common-enough instance of pareidolia (i.e., detecting an image of Jesus or the Virgin or whatever in some substrate) but for the fact that it was dynamic in movement and was experienced as having its own autonomy. Though I had the metacognition at the time to "know" I was seeing this image in the clouds and was able to enjoy it aesthetically, it is very easy to understand how religious individuals might have a very different experience of this phenomenon. Pareidolia seems definitely in play as a partial explanation for aspects of these experiences, but as an explanation, pareidolia would only go so far: making sense of perceived patterns is something we are always doing, constantly. So differentiating "justified" from "unjustified" pareidolia would merely be to redescribe the same old epistemological questions. For a discussion of the most common type of pareidolia, "face pareidolia," see Jiangang Liu et al., "Seeing Jesus in Toast: Neural and Behavioral Correlates of Face Pareidolia," *Cortex* 53 (April 2014): 60–77, doi.org/10.1016/j.cortex.2014.01.013.

98. David Felton and David Dalton, "Charles Manson: The Incredible Story of the Most Dangerous Man Alive," *Rolling Stone*, June 25, 1970, www.rollingstone.com/culture/culture-news/charles-manson-the-incredible-story-of-the-most-dangerous-man-alive-85235/.

99. Jim DeRogatis, "Charles Manson's Musical Ambitions," *New Yorker*, August 19, 2019, www.newyorker.com/culture/cultural-comment/charles-mansons-musical-ambitions.

100. Neurotech@Berkeley, "Psychedelics: A Tragic History of Cults, Drugs, and Promises to the Future," *Medium*, April 10, 2022, ucbneurotech.medium.com/psychedelics-a-tragic-history-of-cults-drugs-and-promises-to-the-future-121ad2bd2b48. This article's examples are drawn from James Robert Douglas, "Inside the Bizarre 1960s Cult, The Family: LSD, Yoga and UFOs," *Guardian*, February 12, 2017, www.theguardian.com/film/2017/feb/13/the-family-great-white-brotherhood-australia-melbourne-cult-anne-hamilton-byrne.

101. Much has been written about this. See Hadley Mears, "The Witches of Westwood and Carlos Castaneda's Sinister Legacy," *LAist*, September 2, 2021, laist.com/news/la-history/carlos-castanedas-sinister-legacy-witches-of-westwood, and Robert Marshall, "The Dark Legacy of Carlos Castaneda," *Salon*, April 12, 2007, www.salon.com/2007/04/12/castaneda/. Many more examples from this period are found in Gary Lachman, *Turn Off Your Mind: The Dedalus Book of the 1960s* (Sawtry, UK: Dedalus, 2001), which recounts the interrelation between psychedelic and "occult" and their relation to popular culture.

102. See Francisco Javier Carod-Artal, "Hallucinogenic Drugs in Pre-Columbian Mesoamerican Cultures," *Neurología* 30, no. 1 (January–February 2015): 42–49, doi.org/10.1016/j.nrleng.2011.07.010.

103. See Carl de Borhegyi (with Suzanne de Borhegyi-Forrest), "The Genesis of a Mushroom/Venus Religion in Mesoamerica," in *Entheogens in the Development of Culture: The Anthropology and Neurobiology of Ecstatic Experience*, ed. John A. Rush (Berkeley, CA: North Atlantic, 2013), 456–462. Examples are also discussed in Matthew W. Johnson, William A. Richards, and Roland R. Griffiths, "Human Hallucinogen Research: Guidelines for Safety," *Journal of Psychopharmacology* 22, no. 6 (August 2008): 3, doi.org/10.1177/0269881108093587, arguing that "indigenous cultures should not be regarded as absolute role models in the clinical use of hallucinogens." See also Richard Evans Schultes, "Teonanacatl: The Narcotic Mushroom of the Aztecs," *American Anthropologist* 42, no. 3 (September 1940): 429–443. But there is some disagreement over this point; e.g., see Harri Hyberg, "Religious Use of Hallucinogenic Fungi: A Comparison between Siberian and Mesoamerican Cultures," which argues, "It has been suggested that the human sacrificial victims of the Aztecs were willing to die because they were drugged with psilocybin. . . . However, the Aztecs thought that the continued existence of the world was guaranteed by sacrifice of human blood and hearts to the sun, and the souls of the sacrifice victims fared better in the afterlife than those of ordinary people. . . . Thus it seems that no drugging was necessary, especially as the Aztec philosophical ideas were thoroughly permeated with the importance of fulfilling one's duty." *Karstenia* 32 (1992): 74, www.samorini.it/doc1/alt_aut/lr/nyberg-religious-use-of-hallucinogenic-fungi.pdf.

104. See Dagmara M. Socha et al., "Use of psychoactive and stimulant plants on the south coast of Peru from the Early Intermediate to Late Intermediate Period," *Journal of Archeological Science* 148 (December 2022), doi.org/10.1016/j.jas.2022.105688.

105. A helpful essay on this issue, with further cultic and historical examples is philosopher Jules Evans, "Do Psychedelics Make You Liberal? Not Always," *Philosophy for Life*, February 15, 2001, www.philosophyforlife.org/blog/do-psychedelics-make-you-liberal-not-always.

106. For the "inherently evil" point of view, see Lewis Ungit, *The Return of the Dragon: The Shocking Way Drugs and Religion Shape People and Societies* (Independently published, 2022).

107. See Carhart-Harris et al., "LSD Enhances Suggestibility in Health Volunteers."

108. Sigmund Freud, *Studies in Hysteria* (New York: Penguin, 2004 [1895]), 303–304.

109. Ross, "Power Trip."

110. Ross, "Power Trip," episodes 6 and 7.

111. See, e.g., Olivia Goldhill, "A Psychedelic Therapist Allegedly Took Millions from a Holocaust Survivor, Highlighting Worries about Elders Taking Hallucinogens," *Stat News*, April 21, 2022, www.statnews.com/2022/04/21/psychedelic-therapist-allegedly-took-millions-from-holocaust-survivor-highlighting-worries-

about-elders-taking-hallucinogens/, and Goldhill, "Psychedelic Therapy Has a Sexual Abuse Problem." See also Evan Lewis-Healey's survey of underground practitioners on the topic, "Preventing Sexual Abuse in Psychedelic Therapy," *Psychedelic Spotlight*, October 15, 2021, psychedelicspotlight.com/preventing-sexual-abuse-in-psychedelic-therapy/; and for information about support resources for victims, see Leia Friedwoman and Katherine MacLean, "Sexual Abuse in Psychedelic Therapy: Important Steps Being Taken to Support Survivors," *Double Blind*, September 15, 2022, doubleblindmag.com/psychedelic-survivors/.

112. Johnson, "Consciousness, Religion, and Gurus," 590.

113. Released as a single July 7, 1967, Capitol Records (US).

114. Pollan, *How to Change Your Mind*, 251.

115. William James, *Varieties of Religious Experience* (New York: Penguin, 1982 [1902]), Lectures 16 and 17.

116. Ludwig Wittgenstein, *Tractatus Logico-Philosophicus*, trans. D. F. Pears and B. F. McGuinness (New York: Humanities Press, 1961 [1922]), 7.

117. Wittgenstein, *Tractatus Logico-Philosophicus*, 6.522.

Chapter 4

1. Timothy Leary, Ralph Metzner, and Richard Alpert, *The Psychedelic Experience: A Manual Based on the Tibetan Book of the Dead* (Toronto: Citadel Press, 1992 [1962]), 3.

2. Friedrich Nietzsche, *The Will to Power*, trans. Walter Kaufmann and R. J. Hollingdale (New York: Vintage Books, 1967 [1901]), §482.

3. See Stanislav Grof, *The Adventure of Self-Discovery: Dimensions of Consciousness and New Perspectives in Psychotherapy and Inner Exploration* (Albany: State University of New York Press, 1988), 3–36.

4. Grof, *The Adventure of Self-Discovery*, 88–89, 105–147. See also Stanislav Grof, "The Experience of Death and Dying: Psychological, Philosophical, and Spiritual Aspects," *Spirituality Studies* 1, no. 2 (Fall 2015), www.spirituality-studies.org/files/1-2-grof.pdf; and *Infinity: The Ultimate Trip—Journey Beyond Death*, documentary film, directed by Jay Weidner (Boulder, CO: Sacred Mystery Productions, 2009).

5. A "distorted sense of time" is listed as among the "comprehensive constituent themes" of DMT experiences in Christopher Cott and Adam Rock, "Phenomenology of N,N-Dimethyltryptamine Use: A Thematic Analysis," *Journal of Scientific Exploration* 22, no. 3 (2008): 363, 366: "Participants routinely referred to the dissolution of Einsteinian space-time during the DMT-induced state." See also Chad Davis, "People Are Tripping on DMT to Lose All Perception of Time and Reality," *Elite Daily*, July 22, 2015, www.elitedaily.com/life/the-implications-of-dmt/1106931. On LSD and psilocybin time distortion, see

Steliana Yanakieva et al., "The Effects of Microdose LSD on Time Perception: A Randomised, Double-Blind, Placebo-Controlled Trial," *Psychopharmacology (Berl)* 236, no. 4 (April 2019): 1159–1170, doi.org/10.1007/s00213-018-5119-x; and Katarina L. Shebloski and James M. Broadway, "Commentary: Effects of Psilocybin on Time Perception and Temporal Control of Behavior in Humans," *Frontiers in Psychology* 7 (May 19, 2016), doi.org/10.3389/fpsyg.2016.00736.

6. Grof, *LSD Psychotherapy*, 11–12.

7. Stanislav Grof, "Forward," in Albert Hofmann, *LSD: My Problem Child*, 14.

8. See Pace and Devenot, "Right-Wing Psychedelia," 1–21.

9. See Patrick Lundborg, *Psychedelia*; Mike Jay, *High Society: The Central Role of Mind-Altering Drugs in History, Science, and Culture* (Rochester, VT: Park Street, 2010); Mike Jay, *Psychonauts*; Davis, *High Weirdness*; Gary Lachman, *Turn Off Your Mind*; Christopher Partridge, *High Culture: Drugs, Mysticism, and the Pursuit of Transcendence in the Modern World* (New York: Oxford University Press, 2018); and Ido Hartogsohn, *American Trip: Set, Setting, and the Psychedelic Experience in the Twentieth Century* (Cambridge: MIT Press, 2020).

10. Davis, *High Weirdness*.

11. See Jonathan Lear, "Inside and Outside the *Republic*," *Phronesis* 37, no. 2 (1992): 184–215.

12. For information on ongoing clinical trials, see National Institutes of Health, "Lysergic Acid Diethylamide (LSD) as Treatment for Cluster Headache (LCH)," U.S. Library of Medicine, May 5, 2022, clinicaltrials.gov/ct2/show/NCT03781128.

13. There is now some evidence specifically concerning ayahuasca and trauma, too, having to do with enabling the reexperiencing of past traumatic life events. See Brandon Weiss et al., "Prevalence and Therapeutic Impact of Adverse Life Event Reexperiencing under Ceremonial Ayahuasca," *Scientific Reports* 13, 9438 (June 9, 2023), doi.org/10.1038/s41598-023-36184-3. They note that a "liberal interpretation" of their results is "our data is the first to systematically demonstrate the association between psychedelic reexperiencing and positive mental health outcomes. It is conceivable that the cognitive mechanisms underlying these changes involve ways of relating to trauma and adverse life events under ayahuasca that are distinctly therapeutic."

14. For a description and photograph, see Charles S. Grob, Anthony P. Bossis, and Roland R. Griffiths, "Use of the Classic Hallucinogen Psilocybin for Treatment of Existential Distress Associated with Cancer," in Jennifer L. Steel and Brian I. Carr, eds., *Psychological Aspects of Cancer: A Guide to Emotional and Psychological Consequences of Cancer, Their Causes and Their Management*, 2nd ed. (Basel: Springer, 2022), 81.

15. The search "Johns Hopkins playlist" on Spotify yields many versions of these playlists. See also Marc Shapiro, "Playlist for a Psychedelic Journey,"

News and Publications, Johns Hopkins Medicine, February 5, 2021, www.hopkinsmedicine.org/news/articles/playlist-for-a-psychedelic-journey.

16. See Nguyen Thanh Tam et al., "Participants' Understanding of Informed Consent in Clinical Trials over Three Decades: Systematic Review and Meta-analysis," *Bull World Health Organ* 93, no. 3 (March 2015): 186–198H, doi.org/10.2471/BLT.14.141390: "The proportion of participants in clinical trials who understood different components of informed consent varied from 52.1% to 75.8%. Investigators could do more to help participants achieve a complete understanding." Also see David Wendler and Christine Grady, "What Should Research Participants Understand about Medical Costs?" *Journal of Medical Ethics* 34, no. 10 (June 2008): 767–770, doi.org/10.1136/jme.2007.023325.

17. Gaby Galvin, "Surprise Medical Bills Have Been Banned Since January. 1 in 5 Americans Say They or Their Family Have Gotten an Unexpected Charge Anyway," *Morning Consult*, July 7, 2022, morningconsult.com/2022/07/07/surprise-medical-billing-ban-unexpected-charges/.

18. See Mo Costandi, "A Brief History of Psychedelic Psychiatry," *Psychologist* (UK) 27, no. 9 (September 2014): 714–716, issuu.com/thepsychologist/docs/psy09_14web/84?e=1106616/9079836.

19. "Acid manufacturing might be one of the last criminal enterprises where those involved are motivated by more than the prospect of making money. Even now, more than three decades on from the Summer of Love, to cook acid is to perform a sacrament, a public service." Peter Wilkinson, "The Acid King," *Rolling Stone*, July 5, 2001, www.rollingstone.com/feature/acid-lsd-king-william-leonard-pickard-prison-pete-wilkinson-184390/.

20. Rustam Yulbarisov, "LSD Capitalism Promises a Bad Trip for Us All," *Jacobin*, April 2, 2022, jacobin.com/2022/04/lsd-capitalism-psychedelics-mdma-ketamine-companies-medical.

21. Davis, *High Weirdness*, 39.

22. Patrick Lee, *We Borrow the Earth: An Intimate Portrait of the Gypsy Folk Tradition and Culture* (Pembrokeshire, Wales: Ravine, 2015), 120–200.

23. Among many sources, see Beatriz Caiuby Labate, Brian T. Anderson, and Henrik Jungaberle, "Ritual Ayahuasca Use and Health: An Interview with Jacques Mabit," In *The Internationalization of Ayahuasca*, ed. Beatriz Caiuby Labate and Henrik Jungaberle, 223–243 (Zurich: Lit Verlag), www.researchgate.net/publication/314404765_Ritual_Ayahuasca_use_and_health_an_interview_with_Jacques_Mabit; see also "Bwiti Tradition," Discover Iboga Church of America, accessed May 21, 2023, ibogausa.org/bwiti-tradition/: "Discover Iboga Church of America is a spiritual learning and healing center. Our mission is to help the community and the people in need with spiritual guidance to reconnect to their self (soul) and the Creator, to provide spiritual support, healing practices and sacred Iboga ceremonies with Bwiti teachings. Iboga is the 'Grandfather and Queen Mother' of all medicinal plants, probably the most powerful plant medicine on earth. In

Gabon, it is known as the tree of life and knowledge. Iboga is a plant medicine that works on all 3 levels: mental, physical, and spiritual healing."

24. Metzner, "Hallucinogenic Drugs and Plants in Psychotherapy and Shamanism."

25. Harner, *The Way of the Shaman*, 93.

26. Jeremy Narby, "Amazonian Perspectives on Invisible Entities," in *DMT Dialogues: Encounters with the Spirit Molecule*, ed. David Luke and Rory Spowers (Rochester, VT: Park Street, 2018), 75.

27. Narby, "Amazonian Perspectives," 77–78.

28. Narby, "Amazonian Perspectives," 79.

29. See Mark Hoffman, "Entheogens (Psychedelic Drugs) and the Ancient Mystery Religions," in *Toxicology in Antiquity*, 2nd ed., ed. Philip Wexler (London: Elsevier, 2019), 359; David DuPuis, "Psychedelics as Tools for Belief Transmission. Set, Setting, Suggestibility, and Persuasion in the Ritual Use of Hallucinogens," *Frontiers in Psychology* 12 (November 23, 2021), doi.org/10.3389/fpsyg.2021.730031; and, for a global survey, Gastón Guzmán, "Sacred Mushrooms and Man: Diversity and Traditions in the World, with Special Reference to *Psilocybe*," in *Entheogens and the Development of Culture: The Anthropology and Neurology of Ecstatic Experience*, ed. John A. Rush (Berkeley, CA: North Atlantic Books, 2012), 485–518.

30. Wasson, Hofmann, and Ruck, *The Road to Eleusis*; Muraresku, *The Immortality Key*; and Karen Polinger Foster, "Psychedelic Art and Ecstatic Visions in the Aegean," in *The Routledge Companion to Ecstatic Experience in the Ancient World*, ed. Diana Stein, Sarah Kielt Costello, and Karen Polinger Foster (London: Routledge, 2021), 489–516.

31. See David J. Lewis-Williams and Jean Clottes, "The Mind in the Cave—the Cave in the Mind: Altered Consciousness in the Upper Paleolithic," *Anthropology and Consciousness* 9, no. 1 (January 2008): 13–21.

32. See Arce and Winkelman, "Psychedelics, Sociality, and Human Evolution." For alleged use of iboga root by mandrills, see Samorini, *Animals and Psychedelics*, 58.

33. See Mark G. Blainey, *Christ Returns from the Jungle: Ayahuasca Religion as Mystical Healing* (Albany: State University of New York Press, 2021).

34. Anthropologist Michael J. Winkelman argues for the adaptive "group bonding" thesis in "Altered Consciousness and Drugs in Human Evolution," 40–45. See also Arce and Winkelman, "Psychedelics, Sociality, and Human Evolution," 1: "the evolutionary scenario put forward suggests that integration of psilocybin into ancient diet, communal practice, and proto-religious activity may have enhanced hominin response to the socio-cognitive niche, while also aiding in its creation. In particular, the interpersonal and prosocial effects of psilocybin may have mediated the expansion of social bonding mechanisms such

as laughter, music, storytelling, and religion, imposing a systematic bias on the selective environment that favored selection for prosociality in our lineage."

35. Mona Sobhani, "Psychedelic Worldview Flips + Secular Society," The Brave New *World of Psychedelic Science*, March 17, 2023, psychedelicrenaissance.substack.com/p/psychedelic-worldview-flips-secular?r=2sz1v.

36. Michael Pollan, *How to Change Your Mind*, 215.

37. See Arce and Winkelman, "Psychedelics, Sociality and Human Evolution."

38. Davis, *High Weirdness*, 55.

39. Davis, *High Weirdness*, 55.

40. Davis, *High Weirdness*, 39.

41. Hart, *Drug Use for Grown-Ups*, 177–193.

42. Hart, *Drug Use for Grown-Ups*, 14.

43. See David Pilgrim, "The Brut Caricature," museum exhibit, The Jim Crow Museum, Ferris State University, Big Rapids, MI, accessed May 21, 2023, www.ferris.edu/jimcrow/brute/; Doris Marie Provine, *Unequal Under the Law: Race in the War on Drugs* (Chicago: University of Chicago Press, 2007), 37–90.

44. Hart, *Drug Use for Grown-Ups*, 23–24; see also Michelle Alexander, *The New Jim Crow: Mass Incarceration in the Age of Colorblindness* (New York: New Press, 2012), 51–54.

45. Hart, *Drug Use for Grown-Ups*, 252–253.

46. MAPS provides a "Psychedelic Integration List: Mental Health Support Practitioners by Location," accessed May 21, 2023, integration.maps.org.

47. A sizeable listing of "entheogenic retreats" may be found at Retreat Guru, "Find Authentic Entheogenic Retreats," accessed May 21, 2023, retreat.guru/be/entheogenic-retreats.

48. See Etnikas Integrative Medicine, "Ayahuasca Healing Retreats," accessed May 21, 2023, etnikas.com; and "Ayahuasca Retreat Programs," Ayahuasca Foundation, accessed May 21, 2023, www.ayahuascafoundation.org/ayahuasca-retreat.

49. Tara Isabella Burton, *Strange Rites: New Religions for a Godless World* (New York: PublicAffairs, 2020), 18.

50. Burton, *Strange Rites*, 20–21.

51. John Rawls, *Political Liberalism* (New York: Columbia University Press, 2005), 24.

52. Blacker, *What's Left of the World?*

53. See Maroukis, *The Peyote Road*, 25.

54. The main relevant federal statutes are the American Indian Religious Freedom Act (AIRFA), Public Law No. 95–341, 92 Stat. 469 (Aug. 11, 1978), and the Religious Freedom Restoration Act of 1993 (RFRA), Public Law No. 103–141, 107 Stat. 1488 (November 16, 1993).

55. Luis Sahagún, "Why Are Some Native Americans Fighting Efforts to Decriminalize Peyote?" *Los Angeles Times*, March 29, 2020.

56. Wisconsin v. Yoder, 406 U.S. 205 (1972).

57. Employment Division, Department of Human Resources v. Smith, 494 U.S. 872 (1990). The RFRA essentially returns the Court to the earlier level of deference of religious belief articulated in the "Sherbert test," from Sherbert v. Verner, 374 U.S. 398 (1963), which had established the higher "strict scrutiny" standard for religious accommodations.

58. There have been many of these challenges. See, e.g., United States v. Jefferson (N.D. Ind. 2001), denying a daily marijuana smoker's petition for release due, essentially, to the government's "compelling interest" in enforcing drug laws outweighing the religious freedom claim. For a more recent relevant news story, see Luis Andres Henao and Kwasi Gymafi Asiedu, "Rastafari Want More Legal Marijuana for Freedom of Worship," *Associated Press*, December 10, 2021, apnews.com/article/health-religion-ohio-marijuana-columbus-d2dc83bc70426d6b6b10449496469557.

59. New Hampshire v Mack (N.H. 2020).

60. "No religious Test shall ever be required as a Qualification to any Office or public Trust under the United States." See also Torcaso v Watkins, 367 US 488 (1961), overturning a Maryland state requirement that required candidates for public office to profess a belief in God.

61. Burwell v. Hobby Lobby Stores, 573 U.S. at 724–5 (2014).

62. Civil Rights Act of 1964 (Public Law 88-352).

63. See West Virginia v. Barnette, 319 U.S. 624 (1943); Boy Scouts of America v. Dale, 530 U.S. 640 (2000); Wisconsin v. Yoder, 406 U.S. 205 (1972); Pierce v. Society of Sisters, 268 U.S. 510 (1925); Prince v. Massachusetts, 321 U.S. 158 (1944); United States v. Seeger, 380 U.S. 163 (1965); Welsh v. United States, 398 U.S. 333 (1970).

64. See, e.g., United States v. Kuch (D.D.C. 1968), denying the religious accommodation claim for marijuana and LSD use. The diverse range of such groups—from benign to silly to downright sinister—is ably cataloged in Mike Marinacci, *Psychedelic Cults and Outlaw Churches: LSD, Cannabis, and Spiritual Sacraments in Underground America* (Rochester, VT: Park Street, 2023).

65. Jacobellis v. Ohio, 378 U.S. 184 (1964), at 197 ("I shall not today attempt further to define the kinds of material I understand to be embraced within that shorthand description, and perhaps I could never succeed in intelligibly doing so").

66. See Lake, *The Law of Entheogenic Churches*, 15–22; U.S. v. Meyers, 906 F. Supp 1494 (D. Wyo. 1995) and U.S. v. Meyers II, F. 3d 1475 (1996).

67. See Rhodes, "Up in Smoke," 339–340. Meyers's "Church" flunked most of the Meyers factors; for example, the Court "concluded there was nothing metaphysical about his beliefs—everything was physical and the objective of the beliefs was simply to smoke marijuana" (339).

68. Lake, *The Law of Entheogenic Churches*, 18–19.

69. Lake, *The Law of Entheogenic Churches*, 19–21.

70. U.S. v. Meyers, 906 F. Supp. 1494 at 1502–03, as quoted in Lake, *The Law of Entheogenic Churches*, 21.

71. Lake, *The Law of Entheogenic Churches*, 16.

72. Edwards v. Aguillard, 482 U.S. 578 (1987); see also Rodney A. Grunes, "Creationism, the Courts, and the First Amendment," *Journal of Church and State* 31, no. 3 (Autumn 1989): 465–486.

73. Office of Legal Counsel, US Department of Justice, "Peyote Exemption for Native American Church," December 22, 1981, www.justice.gov/olc/opinion/peyote-exemption-native-american-church, justifying the exemption against Establishment Clause challenge on the grounds of the special legal status of Native Americans.

74. "It is inappropriate for a reviewing court to attempt to assess the truth or falsity of an announced article of faith. Judges are not oracles of theological verity, and the Founders did not intend for them to be declarants of religious orthodoxy." Africa v. Commonwealth of Pa., 662 F.2d 1025, 1030 (3d Cir. 1981).

75. Sacks, *Hallucinations*, 90–121.

76. Sacks, *Hallucinations*, 106.

77. Sacks, *Hallucinations*, 109.

78. Melissa Shukuroglou et al., "Changes in Music-Evoked Emotion and Ventral Striatal Functional Connectivity after Psilocybin Therapy for Depression," *Journal of Psychopharmacology* 37, no. 1 (January 2023): 70–79, doi.org/10.1177/0269881122112; and Mendel Kaelen et al., "LSD Enhances the Emotional Response to Music," *Journal of Psychopharmacology* 232, no. 19 (October 2015): 3607–3614, doi.org/10.1007/s00213-015-4014-y.

79. Noah Eckstein, "Creating a Sanctuary for Psychedelic Art," *New York Times*, May 28, 2023.

80. Rick Strassman, *DMT and the Soul of Prophecy: A New Science of Spiritual Revelation in the Hebrew Bible* (Rochester, VT: Park Street, 2014).

81. Bache, *LSD and the Mind of the Universe*, 46–50.

82. Bache, *LSD and the Mind of the Universe*, 21; "The magnitude of Love at the fount of the creation of our universe is beyond description" (130).

83. Bache, *LSD and the Mind of the Universe*, 49.

84. Hofmann, *LSD: My Problem Child*, 18–22.

85. Shulgin and Shulgin, *PIHKAL* and *TIHKAL*.

86. See Morris, "Conversation with Dr. David Nichols," at 1:45:13; the Johns Hopkins policy on self-experimentation can be found at "Investigators as Study Participants (Self-Experimentation)," Office of Human Subjects Research, Institutional Review Board, Johns Hopkins Medicine, July 2005, www.hopkinsmedicine.org/institutional_review_board/guidelines_policies/guidelines/self_experimentation.html.

87. Jon Hamilton et al., "Brain Scientists Are Tripping Out Over Psychedelics," *National Public Radio*, December 12, 2022, www.npr.org/2022/12/19/1144306776/brain-scientists-are-tripping-out-over-psychedelics.

88. See Andrew Jacobs, "The Psychedelic Revolution Is Coming. Psychiatry May Never Be the Same," *New York Times*, May 9, 2021, updated November 11, 2021; Rick Doblin discussed the MAPS future on Joe Rogan, "The Joe Rogan Experience #1964—Rich Doblin," March 31, 2023, podcast, 2:49:00, www.jrepodcast.com/episode/joe-rogan-experience-1964-rick-doblin/.

89. "Best Psytrance Festivals Around the Globe," Tribal Reunion, accessed May 22, 2023, tribalreunion.com/festival/best-psytrance-festivals/.

90. See "Alex Grey," accessed May 22, 2023, www.alexgrey.com; "Barbara Takenaga," accessed May 22, 2023, www.barbaratakenaga.com; "Amanda Sage," accessed May 22, 2023, www.amandasage.com; "Martina Hoffmann," accessed May 22, 2023, www.martinahoffmann.com; "Venosa Art," accessed May 22, 2023, www.venosa.com.

91. See Higginbottom, "The 'Psychonauts' Training to Explore Another Dimension."

92. See J. D. Lewis-Williams and T. A. Dowson, "The Signs of All Times: Entoptic Phenomena in Upper Paleolithic Cave Art," *Current Anthropology* 29, no. 2 (April 1988): 201–245; and David W. Robinson et al., "*Datura* Quids at Pinwheel Cave, California, Provide Unambiguous Confirmation of the Ingestion of Hallucinogens at a Rock Art Site," *Proceedings of the National Academy of Sciences* 117, no. 49 (November 23, 2020): 31026–31037, doi.org/10.1073/pnas.2014529117.

93. There are many online commercial sites selling Huichol yarn paintings. For a book-length treatment, see Kathleen Berrin and Thomas K. Seligman, *Art of the Huichol Indians* (New York: Harry N. Abrams, 1978).

94. Lin, *Trip*, 14.

95. Davis, *High Weirdness*, 93.

96. Hart, *Drug Use for Grown-Ups*, 62–63.

97. Tom Wolfe, *The Electric Kool-Aid Acid Test* (New York: Picador, 2008).

98. Jean-Paul Sartre, *Critique of Dialectical Reason, Vol. 1*, trans. Alan Sheridan-Smith (London: Verso, 2004 [1960]), 345–362.

99. Lachman, *Turn Off Your Mind*, 29.

100. Sartre, *Critique of Dialectical Reason*, 351–362.

101. See "Statement from Asbury President Dr. Kevin Brown," Asbury University, February 24, 2023, www.asbury.edu/outpouring/. For video footage, see "LIVE from Asbury University's Spiritual Revival," *CBN News*, February 23, 2023, video, 2:35:10, www.youtube.com/watch?v=4IZL9d-g_fc.

102. See Simon Reynolds, *Energy Flash: A Journey through Rave Music and Dance Culture* (New York: Soft Skull, 2012), on how MDMA "spawned rave culture." For a description of a mushroom rave (in a "mushwomb"), see Michelle

Lhooq, "Inside Shroom Rave: A Radical Experiment in Post-Alcohol Partying," *Double-Blind*, March 3, 2003, doubleblindmag.com/mushwomb-shroom-rave/.

103. Martha Newson et al., "'I Get High With a Little Help From My Friends'—How Raves Can Invoke Identity Fusion and Lasting Co-operation via Transformative Experiences," *Frontiers in Psychology* 12 (September 24, 2021), doi.org/10.3389/fpsyg.2021.719596.

104. A long list of *physical* effects is also available at Josie Kins, "Subjective Effects Index," accessed May 23, 2023, effectindex.com/categories/physical-effects.

105. See Lindsay P. Cameron et al., "A Non-Hallucinogenic Psychedelic Analogue with Therapeutic Potential," *Nature* 589 (January 21, 2021): 474–479, doi.org/10.1038/s41586-020-3008-z; and Katherine M. Nautiyal and David B. Yaden, "Does the Trip Matter? Investigating the Role of the Subjective Effects of Psychedelics in Persisting Therapeutic Effects," *Neuropsychopharmacology* 48 (January 2023): 215–216, doi.org/10.1038/s41386-022-01424-z.

106. Timmermann et al., "Psychedelics Alter Metaphysical Beliefs."

107. For a good example such a festival, see "Voove," *Voove Experience*, accessed May 22, 2023, www.voov-festival.de.

108. G. W. F. Hegel, *Phenomenology of Spirit*, trans. A.V. Miller (New York: Oxford University Press, 1977 [1807]), 2.

109. Samorini, *Animals and Psychedelics*, 16.

110. The classic paper for so-called "Shannon entropy" is Claude E. Shannon, "A Mathematical Theory of Communication," *Bell System Technical Journal* 27 (July–October 1948): 379–423, 623–656. The earliest reference to brain entropy in the psychedelic context that I have found is in ethnobotanist Giorgio Samorini's *Riflessioni lisergiche* (Milan: Flash, 1981), as quoted by Samorini himself in *Animals and Psychedelics*, 85–86.

111. Robin L. Carhart-Harris et al., "The Entropic Brain: a Theory of Conscious States Informed by Neuroimaging Research with Psychedelic Drugs," *Frontiers of Human Neuroscience* 8 (February 3, 2014), doi.org/10.3389/fnhum.2014.00020. For a survey of entropic brain theory research and its proposed application to "disorders of consciousness," see Sidath Rankaduwa and Adrian M. Owen, "Psychedelics, Entropic Brain Theory, and the Taxonomy of Conscious States: A Summary of Debates and Perspectives," *Neuroscience of Consciousness* 2023, no. 1 (April 2023): 1–13, doi.org/10.1093/nc/niad001.

112. Carhart-Harris et al., "The Entropic Brain."

113. Robin L. Carhart-Harris and K. J. Friston, "REBUS and the Anarchic Brain: Toward a Unified Model of the Brain Action of Psychedelics," *Pharmacological Review* 71, no. 3 (July 2019): 319, 326, doi.org/10.1124/pr.118.017160.

114. Carhart-Harris and Friston, "REBUS and the Anarchic Brain," 326.

115. On the notion of priors, see David Nutt, Meg J. Spriggs, and David Erritzoe, "Psychedelics Therapeutics: What We Know, What We Think, and

What We Need to Research," *Neuropharmacology* 223, 109257 (February 1, 2023), doi.org/10.1016/j.neuropharm.2022.109257; and Christopher Timmermann et al., "LSD Modulates Effective Connectivity and Neural Adaptation Mechanisms in an Auditory Oddball Paradigm," *Neuropharmacology* 142 (November 2018): 251–262, doi.org/10.1016/j.neuropharm.2017.10.039.

116. Carhart-Harris and Friston, "REBUS and the Anarchic Brain," 326.

117. Carhart-Harris and Friston, "REBUS and the Anarchic Brain," 317.

118. Carhart-Harris and Friston, "REBUS and the Anarchic Brain," 331–332. See also Robin L. Carhart-Harris et al., "Canalization and Plasticity in Psychopathology," *Neuropharmacology* 226 (March 1, 2023): 109398, doi.org/10.1016/j.neuropharm.2022.109398.

119. These categories and the Good Samaritan example are laid out in Robert Stein, *Biblical Hermeneutics* (Carnas, WA: Biblical Training, 2020). See also Grant R. Osborne, *The Hermeneutical Spiral: A Comprehensive Introduction to Biblical Interpretation* (Downers Grove, IL: IVP Academic, 2006).

120. Gadamer, *Truth and Method*, 395.

121. See Paul Ricoeur, "Schleiermacher's Hermeneutics," *Monist* 60, no. 22 (April 1977): 184.

122. The locus classicus for the application of the principle of charity in philosophy is Donald Davidson, "Radical Interpretation," *Dialectica* 27 (December 1973): 314–328. He also called it "rational accommodation," the idea being to construct an initial interpretation of the other such that it maximizes agreement.

123. Thomas Nagel, *The View from Nowhere* (New York: Oxford University Press, 1989).

124. Hans-Georg Gadamer, "Man and Language," in *Philosophical Hermeneutics*, trans. and ed. David E. Linge (Berkeley: University of California Press, 1976), 66.

125. Gadamer, "Man and Language," 66.

126. The term "fusion of horizons" is meant to overcome the narrowly psychologistic (i.e., having to do with personal beliefs) account of Romantic era hermeneutics. The term "horizon" is from Husserl, where it is also meant to express the region of our intentionality in perception (in both a spatial and temporal sense), somewhat similar to the sense of *Umwelt*, though it is less associated with the biological perceptual apparatus. Gadamer broadens the term to stress cultural and historical situatedness, as well as the context-bound nature of all interpretation. For Gadamer, our horizon "moves with us" as we gain in understanding, strikingly parallel to Luis Eduardo Luna's remark about the indigenous "cosmos" that serves as the epigraph for this chapter.

127. David Ingram, "Hermeneutics and Truth," *Journal of the British Society of Phenomenology* 15, no. 1 (January 1984): 70.

128. On Nietzsche's idea of the eternal recurrence as an ethical test (the ideal that one should be able to affirm living one's life ad infinitum), see Richard

Schacht, *Nietzsche* (London: Routledge, 1983), 258–261; for a refinement of this view, see Eric Oger, "The Eternal Return as Crucial Test," *Journal of Nietzsche Studies* 14 (Autumn 1997): 1–18.

129. Gadamer, *Truth and Method*, 579.

130. Gadamer, *Truth and Method*, 355.

131. Hans-Georg Gadamer, "Text and Interpretation," in *Dialogue and Deconstruction: The Gadamer-Derrida Encounter*, Diane P. Michelfelder and Robert E. Palmer, eds. (Albany: State University of New York Press, 1989), 26.

132. Hegel, *Phenomenology of Spirit*, 2: "the diversity of philosophical systems as the progressive unfolding of truth."

133. On the complexities of ascertaining the DMN's role in psychedelics, see Gattuso et al., "Default Mode Network Modulation by Psychedelics."

134. Gadamer, *Truth and Method*, 358.

135. Timmermann et al., "Psychedelics Alter Metaphysical Beliefs."

136. Gadamer, "Text and Interpretation," 26. Here Gadamer outlines his suspicion of the "psychoanalytic" posture toward others, which, though usually often offered under the banner of wellness and liberation, nonetheless falls into the "knowledge of human nature" category due to its objectivizing tendencies.

137. Gadamer, *Truth and Method*, 268–277.

138. Anil Seth, *Being You: A New Science of Consciousness* (New York: Penguin, 2021), 80.

139. "If hallucination is a kind of uncontrolled perception, then perception right here and right now is also a kind of hallucination, but a controlled hallucination in which the brain's predictions are being reined in by sensory information from the world. In fact, we're all hallucinating all the time, including right now. It's just that when we agree about our hallucinations, we call that reality." Anil Seth, "Your Brain Hallucinates Your Conscious Reality," TED video transcript, filmed April 2017, Vancouver, BC, www.ted.com/talks/anil_seth_your_brain_hallucinates_your_conscious_reality/transcript?language=en.

140. Harry S. Broudy, "The Role of Imagery in Learning," Getty Center for Education in the Arts Occasional Paper 1 (Los Angeles: J. Paul Getty Trust, 1987).

141. Hans-Georg Gadamer, "Plato's Unwritten Dialectic," in *Dialogue and Dialectic: Eight Hermeneutical Studies on Plato*, trans. P. Christopher Smith (New Haven: Yale University Press, 1980), 152.

142. Aristotle, *Politics*, trans. Ernest Baker, rev. R. F. Stalley (New York: Oxford University Press, 1995), 1253a, 26–29.

143. Robert Frost, "A Servant to Servants" [1914], *Poetry Verse*, accessed May 22, 2023, www.poetryverse.com/robert-frost-poems/a-servant-to-servants.

144. Hans-Georg Gadamer, "The Universality of the Hermeneutics Problem," in *Philosophical Hermeneutics*, trans. and ed. David E. Linge (Berkeley: University of California Press, 1976), 3–17.

145. Hans-Georg Gadamer, "Hermeneutics and Social Science," *Cultural Hermeneutics* 2, no. 4 (December 1975): 314, doi.org/10.1177/019145377500200402.

146. See Carhart-Harris and Friston, "REBUS and the Anarchic Brain," 326, and also Robin Carhart-Harris et al., "LSD Enhances Suggestibility in Healthy Volunteers," 785–794.

147. This issue is dramatized in the popular podcast series by journalist Emily Hanford, "Sold a Story: How Teaching Kids to Read Went So Wrong," APM *Reports*, American Public Media, podcast audio, October 20, 2022, features.apmreports.org/sold-a-story/. See also Jan Burkins and Kari Yates, *Shifting the Balance: 6 Ways to Bring the Science of Reading into the Balanced Literacy Classroom* (Portsmouth, NH: Stenhouse, 2021).

148. Doblin, "Walter Pahnke's 'Good Friday' Experiment."

149. Jean-Francois Lyotard, *The Postmodern Condition: A Report on Knowledge*, trans. Geoff Bennington (Minneapolis: University of Minnesota Press, 1984), xxiii–xxiv.

Chapter 5

1. McKenna, *Archaic Revival*, 98.

2. There are interesting subtleties here, though, and research is ongoing. For example, people with sensory deficits such as the blind might be able to receive new experiences with LSD indirectly via synesthesia. See Sara Dell'Erba, David J. Brown, and Michael J. Proulx, "Synesthetic Hallucinations Induced by Psychedelic Drugs in a Congenitally Blind Man," *Consciousness and Cognition* 60 (April 2018): 127–132, doi.org/10.1016/j.concog.2018.02.008: "The phenomenology of the induced hallucinations suggests that experiences acquired through other means, might not give rise to 'visual' experiences in the phenomenological sense, but instead gives rise to novel experiences in the other functioning senses." For a review of earlier decades' research on LSD and perception, see Jacob S. Aday et al., "Psychedelic Drugs and Perception: A Narrative Review of the First Era of Research," *Reviews in the Neurosciences* 32, no. 5 (February 2021): 559–571, doi.org/10.1515/revneuro-2020-0094. There are of course copious data on perceptual alterations, but *enhancements* are another matter.

3. Carhart-Harris and Friston, "REBUS and the Anarchic Brain," 331.

4. Carhart-Harris and Friston, "REBUS and the Anarchic Brain," 332.

5. Ludwig Wittgenstein, *Philosophical Investigations*, trans. G. E. M. Anscombe (New York: Macmillan, 1953), §109.

6. See Marko Rodriguez, "A Methodology for Studying Various Interpretations of the N,N-dimethyltryptamine-Induced Alternate Reality," *Journal of Scientific Exploration* 21, no. 1 (March 2007): 67–84: "provides a methodology for

studying the nature of the DMT-induced alternate reality by means of various simple information theory experiments." See also Andrew R. Gallimore and David P. Luke, "DMT Research from 1956 to the Edge of Time," in *Neurotransmissions: Essays on Psychedelics from Breaking Convention*, ed. Dave King et al. (London: Strange Attractor Press, 2015), 291–316: "perhaps the extraction of useful information would be a better standard by which to judge the objective existence or otherwise of the DMT reality and its inhabitants."

7. Shanon, "The Epistemics of Ayahuasca Visions," 267.

8. For a nuanced view, see Dupuis, "Psychedelics as Tools for Belief Transmission."

9. Kanen et al., "Effect of Lysergic Acid Diethylamide (LSD) on Reinforcement Learning in Humans," 9.

10. The terminology here (viz., "thick," "thin," *modus vivendi*) is taken from political philosophy; see Michael Walzer, *Thick and Thin: Moral Argument at Home and Abroad* (Notre Dame, IN: University of Notre Dame Press, 2019).

11. Alasdair MacIntyre, *After Virtue*, 2nd edition (Notre Dame, IN: University of Notre Dame Press, 1984), 11–12.

12. See Luna, "The Concept of Plants as Teachers," 135–156; and Jeremy Narby, *Plant Teachers: Ayahuasca, Tobacco, and the Pursuit of Knowledge* (Novato, CA: New World Library, 2021).

13. Shanon, *The Antipodes of the Mind*, 163–164.

14. Chris Letheby and Jaipreet Mattu, "Philosophy and Classic Psychedelics: A Review of Some Emerging Themes," *Journal of Psychedelic Studies* 5, no. 3 (February 2022): 172, doi.org/10.1556/2054.2021.00191.

15. Virginia Ballesteros, "Applied Mysticism: A Drug-Enabled Visionary Experience Against Moral Blindness," *Zygon* 54, no. 3 (August 2019): 731–755, doi.org/10.1111/zygo.12544.

16. Plato, *Phaedrus*, trans. Robin Waterfield (New York: Oxford University Press, 2002), 253d–254e. It is interesting to note that the *Upanishads* utilizes similar imagery: "Know the Self as Lord of the chariot, / The body as the chariot itself, / The discriminating intellect as / The charioteer, and the mind as the reins. / The senses, say the wise, are the horses; / Selfish desires are the roads they travel. . . . When a person lacks discrimination / And his mind is undisciplined, the senses / Run hither and thither like wild horses." "The Katha Upanishad" 1.3.3–4, in *The Upanishads*, trans. Eknath Easwaran (Tomales, CA: Nilgiri Press, 2007), 81.

17. John Rawls, *Lectures on the History of Moral Philosophy* (Cambridge, MA: Harvard University Press, 2000), 29. Portions of the foregoing discussion of Hume are drawn, in substantially altered form, from Blacker, *Democratic Education Stretched Thin*, 154–159.

18. David Hume, *A Treatise of Human Nature* (New York: Oxford University Press, 1985 [1740]), 415.

19. Bernard Williams, *Morality: An Introduction to Ethics* (Cambridge: Cambridge University Press, 1972), 3.

20. Hume, *A Treatise of Human Nature*, 416.

21. One should not take this label too far, though. As Dorothy Coleman rightly suggests, it would be anachronistic to ascribe to Hume a position in internalism-externalism debates among contemporary philosophers. See Dorothy Coleman, "Hume's Internalism," *Hume Studies* 18 (1992): 331–347. In short, similar to contemporary evolutionary biologists, Hume's aim is to give a naturalistic account of how moral judgments are made. He does not undertake to justify morality as such (his skepticism is too encompassing for that), as he holds that certain end-of-the-line "sympathies" are definitive of humanity itself, e.g., our impulses toward sociality. He writes, "It is needless to push our researches so far as to ask, why we have humanity or fellow-feeling with others. It is sufficient, that this is experienced to be a principle of human nature." David Hume, *Enquiry Concerning the Principles of Morals* (Indianapolis: Hackett, 1983 [1748]), 219–220).

22. See Coleman, "Hume's Internalism," 331; and Rawls, *Lectures on the History of Moral Philosophy*, 28.

23. Rawls, *Lectures on the History of Moral Philosophy*, 32.

24. Annette Baier develops this point from a "care" perspective in *Moral Prejudices: Essays on Ethics* (Cambridge, MA: Harvard University Press, 1994), 64.

25. *Republic*, 518d, trans. Robin Waterfield (New York: Oxford University Press, 1993) (translation altered by the author, "soul" for "mind"). For a full discussion, see Damien Storey, "The Soul-Turning Metaphor in Plato's *Republic* Book 7," *Classical Philology* 117, no. 3 (July 2022): 525–542, doi.org/10.1086/720177.

26. "NYC Woman Gets 21 Years in Attempted Cheesecake Poisoning of Lookalike Friend," CBS News, April 20, 2023, www.cbsnews.com/news/attempted-cheesecake-poisoning-lookalike-friend-sentencing/.

27. Woody Allen, dir., *Sleeper* (Los Angeles: United Artists, 1973), DVD. Video clips of the scene in question are readily found on YouTube.

28. Here, I follow Rawls's categorization in *Lectures on the History of Moral Philosophy*, 33.

29. Rawls, *Lectures on the History of Moral Philosophy*, 33.

30. David Hume, *A Treatise of Human Nature*, 417.

31. Jean-Paul Sartre, *Existentialism and Humanism* (London: Methuen, 1968), 35–37.

32. Max Scheler, *Selected Philosophical Essays*, trans. David Lachterman (Evanston, IL: Northwestern University Press, 1973).

33. Hume, *Enquiry Concerning the Principles of Morals*, 297; and Baier, *Moral Prejudices*, 71.

34. Baier, *Moral Prejudices*, 70.

35. Isaiah Berlin, *The Hedgehog and the Fox: An Essay on Tolstoy's view of History* (Princeton, NJ: Princeton University Press, 2013), 1.

36. Berlin, *The Hedgehog and the Fox*, 2.
37. Strassman, *DMT and the Soul of Prophecy*, 204.
38. Strassman, *DMT and the Soul of Prophecy*, 205.
39. Strassman, *DMT and the Soul of Prophecy*, 46.
40. Strassman, *DMT and the Soul of Prophecy*, 56.
41. For more documentation of subjects' perception of DMT entities and their relational aspects, see David Wyndham Lawrence et al., "Phenomenology and Content of the Inhaled N, N-dimethyltryptamine (N, N-DMT) Experience," *Nature Scientific Reports* 12, 8562 (May 24, 2022), doi.org/10.1038/s41598-022-11999-8. There are also reported "God-encounter" experiences on DMT and other psychedelics that may fit Strassman's framing here; see Griffiths et al., "Survey of Subjective 'God Encounter Experiences.'"
42. Strassman, *DMT and the Soul of Prophecy*, 23.
43. This is the so-called "biblical entheogen hypothesis"; see Benny Shanon, "Biblical Entheogens: a Speculative Hypothesis," *Time and Mind* 1, no. 1 (2008): 51–74, doi.org/10.2752/175169608783489116. One can only agree with Shanon that the hypothesis is "intriguing."
44. David Lukes, *Otherworlds: Psychedelics and Exceptional Human Experience* (London: Muswell Hill, 2017), 85.
45. Strassman, *DMT and the Soul of Prophecy*, 107–108.
46. Strassman, *DMT and the Soul of Prophecy*, 28–29.
47. Strassman, *DMT and the Soul of Prophecy*, 57.
48. Strassman, *DMT and the Soul of Prophecy*, 58.
49. Benton Rooks, "Unified Psychedelic Theory: An Interview with Patrick Lundborg R.I.P.," *Reality Sandwich*, June 20, 2014, realitysandwich.com/unified-psychedelic-theory-an-interview-with-patrick-lundborg-r-i-p/.
50. I detail the Gaian worldview in Blacker, *What's Left of the World*, 183–193. Davis colorfully invokes 75 years of underground acid culture as well: "the chaotic underground lineage of the psychedelic counterculture may paradoxically hold the sort of 'traditional values' that could help guide us through the ferocious new psychedelic frontier, where the digital railway networks unload a fresh swarm of carpetbaggers, snake-oil salesmen, and robber barons to be on a daily basis." Erik Davis, "The Elephant LSD: Thoughts on a Euro-American Ally," *Burning Shore*, April 27, 2022, www.burningshore.com/p/the-elephant-lsd.
51. William Richards, *Sacred Knowledge: Psychedelics and Religious Experiences* (New York: Columbia University Press, 2018), 6.
52. Richards, *Sacred Knowledge*, 6.
53. William Richards, "Ineffability and Revelation on the Frontiers of Knowledge," in *DMT Entity Encounters: Dialogues on the Spirit Molecule*, ed. David Luke and Rory Spowers (Rochester, VT: Park Street, 2021), 139.
54. See Michael Casey, "Psychedelic Churches in US Pushing Boundaries of Religion," *Associated Press*, February 2, 2023, apnews.com/article/psychedelic-churches-ayahuasca-5101fe47fe9a6e28de686272ed96ff46; Don Lattin,

"Pioneering Clergy of Diverse Religions Embrace Psychedelics," *Lucid News*, April 20, 2022, www.lucid.news/pioneering-clergy-of-diverse-religions-embrace-psychedelics/; and Manisha Krishnan, "Ex-Mormons Are Running a Magic Mushroom Church," *Vice News*, February 15, 2023, www.vice.com/en/article/akexaa/magic-mushroom-mormon-church-utah. See also The Sacred Plant Alliance, www.sacredplantalliance.org/, accessed May 22, 2023: "a self-regulating organization and professional society of spiritual practitioners with religious communities dedicated to the advancement of the ceremonial use of psychedelic sacraments within the United States."

55. Downloadable at "The Four Cups of Consciousness: A Shefa Haggadah Companion," Shefa Jewish Psychedelic Support, accessed May 22, 2023, www.shefaflow.org/haggadah-companion. In addition, they put a psychedelic spin on Hanukkah with their "Higher Life Hanukkah Companion," Shefa Jewish Psychedelic Support, accessed May 22, 2023, drive.google.com/file/d/1dcJrmXtbrSvT-VbfIwJwETpFQvdWzc4O/view.

56. See Karen Armstrong, *The Great Transformation: The Beginning of Our Religious Traditions* (New York: Anchor, 2006), 3–56.

57. Strassman, *DMT and the Soul of Prophecy*, 292.

58. Strassman, *DMT and the Soul of Prophecy*, 291. He continues, wisely adding that "higher doses would necessitate laying down with the text and attending to the visions it has elicited in a more private, internalized manner."

59. Richards, *Sacred Knowledge*, 154.

60. Richards, *Sacred Knowledge*, 154–155.

61. See Doblin, "Walter Pahnke's 'Good Friday Experiment,'" 22–23; see also Pollan, *How to Change Your Mind*, 46.

62. Louis Althusser, "Ideology and Ideological State Apparatuses," in *Lenin and Philosophy and Other Essays*, trans. Ben Brewster (New York: Monthly Review Press, 1971), 162–167.

63. Charles Taylor, *A Secular Age* (Cambridge: Harvard University Press, 2007), 299–313.

64. Taylor, *A Secular Age*, 3.

65. For an example, see Leor Roseman et al., "Relational Processes in Ayahuasca Groups of Palestinians and Israelis," *Frontiers in Pharmacology* 12, 607529 (May 19, 2021), doi.org/10.3389/fphar.2021.607529: "psychedelic ceremonies have the potential to contribute to peacebuilding."

Conclusion

1. "Nevertheless, it is—as a matter of evidence and probative force—far easier to satisfy triers that beliefs are religious if they are widely-held and

clothed in substantial historical antecedent and traditional concepts of a deity than it is where such factors are absent." Stevens v. Berger, 428 F. Supp. 896, 900 (E.D.N.Y. 1977). On the "lineage" requirement, see George G. Lake, *The Law of Entheogenic Churches, Volume II* (Self-pub., 2022), 6–18.

2. W. J. Rorabaugh, *Prohibition: A Very Short Introduction* (New York: Oxford University Press, 2020), 58–62, 79. See also Megan Gambino, "During Prohibition, Your Doctor Could Write You a Prescription for Booze," *Smithsonian Magazine*, October 7, 2013, www.smithsonianmag.com/history/during-prohibition-your-doctor-could-write-you-prescription-booze-180947940/; and Bartlett C. Jones, "A Prohibition Problem: Liquor as Medicine 1920–1933," *Journal of the History of Medicine and Allied Sciences* 18, no. 4 (October 1963): 353–369.

3. Osiris Sinuhé González Romero, "Decolonizing the Philosophy of Psychedelics," in *Philosophy and Psychedelics Frameworks for Exceptional Experience*, ed. Christine Hauskeller and Peter Sjöstedt-Hughes (London: Bloomsbury, 2022), 91.

4. See Rick Doblin, "Dr. Leary's Concord Prison experiment: A 34-Year Follow-up Study." *Journal of Psychoactive Drugs* 30, no. 4 (October 1998): 419–426, showing misleading reporting of research results; and, regarding the famous study conducted under Leary's supervision, from Doblin, "Walter Pahnke's 'Good Friday Experiment'": "the long-term follow-up also uncovered data that should have been reported in the original thesis. Pahnke failed to report the administration of the tranquilizer Thorazine to one of the subjects who received psilocybin. There is no justification for this omission no matter how unfairly the critics of this research may have used the information and no matter how minimal were the negative persisting effects reported by the subject. In addition, Pahnke underemphasized the difficult psychological struggles experienced by most of the psilocybin subjects. These very serious omissions point to an important incompleteness in Pahnke's interpretation of the effects of psilocybin." For the surrounding context of both experiments, see Hartogsohn, *American Trip*, 109–119; and for a general description of Leary's well-documented erratic and cultic-guru behavior, see Lachman, *Turn Off Your Mind*, 162–200.

5. For a responsible assessment of scientific literature on adverse effects (concluding that although they exist they are minimal), see Anne K. Schlag et al., "Adverse Effects of Psychedelics: From Anecdotes and Misinformation to Systematic Science," *Journal of Psychopharmacology* 36, no. 3 (February 2022): 258–272, doi.org/10.1177/02698811211069100. On concrete attempts to mitigate adverse psychedelic effects at festivals and the like, see Lydia Laurenson, "Spirituality, Psychedelics and Psychotic Risk: Ryan Jay Beauregard and the Zendo Project," *The New Modality*, November 11, 2019, thenewmodality.com/spirituality-psychedelics-and-psychotic-risk-ryan-jay-beauregard-and-the-zendo-project/; and "Psychedelic Peer: Support: Creating Communities of Compassionate Care," The Zendo Project, accessed May 22, 2023, zendoproject.org: "The Zendo Project

provides professional comprehensive harm reduction education and support for communities to help inform and transform difficult psychedelic experiences into opportunities for learning and growth."

6. See Hart, *Drug Use for Grown-Ups*, 32, 193; the phrase "cognitive liberty" was coined by Richard Glen Boire. For a general defense of cognitive liberty, see his amicus curiae brief for Sell v. United States, 539 U.S. 166 (2003), "Cognitive Liberty," cognitive-liberty.online/wp-content/uploads/2018/11/Boire20_On_Cognitive_Liberty1.pdf; for a defense of cognitive liberty in the context of psychedelics, see Charlotte Walsh, "Beyond Religious Freedom: Psychedelics and Cognitive Liberty," in *Prohibition, Religious Freedom, and Human Rights: Regulating Traditional Drug Use*, ed. B. Labate and C. Cavnar (New York: Springer, 2014), 211–233.

7. Although even here there is ongoing research of possible benefits to schizophrenia patients. See Gilly Wolf et al., "Could Psychedelic Drugs Have a Role in the Treatment of Schizophrenia? Rationale and Strategy for Safe Implementation," *Molecular Psychiatry* 28, no. 1 (January 2023): 44–58, doi.org/10.1038/s41380-022-01832-z: "Careful research in this area could significantly impact the treatment of one of the most severe and socially debilitating psychiatric disorders and open an exciting new frontier in psychopharmacology"; yet see also a disturbing cautionary tale (disturbing on a number of levels, including forcing psychedelics as "treatment" for homosexuality) from the first wave of psychiatric interventions with institutionalized patients in Petter Grahl Johnstad, "A Dangerous Method? Psychedelic Therapy at Modum Bad, Norway, 1961–76," *History of Psychiatry* 31, no. 2 (January 2020): 217–226: "The psychiatrists there initially regarded the psychedelic treatment as efficacious and without serious negative reactions, but reports of long-term harm have since surfaced."

8. Ernst Jünger, *Approaches: Drugs and Altered States*, trans. Thomas Friese, ed. Russell A. Berman (Candor, NY: Telos, 2022), 295.

References

Aday, Jacob S., Cayla M. Mitzkovitz, Emily K. Bloesch, Christopher C. Davoli, and Alan T. Davis. "Long-Term Effects of Psychedelic Drugs: A Systematic Review." *Neuroscience & Biobehavioral Reviews* 113 (June 2020): 179–189. doi.org/10.1016/j.neubiorev.2020.03.017.

Aday, Jacob S., Julia T. Wood, Emily K. Bloesch, and Christopher C. Davoli. "Psychedelic Drugs and Perception: A Narrative Review of the First Era of Research." *Reviews in the Neurosciences* 32, no. 5 (February 2021): 559–571. doi.org/10.1515/revneuro-2020-0094.

Agin-Liebes, Gabrielle, Tara Malone, Matthew M. Yalch, Sarah E. Mennenga, K Linnae Ponté, Jeffrey Guss, Anthony P. Bossis, Jim Grigsby, Stacy Fischer, and Stephen L. Ross. "Long-Term Follow-Up of Psilocybin-Assisted Psychotherapy for Psychiatric and Existential Distress in Patients with Life-Threatening Cancer." *Journal of Psychopharmacology* 34, no. 2 (February 2020): 155–166. doi.org/10.1177/0269881119897615.

Alexander, Michelle. *The New Jim Crow: Mass Incarceration in the Age of Colorblindness*. New York: New Press, 2012.

Allen, Woody, dir. *Sleeper*. Los Angeles: United Artists, 1973. DVD.

Althusser, Louis. "Ideology and Ideological State Apparatuses." In *Lenin and Philosophy and Other Essays*, translated by Ben Brewster, 85–126. New York: Monthly Review Press, 1971.

Aqil, Marco, and Leor Roseman. "More than Meets the Eye: The Role of Sensory Dimensions in Psychedelic Brain Dynamics, Experience, and Therapeutics." *Neuropharmacology* 223 (November 2, 2022): 109300. doi.org/10.1016/j.neuropharm.2022.109300.

Aristotle. *Nicomachean Ethics*. Translated by Terence Irwin. Indianapolis: Hackett, 2019.

———. *Politics*. Translated by Ernest Baker and revised by R. F. Stalley. New York: Oxford University Press, 1995.

Armstrong, Karen. *The Great Transformation: The Beginning of Our Religious Traditions*. New York: Anchor, 2006.

Aurelius, Marcus. *Meditations*. Translated by Robin Waterfield. New York: Basic Books, 2021.
Bache, Christopher M. *LSD and the Mind of the Universe: Diamonds from Heaven*. Rochester, VT: Park Street, 2019.
Baier, Annette. *Moral Prejudices: Essays on Ethics*. Cambridge, MA: Harvard University Press, 1994.
Bakhtin, Mikhail. *Rabelais and His World*. Translated by Helene Iswolsky. Bloomington: Indiana University Press, 2009 [1940].
Ballesteros, Virginia. "Applied Mysticism: A Drug-Enabled Visionary Experience Against Moral Blindness." *Zygon* 54, no. 3 (August 2019): 731–755. doi.org/10.1111/zygo.12544.
Barsuglia, Joseph P., Alan T. Davis, Robert D. Palmer, Rafael Lancelotta, Austin-Marley Windham-Herman, Kristel Peterson, Martin Polanco, Robert M. Grant, and Roland R. Griffiths. "Intensity of Mystical Experiences Occasioned by 5-MeO-DMT and Comparison with a Prior Psilocybin Study." *Frontiers in Psychology* 9 (December 6, 2018). doi.org/10.3389/fpsyg.2018.02459.
Basen, Ryan. "Academic Centers Start to Take Psychedelics Seriously." *MedPage Today*, November 24, 2021. www.medpagetoday.com/special-reports/exclusives/95865.
Bauman, Zygmunt. *Liquid Modernity*. London: Polity, 2000.
———. *Mortality, Immortality and Other Life Strategies*. Cambridge: Polity, 2013.
Beatles, The. "All You Need is Love." Los Angeles: Capitol Records, 1967.
———. *Sgt. Pepper's Lonely Hearts Club Band*. London: Parlophone, 1967.
Beckett, Samuel. *Nohow On: Company, Ill Seen Ill Said, Worstward Ho: Three Novels*. New York: Grove, 1995.
Beiner, Alexander. *The Bigger Picture: How Psychedelics Can Help Us Make Sense of the World*. London: Hay House, 2023.
Bennett, Drake. "Dr. Ecstasy." *New York Times Magazine*, November 17, 2011.
Bergson, Henri. *Introduction to Metaphysics*. Translated by T. E. Hulme. Indianapolis: Hackett, 1999 [1912].
Berlin, Isaiah. *The Hedgehog and the Fox: An Essay on Tolstoy's view of History*. Princeton, NJ: Princeton University Press, 2013.
Berrin, Kathleen, and Thomas K. Seligman. *Art of the Huichol Indians*. New York: Harry N. Abrams, 1978.
Blacker, David J. "Allowing Educational Technologies to Reveal: A Deweyan Perspective." *Educational Theory* 43, no. 2 (Spring 1993): 181–194. doi.org/10.1111/j.1741-5446.1993.00181.x.
———. *Democratic Education Stretched Thin: How Complexity Challenges a Liberal Ideal*. Albany: State University of New York Press, 2007.
———. *Dying to Teach: The Educator's Search for Immortality*. New York: Columbia University Teachers College Press, 1997.

———. *What's Left of the World? Education, Identity and the Post-Work Political Imagination*. Winchester, MA: Zer0 Books, 2019.
Blacker, H. Martin. "Volitional Sympathetic Control." *Anesthesia and Analgesia* 59, no. 10 (October 1980): 785–788.
Blainey, Mark G. *Christ Returns from the Jungle: Ayahuasca Religion as Mystical Healing*. Albany: State University of New York Press, 2021.
Block, Ned. "Paradox and Cross Purposes in Recent Work on Consciousness." *Cognition* 79, no. 1–2 (April 2001): 197–219. doi.org/10.1016/s0010-0277(00)00129-3.
Boire, Richard Glenn. "On Cognitive Liberty." *Journal of Cognitive Liberties* 1, no. 1 (Winter 1999–2000): 7–13. www.cognitiveliberty.org/on-cognitive-liberty-boire/.
Bostrom, Nick. "Are We Living in a Computer Simulation?" *Philosophical Quarterly* 53, no. 211 (2003): 243–255. www.simulation-argument.com.
Boswell, James. *The Life of Samuel Johnson*. New York: Penguin, 1979 [1791].
Brennan, William J., Margo A. Jackson, Katherine MacLean, and Joseph G. Ponterotto. "A Qualitative Exploration of Relational Ethical Challenges and Practices in Psychedelic Healing." *Journal of Humanistic Psychology* (September 16, 2021). doi.org/10.1177/00221678211045265.
Brooks, Xan. "Cary Grant: How 100 Acid Trips in Tinseltown 'Changed My Life.'" *Guardian*, May 12, 2017. www.theguardian.com/film/2017/may/12/cary-grant-how-100-acid-trips-in-tinseltown-changed-my-life-lsd-documentary.
Broudy, Harry S. "The Humanities and Their Uses: Proper Claims and Expectations." *Journal of Aesthetic Education* 17, no. 4 (Winter 1983): 125–138.
———. "The Role of Imagery in Learning." Getty Center for Education in the Arts Occasional Paper 1. Los Angeles: J. Paul Getty Trust, 1987.
Broughton, Janet. *Descartes's Method of Doubt*. Princeton, NJ: Princeton University Press, 2002.
Brown, Jerry B., and Julie M. Brown. "Entheogens in Christian Art: Wasson, Allegro, and the Psychedelic Gospels." *Journal of Psychedelic Studies* 3, no. 2 (June 2019): 142–163. doi.org/10.1556/2054.2019.019.
Bryn, Brandon. "Inaugural Class of Invention Ambassadors Highlights Need for Innovation." *American Association for the Advancement of Science*, July 18, 2014. www.aaas.org/news/inaugural-class-invention-ambassadors-highlights-need-innovation.
Burkins, Jan and Kari Yates, *Shifting the Balance: 6 Ways to Bring the Science of Reading into the Balanced Literacy Classroom*. Portsmouth, NH: Stenhouse, 2021.
Burnyeat, Miles. "Can the Skeptic Live His Skepticism?" In *The Skeptical Tradition*, edited by Miles Burnyeat, 117–148. Berkeley: University of California Press, 1983.

———. "The Skeptic in His Place and Time." In *The Original Skeptics: A Controversy*, edited by Miles Burnyeat and Michael Frede, 92–126. Indianapolis: Hackett, 1997.

Burroughs, William S. "The Art of Fiction, No. 36." Interview by Conrad Knickerbocker. *Paris Review* 35, Fall 1965. www.theparisreview.org/interviews/4424/the-art-of-fiction-no-36-william-s-burroughs.

Burton, Tara Isabella. *Strange Rites: New Religions for a Godless World.* New York: PublicAffairs, 2020.

Calder, Abigail E., and George Hasler. "Towards an Understanding of Psychedelic-Induced Neuroplasticity." *Neuropsychopharmacology* 48 (2023): 104–112.

Cameron, Lindsay P., Robert J. Tombari, Ju Lu, Alexander J. Pell, Zefan Q. Hurley, Yann Ehinger, Maxemiliano V. Vargas, Matthew N. McCarroll, Jack C. Taylor, Douglas Myers-Turnbull, Taohui Liu, Bianca Yaghoobi, Lauren J. Laskowski, Emilie I. Anderson, Guoliang Zhang, Jayashri Viswanathan, Brandon M. Brown, Michelle Tjia, Lee E. Dunlap, Zachary T. Rabow, Oliver Fiehn, Heike Wulff, John D. McCorvy, Pamela J. Lein, David Kokel, Dorit Ron, Jamie Peters, Yi Zuo, and David E. Olson. "A Non-Hallucinogenic Psychedelic Analogue with Therapeutic Potential." *Nature* 589 (January 21, 2021): 474–479. doi.org/10.1038/s41586-020-3008-z.

Campbell, Joseph. *The Hero with a Thousand Faces.* Princeton, NJ: Princeton University Press, 1949.

Camus, Albert. *The Stranger.* New York: Vintage, 1954.

Cantor, Lea. "Thales–the 'First Philosopher'? A Troubled Chapter in the Historiography of Philosophy." *British Journal for the History of Philosophy* 30, no. 5 (March 2022): 727–750. doi.org/10.1080/09608788.2022.2029347.

Carhart-Harris, Robin L., Shamil Chandaria, David Erritzoe, Adam Gazzaley, Manesh Girn, Hannes Kettner, Pedro A. M. Mediano, David John Nutt, Fernando E. Rosas, Leor Roseman, Christopher B. Timmermann, Brandon M. Weiss, Richard J. Zeifman, and Karl J. Friston. "Canalization and Plasticity in Psychopathology." *Neuropharmacology* 226 (March 1, 2023): 109398. doi.org/10.1016/j.neuropharm.2022.109398.

Carhart-Harris, Robin L., David Erritzoe, Eline Haijen, Mendel Kaelen, and Richard A. Watts. "Psychedelics and Connectedness." *Psychopharmacology* 235, no. 2 (February 2018): 547–550. doi.org/10.1007/s00213-017-4701-y.

Carhart-Harris, Robin L., and K. J. Friston, "REBUS and the Anarchic Brain: Toward a Unified Model of the Brain Action of Psychedelics." *Pharmacological Review* 71, no. 3 (July, 2019): 316–344. doi.org/10.1124/pr.118.017160.

Carhart-Harris, Robin L., Mendel Kaelen, Matthew G. Whalley, Mark Bolstridge, Amanda Feilding, and David J. Nutt. "LSD Enhances Suggestibility in Healthy Volunteers." *Psychopharmacology* 232, no. 4 (February 1, 2015): 785–794. doi.org/10.1007/s00213-014-3714-z.

Carhart-Harris, Robin L., Robert Leech, Peter J. Hellyer, Murray Shanahan, Amanda Feilding, Enzo Tagliazucchi, Dante R. Chialvo, and David J. Nutt. "The Entropic Brain: A Theory of Conscious States Informed by Neuroimaging Research with Psychedelic Drugs." *Frontiers in Human Neuroscience* 8 (February 3, 2014). doi.org/10.3389/fnhum.2014.00020.

Carhart-Harris, Robin L., Leor Roseman, Mark Bolstridge, Lysia Demetriou, J. Nienke Pannekoek, Matthew B. Wall, Mark A. Tanner, Mendel Kaelen, John McGonigle, Kevin Murphy, Robert Leech, H. Valerie Curran, and David J. Nutt. "Psilocybin for Treatment-Resistant Depression: FMRI-Measured Brain Mechanisms." *Scientific Reports* 7, 13187 (October 13, 2017). doi.org/10.1038/s41598-017-13282-7.

Carod-Artal, Francisco Javier. "Hallucinogenic Drugs in Pre-Columbian Mesoamerican Cultures." *Neurología* 30, no. 1 (January–February 2015): 42–49. doi.org/10.1016/j.nrleng.2011.07.010.

Carroll, Lewis. *Alice's Adventures in Wonderland*. New York: Penguin, 1998 [1865].

Casey, Michael. "Psychedelic Churches in US Pushing Boundaries of Religion." *Associated Press*, February 2, 2023. apnews.com/article/psychedelic-churches-ayahuasca-5101fe47fe9a6e28de686272ed96ff46.

Chacruna Institute for Psychedelic Plant Medicines. "Queering Psychedelics." Conference, San Francisco, June 1–2, 2019. chacruna.net/queering-psychedelics/.

Chalmers, David. "Facing Up to the Problem of Consciousness." *Journal of Consciousness Studies* 2, no. 3 (1995): 200–219.

Chen, Guang, Gang Yu, Zheng Yong, Hui Yan, Ruibin Su, and Huijun Wang. "A Large Dose of Methamphetamine Inhibits Drug-Evoked Synaptic Plasticity via ER Stress in the Hippocampus." *Molecular Medicine Reports* 23, no. 4 (February 11, 2021): 278. doi.org/10.3892/mmr.2021.11917.

Coleman, Dorothy. "Hume's Internalism." *Hume Studies* 18 (1992): 331–347.

Copland, Aaron. *What to Listen for in Music*. New York: New American Library, 2009 [1937].

Corrigan, Kate, Maeve Haran, Conor McCandliss, Roisin McManus, Shannon Cleary, Rebecca Trant, Yazeed Kelly, Kathryn Ledden, Gavin Rush, Veronica O'Keane, and John R. Kelly "Psychedelic Perceptions: Mental Health Service User Attitudes to Psilocybin Therapy." *Irish Journal of Medical Science* 191, no. 3 (June 15, 2022): 1385–1397. doi.org/10.1007/s11845-021-02668-2.

Cosimano, Mary. "The Role of the Guide in Psychedelic Assisted Treatment." In *Handbook of Medical Hallucinogens*, edited by Charles S. Grob and Jim Grigsby, 377–394. New York: Guilford, 2021.

Costa, Miguel Ângelo. "A Dose of Creativity: An Integrative Review of the Effects of Serotonergic Psychedelics on Creativity." *Journal of Psychoactive Drugs* 55, no. 3 (2023). doi.org/10.1080/02791072.2022.2106805.

Costandi, Mo. "A Brief History of Psychedelic Psychiatry." *Psychologist* (UK) 27, no. 9 (September 2014): 714–716. issuu.com/thepsychologist/docs/psy09_14web/84?e=1106616/9079836.

Cott, Christopher, and Adam Rock. "Phenomenology of N,N-Dimethyltryptamine Use: A Thematic Analysis." *Journal of Scientific Exploration* 22, no. 3 (2008): 359–370.

Crawford, Matthew B. *Shop Class as Soulcraft: An Inquiry into the Value of Work.* New York: Penguin, 2010.

Dance, Amber. "Quest for Clues to Humanity's First Fires." *Scientific American*, June 19, 2017. www.scientificamerican.com/article/quest-for-clues-to-humanitys-first-fires/.

Dannaway, Frederick. R, Alan Piper, and Peter Webster. "Bread of Heaven or Wines of Light: Entheogenic Legacies and Esoteric Cosmologies." *Journal of Psychoactive Drugs* 38, no. 4 (2006): 493–503.

Davidson, Donald. "Radical Interpretation." *Dialectica* 27 (December 1973): 314–328.

Davis, Chad. "People Are Tripping on DMT to Lose All Perception of Time and Reality." *Elite Daily*, July 22, 2015. www.elitedaily.com/life/the-implications-of-dmt/1106931.

Davis, Erik. "The Elephant LSD: Thoughts on a Euro-American Ally." *Burning Shore*, April 27, 2022. www.burningshore.com/p/the-elephant-lsd.

———. *High Weirdness: Drugs, Esoterica and Visionary Experiences in the Seventies.* Cambridge, MA: MIT Press, 2019.

Daws, Richard E., Christopher Timmermann, Bruna Giribaldi, James Sexton, Matthew B. Wall, David Erritzoe, Leor Roseman, David J. Nutt, and Robin L. Carhart-Harris. "Increased Global Integration in the Brain after Psilocybin Therapy for Depression." *Nature Medicine* 28, no. 4 (April 11, 2022): 844–851. doi.org/10.1038/s41591-022-01744-z.

de Borhegyi, Carl, with Suzanne de Borhegyi-Forrest. "The Genesis of a Mushroom/Venus Religion in Mesoamerica." In *Entheogens in the Development of Culture: The Anthropology and Neurobiology of Ecstatic Experience*, edited by John A. Rush, 456–462. Berkeley, CA: North Atlantic, 2013.

de Vos, Cato H. M., Natasha L. Mason, and Kim P.C. Kuypers. "Psychedelics and Neuroplasticity: A Systematic Review Unraveling the Biological Underpinnings of Psychedelics." *Frontiers in Psychology* 12 (September 10, 2021): 1–17. doi.org/10.3389/fpsyt.2021.724606.

Dell'Erba, Sara, David J. Brown, and Michael J. Proulx. "Synesthetic Hallucinations Induced by Psychedelic Drugs in a Congenitally Blind Man." *Consciousness and Cognition* 60 (April 2018): 127–132. doi.org/10.1016/j.concog.2018.02.008.

DeRogatis, Jim. "Charles Manson's Musical Ambitions." *New Yorker*, August 19, 2019. www.newyorker.com/culture/cultural-comment/charles-mansons-musical-ambitions.

Descartes, René. *Meditations on First Philosophy*. Translated by Donald A. Cress. Indianapolis: Hackett, 1980.

———. *Oeuvres de Descartes*, revised edition, 12 vols. Edited by Charles Adam and Paul Tannery. Paris: Vrin/CNRS, 1964–1976.

———. *The Philosophical Writings of Descartes*, 2 vols. Translated by John Cottingham, Robert Stoothoff, and Dugald Murdoch. Cambridge: Cambridge University Press, 1985.

Devereux, Paul. *The Long Trip: A Prehistory of Psychedelia*. Brisbane: Daily Grail, 2008.

Dewey, John. *Art as Experience* [1934]. In *The Later Works, 1925–1953*, vol. 10, edited by Joanne Boydston. Carbondale: Southern Illinois University Press, 1989.

———. *Experience and Nature* [1925]. In *The Later Works, 1925–1953*, vol. 1, edited by Joanne Boydston. Carbondale: Southern Illinois University Press, 1981.

Doblin, Rick. "Dr. Leary's Concord Prison Experiment: A 34-Year Follow-up Study." *Journal of Psychoactive Drugs* 30, no. 4 (October 1998): 419–246. doi.org/10.1080/02791072.1998.10399715.

———. "Walter Pahnke's 'Good Friday Experiment': A Long-Term Follow-up and Critique." *Journal of Transpersonal Psychology* 23 (January 1991). maps.org/research-archive/cluster/psilo-lsd/goodfriday.pdf.

Dodds, E. R. *The Greeks and the Irrational*. Berkeley: University of California Press, 1951.

Douglas, James Robert. "Inside the Bizarre 1960s Cult, The Family: LSD, Yoga and UFOs." *Guardian*, February 12, 2017. www.theguardian.com/film/2017/feb/13/the-family-great-white-brotherhood-australia-melbourne-cult-anne-hamilton-byrne.

Doyle, Rich. "Hyperbolic: Divining Ayahuasca." *Discourse* 27, no. 1 (Winter 2005): 6–33.

Duerler, Patricia, Leonhard Schilbach, Philipp Stämpfli, Franz X. Vollenweider, and Katrin H. Preller. "LSD-Induced Increases in Social Adaptation to Opinions Similar to One's Own Are Associated with Stimulation of Serotonin Receptors." *Scientific Reports* 10, 12181 (July 22, 2020). doi.org/10.1038/s41598-020-68899-y.

DuPuis, David. "Psychedelics as Tools for Belief Transmission. Set, Setting, Suggestibility, and Persuasion in the Ritual Use of Hallucinogens." *Frontiers in Psychology* 12 (November 23, 2021). doi.org/10.3389/fpsyg.2021.730031.

Eagleman, David. *Livewired: The Inside Story of the Ever-Changing Brain*. New York: Vintage, 2021.

Echard, William. *Psychedelic Popular Music: A History through Musical Topic Theory*. Bloomington: Indiana University Press, 2017.

Eckstein, Noah. "Creating a Sanctuary for Psychedelic Art." *New York Times*, May 28, 2023.

Eliade, Mircea. *The Myth of the Eternal Return: Or, Cosmos and History.* Translated by Willard Trask. Princeton, NJ: Princeton University Press, 1957.

———. *Shamanism: Archaic Techniques of Ecstasy.* Translated by William R. Trask. Princeton, NJ: Princeton University Press, 1964.

Epicurus, "Letter to Menoeceus." In *The Hellenistic Philosophers Volume 1: Translation of the Principal Sources with Philosophical Commentary,* edited and translated by A. A. Long and D. N. Snedley, 124–127. New York: Cambridge University Press, 1987.

Ermakova, Anna O., Fiona Dunbar, James Rucker, and Matthew P. Johnson. "A Narrative Synthesis of Research with 5-MeO-DMT." *Journal of Psychopharmacology* 36, no. 3 (March 2022): 273–294. doi.org/10.1177/02698811211050543.

Ernst, Sara Willa. "Psychedelic Therapy Research is on the Horizon for Texas Veterans with PTSD." *Houston Public Media,* November 11, 2021. www.houstonpublicmedia.org/articles/news/in-depth/2021/11/11/413205/.

Estévez Pérez, Nancy. "Neuroplasticity and the Zone of Proximal Development: A Neurobiological Reflection on a Key Psychological Construct," *IBRO/IBE-UNESCO Science of Learning Briefings.* June 23, 2020. solportal.ibe-unesco.org/articles/neuroplasticity-and-the-zone-of-proximal-development-a-neurobiological-reflection-on-a-key-psychological-construct/.

Evans, Jules. *The Art of Losing Control: A Philosopher's Search for Ecstatic Experience.* London: Canongate, 2017.

———. "Do Psychedelics Make You Liberal? Not Always." *Philosophy for Life,* February 15, 2001. www.philosophyforlife.org/blog/do-psychedelics-make-you-liberal-not-always.

———. "What Helps with Challenging Psychedelic Experiences?" *The Psychedelic Society,* accessed May 21, 2023. psychedelicsociety.org.uk/media/what-helps-with-challenging-psychedelic-experiences.

Fadiman, James. *The Psychedelic Explorer's Guide: Safe, Therapeutic, and Sacred Journeys.* Rochester, VT: Park Street, 2011.

Fadiman, James, and Sophia Korb. "Might Microdosing Psychedelics Be Safe and Beneficial? An Initial Exploration." *Journal of Psychoactive Drugs* 51, no. 2 (April 2019): 118–122. doi.org/10.1080/02791072.2019.1593561.

Felton, David, and David Dalton. "Charles Manson: The Incredible Story of the Most Dangerous Man Alive." *Rolling Stone,* June 25, 1970. www.rollingstone.com/culture/culture-news/charles-manson-the-incredible-story-of-the-most-dangerous-man-alive-85235/.

Fern, Maya, and Hannah McClane, *Trans-Affirming Care in the Psychedelic Space: A Guide for Therapists, Clinicians, Facilitators and Healers.* Philadelphia: Sound Mind Institute, 2022. drive.google.com/file/d/1TGP9LbVZ0C7JZGKATx5JYdw2qboPMIJa/view.

Fine, Gail. "Descartes and Ancient Skepticism." *Philosophical Review* 109 (2000): 195–234.
Fontanilla, Dominique, Molly Johannessen, Abdol R. Hajipour, Nicholas V. Cozzi, Meyer B. Jackson, and Arnold E. Ruoho. "The Hallucinogen N,N-Dimethyltryptamine (DMT) Is an Endogenous Sigma-1 Receptor Regulator." *Science* 323, no. 5916 (February 13, 2009): 934–937. doi.org/10.1126/science.1166127.
Forstmann, Matthias, Daniel A. Yudkin, Annayah M.B. Prosser, Simon Heller, and Molly J. Crockett. "Transformative Experience and Social Connectedness Mediate the Mood-Enhancing Effects of Psychedelic Use in Naturalistic Settings." *Proceedings of the National Academy of Sciences of the United States of America* 117, no. 5 (February 4, 2020): 2338–2346. doi.org/10.1073/pnas.1918477117.
Foster, John Bellamy. "Marx's Theory of Metabolic Rift: Classical Foundations for Environmental Sociology." *American Journal of Sociology* 105, no. 2 (September 1999): 366–405.
Foster, Karen Polinger. "Psychedelic Art and Ecstatic Visions in the Aegean." In *The Routledge Companion to Ecstatic Experience in the Ancient World*, edited by Diana Stein, Sarah Kielt Costello, and Karen Polinger Foster, 489–516. London: Routledge, 2021.
Frankfurt, Harry G. *Demons, Dreamers and Madmen: The Defense of Reason in Descartes's Meditations*. New York: Bobbs-Merrill, 1970.
Frecska, Ede, Mihály Hoppál, and Luis Muñiz Luna. "Nonlocality and the Shamanic State of Consciousness." *NeuroQuantology* 14, no. 2 (May 2016): 155–165. real.mtak.hu/36545/1/2016_Frecska_E_Nonlocality_and_SSC_u.pdf.
Freud, Sigmund. *Civilization and Its Discontents*. Translated by James Strachey. New York: Norton, 1961 [1930].
———. *Studies in Hysteria*. New York: Penguin, 2004 [1895].
Friedwoman, Leia, and Katherine MacLean. "Sexual Abuse in Psychedelic Therapy: Important Steps Being Taken to Support Survivor." *Double Blind*, September 15, 2022. doubleblindmag.com/psychedelic-survivors/.
Frost, Robert. "A Servant to Servants" [1914]. *Poetry Verse*. Accessed May 22, 2023. www.poetryverse.com/robert-frost-poems/a-servant-to-servants.
Fuchs, Eberhard, and Gabriele Flügge. "Adult Neuroplasticity: More than 40 Years of Research," *Neural Plasticity* 2014, 541870 (May 2014). doi:10.1155/2014/541870.
Gadamer, Hans-Georg. "Hermeneutics and Social Science." *Cultural Hermeneutics* 2, no. 4 (December 1975): 307–316. doi.org/10.1177/019145377500200402.
———. "Man and Language." In *Philosophical Hermeneutics*, translated and edited by David E. Linge, 59–68. Berkeley: University of California Press, 1976.

———. *Philosophical Apprenticeships*. Cambridge, MA: MIT Press, 1985.

———. "Plato's Unwritten Dialectic." In *Dialogue and Dialectic: Eight Hermeneutical Studies on Plato*, translated by P. Christopher Smith, 124–155. New Haven: Yale University Press, 1980.

———. "Text and Interpretation." In *Dialogue and Deconstruction: The Gadamer-Derrida Encounter*, edited by Diane P. Michelfelder and Richard E. Palmer, 21–51. Albany: State University of New York Press, 1989.

———. *Truth and Method*. Translated by Joel Weinsheimer and Donald G. Marshall. New York: Continuum, 1989.

———. "The Universality of the Hermeneutics Problem." In *Philosophical Hermeneutics*, trans. and ed. David E. Linge, 3–17. Berkeley: University of California Press, 1976.

Gallimore, Andrew. *Reality Switch Technologies: Psychedelics as Tools for the Discovery and Exploration of New Worlds*. Tokyo: Strange Worlds, 2022.

Gallimore, Andrew R., and David P. Luke. "DMT Research from 1956 to the Edge of Time." In *Neurotransmissions: Essays on Psychedelics from Breaking Convention*, edited by Dave King, David Luke, Ben Sessa, Cameron Adams, and Aimie Tollen, 291–316. London: Strange Attractor Press, 2015.

Gallimore, Andrew R., and Rick J. Strassman. "A Model for the Application of Target-Controlled Intravenous Infusion for a Prolonged Immersive DMT Psychedelic Experience." *Frontiers in Pharmacology* 7 (July 14, 2016). doi.org/10.3389/fphar.2016.00211.

Galvin, Gaby. "Surprise Medical Bills Have Been Banned Since January. 1 in 5 Americans Say They or Their Family Have Gotten an Unexpected Charge Anyway." *Morning Consult*, July 7, 2022. morningconsult.com/2022/07/07/surprise-medical-billing-ban-unexpected-charges/.

Gambino, Megan. "During Prohibition, Your Doctor Could Write You a Prescription for Booze." *Smithsonian Magazine*, October 7, 2013. www.smithsonianmag.com/history/during-prohibition-your-doctor-could-write-you-prescription-booze-180947940/.

Gascoigne, Neil. *Scepticism*. Montreal: McGill-Queen's University Press, 2002.

Gattuso, James J., Daniel Perkins, Simon Ruffell, Andrew J. Lawrence, Daniel Hoyer, Laura H. Jacobson, Christopher Timmermann, David Castle, Susan L. Rossell, Luke A. Downey, Broc A. Pagni, Nicole L. Galvão-Coelho, David Nutt, and Jerome Sarris. "Default Mode Network Modulation by Psychedelics: A Systematic Review." *International Journal of Neuropsychopharmacology* 26, no. 3 (March 2023): 155–188. doi.org/10.1093/ijnp/pyac074.

Gearin, Alex K., and Oscar Calavia Sáez. "Altered Vision: Ayahuasca Shamanism and Sensory Individualism." *Current Anthropology* 62, no. 2 (April 2021): 138–163.

Georgiou, Aristos. "Depression and Grief Wrecked a Man's Life—Until He Took Magic Mushroom Ingredient." *Newsweek*, December 26, 2021. www.news-

week.com/depression-grief-wrecked-man-life-magic-mushroom-ingredient-psilocybin-therapy-trial-kirk-rutter-1660581.
Gerassi, John. "When Sartre Talked to Crabs (It Was Mescaline)." *New York Times*, November 14, 2009.
Girn, Manesh. "The Psychedelic Scientist." *The Psychedelic Scientist*. Accessed May 20, 2023. www.youtube.com/@ThePsychedelicScientist.
Girn, Manesh, Fernando Rosas, Richard E. Daws, Courtney L. Gallen, Adam Gazzaley, and Robin L. Carhart-Harris. "A Complex Systems Perspective on Psychedelic Brain Action." *Trends in Cognitive Sciences* 27, no. 5 (May 2023): 433–445. doi.org/10.1016/j.tics.2023.01.003.
Giza, Christopher C., and Mayumi L. Prins. "Is Being Plastic Fantastic? Mechanisms of Altered Plasticity after Developmental Traumatic Brain Injury." *Developmental Neuroscience* 28, no. 4–5 (August 1, 2006): 364–379. doi.org/10.1159/000094163.
Glinton, Sonari. "Big Pharma's Bet on Psychedelics." Podcast episode. *Slate Magazine*, August 14, 2022. slate.com/podcasts/what-next-tbd/2022/08/the-corporatization-of-psychedelics.
Godfrey-Smith, Peter. *Other Minds: The Octopus, the Sea, and the Deep Origins of Consciousness*. Farrar, Straus & Giroux, 2016.
Goldhill, Olivia. "A Psychedelic Therapist Allegedly Took Millions from a Holocaust Survivor, Highlighting Worries about Elders Taking Hallucinogens." *Stat News*, April 21, 2022. www.statnews.com/2022/04/21/psychedelic-therapist-allegedly-took-millions-from-holocaust-survivor-highlighting-worries-about-elders-taking-hallucinogens/.
———. "Psychedelic Therapy Has a Sexual Abuse Problem." *Quartz*, May 13, 2020. qz.com/1809184/psychedelic-therapy-has-a-sexual-abuse-problem-3/.
González Romero, Osiris Sinuhé. "Decolonizing the Philosophy of Psychedelics." In *Philosophy and Psychedelics Frameworks for Exceptional Experience*, edited by Christine Hauskeller and Peter Sjöstedt-Hughes, 77–94. London: Bloomsbury, 2022.
Götz, Ignacio. *The Psychedelic Teacher*. Philadelphia: Westminster, 1972.
Graukroger, Stephen. *Descartes: An Intellectual Biography*. New York: Oxford University Press, 1995.
Gravitz, Lauren. "Hope that Psychedelic Drugs Can Erase Trauma." *Nature Outlook*, September 28, 2002. www.nature.com/articles/d41586-022-02870-x.
Griffiths, Roland R., and Charles C. Grob. "Hallucinogens as Medicine." *Scientific American*, December 1, 2010. www.scientificamerican.com/article/hallucinogens-as-medicine/.
Griffiths, Roland R., Ethan Hurwitz, Alan T. Davis, Matthew P. Johnson, and Robert L. Jesse. "Survey of Subjective 'God Encounter Experiences': Comparisons among Naturally Occurring Experiences and Those Occasioned

by the Classic Psychedelics Psilocybin, LSD, Ayahuasca, or DMT." *PLOS ONE* 14, no. 4 (April 2019). doi.org/10.1371/journal.pone.0214377.

Griffiths, Roland R., Matthew P. Johnson, Michael A. Carducci, Annie Umbricht, William G. Richards, Brian K. Richards, Mary P Cosimano, and Margaret A. Klinedinst. "Psilocybin Produces Substantial and Sustained Decreases in Depression and Anxiety in Patients with Life-Threatening Cancer: A Randomized Double-Blind Trial." *Journal of Psychopharmacology* 30, no. 12 (December 2016): 1181–1197. doi.org/10.1177/0269881116675513.

Griffiths, Roland R., Matthew P. Johnson, William G. Richards, Brian K. Richards, Robert L. Jesse, Katherine A. MacLean, Frederick S. Barrett, Mary P. Cosimano, and Margaret A. Klinedinst. "Psilocybin-Occasioned Mystical-Type Experience in Combination with Meditation and Other Spiritual Practices Produces Enduring Positive Changes in Psychological Functioning and in Trait Measures of Prosocial Attitudes and Behaviors." *Journal of Psychopharmacology* 32, no. 1 (January 2018): 49–69. doi.org/10.1177/0269881117731279.

Griffiths, Roland R., William G. Richards, Matthew P. Johnson, Una D. McCann, and Robert L. Jesse. "Mystical-Type Experiences Occasioned by Psilocybin Mediate the Attribution of Personal Meaning and Spiritual Significance 14 Months Later." *Journal of Psychopharmacology* 22, no. 6 (August 2008): 621–632. doi.org/10.1177/0269881108094300.

Grob, Charles S., Alicia L. Danforth, Gurpreet S. Chopra, Marycie Hagerty, Charles R. McKay, Adam L. Halberstadt, and George Greer. "Pilot Study of Psilocybin Treatment for Anxiety in Patients with Advanced-Stage Cancer." *Archives of General Psychiatry* 68, no. 1 (January 3, 2011): 71–78. doi.org/10.1001/archgenpsychiatry.2010.116.

Grob, Charles S., Anthony P. Bossis, and Roland R. Griffiths. "Use of the Classic Hallucinogen Psilocybin for Treatment of Existential Distress Associated with Cancer." In *Psychological Aspects of Cancer: A Guide to Emotional and Psychological Consequences of Cancer, Their Causes and Their Management*, 2nd ed., edited by Jennifer L. Steel and Brian I. Carr, 69–90. Basel: Springer, 2022.

Grof, Stanislav. *The Adventure of Self-Discovery: Dimensions of Consciousness and New Perspectives in Psychotherapy and Inner Exploration* (Albany: State University of New York Press, 1988).

———. "The Experience of Death and Dying: Psychological, Philosophical, and Spiritual Aspects." *Spirituality Studies* 1, no. 2 (Fall 2015). www.spirituality-studies.org/files/1-2-grof.pdf.

———. "Forward." In Albert Hofmann, *LSD My Problem Child: Reflections on Sacred Drugs, Mysticism and Science*, 4th ed. Santa Cruz, CA: MAPS, 2017.

———. In *Infinity: The Ultimate Trip—Journey Beyond Death*. Documentary film. Directed by Jay Weidner. Boulder, CO: Sacred Mystery Productions, 2009.

———. *LSD Psychotherapy: The Healing Potential of Psychedelic Medicine*, 4th ed. Santa Cruz: MAPS, 2008.

———. *Realms of the Human Unconscious: Observations from LSD Research*. London: Souvenir, 2019.

Grunes, Rodney A. "Creationism, the Courts, and the First Amendment," *Journal of Church and State* 31, no. 3 (Autumn 1989): 465–486.

Guenther, Matthew. *Human-Animal Relationships in San and Hunter-Gatherer Cosmology, Volume I: Therianthropes and Transformation*. New York: Palgrave Macmillan, 2019.

Guerra-Doce, Elisa. "Psychoactive Substances in Prehistoric Times: Examining the Archaeological Evidence." *Time and Mind* 8 (2015): 11–91.

Gukasyan, Natalie, Alan T. Davis, Frederick S. Barrett, Mary P. Cosimano, Nathan D. Sepeda, Matthew P. Johnson, and Roland R. Griffiths. "Efficacy and Safety of Psilocybin-Assisted Treatment for Major Depressive Disorder: Prospective 12-Month Follow-Up." *Journal of Psychopharmacology* 36, no. 2 (February 2022): 151–158. doi.org/10.1177/02698811211073759.

Guzmán, Gastón. "Sacred Mushrooms and Man: Diversity and Traditions in the World, with Special Reference to *Psilocybe*." In *Entheogens and the Development of Culture: The Anthropology and Neurology of Ecstatic Experience*, edited by John A. Rush, 485–518. Berkeley, CA: North Atlantic Books, 2012.

Gwynn, S. C. *Empire of the Summer Moon: Quanah Parker and the Rise and Fall of the Comanches, the Most Powerful Indian Tribe in American History*. New York: Scribner, 2010.

Hadot, Pierre. *Philosophy as a Way of Life*. Edited by Arnold I. Davidson and translated by Michael Chase. London: Blackwell, 1995.

———. *What is Ancient Philosophy?* Translated by Michael Chase. Cambridge, MA: Harvard University Press, 2002.

Hall, Manly, T. *The Secret Teachings of All Ages*. New York: Penguin, 2003.

Hamilton, Jon, Aaron Scott, Thomas Lu, and Gabriel Spitzer. "Brain Scientists Are Tripping Out Over Psychedelics." *National Public Radio*, December 12, 2022. www.npr.org/2022/12/19/1144306776/brain-scientists-are-tripping-out-over-psychedelics.

Hancock, Graham, ed. *The Divine Spark: Psychedelics, Consciousness and the Birth of Civilization*. San Francisco: Disinformation Books, 2015.

Hancock, Graham. *Visionary: The Mysterious Origins of Human Consciousness*. Newburyport, MA: New Page Books, 2022.

Hancock, Graham, and Andrew Gallimore. "DMTx Breakthrough Panel Moderated by Graham Hancock, Dr. Andrew Gallimore & Dr. Rick Strassman." *Noonautics*, May 23, 2023. Video, 2:27:58. www.youtube.com/watch?v=Myq_Hc_39aI.

Hanford, Emily. "Sold a Story: How Teaching Kids to Read Went So Wrong." *APM Reports*. American Public Media. Podcast audio. October 20, 2022. features.apmreports.org/sold-a-story/.

Harner, Michael. *The Way of the Shaman*. New York: Harper, 1990.
Harris, Sam. "Drugs and the Meaning of Life." *Making Sense Podcast*, July 4, 2011. www.samharris.org/podcasts/making-sense-episodes/drugs-and-the-meaning-of-life.
Hart, Carl. *Drug Use for Grown-Ups: Chasing Liberty in the Land of Fear*. New York: Penguin, 2021.
Hartogsohn, Ido. *American Trip: Set, Setting, and the Psychedelic Experience in the Twentieth Century*. Cambridge, MA: MIT Press, 2020.
Hegel, G. W. F. *Phenomenology of Spirit*. Translated by A. V. Miller. New York: Oxford University Press, 1977 [1807].
Heidegger, Martin. *Being and Time*. Translated by John Macquarrie and Edward Robinson. New York: Harper &Row, 1962 [1927].
———. *Discourse on Thinking*. Translated by John M. Anderson and E. Hans Freund. New York: Harper & Row, 1966.
———. "Only a God Can Save Us Now." *Graduate Faculty Philosophy Journal* 6 (Winter 1977): 1–23.
———. "On the Essence of Truth." In *Martin Heidegger: Basic Writings*, edited by David Farrell Krell, 113–142. New York: Harper, 2008.
———. "On the Origin of the Work of Art." In *Martin Heidegger: Basic Writings*, edited by David Farrell Krell, 162–181. New York: Harper, 2008.
———. *Ponderings XII–XV Black Notebooks, 1939–1941*. Translated by Richard Rocjewicz. Bloomington: Indiana University Press, 2017.
———. "The Question Concerning Technology." In *The Question Concerning Technology and Other Essays*, translated by William Lovitt, 3–35. New York: Garland, 1977.
Henao, Luis Andres and Kwasi Gymafi Asiedu. "Rastafari Want More Legal Marijuana for Freedom of Worship." *Associated Press*, December 10, 2021. apnews.com/article/health-religion-ohio-marijuana-columbus-d2dc83bc70426d6b6b10449496469557.
Heraclitus, "Heraclitus of Ephesus." In *The First Philosophers: The Presocratics and Sophists*, translated and edited by Robin Waterfield, 32–48. New York: Oxford University Press, 2000.
Herrington, A. J. "Alberta to Be First Canadian Province to Regulate Psychedelics for Therapeutic Use." *Forbes*, October 6, 2022. www.forbes.com/sites/ajherrington/2022/10/06/alberta-to-be-first-canadian-province-to-regulate-psychedelics-for-therapeutic-use/?sh=7ae14a5e85ea.
———. "House Lawmakers Launch Bipartisan Psychedelics Caucus." *High Times*, November 21, 2022. hightimes.com/psychedelics/house-lawmakers-launch-bipartisan-psychedelics-caucus/.
Higginbottom, Justin. "The 'Psychonauts' Training to Explore Another Dimension." *New Republic*, January 3, 2023. newrepublic.com/article/169525/psychonauts-training-psychedelics-dmt-extended-state.

References

Hill, Amelia. "LSD Could Help Alcoholics Stop Drinking, AA Founder Believed." *Guardian*, August 23, 2012. www.theguardian.com/science/2012/aug/23/lsd-help-alcoholics-theory.

Hipólito, Inês, Jonas Mago, Fernando Rosas, and Robin Carhart-Harris. "Pattern Breaking: A Complex Systems Approach to Psychedelic Medicine." *PsyArXiv Preprints* (July 13, 2022). doi.org/10.31234/osf.io/ydu3h.

Hodges, Nicolle. "How Psychedelics Help with Gender Identity and Transition." *Double Blind*, updated May 26, 2021. doubleblindmag.com/psychedelics-transgender/.

Hoffman, Mark. "Entheogens (Psychedelic Drugs) and the Ancient Mystery Religions." In *Toxicology in Antiquity*, 2nd ed., edited by Philip Wexler, 353–362. London: Elsevier, 2019.

Hofmann, Albert. *LSD and the Divine Scientist: The Final Thoughts and Reflections of Albert Hofmann*. New York: Simon & Schuster, 2013.

———. *LSD My Problem Child: Reflections on Sacred Drugs, Mysticism and Science*, 4th ed. Santa Cruz, CA: MAPS, 2017.

Hölderlin, Friedrich. *Selected Poems and Fragments*. Translated by Michael Hamburger. New York: Penguin, 1998.

Holloway, Kali. "The Secret Black History of LSD." *The Nation*. March 22, 2022. www.thenation.com/article/society/lsd-acid-black-history/.

Hood, R. W. Jr. "Chemically Assisted Mysticism and the Question of Veridicality." In *Seeking the Sacred with Psychoactive Substances: Chemical Paths to Spirituality and God. Volume I: History and Practices*, edited by J. Harold Ellens, 395–410. Santa Barbara, CA: Praeger, 2014.

Horowitz, Alexandra. *Inside of a Dog: What Dogs See, Smell, and Know*. New York: Simon & Schuster, 2012.

Huberman, Andrew. "How to Focus to Change Your Brain." Podcast episode. *Huberman Lab*. February 8, 2021. hubermanlab.com/how-to-focus-to-change-your-brain/.

———. "Psychedelic Medicine with Dr. Matthew Johnson." Podcast episode. *Huberman Lab*, September 2021. hubermanlab.com/dr-matthew-johnson-psychedelic-medicine/.

Hughes, Robert. *The Shock of the New: The Hundred-Year History of Modern Art—Its Rise, Its Dazzling Achievement, Its Fall*. New York: Knopf, 1991.

Hume, David. *A Treatise of Human Nature*. New York: Oxford University Press, 1985 [1740].

———. *Enquiry Concerning Human Understanding*. New York: Oxford University Press, 1999 [1777].

———. *Enquiry Concerning the Principles of Morals*. Indianapolis: Hackett, 1983 [1748].

———. *Hume: Moral and Political Philosophy*. Edited by Henry D. Aiken. New York: Hafner, 1948.

Husserl, Edmund. *Cartesian Meditations: An Introduction to Phenomenology*. Edited by Dorion Cairns. The Hague: Martinus Nijhoff, 1960.
———. *Logical Investigations Volume II*. London: Routledge, 2001 [1921].
Huxley, Aldous. *The Doors of Perception and Heaven and Hell*. New York: Harper, 2009.
———. *Island*. New York: Harper, 2009.
Hyberg, Harri. "Religious use of Hallucinogenic Fungi: A Comparison between Siberian and Mesoamerican Cultures." *Karstenia* 32 (1992): 74, www.samorini.it/doc1/alt_aut/lr/nyberg-religious-use-of-hallucinogenic-fungi.pdf.
Hyde, Lewis. *Trickster Makes This World: Mischief, Myth and Art*. New York: Farrar, Straus & Giroux, 2010.
Ihde, Don. *Technology and the Lifeworld: From Garden to Earth*. Bloomington: Indiana University Press, 1990.
Ingram, David. "Hermeneutics and Truth." *Journal of the British Society of Phenomenology* 15, no. 1 (January 1984): 62–78.
Ivanhoe, Philip J., Owen J. Flanagan, Victoria Harrison, Hagop Sarkissian, and Eric Schwitzgebel, eds. *The Oneness Hypothesis: Beyond the Boundary of the Self*. New York: Columbia University Press, 2018.
Jacobs, Andrew. "The Psychedelic Revolution Is Coming. Psychiatry May Never Be the Same." *New York Times*, May 9, 2021, updated November 11, 2021.
Jaeger, Werner. *Paideia: The Ideals of Greek Culture*. 3 vols. Translated by Gilbert Highet. New York: Oxford University Press, 1986.
James, William. *Principles of Psychology*. New York: Henry Holt, 1918 [1890].
———. *Varieties of Religious Experience*. New York: Penguin, 1982 [1902].
Jay, Mike. *High Society: The Central Role of Mind-Altering Drugs in History, Science, and Culture*. Rochester, VT: Park Street, 2010.
———. *Mescaline: A Global History of the First Psychedelic*. New Haven, CT: Yale University Press, 2019.
———. *Psychonauts: Drugs and the Making of the Modern Mind*. New Haven, CT: Yale University Press, 2023.
Jeffers, Robinson. "The Answer." In *Selected Poetry of Robinson Jeffers*, 522. Edited by Tim Hunt. Stanford: Stanford University Press, 2002.
Johnson, Matthew W. "Consciousness, Religion, and Gurus: Pitfalls of Psychedelic Medicine." *ACS Pharmacology & Translational Science* 4, no. 2 (December 16, 2020): 578–581. doi.org/10.1021/acsptsci.0c00198.
Johnson, Matthew W., William G. Richards, and Roland R. Griffiths. "Human Hallucinogen Research: Guidelines for Safety." *Journal of Psychopharmacology* 22, no. 6 (May 30, 2008): 603–620. doi.org/10.1177/0269881108093587.
Johnson, Matthew W., and David B. Yaden. "There's No Good Evidence That Psychedelics Can Change Your Politics or Religion." *Scientific American*, November 5, 2020. www.scientificamerican.com/article/theres-no-good-evidence-that-psychedelics-can-change-your-politics-or-religion/.

Johnstad, Petter Grahl. "A Dangerous Method? Psychedelic Therapy at Modum Bad, Norway, 1961–76." *History of Psychiatry* 31, no. 2 (January 2020): 217–226. doi.org/10.1177/0957154x19894537.

Jones, Bartlett C. "A Prohibition Problem: Liquor as Medicine 1920–1933." *Journal of the History of Medicine and Allied Sciences* 18, no. 4 (October 1963): 353–369.

Jünger, Ernst. *Approaches: Drugs and Altered States*. Translated by Thomas Friese, edited by Russell A. Berman. Candor, NY: Telos, 2022.

Kaelen, Mendel, Frederick S. Barrett, Leor Roseman, Romy Lorenz, Neiloufar Family, Mark Bolstridge, H. Valerie Curran, Amanda Feilding, David J. Nutt, and Robin L. Carhart-Harris. "LSD Enhances the Emotional Response to Music." *Psychopharmacology* 232, no. 19 (October 2015): 3607–3614. doi.org/10.1007/s00213-015-4014-y.

Kanen, Jonathan W., Qiang Luo, Mojtaba Rostami Kandroodi, Rudolf N. Cardinal, Trevor W. Robbins, David J Nutt, Robin L. Carhart-Harris, and Hanneke E. M. Den Ouden. "Effect of Lysergic Acid Diethylamide (LSD) on Reinforcement Learning in Humans." *Psychological Medicine* 53, no. 14 (October 2023), 6434–6445. doi.org/10.1017/s0033291722002963.

Kant, Immanuel. *Critique of Judgment*. Translated by James Creed Meredith, revised by Nicholas Walker. New York: Oxford University Press, 2007 [1790].

———. *Critique of Pure Reason*. Translated by Norman Kemp Smith. New York: St. Martin's, 1965 [1781].

Kempis, Thomas à. *The Imitation of Christ*. New York: Vintage, 1998 [c. 1420].

Kheir, Ala, John Burns, and Ibrahim Algrefwi. "The Psychedelic World of Sudan's Sufis—In Pictures." *Guardian*, February 5, 2016. www.theguardian.com/world/gallery/2016/feb/05/the-psychedelic-world-of-sudans-sufis-in-pictures.

Khoury, George. *The Extraordinary Works of Alan Moore*. Raleigh, NC: TwoMorrows Publishing, 2003.

Kimmerer, Robin Wall. *Braiding Sweetgrass: Indigenous Wisdom, Scientific Knowledge and the Teachings of Plants*. Minneapolis: Milkweed, 2013.

Kingsland, James. *Am I Dreaming? The Science of Altered States, from Psychedelics to Virtual Reality, and Beyond*. London: Atlantic Books, 2019.

Kins, Josie. "Subjective Effect Index." *Effect Index*. Accessed May 20, 2023. effectindex.com/effects/.

Klein, Joanna. "A Mushroom Out of a Fairy Tale You Might Find in the Forest." *New York Times*, October 17, 2017.

Kolaczynska, Karolina E., Dino Luethi, Daniel Trachsel, Marius C. Hoener, and Matthias E. Liechti. "Receptor Interaction Profiles of 4-Alkoxy-3,5-Dimethoxy-Phenethylamines (Mescaline Derivatives) and Related Amphetamines." *Frontiers in Pharmacology* 12 (February 9, 2022). doi.org/10.3389/fphar.2021.794254.

Korzybski, Alfred. *Science and Sanity: An Introduction to Non-Aristotelian Systems and General Semantics*, 5th ed. Lancaster, PA: International Non-Aristotelian Library, 1933. Available at esgs.free.fr/uk/art/sands.htm.

Kovacic, Peter, and Ratnasamy Somanathan. "Novel, Unifying Mechanism for Mescaline in The Central Nervous System: Electrochemistry, Catechol Redox Metabolite, Receptor, Cell Signaling and Structure Activity Relationships." *Oxidative Medicine and Cellular Longevity* 2, no. 4 (January 1, 2009): 181–90. doi.org/10.4161/oxim.2.4.9380.

Krishnan, Manisha. "Ex-Mormons Are Running a Magic Mushroom Church." *Vice News*, February 15, 2023. www.vice.com/en/article/akexaa/magic-mushroom-mormon-church-utah.

Kuhn, Thomas S. *The Structure of Scientific Revolutions*. Chicago: University of Chicago Press, 2012 [1962].

Labate, Beatriz Caiuby, Brian T. Anderson, and Henrik Jungaberle. "Ritual Ayahuasca Use and Health: An Interview with Jacques Mabit." In *The Internationalization of Ayahuasca*, edited by Beatriz Caiuby Labate and Henrik Jungaberle, 223–243. Zurich: Lit Verlag. www.researchgate.net/publication/314404765_Ritual_Ayahuasca_use_and_health_an_interview_with_Jacques_Mabit.

Lachman, Gary. *Turn Off Your Mind: The Dedalus Book of the 1960s*. Sawtry, UK: Dedalus, 2001.

Lake, George F. *The Law of Entheogenic Churches in the United States*. Self-pub., 2021.

———. *The Law of Entheogenic Churches Volume II*. Self-pub., 2022.

Langlitz, Nicholas. "Rightist Psychedelia." *Society for Cultural Anthropology*, July 21, 2020. culanth.org/fieldsights/rightist-psychedelia.

Laurenson, Lydia. "Spirituality, Psychedelics and Psychotic Risk: Ryan Jay Beauregard and the Zendo Project." *New Modality*, November 11, 2019. thenewmodality.com/spirituality-psychedelics-and-psychotic-risk-ryan-jay-beauregard-and-the-zendo-project/.

Lattin, Don. "Pioneering Clergy of Diverse Religions Embrace Psychedelics." *Lucid News*, April 20, 2022. www.lucid.news/pioneering-clergy-of-diverse-religions-embrace-psychedelics/.

Lawrence, David Wyndham, Robin Carhart-Harris, Roland Griffiths, and Christopher Timmermann. "Phenomenology and Content of the Inhaled N,N-Dimethyltryptamine (N, N-DMT) Experience." *Scientific Reports* 12, 8562 (May 24, 2022). doi.org/10.1038/s41598-022-11999-8.

Lear, Jonathan. *Imagining the End: Mourning and Ethical Life*. Cambridge, MA: Harvard University Press, 2022.

———. "Inside and Outside the *Republic*." *Phronesis* 37, no. 2 (1992): 184–215.

Leary, Timothy, Ralph Metzner, and Richard Alpert. *The Psychedelic Experience: A Manual Based on the Tibetan Book of the Dead*. Toronto: Citadel Press, 1992 [1962].

Lee, Martin A., and Bruce Shlain. *Acid Dreams: The Complete Social History of LSD: The CIA, the Sixties, and Beyond.* New York: Grove Press, 1994.
Lee, Patrick. *We Borrow the Earth: An Intimate Portrait of the Gypsy Folk Tradition and Culture.* Pembrokeshire, Wales: Ravine, 2015.
Letheby, Chris. *Philosophy of Psychedelics.* New York: Oxford University Press, 2021.
Letheby, Chris, and Philip Gerrans. "Self Unbound: Ego Dissolution in Psychedelic Experience." *Neuroscience of Consciousness* 2017, no. 1 (June 30, 2017). doi.org/10.1093/nc/nix016.
Letheby, Chris, and Jaipreet Mattu. "Philosophy and Classic Psychedelics: A Review of Some Emerging Themes. *Journal of Psychedelic Studies* 5, no. 3 (February 2022): 166–175. doi.org/10.1556/2054.2021.00191.
Lewis-Healey, Evan. "Preventing Sexual Abuse in Psychedelic Therapy." *Psychedelic Spotlight*, October 15, 2021. psychedelicspotlight.com/preventing-sexual-abuse-in-psychedelic-therapy/.
Lewis-Williams, David. *A Cosmos in Stone: Interpreting Religion and Society through Rock Art.* Lanham, MD: AltaMira Press, 2002.
Lewis-Williams, David J., and Jean Clottes. "The Mind in the Cave—the Cave in the Mind: Altered Consciousness in the Upper Paleolithic." *Anthropology and Consciousness* 9, no. 1 (January 2008): 13–21.
Lewis-Williams, J. D., and T. A. Dowson. "The Signs of All Times: Entoptic Phenomena in Upper Paleolithic Cave Art." *Current Anthropology* 29, no. 2 (April 1988): 201–245.
Lhooq, Michelle. "Inside Shroom Rave: A Radical Experiment in Post-Alcohol Partying." *Double-Blind*, March 3, 2003. doubleblindmag.com/mushwomb-shroom-rave/.
Lin, Tao. *Trip: Psychedelics, Alienation, and Change.* New York: Vintage, 2018.
Liu, Jiangang, Jun Li, Lu Feng, Ling Li, Jie Tian, and Kang Lee. "Seeing Jesus in Toast: Neural and Behavioral Correlates of Face Pareidolia." *Cortex* 53 (April 2014): 60–77. doi.org/10.1016/j.cortex.2014.01.013.
Loder, Natasha. "Ketamine, Psilocybin and Ecstasy are Coming to the Medicine Cabinet." *Economist*, September 21, 2022. www.economist.com/technology-quarterly/2022/09/21.
Loeb, Louis E. "Sextus, Hume and Peirce: On Securing Settled Doxastic States." *NOÛS* 32 (1998): 205–230.
Lonergan, Eric. "Psychedelics are Pluripotent." *Mind Foundation*, April 27, 2021. mind-foundation.org/psychedelics-politically-pluripotent/.
Lordi, Emily. "The Radical Experimentation of Black Psychedelia." *New York Times Style Magazine*, February 10, 2022.
Lucretius. *The Nature of Things.* Translated by A. E. Stallings. New York: Penguin, 2007.
Lukes, David. *Otherworlds: Psychedelics and Exceptional Human Experience.* London: Muswell Hill, 2017.

Luna, Luis Eduardo. "The Concept of Plants as Teachers among Four Mestizo Shamans of Iquitos, Northeastern Peru." *Journal of Ethnopharmacology* 11, no. 2 (July 1984): 135–516. doi.org/10.1016/0378-8741(84)90036-9.

———. "On Encounters with Entities in the Ayahuasca Realm." In *DMT Entity Encounters: Dialogues on the Spirit Molecule*, edited by David Luke and Rory Spowers, 3–29. Rochester, VT: Park Street, 2021.

Lundborg Patrick. *Psychedelia: Ancient Culture, a Modern Way of Life*. Stockholm: Lysergia, 2012.

Lyotard, Jean-Francois. *The Postmodern Condition: A Report on Knowledge*. Translated by Geoff Bennington. Minneapolis: University of Minnesota Press, 1984.

MacIntyre, Alasdair. *After Virtue*, 2nd edition. Notre Dame, IN: University of Notre Dame Press, 1984.

MacLean, Katherine A., Jeannie Marie S. Leoutsakos, Matthew P. Johnson, and Roland R. Griffiths. "Factor Analysis of the Mystical Experience Questionnaire: A Study of Experiences Occasioned by the Hallucinogen Psilocybin." *Journal for the Scientific Study of Religion* 51, no. 4 (December 2012): 721–737. doi.org/10.1111/j.1468-5906.2012.01685.x.

Marchese, David. "A Psychedelics Pioneer Takes the Ultimate Trip." *New York Times Magazine*, April 7, 2023.

Marinacci, Mike. *Psychedeic Cults and Outlaw Churches: LSD, Cannabis, and Spiritual Sacraments in Underground America*. Rochester, VT: Park Street, 2023.

Marks, Mason, Brent M. Kious, Carmel Shachar, and I. Glenn Cohen. "Introducing Psychedelics to End-of-Life Mental Healthcare." *Nature Mental Health* 1, no. 12 (November 8, 2023): 920–922. doi.org/10.1038/s44220-023-00166-1.

Maroukis, Thomas C. *The Peyote Road: Religious Freedom and the Native American Church*. Norman: University of Oklahoma Press, 2010.

Marshall, Robert. "The Dark Legacy of Carlos Castaneda." *Salon*, April 12, 2007. www.salon.com/2007/04/12/castaneda/.

Marx, Karl, and Frederick Engels, *Manifesto of the Communist Party*. Translated by Samuel Moore in cooperation with Frederick Engels. In *Marx/Engels Selected Works*, vol. 1, 98–137. Moscow: Progress Publishers, 1969 [1848]. www.marxists.org/archive/marx/works/1848/communist-manifesto/index.htm.

Matossian, Mary. "Ergot and the Salem Witchcraft Affair." *American Scientist* 70, no. 4 (July–August 1982), 355–357.

———. *Poisons of the Past: Molds, Epidemics, and History*. New Haven: Yale University Press, 1991.

McClintock, Sean. "Why Investors Are Turning toward Psychedelic Health Care Companies." *Forbes*, September 4, 2021. fortune.com/2021/09/04/psychedelic-industry-investment-growth-stocks-companies/.

McKenna, Terence. *Archaic Revival: Speculations on Psychedelic Mushrooms, the Amazon, Virtual Reality, UFOs, Evolution, Shamanism, the Rebirth of the Goddess, and the End of History*. New York: HarperCollins, 1992.

———. *Food of the Gods: The Search for the Original Tree of Knowledge: A Radical History of Plants, Drugs, and Human Evolution.* New York: Bantam, 1993.

———. *True Hallucinations: Being an Account of the Author's Extraordinary Adventures in the Devil's Paradise.* New York: HarperOne, 1994.

Mears, Hadley. "The Witches of Westwood and Carlos Castaneda's Sinister Legacy." *LAist,* September 2, 2021. laist.com/news/la-history/carlos-castanedas-sinister-legacy-witches-of-westwood.

Metzner, Ralph. "Hallucinogenic Drugs and Plants in Psychotherapy and Shamanism." *Journal of Psychoactive Drugs* 30, no. 4 (October–December 1998): 333–341. doi.org/10.1080/02791072.1998.10399709.

Michael, Pascal, David Luke, and Oliver Robinson. "An Encounter with the Other: A Thematic and Content Analysis of DMT Experiences From a Naturalistic Field Study." *Frontiers in Psychology* 12, 720717 (December 16, 2021). doi.org/10.3389/fpsyg.2021.720717.

Miller, Richard Louis, and Mariavittoria Mangini. "Psychedelics and the Social Matrix." In *Psychedelic Wisdom: The Astonishing Rewards of Mind-Altering Substances,* edited by Richard Louis Miller. Rochester, VT: Park Street, 2022.

Minutaglio, Bill, and Stephen L. David. *The Most Dangerous Man in America: Timothy Leary, Richard Nixon and the Hunt for the Fugitive King of LSD.* New York: Twelve, 2018.

Morgenson, Kat. "Fly Agaric (*Amanita muscaria*)." *Sacred Earth,* November 11, 2020. sacredearth.com/2020/11/11/fly-agaric-amanita-muscaria/.

Morris, Hamilton. "A Four Hour Long Conversation with Dr. David Nichols." *The Hamilton Morris Podcast,* November 23, 2022. Audio, 4:02:49. hamiltonmorris.buzzsprout.com/1870388/11732744-a-four-hour-long-conversation-with-dr-david-nichols.

———. "The Psychedelic Toad." *Hamilton's Pharmacopeia,* season 2, episode 1. Directed by Hamilton Morris. Vice TV, November 28, 2017. Video, 44:05. www.vicetv.com/en_us/video/hamiltons-pharmacopeia-the-psychedelic-toad/59cd5cd7c6e1eb5725458fdc.

Murakami, Haruki, *Killing Commendatore.* New York: Knopf Doubleday, 2018.

Muraresku, Brian C. *The Immortality Key: The Secret History of the Religion with No Name.* New York: St. Martin's, 2020.

Murdoch, Iris. *The Sovereignty of the Good.* New York: Routledge, 2000.

Nagel, Thomas. *The View from Nowhere.* New York: Oxford University Press, 1989.

———. "What Is It Like to Be a Bat?" *Philosophical Review* 83, no. 4 (October 1974): 435–450.

Narby, Jeremy. "Amazonian Perspectives on Invisible Entities." In *DMT Dialogues: Encounters with the Spirit Molecule,* edited by David Luke and Rory Spowers, 69–94. Rochester, VT: Park Street, 2018.

———. *Plant Teachers: Ayahuasca, Tobacco, and the Pursuit of Knowledge.* Novato, CA: New World Library, 2021.

National Institutes of Health, "Marijuana and Hallucinogen use Among Young Adults Reached All-Time High in 2021." *New Releases*, August 22, 2022. www.nih.gov/news-events/news-releases/marijuana-hallucinogen-use-among-young-adults-reached-all-time-high-2021.

National Institutes of Health. "Lysergic Acid Diethylamide (LSD) as Treatment for Cluster Headache (LCH)." U.S. Library of Medicine, May 5, 2022. clinicaltrials.gov/ct2/show/NCT03781128.

Nautiyal, Katherine M., and David B. Yaden. "Does the Trip Matter? Investigating the Role of the Subjective Effects of Psychedelics in Persisting Therapeutic Effects." *Neuropsychopharmacology* 48 (January 2023): 215–216. doi.org/10.1038/s41386-022-01424-z.

Nayak, Sandeep M., and Roland R. Griffiths. "A Single Belief-Changing Psychedelic Experience Is Associated with Increased Attribution of Consciousness to Living and Non-living Entities." *Frontiers in Psychology* 13, no. 852248 (March 2022). doi.org/10.3389/fpsyg.2022.852248.

Neurotech@Berkeley. "Psychedelics: A Tragic History of Cults, Drugs, and Promises to the Future." *Medium*, April 10, 2022. ucbneurotech.medium.com/psychedelics-a-tragic-history-of-cults-drugs-and-promises-to-the-future-121ad2bd2b48.

Newson, Martha, Ragini Khurana, Freya Cazorla, and Valerie Van Mulukom. "'I Get High With a Little Help From My Friends'—How Raves Can Invoke Identity Fusion and Lasting Co-Operation via Transformative Experiences." *Frontiers in Psychology* 12 (September 24, 2021). doi.org/10.3389/fpsyg.2021.719596.

Nguyen Thanh Tam, Nguyen Tien Huy, Le Thi Bich Thoa, Nguyen Phuoc Long, Nguyen Thi Huyen Trang, Kenji Hirayama, and Juntra Karbwang. "Participants' Understanding of Informed Consent in Clinical Trials over Three Decades: Systematic Review and Meta-Analysis." *Bull World Health Organ* 93, no. 3 (March 2015): 186–198H. doi.org/10.2471/blt.14.141390.

Nichols, David E. "Studies of the Relationship between Molecular Structure and Hallucinogenic Activity." *Pharmacology Biochemistry and Behavior* 24, no. 2 (1986): 335–340. doi.org/10.1016/0091-3057(86)90362-X.

Nietzsche, Friedrich. *The Gay Science*. Translated by Josefine Nauckhoff. New York: Cambridge University Press, 2001 [1882].

———. *Human, All-Too-Human, Part II: The Wanderer and His Shadow*. Translated by Paul V. Cohn. New York: MacMillan, 1913 [1880]. www.gutenberg.org/files/37841/37841-h/37841-h.html.

———. *Thus Spoke Zarathustra: A Book for Everyone and No One*. Translated by R. J. Hollingdale. New York: Penguin, 1961.

———. *The Will to Power*. Translated by Walter Kaufmann and R. J. Hollingdale. New York: Vintage Books, 1967 [1901].

Nikolaidis, Aki, Rafaelle Lancelotta, Natalie Gukasyan, Roland R Griffiths, Frederick S Barrett, and Alan K Davis. "Subtypes of the Psychedelic

Experience Have Reproducible and Predictable Effects on Depression and Anxiety Symptoms." *Journal of Affective Disorders* 324 (March 1, 2023): 239–249. doi.org/10.1016/j.jad.2022.12.042.

Nour, Matthew M., Lisa Evans, David J. Nutt, and Robin L. Carhart-Harris. "Ego-Dissolution and Psychedelics: Validation of the Ego-Dissolution Inventory (EDI)." *Frontiers in Human Neuroscience* 10 (June 14, 2016). doi.org/10.3389/fnhum.2016.00269.

Novak, S. J. "LSD Before Leary: Sidney Cohen's Critique of 1950s Psychedelic Drug Research." *Isis* 88, no. 1 (March 1997): 87–110. doi.org/10.1086/383628.

Nussbaum, Martha C. *The Therapy of Desire*. Princeton, NJ: Princeton University Press, 1994.

Nutt, David, Meg J. Spriggs, and David Erritzoe. "Psychedelics Therapeutics: What We Know, What We Think, and What We Need to Research." *Neuropharmacology* 223, 109257 (February 1, 2023). doi.org/10.1016/j.neuropharm.2022.109257.

O'Neill, Tom. *Chaos: Charles Manson, the CIA and the Secret History of the Sixties*. New York: Little, Brown, 2019.

Office of Legal Counsel, US Department of Justice. "Peyote Exemption for Native American Church." December 22, 1981. www.justice.gov/olc/opinion/peyote-exemption-native-american-church.

Oger, Eric. "The Eternal Return as Crucial Test." *Journal of Nietzsche Studies* 14 (Autumn 1997): 1–18.

Ohio State University. "Breaking the Shackles of Anxiety and Depression: How Psychedelic Experiences May Improve Mental Health." *SciTech Daily*, February 25, 2023. scitechdaily.com/breaking-the-shackles-of-anxiety-and-depression-how-psychedelic-experiences-may-improve-mental-health/.

Okrent, Daniel. *Last Call: The Rise and Fall of Prohibition*. New York: Scribner, 2010.

Orth, Taylor. "One in Four Americans Say They've Tried at Least One Psychedelic Drug." *YouGov (US)*, July 18, 2022. today.yougov.com/topics/society/articles-reports/2022/07/28/one-in-four-americans-have-tried-psychedelic-drugs.

Osborne, Grant R. *The Hermeneutical Spiral: A Comprehensive Introduction to Biblical Interpretation*. Downers Grove, IL: IVP Academic, 2006.

Pace, Brian. "Lucy in the Sky with Nazis: Psychedelics and the Right Wing." *Psymposia*, February 3, 2020. www.psymposia.com/magazine/lucy-in-the-sky-with-nazis-psychedelics-and-the-right-wing/.

Pace, Brian A., and Neşe Devenot. "Right-Wing Psychedelia: Case Studies in Cultural Plasticity and Political Pluripotency." *Frontiers in Psychology* 12 (December 10, 2021). doi.org/10.3389/fpsyg.2021.733185.

Palhano-Fontes, Fernanda, Katia Andrade, Luís Fernando Tófoli, Antonio Carlos Dos Santos, José Alexandre De Souza Crippa, Jaime Eduardo Cecílio Hallak, Sidarta Ribeiro, and Dráulio Barros De Araújo. "The Psychedelic

State Induced by Ayahuasca Modulates the Activity and Connectivity of the Default Mode Network." *PLOS ONE* 10, no. 2 (February 2015). doi.org/10.1371/journal.pone.0118143.

Partridge, Christopher. *High Culture: Drugs, Mysticism, and the Pursuit of Transcendence in the Modern World*. New York: Oxford University Press, 2018.

Pedersen, Willy, Heith Copes, and Liridona Gashi. "Narratives of the Mystical among Users of Psychedelics." *Acta Sociologica* 64, no. 2 (January 2021): 230–246. doi.org/10.1177/0001699320980050.

Perez, Erika. "How Often Should You Take Psilocybin Mushrooms?" *Psychedelic Passage*, June 6, 2022. www.psychedelicpassage.com/how-often-should-you-take-psilocybin-mushrooms/.

Perutz, Leo. *Saint Peter's Snow*. London: Pushkin Vertigo, 2014 [1933].

Pilgrim, David. "The Brut Caricature." Museum exhibit. The Jim Crow Museum, Ferris State University, Big Rapids, MI. Accessed May 21, 2023, www.ferris.edu/jimcrow/brute/.

Piper, Alan. "Leo Perutz and the Mystery of St. Peter's Snow." *Time and Mind: The Journal of Archaeology, Consciousness and Culture* 6, no. 2 (July 2013): 175–198.

Plato. *Meno*. Translated by Robin Waterfield. New York: Oxford University Press, 2005.

———. *Phaedo*. Translated by G. M. A. Grube. Indianapolis: Hackett, 2002.

———. *Phaedrus*. Translated by Robin Waterfield. New York: Oxford University Press, 2002.

———. *Republic*. Translated by Robin Waterfield. New York: Oxford University Press, 2008.

———. *Theaetetus*. Translated by Robin Waterfield. New York: Oxford University Press, 2008.

———. *Timaeus*. Translated by Robin Waterfield. New York: Oxford University Press, 2008.

Plotinus, "The Good or the One" [from the *Enneads*]. In *The Essential Plotinus*. Edited and translated by Elmer O'Brian, SJ, 72–89. Indianapolis: Hackett, 1964.

Pollan, Michael. *How to Change Your Mind: What the New Science of Psychedelics Teaches Us About Consciousness, Dying, Addiction, Depression, and Transcendence*. New York: Penguin, 2018.

———. *This is Your Mind on Plants*. New York: Penguin, 2021.

Popkin Richard. *The History of Skepticism: From Savonarola to Boyle*. Revised and expanded edition. New York: Oxford University Press, 2003.

Provine, Doris Marie. *Unequal Under the Law: Race in the War on Drugs*. Chicago: University of Chicago Press, 2007.

Raetsch, Christopher. *The Encyclopedia of Psychoactive Plants: Ethnopharmacology and Its Applications*. Rochester, VT: Park Street, 2005.

Rankaduwa, Sidath, and Adrian M. Owen. "Psychedelics, Entropic Brain Theory, and the Taxonomy of Conscious States: A Summary of Debates and Perspectives." *Neuroscience of Consciousness* 2023, no. 1 (April 2023): 1–13. doi.org/10.1093/nc/niad001.

Rawls, John. *Lectures on the History of Moral Philosophy*. Cambridge, MA: Harvard University Press, 2000.

———. *Political Liberalism*. New York: Columbia University Press, 2005.

Reed, Betsy. "Australia to Allow Prescription of MDMA and Psilocybin for Treatment-Resistant Mental Illnesses." *Guardian*, February 3, 2023. www.theguardian.com/australia-news/2023/feb/03/australia-to-allow-prescription-of-mdma-and-psilocybin-for-treatment-resistant-mental-illnesses.

Reynolds, Simon. *Energy Flash: A Journey through Rave Music and Dance Culture*. New York: Soft Skull, 2012.

Rhodes, John. "Up in Smoke: The Religious Freedom Restoration Act and Federal Marijuana Prosecutions." *Oklahoma City Law Review* 38, no. 3 (Fall 2013): 319–366.

Richards, William. "Ineffability and Revelation on the Frontiers of Knowledge." In *DMT Entity Encounters: Dialogues on the Spirit Molecule*. Edited by David Luke and Rory Spowers, 118–143. Rochester, VT: Park Street, 2021.

———. *Sacred Knowledge: Psychedelics and Religious Experiences*. New York: Columbia University Press, 2018.

Ricoeur, Paul. "Schleiermacher's Hermeneutics." *Monist* 60, no. 22 (April 1977): 181–197.

Rig Veda. Translated and edited by Wendy Doniger. New York: Penguin, 2005.

Robinson, David W., Kelly L. Brown, M. L. Mcmenemy, Lynn Dennany, Matthew J. Baker, Pamela Allan, Caroline R. Cartwright, Julienne Bernard, Fraser Sturt, Elena Kotoula, Christopher Jazwa, Kristina M. Gill, Patrick Randolph-Quinney, Thomas Ash, Clare Bedford, Devlin Gandy, Matthew Armstrong, James Miles, and David Haviland. "*Datura* Quids at Pinwheel Cave, California, Provide Unambiguous Confirmation of the Ingestion of Hallucinogens at a Rock Art Site." *Proceedings of the National Academy of Sciences* 117, no. 49 (November 23, 2020): 31026–31037. doi.org/10.1073/pnas.2014529117.

Rodriguez, Marko A. "A Methodology for Studying Various Interpretations of the N,N-dimethyltryptamine-Induced Alternate Reality." *Journal of Scientific Exploration* 21, no. 1 (March 2007): 67–84.

Rodriguez Arce, José Manuel, and Michael Winkelman. "Psychedelics, Sociality, and Human Evolution." *Frontiers in Psychology* 12 (January 1, 2021). doi.org/10.3389/fpsyg.2021.729425.

Rooks, Benton. "Unified Psychedelic Theory: An Interview with Patrick Lundborg R.I.P." *Reality Sandwich*, June 20, 2014. realitysandwich.com/unified-psychedelic-theory-an-interview-with-patrick-lundborg-r-i-p/.

Rorabaugh, W. J. *Prohibition: A Very Short Introduction*. New York: Oxford University Press, 2020.

Rorty, Richard. *Contingency, Irony, and Solidarity*. Cambridge: Cambridge University Press, 1989.

Roseman, Leor, Yiftach Ron, Aldaz Saca, Natalie Lyla Ginsberg, Lisa Luan, Nadeem Karkabi, Rick Doblin, and Robin L. Carhart-Harris. "Relational Processes in Ayahuasca Groups of Palestinians and Israelis." *Frontiers in Pharmacology* 12, 607529 (May 19, 2021). doi.org/10.3389/fphar.2021.607529.

Ross, Lilly Kay. "Cover Story: Power Trip." Podcast. *New York Magazine*. Aired November 2021–February 2022. nymag.com/podcasts.

Rousseau, Jean-Jacques. *Emile*. Translated by Barbara Foxley. Project Gutenberg, 2011 [1762]. Updated 2018. www.gutenberg.org/files/5427/5427-h/5427-h.htm.

Ruck, Carl A. P. "Entheogens in Ancient Times: Wine and the Rituals of Dionysus." In *Toxicology in Antiquity*, 2nd ed., edited by Philip Wexler, 343–352. Cambridge, MA: Academic Press, 2019.

Ruck, Carl A. P., Jeremy Bigwood, Danny Staples, Jonathan Ott, and R. Gordon Wasson. "Entheogens." *Journal of Psychedelic Drugs* 11, no. 1–2 (1979): 145–146.

Ruck, Carl A. P., and Mark Hoffman. *Entheogens, Myth and Human Consciousness*. Oakland, CA: Ronin, 2013.

Ruck, Carl A. P., Blaise Daniel Staples, and Clark Heinrich. *The Apples of Apollo: Pagan and Christian Mysteries of the Eucharist*. Durham, NC: Carolina Academic Press, 2001.

Sacks, Oliver. *Hallucinations*. New York: Vintage, 2012.

Sahagún, Luis. "Why Are Some Native Americans Fighting Efforts to Decriminalize Peyote?" *Los Angeles Times*, March 29, 2020.

Sakellardis, Faye. "How Ibogaine Emerged as an Addiction Treatment in the West." *Lucid News*, June 1, 2022. www.lucid.news/ibogaine-addiction-treatment-in-the-west/.

Samenow, Deborah. Kristi Kung, and Rachel Ludwig. "State Psychedelic Regulation: Oregon and Colorado Taking the Lead." *DLA Piper*, January 11, 2023. www.dlapiper.com/en/insights/publications/2023/01/state-psychedelic-regulation-oregon-and-colorado-taking-the-lead.

Samorini, Giorgio. *Animals and Psychedelics: The Natural World and the Instinct to Alter Consciousness*. Rochester, VT: Park Street, 2002.

———. *Riflessioni lisergiche*. Milan: Flash, 1981.

Sartre, Jean-Paul. *Being and Nothingness*. Translated by Hazel E. Barnes. New York: Philosophical Library, 1956.

———. *Critique of Dialectical Reason, Vol. 1*. Translated by Alan Sheridan-Smith. London: Verso, 2004 [1960].

———. *Existentialism and Humanism*. London: Methuen, 1968.

———. *Nausea*. Translated by Lloyd Alexander. New York: New Directions, 1964 [1938].
Schacht, Richard. *Nietzsche*. London: Routledge, 1983.
Scharper, Julie. "Crash Course in the Nature of Mind: Roland Griffiths' Psilocybin Experiments Have Produced Striking Evidence for Therapeutic Uses of Hallucinogens." *Johns Hopkins Magazine*, Fall 2017. hub.jhu.edu/magazine/2017/fall/roland-griffiths-magic-mushrooms-experiment-psilocybin-depression/.
Scheler, Max. *Selected Philosophical Essays*. Translated by David Lachterman. Evanston, IL: Northwestern University Press, 1973.
Schlag, Anne Katrin, Jacob S. Aday, I. Salam, Jo C. Neill, and David J. Nutt. "Adverse Effects of Psychedelics: From Anecdotes and Misinformation to Systematic Science." *Journal of Psychopharmacology* 36, no. 3 (February 2, 2022): 258–272. doi.org/10.1177/02698811211069100.
Schopenhauer, Arthur. "Psychological Remarks." In *Parerga and Paralipomena*, vol. 2, Translated and edited by Adrian Del Caro and Christopher Janaway, 520–549. New York: Cambridge University Press, 2015.
Schulte, Gabriela. "Poll: 65 Percent of Voters say Psychedelic Substances Do Not Have Medical Use." *The Hill*, June 1, 2021. thehill.com/hilltv/what-americas-thinking/556304-poll-65-percent-of-voters-say-psychedelic-substances-do-not/.
Schultes, Richard Evans. "Teonanacatl: The Narcotic Mushroom of the Aztecs." *American Anthropologist* 42, no. 3 (September 1940): 429–443.
Schultes, Richard Evans, Albert Hofmann, and Christian Rätsch. *Plants of the Gods: Their Sacred, Healing, and Hallucinogenic Powers*. Rochester, VT: Healing Arts Press, 1998.
Segall, Matthew D. "Altered Consciousness after Descartes: Whitehead's Philosophy of Organism as Psychedelic Realism." In *Philosophy and Psychedelics: Frameworks for Exceptional Experience*, edited by Christine Hauskeller and Peter Sjöstedt-Hughes, 195–210. London: Bloomsbury, 2022.
Sessa, Ben. *The Psychedelic Renaissance: Reassessing the Role of Psychedelic Drugs in 21st Century Psychiatry and Society*, 2nd ed. London: Aeon, 2019.
Seth, Anil. *Being You: A New Science of Consciousness*. New York: Penguin, 2021.
———. "Your Brain Hallucinates Your Conscious Reality." TED video transcript. Filmed April 2017, Vancouver, BC. www.ted.com/talks/anil_seth_your_brain_hallucinates_your_conscious_reality/transcript?language=en.
Shannon, Claude E. "A Mathematical Theory of Communication." *Bell System Technical Journal* 27 (July–October 1948): 379–423, 623–656.
Shanon, Benny. *The Antipodes of the Mind: Charting the Phenomenology of the Ayahuasca Experience*. New York: Oxford University Press, 2003.
———. "Biblical Entheogens: a Speculative Hypothesis." *Time and Mind* 1, no. 1 (2008): 51–74. doi.org/10.2752/175169608783489116.

———. "A Cognitive-Psychological Study of Ayahuasca." *Newsletter of the Multidisciplinary Association for Psychedelic Studies* 7, no. 3 (Summer 1997): 13–15.

———. "The Epistemics of Ayahuasca Visions." *Phenomenology and the Cognitive Sciences* 9, no. 2 (June 2010): 263–280. doi.org/10.1007/s11097-010-9161-3.

Shapiro, Marc. "Playlist for a Psychedelic Journey." *News and Publications*, Johns Hopkins Medicine, February 5, 2021. www.hopkinsmedicine.org/news/articles/playlist-for-a-psychedelic-journey.

Shebloski, Katarina L., and James M. Broadway. "Commentary: Effects of Psilocybin on Time Perception and Temporal Control of Behavior in Humans." *Frontiers in Psychology* 7 (May 19, 2016). doi.org/10.3389/fpsyg.2016.00736.

Sheldrake, Melvin. *Entangled Life: How Fungi Make Our Worlds, Change Our Minds and Shape Our Futures.* New York: Random House, 2020.

Shukuroglou, Melissa, Leor Roseman, Matt Wall, David Nutt, Mendel Kaelen, and Robin Carhart-Harris. "Changes in Music-Evoked Emotion and Ventral Striatal Functional Connectivity after Psilocybin Therapy for Depression." *Journal of Psychopharmacology* 37, no. 1 (January 2023): 70–79. doi.org/10.1177/0269881122112.

Shulgin, Alexander and Ann Shulgin. *PIHKAL: A Love Story.* Berkeley, CA: Transform, 1990.

———. *TIHKAL: The Continuation.* Berkeley, CA: Transform, 2002.

Siegel, Ronald K. *Intoxication: The Universal Drive for Mind-Altering Substances.* Rochester, VT: Park Street, 2005.

Singleton, S. Parker, Andrea I. Luppi, Robin Carhart-Harris, Josephine Cruzat, Leor Roseman, David J. Nutt, Gustavo Deco, Morten L. Kringelbach, Emmanuel Stamatakis, and Amy Kuceyeski. "Receptor-Informed Network Control Theory Links LSD and Psilocybin to a Flattening of the Brain's Control Energy Landscape." *Nature Communications* 13, 5812 (October 3, 2022). doi.org/10.1038/s41467-022-33578-1.

Sjöstedt-Hughes, Peter. *Modes of Sentience: Psychedelics, Panpsychism, Metaphysics.* London: Psychedelic Press, 2021.

———. *Noumenautics: Metaphysics, Meta-Ethics, Psychedelics.* Falmouth, UK: Psychedelic Press, 2015.

———. "On the Need for Metaphysics in Psychedelic Therapy and Research." *Frontiers in Psychology* 14 (March 2023): 1–17. doi.org/10.3389/fpsyg.2023.1128589.

Smart, Ninian. "Understanding Religious Experience." In *Mysticism and Philosophical Analysis*, edited by Steven T. Katz, 10–21. New York: Oxford University Press, 1978.

Smith, Huston. *Cleansing the Doors of Perception: The Religious Significance of Entheogenic Plants and Chemicals.* New York: Tarcher/Putnam, 2000.

Sobhani, Mona. "Psychedelic Worldview Flips + Secular Society." *The Brave New World of Psychedelic Science*, March 17, 2023. psychedelicrenaissance.substack.com/p/psychedelic-worldview-flips-secular?r=2sz1v.
Socha, Dagmara M., Marzena Sykutera, and Giuseppe Orefici. "Use of Psychoactive and Stimulant Plants on the South Coast of Peru from the Early Intermediate to Late Intermediate Period." *Journal of Archaeological Science* 148 (December 2022): 105688. doi.org/10.1016/j.jas.2022.105688.
Spinoza, Baruch. *Ethics*. In *Spinoza: Complete Works*. Edited by Michael L. Morgan and translated by Samuel L. Shirley. Indianapolis: Hackett, 2002 [1677].
Stace, W. T. *Mysticism and Philosophy*. Philadelphia: Lippincott, 1960.
Stamets, Paul, ed. *Fantastic Fungi: How Mushrooms can Heal, Shift Consciousness and Save the Planet*. San Rafael, CA: Earth Aware, 2019.
Stamets, Paul. *Growing Gourmet and Medicinal Mushrooms*. New York: Ten Speed, 2000.
———. *Mycelium Running: How Mushrooms Can Help Save the World*. New York: Ten Speed, 2005.
Stephen, James. "R. Gordon Wasson & Maria Sabina: First Contact with Magic Mushrooms." *Truffle Report*, November 10, 2020. truffle.report/maria-sabina-and-r-gordon-wasson-psychedelic-first-contact-warning/.
Stein, Robert. *Biblical Hermeneutics*. Carnas, WA: Biblical Training, 2020.
Storey, Damien. "The Soul-Turning Metaphor in Plato's *Republic* Book 7." *Classical Philology* 117, no. 3 (July 2022): 525–542. doi.org/10.1086/720177.
Strassman, Rick. *The Psychedelic Handbook: A Practical Guide to Psilocybin, LSD, Ketamine, MDMA, and DMT/Ayahuasca*. Berkeley, CA: Ulysses Press, 2022.
———. *DMT and the Soul of Prophecy: A New Science of Spiritual Revelation in the Hebrew Bible*. Rochester, VT: Park Street, 2014.
———. *DMT and the Soul of Prophecy*. Rochester, VT: Park Street, 2014.
———. *DMT: The Spirit Molecule: A Doctor's Revolutionary Research into the Biology of Near-Death and Mystical Experiences*. Rochester, VT: Park Street, 2001.
Stringer, Maya, "Could the Embrace of Psychedelics Lead to a Mental-Health Revolution?" *Vogue*, February 12, 2001. www.vogue.com/article/psychededlic-wellness-mental-health.
Sullivan, Walter. "New Study Backs Thesis on Witches." *New York Times*, August 29, 1982.
Suzuki, Shunryu. *Zen Mind, Beginner's Mind: Informal Talks on Zen Meditation and Practice*. Boulder, CO: Shambhala, 1970.
Swanson, Link R. "Unifying Theories of Psychedelic Drug Effects." *Frontiers in Pharmacology* 9, no. 172 (March 2018). doi.org/10.3389/fphar.2018.00172.
Szabo, Attila, Attila Kovács, Jordi Riba, Srdjan Djurovic, Éva Rajnavölgyi, and Ede Frecska. "The Endogenous Hallucinogen and Trace Amine N,N-Dimethyltryptamine (DMT) Displays Potent Protective Effects against

Hypoxia via Sigma-1 Receptor Activation in Human Primary IPSC-Derived Cortical Neurons and Microglia-Like Immune Cells." *Frontiers in Neuroscience* 10 (September 14, 2016). doi.org/10.3389/fnins.2016.00423.

Szára, Stephen. "Dimethyltryptamin: its Metabolism in Man; the Relation to its Psychotic Effect to the Serotonin Metabolism." *Experientia* 12, no. 11 (November 15, 1956): 441–442.

Taylor, Charles. *A Secular Age*. Cambridge: Harvard University Press, 2007.

Tersavich, Chelsea. "Why the 'Trust, Let Go, Be Open' Mantra is Important in Psychedelic Healing." *Mindbloom*, August 15, 2022. www.mindbloom.com/blog/exploring-the-trust-let-go-be-open-tlo-mantra.

Thompson, Hunter S. *Fear and Loathing in Las Vegas: A Savage Journey to the Heart of the American Dream*. New York: Vintage, 2010 [1972].

Thompson, Hunter S., and Ralph Steadman. *The Curse of Lono*. Los Angeles: Taschen, 2005.

Timmermann, Christopher, Hannes Kettner, Chris Letheby, Leor Roseman, Fernando Rosas, and Robin L. Carhart-Harris. "Psychedelics Alter Metaphysical Beliefs." *Scientific Reports* 11, 22166 (November 23, 2021). doi.org/10.1038/s41598-021-01209-2.

Timmermann, Christopher, Meg J. Spriggs, Mendel Kaelen, Robert Leech, David J. Nutt, Rosalyn J. Moran, Robin L. Carhart-Harris, and Suresh D. Muthukumaraswamy. "LSD Modulates Effective Connectivity and Neural Adaptation Mechanisms in an Auditory Oddball Paradigm." *Neuropharmacology* 142 (November 2018): 251–262. doi.org/10.1016/j.neuropharm.2017.10.039.

Tupper, Kenneth W. "Could Psychedelics Become a Crucial Part of Our Education?" Interview by Paul Austin. *The Psychedelic Podcast by Third Wave*, episode 31, July 23, 2017. thethirdwave.co/podcast/episode-31-ken-tupper/.

———. "Entheogenic Education: Psychedelics as Tools of Wonder and Awe." *MAPS Bulletin* 24, no. 1 (2014): 14–19.

———. "Entheogens and Education: Exploring the Potential of Psychoactives as Educational Tools." *Journal of Drug Education and Awareness* 1, no. 2 (January 2003): 145–161.

Uexküll, Jacob von. *A Foray into the Worlds of Animals and Humans*. Translated by Joseph D. O'Neill. Minneapolis: University of Minnesota Press, 2010 [1934].

Ungit, Lewis. *The Return of the Dragon: The Shocking Way Drugs and Religion Shape People and Societies*. Independently published, 2022.

United Nations, Human Rights, Office of the High Commissioner. "Istanbul Protocol: Manual on the Effective Investigation and Documentation of Torture and Other Cruel, Inhuman or Degrading Treatment or Punishment." New York: United Nations, 2022. www.ohchr.org/sites/default/files/documents/publications/2022-06-29/Istanbul-Protocol_Rev2_EN.pdf.

The Upanishads. Translated by Eknath Easwaran. Tomales. CA: Nilgiri Press, 2007.

Vargas, Maxemiliano V., Lee E. Dunlap, Chunyang Dong, Samuel J. Carter, Robert J. Tombari, Shekib A. Jami, Lindsay P. Cameron, Seona D. Patel, Joseph J. Hennessey, Hannah N. Saeger, John D. McCorvy, John A. Gray, Lin Tian, and David E. Olson. "Psychedelics Promote Neuroplasticity through the Activation of Intracellular 5-HT2A Receptors." *Science* 379, no. 6633 (February 16, 2023): 700–706. doi.org/10.1126/science.adf0435.

Vis, Pieter, Anneke E. Goudriaan, Bastiaan C. Ter Meulen, and Jan Dirk Blom. "On Perception and Consciousness in HPPD: A Systematic Review." *Frontiers in Neuroscience* 15 (August 11, 2021). doi.org/10.3389/fnins.2021.675768.

Vlastos, Gregory. "The Unity of the Virtues in the "Protagoras." *Review of Metaphysics* 24, no. 3 (March 1972): 415–458.

Von Rotz, Robin, Eva M Schindowski, Johannes Jungwirth, Anna Schuldt, Nathalie M. Rieser, Katharina Zahoranszky, Erich Seifritz, Albina Nowak, Peter Nowak, Lutz Jäncke, Katrin H. Preller, and Franz X. Vollenweider "Single-Dose Psilocybin-Assisted Therapy in Major Depressive Disorder: A Placebo-Controlled, Double-Blind, Randomised Clinical Trial." *eClinical Medicine* 56 (February 2023). doi.org/10.1016/j.eclinm.2022.101809.

Vygotsky, L. S. *Mind in Society: The Development of Higher Psychological Processes.* Cambridge, MA: Harvard University Press, 1978.

Waldman, Ayelet. *A Really Good Day: How Microdosing Made a Mega Difference in My Mood, My Marriage, and My Life.* New York: Alfred A. Knopf, 2017.

Walsh, Charlotte. "Beyond Religious Freedom: Psychedelics and Cognitive Liberty." In *Prohibition, Religious Freedom, and Human Rights: Regulating Traditional Drug Use*, edited by Beatriz Caiuby Labate and Clancy Cavnar, 211–233. New York: Springer, 2014.

Walsh, Roger and Charles S. Grob, eds. *Higher Wisdom: Eminent Elders Explore the Continuing Impact of Psychedelics.* Albany: State University of New York Press, 2005.

Walzer, Michael. *Thick and Thin: Moral Argument at Home and Abroad.* Notre Dame, IN: University of Notre Dame Press, 2019.

Wasson, Valentina P. "I Ate the Sacred Mushrooms." *This Week*, May 19, 1957. bibliography.maps.org/bibliography/default/resource/17683.

Wasson, R. Gordon. "Drugs: The Sacred Mushroom." *New York Times*, September 26, 1970.

Wasson, R. Gordon, Albert Hofmann, and Carl A. P. Ruck, *The Road to Eleusis: Unveiling the Secrets of the Mysteries.* Berkeley, CA: North Atlantic, 2008.

Watson, Richard. *Cogito Ergo Sum: The Life of René Descartes.* Boston: Godine, 2007.

Watts, Alan. *The Joyous Cosmology: Adventures in the Chemistry of Consciousness.* New York: Pantheon, 1962.

Weisberg, Deena Skolnick, Audrey Kittredge, Kathy Hirsh-Pasek, Roberta Golinkoff, and David Klahr. "Making Play Work for Education." *Phi Delta Kappan* 96, no. 8 (May 2015): 8–13. doi.org/10.1177/0031721715583955.

Weiss, Brandon, Aleksandra Wingert, David Erritzoe, and W. Keith Campbell. "Prevalence and Therapeutic Impact of Adverse Life Event Reexperiencing under Ceremonial Ayahuasca." *Scientific Reports* 13, 9438 (June 9, 2023). doi.org/10.1038/s41598-023-36184-3.

Wendler, David, and Christine Grady. "What Should Research Participants Understand about Medical Costs?" *Journal of Medical Ethics* 34, no. 10 (June 2008): 767–770. doi.org/10.1136/jme.2007.023325.

Wilcox, Anna. "Machine Elves or 'DMT Elves': A Journey Into The DMT Spirit World." *Double Blind*, September 4, 2020. doubleblindmag.com/machine-elves-clockwork-elves-dmt-rick-strassman-terence-mckenna/.

Wilkinson, Peter. "The Acid King." *Rolling Stone*, July 5, 2001. www.rollingstone.com/feature/acid-lsd-king-william-leonard-pickard-prison-pete-wilkinson-184390/.

Williams, Bernard. *Morality: An Introduction to Ethics.* Cambridge: Cambridge University Press, 1972.

Winkelman, Michael James. "Altered Consciousness and Drugs in Human Evolution." In *Entheogens and the Development of Culture: The Anthropology and Neurobiology of Ecstatic Experience*, edited by John A. Rush, 23–49. Berkeley, CA: North Atlantic, 2012.

Wired Staff. "Terence McKenna's Last Trip." *Wired*, May 1, 2000. www.wired.com/2000/05/mckenna/.

Wittgenstein, Ludwig. *On Certainty.* Translated by Denis Paul and G. E. M. Anscombe. New York: Harper, 1969.

———. *Philosophical Investigations.* Translated by G. E. M. Anscombe. New York: Macmillan, 1953.

———. *Tractatus Logico-Philosophicus.* Translated by D. F. Pears and B. F. McGuinness. New York: Humanities Press, 1961 [1922].

Wittman, Mark. *Altered States of Consciousness: Experiences out of Time and Self.* Cambridge, MA: MIT Press, 2018.

Wolf, Gilly, Sandeep Singh, Karin Blakolmer, Leonard Lerer, Tzuri Lifschytz, Uriel Heresco-Levy, Amit Lotan, and Bernard Lerer. "Could Psychedelic Drugs Have a Role in the Treatment of Schizophrenia? Rationale and Strategy for Safe Implementation." *Molecular Psychiatry* 28, no. 1 (January 2023): 44–58. doi.org/10.1038/s41380-022-01832-z.

Wolfe, Tom. *The Electric Kool-Aid Acid Test.* New York: Picador, 2008 [1968].

Wolin, Richard. *Heidegger in Ruins: Between Philosophy and Ideology.* New Haven, CT: Yale University Press, 2023.

Woolfe, Sam. "The Psychedelic Nature of Islamic Art and Architecture." *Sam Woolfe*, October 1, 2018. www.samwoolfe.com/2018/10/the-psychedelic-nature-of-islamic-art-and-architecture.html.

———. "Why Do Jesters and Tricksters Appear in the DMT Experience?" *Sam Woolfe*, September 19, 2019. www.samwoolfe.com/2019/02/jesters-tricksters-dmt-experience.html.

Wrathall, Mark A., ed. *The Cambridge Heidegger Lexicon*. Cambridge: Cambridge University Press, 2021. doi.org/10.1017/9780511843778.089.

Yaden, David Bryce, Jonathan Haidt, Ralph W. Hood Jr., David R. Vago, and Andrew B. Newberg. "The Varieties of Self-Transcendent Experience." *Review of General Psychology* 21, no. 2 (June 2017): 143–160. doi.org/10.1037/gpr0000102.

Yakowicz, Will. "U.S. Government Will Test Ibogaine Derivative as an Addiction Treatment." *Forbes*, December 7, 2021. www.forbes.com/sites/willyakowicz/2021/12/07/us-government-will-test-ibogaine-as-an-addiction-treatment/?sh=329d426d4c4e.

Yanakieva, Steliana, N. Polychroni, Neiloufar Family, Luke Williams, David Luke, and Devin Blair Terhune. "The Effects of Microdose LSD on Time Perception: A Randomised, Double-Blind, Placebo-Controlled Trial." *Psychopharmacology* 236, no. 4 (April 2019): 1159–1170. doi.org/10.1007/s00213-018-5119-x.

Yong, Ed. *An Immense World: How Animal Senses Reveal the Hidden Realm around Us*. New York: Random House, 2022.

Yulbarisov, Rustam. "LSD Capitalism Promises a Bad Trip for Us All." *Jacobin*, April 2, 2022. jacobin.com/2022/04/lsd-capitalism-psychedelics-mdma-ketamine-companies-medical.

Zhou, Katie, David De Wied, Robin Carhart-Harris, and Hannes Kettner. "Predictors of Hallucinogen Persisting Perception Disorder Symptoms, Delusional Ideation and Magical Thinking Following Naturalistic Psychedelic Use." *PsyArXiv Preprints* (November 15, 2022). doi.org/10.31234/osf.io/txzha.

Zemon, Matt, ed. *Psychedelics for Everyone: A Beginner's Guide to these Powerful Medicines for Anxiety, Depression, Addiction, PTSD, and Expanding Consciousness*. Miami: Psyched Publishing, 2022.

Zimmerman, Michael. *Heidegger's Confrontation with Modernity*. Bloomington: Indiana University Press, 1990.

Index

2-CB, xiii, 6
5-MeO-DMT, xiii, 5, 12, 20, 23, 35, 97, 101, 113, 120, 122, 259n36, 269n67

abuse (sexual), 13, 42, 146, 148, 208–210, 230, 278–279n111
addiction, x, 7, 10, 16, 155–156. *See also* substance abuse
alcohol (and alcoholism), 3, 6, 7, 24, 78, 179, 240–241
Allen, Woody, 219–220
Amanita muscaria, 4, 160
animals, 8, 22, 98–99, 108, 118, 161, 108, 188, 207, 255n5, 273n40
archetypes (Jungian), 30, 62, 53, 109, 119, 148, 229 263n80
ataraxia, 27, 36, 129
Aristotle, 58, 140–141, 183, 201
Aurelius, Marcus, 103
ayahuasca, xiii, 6, 12, 14, 78, 82, 89, 100, 101, 108, 117, 118, 122, 128, 142, 145, 161, 169, 173, 207, 224, 230, 241, 257–258n24, 280n13, 281n23
Aztecs (Nahua), 90, 145, 163, 278n103

Bauman, Zygmunt, 114, 143
Bache, Christopher, 133, 176–177

Beatles (band) 7, 147, 180, 249n26
Beckley Foundation (UK), 11
Bergson, Henri, 126
Berlin, Isaiah, 223–224
Blacker, H. Martin, 100
Block, Ned, 106–107
Broudy, Harry, 38, 201, 260n47
Buddhism (and Buddhist), 15, 23, 27, 35, 230, 236
Burroughs, William S., 6, 181

Camus, Albert, 83
Carhart-Harris, Robin, 52, 110, 188, 189–191, 203, 206, 287n111
Carroll, Lewis, 30
Cartesian, 84, 98, 122–129, 133–140, 143, 185, 213, 274n58, 276n82. *See also* doubt (Cartesian)
Castaneda, Carlos, 145, 277n101
Catholicism, 163, 165, 230. *See also* Christianity
Cézanne, Paul, 92–93
Christianity (and Christian), 23, 27, 29, 37, 41, 49, 138–139, 162, 165, 173, 204, 209, 212, 227, 230, 232. *See also* Catholicism
classic psychedelics, xii–xiv, 14, 22, 70, 174, 228
cognitive liberty, 13, 166, 242, 296n6
Cohen, Sidney, 6, 248n22

connectedness (and interconnectedness), 23, 35, 43, 48, 52, 88, 106, 108, 110, 114, 117–118, 128, 164, 186, 218, 224–225. *See also* unitive experience
consciousness, 8, 19, 20, 25–26, 45–46, 83, 101, 110, 113, 136, 188, 194, 197, 213, 234–235
consciousness alteration, 3, 14, 18, 21, 22, 25, 27, 59, 147–148, 160, 183, 241–243, 262n66, 279–280n5, 282–283n34
Copland, Aaron, 141–142, 242
cult problem, 7, 144–146, 154, 184, 226, 230, 241, 277n100

Dasein (being-there), 26–27, 31–32, 74, 85, 86, 88, 152, 225
Davis, Erik, 16–17, 165, 182, 249n27, 293n50
death (and mortality), 19, 27, 33, 36, 84, 91, 107–109, 114, 116, 118, 224, 225, 138
death anxiety, x, 10, 24, 111, 116, 118, 224, 256n14
Default Mode Network (DMN), 188, 197, 257–258n24
depression (and anxiety), x, 3, 10, 11, 42, 66, 124, 156, 158, 159, 237, 256n256, 258–259n31
Descartes, René, 46, 88, 121–140, 152, 154, 215, 274n49, 274n56, 275n75, 276n81. *See also* Cartesian
Dewey, John, 54, 75
DMT, xii, 10, 12, 14, 16, 23, 34, 38, 47, 48, 60, 69, 70, 73, 77, 82, 89, 101, 106, 113, 115, 120, 123, 136, 143, 153, 155, 166, 175, 181, 184, 212, 227, 229–230, 253n60, 279–280n5; extended state (DMTx), 78, 181, 262–263n71, 263n75, 265n5, 279n5, 290–291n6

DMT entities, 60, 89, 120, 154, 206, 210, 229, 262–263n71, 293n41
Doblin, Rick, 253n58, 295n4
doubt (Cartesian and hyperbolic), 46, 123–136, 139, 143, 213
doxastic enhancement, 50–53, 205, 207, 209–211, 215, 217, 219, 221, 223, 225–227, 243
DPT, xiii
Drug Abuse Control Amendments of 1965, 1
Duchamp, Marcel, 93

education (and educational), 17–19, 24, 31, 39, 77–78, 97, 103, 116, 140, 152, 199–200, 226, 234, 245, 254n64. *See also* learning
ego death (and dissolution), 20, 35, 105–108, 111, 112–114, 116, 117, 120, 142, 153
Ego-Dissolution Inventory (EDI), 111–112, 114, 116
Eleusinian Mysteries, 13, 23, 29, 41, 44, 109, 114, 116, 160, 162, 224, 231
Eliade, Mircea, 40
emotivism, 209–210, 211, 212
entheogen (and entheogenic), 14–15, 23, 30, 39–54, 142, 160, 162–163, 165–179, 232–234, 240–242, 252–253n54
entropy (brain), 96, 127, 188–189, 197, 203, 214, 287n110, 287n111
envelopment, 39, 52, 149, 151, 154–155, 186, 241; intellectual, 42–43, 45, 173–182; medical or therapeutic, 41–42, 45, 155–161, 198, 208; recreational, 44–45, 182–185, 242–243, 252n46; shamanic, 39–40, 41, 45, 159–161; theological/entheogenic), 40–41, 45, 162–173, 230, 233

Index

Epicurus (and Epicureanism), 26, 27, 36, 107
epistemic loosening, 33, 35, 39, 46, 50, 57, 60–66, 76, 90, 94–98, 103, 123, 124, 126, 154, 164, 190, 210, 214, 225, 243
ergot, xiii, 2, 162
Erowid (erowid.org), 13, 111, 116, 174, 262n71
Establishment Clause, 168, 285n74. *See also* First Amendment
Evans, Jules, 25, 48, 269n68, 278n105
exploitation problem (ethics), 146–148, 154, 208

Fadiman, James, 133, 252n46
First Amendment, 14, 68, 142, 168. *See also* Free Exercise Clause
Free Exercise Clause, 14, 168, 170, 173. *See also* First Amendment
Freud, Sigmund, 2, 29, 146
Friston, K. J., 189–191, 206. *See also* Carhart-Harris, Robin
fusion of horizons, 48, 54, 195–196, 201, 288n126

Gadamer, Hans-Georg, 47–48, 49, 54, 186–202, 289n136
Gallimore, Andrew, 1, 19, 65–66, 68, 69, 164
Gelassenheit (releasement), 91–93, 105
Gestell, 79–82, 91, 92
Good Friday Experiment, 15, 48, 143, 204, 235, 253n58, 295n4
Götz, Ignacio, 254n64
Grateful Dead, 6, 43, 175, 179–180, 184
Grey, Alex (and Allyson), 31, 175–176, 177, 180
Griffiths, Roland, 9–10, 24, 87, 106, 109, 111, 155, 232, 250n36, 256–257n14, 259n32

Grob, Charles, 10, 111, 155
Grof, Stanislav (and Grofian), 3, 18, 49–50, 52, 59–60, 61, 117, 152, 154, 164, 176, 178, 204, 237
Guild of Guides, 133, 156, 276n80

Hadot, Pierre, 132, 276n82
hallucinations, 32, 47, 61, 68, 89, 256n7, 289n139, 290n2. *See also* pareidolia
Hallucinogen Persisting Perception Disorder (HPPD), 127
Hart, Carl, 13, 166–167, 183, 242
Hegel, G. W. F. (and Hegelian), 187–188, 195, 196, 197, 211, 212, 247n1
Heidegger, Martin, 26–28, 31–33, 67–93, 98, 105, 152, 190, 192, 225, 227, 267n36
Heraclitus, 57–58, 103, 212, 265n3
hermeneutics, philosophical, 48, 191–204, 207, 210, 211, 214, 225, 288n126; biblical, 191–193, 288n119
Hinduism, 23, 70, 164, 211, 291n16. *See also* soma
Hofmann, Albert, 2, 4, 5, 110, 120, 158, 177
Hubbard, Al ("Captain"), 6, 149
human sacrifice, 37, 145, 227, 278n103
Hume, David (and Humean), 129–132, 183, 214–223, 225, 233, 237, 292n21
Husserl, Edmund, 45–46, 83–84, 89, 135–138, 139, 197, 213, 262n64, 288n126
Huxley, Aldous, 4, 5, 43, 93, 111, 120, 181, 189, 258n29
hyperbolic doubt (or Cartesian doubt), 123–125, 127–129, 131, 133–140, 142, 213

hypertrophic identification, 37, 52, 103, 109–111, 114, 121, 148, 153, 164, 187, 206, 225

ibogaine, xiii, 11, 101, 127, 281–282n23

immortality, 36, 114–116, 118, 264n84

indigenous traditions (communities and culture), xii, 5, 16, 142, 145, 159–161, 173, 204, 232, 242, 265n14

insight, ix, 54–55, 68, 105, 202, 208–210, 218, 237, 241–242, 244

integration (psychological), 38, 121, 128, 139, 148, 164, 204, 205–206, 215, 223, 225, 244

introspection, 120–121, 138, 152, 162, 258n24

Islam, 15, 41, 227, 253n60. *See also* Sufism

James, William, 2, 68, 148, 174

Johns Hopkins University (Center for Psychedelic Research), 10, 24, 44, 87, 109, 142, 157, 175, 232, 250n36, 275n62, 285n86

Johnson, Matthew, 43, 147

Johnson, Samuel, 25

Judaism (Jewish), 15, 41, 176, 231, 232–234, 252, 294n55

Jung, Carl (and Jungian), 53, 119, 229. *See also* archetypes

Kant, Immanuel (and Kantian), 27, 28, 51, 86, 135, 172, 217

Kempis, Thomas à, 37, 260n45

Kesey, Ken, 2, 6, 43, 184. *See also* Merry Pranksters

Kins, Josie, 14, 111–112. *See also* Subjective Effects Index

ketamine, xiii, 11, 23, 35, 70

learning, ix, 18–19, 24, 28, 37, 38, 47, 49, 50, 54, 96, 105, 121, 136, 140, 214, 218–219, 238. *See also* education

Leary, Timothy, 6, 7, 10, 141, 149, 241, 295n4

Leeuwenhoek, Antonie van, 68, 69–70, 76

Letheby, Chris, 17, 34, 87–88, 104, 105, 109, 212, 254n64

Lin, Tao, 181–182

LSD, xii, xiii, 1, 2–3, 4, 6, 7, 8, 12, 16, 22, 34, 35, 54, 59, 77, 95–96, 101, 117, 120, 122, 127, 133, 144, 145, 152, 155, 158, 162, 171, 174, 176–178, 183, 184, 186, 206, 208, 253–254n62, 256n10, 284n64, 290n2

Lucretius, 36

Luna, Luis Eduardo, 149, 265n14, 288n126

Lundborg, Patrick, 231, 249n29

Lyotard, Jean-Francois, 204

MacIntyre, Alasdair, 209–210, 211, 212

Manson, Charles, 2, 7, 43, 144, 209, 227

Maya, 49, 145, 163

marijuana (and cannabis), 11, 16, 24, 41, 122, 166, 169, 171, 253–254n64, 284n58, 284n64, 284n67

Marx, Karl, 82, 123, 142, 247n1, 276n94

McKenna, Dennis, 8, 249n31

McKenna, Terence, 8–9, 35, 44, 48, 89, 101, 119, 121, 174, 182, 184, 206, 239, 249n32, 259n37, 262n71, 265n5

MDMA, xiii, 6, 11, 22, 146, 156, 177, 179, 253–254n62

Meno's paradox, 28–29, 49

Merry Pranksters, 6, 43, 184–185, 206. *See also* Kesey, Ken
mescaline, xiii, 3–4, 6, 108, 111, 120, 122, 145, 174, 253–254n64
Mesoamerica, 145, 163, 185, 227, 231, 256n10, 278n103
methamphetamine, 13, 19
Meyers factors, 171–173, 284n67
microdosing, 132, 156, 252n46
MK-ULTRA, Project (CIA), 2, 37, 155, 199
modernity, 80, 81, 82, 143, 168, 204, 236
modernist West, x, 10, 155, 163, 206, 207, 209, 211, 230–231, 235, 236, 238, 239, 242
Morris, Hamilton, 259n36
Multidisciplinary Association for Psychedelic Studies (MAPS), 11, 156, 179, 283n46
Muraresku, Brian, 13, 114
music, x, 6, 8, 65, 141–142, 144, 156, 157, 175, 180, 181, 185, 223, 226, 242–243, 280n15
mysticism (and mystical), 35, 68, 87, 90, 107, 228, 256n14, 263n80, 271n9

Nagel, Thomas, 100, 270n75
Native American Church (NAC), 14, 15, 41, 163, 168–169, 173, 285n73
near-death experiences (NDE), 113
neuroplasticity, 19, 34, 50, 188–191, 203–204, 255n69, 263n79, 266n20
neuroscience, xii, xiv, 13, 50, 178
New Age, 7, 45, 165–166
Nichols, David, 10, 21, 44, 177, 247n1
Nietzsche, Friedrich, 40, 51, 92, 105, 151, 196, 288–289n128

non-specific amplification, 18, 49, 154, 213, 214, 226, 237. *See also* pluripotency

opioids, 11, 13, 24, 166, 174
Osmond, Humphrey, 6, 54, 178, 258n29

Pahnke, Walter, 15, 143, 204, 235, 253n58, 295n4. *See also* Good Friday Experiment
pareidolia, 277n97
Parker, Quanah, 14
perception, 32–33, 35, 46, 50, 57–62 passim, 82, 86, 88, 100, 123, 138, 139, 150, 206, 224, 270n2; distorted, 46, 60–63, 87, 88, 279n5, 290n2
perinatal matrices, 3, 59, 61, 117, 152176
peyote, 3, 5, 14–15, 23, 29, 41, 142, 168–173 passim, 253–254n64
phenethylamine, xiii, 6, 70
phenomenology, 45, 135, 138, 197, 213
philosophy, x, xi, 4, 13, 17, 57–59, 67, 171, 198, 234
plasticity. *See* neuroplasticity
Plato (and Platonism), 28, 36–37, 41, 52, 57, 58, 115–117, 118, 154, 206, 213, 215–216, 218–219, 224, 234, 257n22, 264n84
Plotinus, 116–117, 118, 138
pluripotency, 49, 88, 139, 154, 204, 224, 227, 261n59. *See also* non-specific amplification
Pollan, Michael, 12, 21, 44, 147, 174, 237
Post-Traumatic Stress Disorder (PTSD), x, 10, 42, 156, 189, 198, 203, 208
Pre-Socratics, 57–59, 63, 123

prohibition (and prohibitionism), 133, 144, 147, 163, 166, 170, 240–242
Psilocybe cubensis, 8–9
psilocybin ("magic mushrooms"), xii, 4, 8–9, 10, 11, 16, 21, 22, 23, 24, 32, 35, 45, 47, 53, 87, 95, 101, 106, 111, 120, 133, 136, 155, 156, 166, 183, 224, 241, 253–254n64, 256n12, 256n14, 258–259n31, 265n11
psytrance, 180, 187
Pyrrho of Ellis, 129, 131
Pythagoras (and Pythagorean), ix, 36–37, 44, 58, 115, 264n84

qualia (sensory), 26, 32, 72–78 passim, 87, 97, 98, 101, 116, 121, 122, 136, 140, 148, 152–154, 165, 175, 186, 215, 225

raves, 120, 182, 185, 286–287n102
Rawls, John, 216–217
REBUS Model, 186–205, 211, 214, 233
religion (and religious), x, 14, 15–16, 23, 37, 41, 65, 106, 117, 139, 159, 163, 164, 168, 170–171, 173, 197, 198, 209, 227–231, 236, 240, 293–294n54; legal definition of, 15, 171–173. See also *Meyers* factors
Religious Freedom Restoration Act of 1993 (RFRA), 14, 169, 171–173, 284n57
Richards, William, 223, 231–232, 234–235
Rorty, Richard 67, 86, 87
Ross, Lily Kay, 146, 261n58
Ruck, Carl A. P., 8, 29, 39, 252–253n54, 256n12

Sabina, Maria, 4–5, 248n18
Sacks, Oliver, 22, 174–175
salvinorin A, xiii
Santa Muerte, 143
Santo Daime (Church), 14, 15, 169–170, 173, 230
Sartre, Jean-Paul, 3–4, 27, 184–185, 221, 262n64
Scheler, Max, 221
schizophrenia, 203, 243, 296n7
Schopenhauer, Arthur, 19
Schleiermacher, Friedrich, 192, 193
self (the), xi, 35, 105, 117, 119, 138, 152, 187, 201, 222, 244, 291n16. See also self-understanding
self-understanding (and self-model), 17, 83, 87, 105, 109–114 passim, 118, 119, 150, 153, 198, 236–237
self-transcendent experience (STE), 106–108
set and setting, 34, 37–39, 46, 48, 50, 54, 96, 122, 149–153, 176, 187, 261
Seth, Anil, 200, 289n139
Sextus Empiricus, 129, 130
shamanism (and shamanic), 4, 5, 29, 34, 39–41, 44, 48, 82, 100, 100, 108, 159–163, 167, 206, 210, 230, 243, 271n12, 273n47
Shanon, Benny, 108, 117, 118, 141–142, 206–207, 211–212, 293n43
Shulgin, Alexander, 6, 44, 177, 205, 213, 249n25
Sjöstedt-Hughes, Peter, 16, 17, 254n64, 270n75
skepticism (philosophical), 58, 125–126, 128–132, 292n21; Pyrrhonian, 129–132
Socrates (and Socratic), 26, 28, 30, 33, 34, 41, 47, 63, 151, 190, 205
soma, 23, 256n13

Spinoza, Baruch (and Spinozism), 36–37, 53, 106, 197, 260n44
spirituality (and spiritualism), 29, 65, 71, 159–160, 164, 165–168, 242, 254n64, 256–257n14, 293–294n54
Stamets, Paul, 8, 9, 13, 178, 250n34, 264n86
Stoicism, 27, 36, 106, 129, 134, 276n82
Strassman, Rick, 9–10, 155, 176, 227–231, 233–234, 263n75
"stoned ape theory," 8–9, 182
Subjective Effects Index, 14, 111–115, 117–118, 272n28, 287n104. *See also* Kins, Josie
substance abuse, 42, 155, 158
Sufism, 41, 253n60
synesthesia, 46, 68, 290n2

Taylor, Charles 235–237
technology, 65, 67, 73, 79–80, 91–92, 100; psychedelics as, 65, 67–77
technological withdrawal, 73–75, 77
Thales, 57, 264n1
therapy (and therapeutic), 38, 59–60, 87, 139–140, 152, 156–157, 159, 182, 199–200, 257–258n24, 270n2, 280n13
Thompson, Hunter S., 7, 63, 120, 181

trip reports, ix, 13, 24, 31, 39, 50, 82, 103, 115, 174, 176, 183, 213
Tupper, Kenneth, 17, 254n64
tryptamine, xiii, 10, 64, 70, 77

Uexküll, Jakob von, 98–99
Umwelt, 97–102, 108, 136, 153, 187, 188, 207, 213, 236, 288n128
understanding, 22, 49, 53–54, 84, 128, 192–196, 200–202. *See also* self-understanding
União do Vegetal (UDV) Church, 14, 15, 169–170, 173, 230
unitive experience, 35, 48, 52, 108, 110–111, 117, 164, 188, 227, 228, 259n40. *See also* connectedness

Van Gogh, Vincent, 92
visual arts, 6, 31, 180–181, 256n12

Wasson, R. Gordon, 4–5, 248n18
Watts, Alan, 15, 19, 78, 128, 255n69
wellness, 12, 16, 42, 45, 66, 140, 155–156, 159, 165, 165, 176, 178, 182, 209, 260n55, 289n136
Winkelman, Michael J., 282–283n34
Wittgenstein, Ludwig, 148, 206, 207, 214
Woolfe, Sam, 253n60, 267n38
Woodstock (festival), 7, 184